Poets, Politics a

V

# Poets, Politics and
the People

V.G. KIERNAN

Edited and Introduced by
Harvey J. Kaye

**VERSO**

London · New York

This collection published by Verso 1989
© 1989 V.G. Kiernan
© 1989 Introduction, H.J. Kaye

**Verso**
UK: 6 Meard Street, London W1V 3HR
USA: 29 West 35th Street, New York, NY 10001-2291

Verso is the imprint of New Left Books

**British Library Cataloguing in Publication Data**

Kiernan, V.G. (Victor Gordon), *1931-*
    Poets, politics and the people.
    1. Great Britain — History
    I. Title II. Kaye, Harvey J.
    941

    ISBN 0-86091-245-0
    ISBN 0-86091-957-9


**Library of Congress Cataloging-in-Publication Data**

Kiernan, V.G. (Victor Gordon), 1913-
    Poets, politics, and the people.

    Includes index.
    1. English literature—History and criticism.
2. Marxist criticism—Great Britain.    3. Politics and
literature—Great Britain.    4. Literature and society
—Great Britain.    5. Great Britain—Politics and govern-
ment.    I. Kaye, Harvey J.    II. Title.
PR99.K445    1989        820'9'358        88-29662
ISBN 0-86091-245-0
ISBN 0-86091-957-9 (pbk.)


Typeset by Leaper & Gard Ltd, Bristol, England
Printed in Great Britain by Bookcraft (Bath) Ltd

*For Iqbal Singh*

– a writer of vision on History,
  Politics and Philosophy,

– a true representative of both Indian
  and European civilization

– and an ideal friend of half a
  century.

*And in memory of PAT*

V.G.K.

# Contents

Editor's Preface
ix

Acknowledgements
xi

INTRODUCTION
*Marxism, History and the Necessity of Poetry*
1

CHAPTER 1
*Patterns of Protest in English History*
18

CHAPTER 2
*The Covenanters: A Problem of Creed and Class*
40

CHAPTER 3
*Evangelicalism and the French Revolution*
65

CHAPTER 4
*Human Relationships in Shakespeare*
78

CHAPTER 5
*Wordsworth and the People*
96

CHAPTER 6
*Tennyson, King Arthur and Imperialism*
129

CHAPTER 7
*Labour and the Literate in Nineteenth-Century Britain*
152

CHAPTER 8
*Herbert Norman's Cambridge*
178

CHAPTER 9
*On Treason*
193

CHAPTER 10
*Socialism, the Prophetic Memory*
204

Index
229

# Editor's Preface

This is actually the second of four projected volumes of the Collected Essays of Victor Kiernan. The first, *History, Classes and Nation-States* (Oxford and New York 1988), is composed of writings on Marxism and history, the formation of nation-states and the centrality of class struggle in the making of modern Europe. The present book brings together a selection of his essays in English studies – or, better, British studies, for it includes one piece on a specifically Scottish subject. These essays take up writers and literature, the politics and ideas of popular protest, religion and social struggles, and Marxism and the socialist tradition in England. The next two volumes are to be titled *Europe, Britain and the World*, and *Intellectuals, Culture and History*. The former will consist of writings on European imperialism and its historical contradictions and consequences, treating the experiences of both the colonizers and the colonized; and the latter will contain essays on non-English writers and socialist thinkers and general considerations of the experience and agency of intellectuals in history. (It should be noted that although determination of the articles to be included in each volume has been pursued in consultation with Professor Kiernan, the final decisions on contents were made by the editor.)

Once again, I must thank Victor Kiernan for the opportunity to edit and introduce his collected essays, and also record my appreciation for his confidence and support in my efforts both on this project and on others not so directly concerned with his own work. As I stated in *History, Classes and Nation-States*, though we are not in agreement on all matters historical and political, I feel quite strongly that his writings on topics past and present represent a model to which we ought to attend. His historical scholarship for the past fifty years clearly attests to the value of 'seeing things historically'. I should add that in my attempts to address the encyclopaedic range of Professor Kiernan's work, I have found myself a student again, with all the anxieties of my university days. Originally trained as a Latin Americanist, my work on the British Marxist historians has represented a dramatic change in area of study: confronting the responsibility of Kiernan's collected essays, I have found myself all over the globe, across centuries of time. In an age of academic specialization – indeed, narrowing *over*-specialization – I find the experience exhilarating though I make no claim to dramatic accomplishments. (Here it should be noted that I am fortunate that my home university has been an interdisciplinary institution since its foundation. There are always pressures upon it to conform, but I hope the day never comes when it does.)

For their encouragement and assistance in the preparation and publication of this volume, I am grateful to Heather Kiernan and Ellen Meiksins Wood. And for their never-flagging enthusiasm and eagerness to help out, I thank my daughters, Rhiannon and Fiona, and my best friend and collaborator, Lorna.

HJK
University of Wisconsin–Green Bay
September 1988

# Acknowledgements

Except for the Editor's Introduction, the articles collected here were originally published elsewhere. For permission to reprint them, we thank and acknowledge the following:

1. Allen & Unwin for 'Patterns of Protest in English History', originally published in R. Benewick and T. Smith, eds, *Direct Action and Democratic Politics*, London 1973.

2. Concordia University and Basil Blackwell Publishers for 'The Covenanters: A Problem of Creed and Class' originally published in F. Krantz, ed, *History from Below: Studies in Honour of George Rudé*, Montreal 1985 and Oxford 1988.

3. The Past & Present Society for 'Evangelicalism and the French Revolution', originally published in *Past & Present* 1, February 1952.

4. Lawrence & Wishart for 'Human Relations in Shakespeare', originally published in A. Kettle, *Shakespeare in a Changing World*, London 1964.

5. Lawrence & Wishart for 'Wordsworth and the People', originally published in J. Saville, ed., *Democracy and the Labour Movement*, London 1954; and Penguin Books for the postscript, which appeared with the article in D. Craig, ed., *Marxists on Literature*, Harmondsworth 1975.

6. Routledge & Kegan Paul for 'Tennyson, King Arthur and Imperialism', originally published in R. Samuel and G. Stedman Jones, eds, *Culture, Ideology and Politics: Essays for Eric Hobsbawm*, London 1983.

7. Croom Helm for 'Labour and the Literate', originally published in D. Rubinstein, ed., *Ideology and the Labour Movement: Essays Presented to John Saville*, London 1979.

8. University of Toronto Press for 'Herbert Norman's Cambridge', originally published in R. Bowen, ed., *E.H. Norman: His Life and Scholarship*, Toronto 1984.

9. *London Review of Books* for 'On Treason', originally published in The *London Review of Books*, 25 June 1987.

10. Croom Helm for 'Socialism, the Prophetic Memory', originally published in B. Parekh, ed., *The Concept of Socialism*, London 1975.

# Introduction: Marxism, History and the Necessity of Poetry

*Harvey J. Kaye*

To some this volume may come as a bit of a surprise, for Victor Kiernan's scholarly reputation is most evidently based on his many books and innumerable articles and critical essays on European imperialism in the nineteenth and twentieth centuries, the class struggles and politics of revolution and nation-state formation, and a remarkable variety of other political and cultural topics in international history. However, as the present work attests, he has also been a most active contributor and critic of English and British studies. If he is less renowned in this area it may be due not only to the volume and scholarly importance of his international studies, but to the fact that the critical writings have been less accessible as a body of work for they have appeared in a wide variety of journals, periodicals, and edited books on diverse subjects.[1] Thus, a primary purpose of the present collection is to make available in a single volume a selection of Kiernan's finest essays on English and British political and cultural history.[2] But that is not all. During the past several years there has been a dramatic renewal of interest in history and historical questions within both the humanities and the social sciences, from literature to sociology – referred to by many literary critics (with apparent pleasure) as 'the return to history'.[3] This collection can be read as addressed to those developments, for it includes essays not only in political and social history, but also in literary history and historical literary criticism.

History, however, has not only returned to the centre of scholarly and academic practice. After a generation (or more) of what many had referred to as its 'marginalization' in political and cultural life, history – as the relation between past and present – has become a central issue of political and cultural discourse for both the right and the left. This has been most evident in Britain in the phenomenal expansion of the 'heritage industry', the rhetoric of politicians (most crudely of the new right), and the present Conservative government's plans for a national educational curriculum in which history is to play a principal role.[4] Similar developments have been visible in the United States.

Paralleling, and probably linked to the 'crisis of history' has been the so-called 'crisis of socialism', which itself has entailed discussion and debate about both the making and writing of history.[5] The chapters of the present work are offered, then, not merely as contributions to the scholarly 'return to history' but just as much to the arguments underway on the left regarding such issues as the place of class struggle in democratic and socialist politics, the emergence of the 'new social movements' and their potential as forces for progressive social change, and the role of intellectuals and artists as political and cultural actors.

Although he has been closely identified with that outstanding generation of British Marxist historians which includes Rodney Hilton, Christopher Hill, Eric Hobsbawm, George Rudé, John Saville and Dorothy and E.P. Thompson, Kiernan's own work has been quite distinct. Along with his former comrades of the Communist Party Historians' Group, Kiernan has sought to explore and reveal the past (and the present) in terms of Marx and Engels's grand hypothesis that 'the history of all hitherto existing society is the history of class struggle'; and his work too has regularly been framed by the historical problematic of the transition from feudalism to capitalism. Nevertheless – in the bright light of his studies on imperialism and nation-state formation – his scholarly labours have appeared to be much less involved with his colleagues' efforts to recover and redeem the experience and agency of the English common people and to reappropriate the history of a radical democratic tradition in which alternative, or counter-hegemonic, conceptions of equality, liberty and community have been asserted.[6] The intention of the British Marxist historians has generally been to demonstrate that radical democracy *and* socialism – far from being Continental or 'Eastern' imports – have deep historical and, in fact, original roots in Britain, expressed in both popular protest and struggle and the writings and ideas of selected political and literary figures. Kiernan, in contrast, has seemed more concerned with recalling the experience and agency of 'the powers that be' such as feudal aristocrats, capitalist entrepreneurs, state bureaucrats, and colonial officials, civil and military – though he never fails to situate these in their historically specific social and class structures and struggles. Perhaps even more than the others, it might be said that Kiernan subscribes to Walter Benjamin's observation that class consciousness and sacrifice are sustained more by the memory of 'enslaved ancestors' than by the vision of 'liberated grandchildren'.[7]

In the chapters which follow, however, Kiernan's work can be seen moving quite close to and, indeed, intersecting with the initiatives of his fellow Marxist historians to rewrite British history from below and to affirm the centrality of radical democratic and socialist struggles. In 'Patterns of Protest in English History' (Chapter 1), he offers a historical survey of the politics of 'direct action' carried out by the 'people' against the prevailing powers of the State and its governors. With some apparent pride he notes that 'It was in the English-speaking world that direct action as a concept originated and found a name,

like so many political things before that have passed into currency everywhere'
(referring to particular twentieth-century events in Britain, the United States
and India). Mobilizing the historical studies of his comrades on the Peasant
Rising of 1381, the English Revolution of the seventeenth century, the crowds
of Hanoverian London, the 'making of the English working class' and
Chartism, Kiernan writes to undermine further the myth that English liberal
and democratic political development was a continuous, progressive, smooth
and evolutionary process. He does not deny the element of reality in the
progressive model, but he is insistent that the forward motion of change has
been motivated by struggles from below. (I would just add that contrary to
recent tendencies on the left to eschew – if not denigrate – this project of
reappropriation it remains a crucial task in the face of Conservative and new
right attacks portraying radical-democratic and socialist politics as alien to
British life.) History from the bottom up – in the specific sense of recovering
the history lived and made by the common people or 'lower orders' – is
also well represented by 'The Covenanters: A Problem of Creed and Class'
(Chapter 2), a study of the Scottish peasant, small tenant farmer, and artisan
movement of the seventeenth and early eighteenth centuries which fought for
the reformation (or restoration) of the Kirk on the basis of the National
Covenant of 1638, a manifesto directed against Charles I's interference in
Church governance and practice. As Kiernan reveals, the Covenanters were
inspired by a popular Calvinism and Scottish nationalism. And yet, although
their aspirations were essentially conservative, their struggle was expressive of a
democratic spirit – for their vision of the Kirk was a people's church controlled
by the people.

Though rather different in subject matter, Kiernan's essays 'Wordsworth
and the People' (Chapter 5) and 'Socialism, the Prophetic Memory' (Chapter
10), are also intimately linked to these labours. In fact, the article on
Wordsworth originally appeared as a chapter in the book, *Democracy and the
Labour Movement*, prepared by the members of the Historians' Group in 1954
both to honour one of their mentors, Dona Torr, and to provide a showcase for
their scholarship. The title of the work declares their project, and in the
foreword John Saville and his co-editors affectionately record their appreciation of Torr's influence and contributions and enunciate the spirit informing
their development of history from the bottom up: 'She has taught us historical
*passion* . . . . History was not words on a page, not the goings on of kings and
prime ministers, not mere events. History was the sweat, blood, tears and
triumphs of the common people, our people.'[8]

Kiernan introduces Wordsworth as having 'devoted the greater part of his
life to the study of political and social questions . . .'; indeed, several years later
in a review essay in *The New Reasoner*, he wrote that 'Wordsworth stands out,
with perhaps only Dante, Shakespeare, and Milton beside him, among the
greatest of political poets, interpreters that is of the hopes, fears, passions of

political life.'[9] Specifically, in the article, Kiernan considers Wordsworth's perception of the growing chasm, the alienation separating poet and people and his desire to secure a means by which to span the distance between 'himself and the world of men'. He notes how Wordsworth, 'disgusted with his own sort of people ... turn[ed] away from the educated classes to the "common people", towards whom history was, as it were, forcing him all through his years as a great poet'. Kiernan's assessments of Wordsworth's attempts to connect with and articulate the experiences of the 'lower orders' are critical (a point to which I shall return), but even as he chronicles the poet's incapacity to bridge the gap, he does not fail to appreciate his ambitions and sympathies, and to admire the development, however problematic, of a '*democratic* theory of diction'.

Written twenty years later, 'Socialism, the Prophetic Memory' considers the varied roots of socialist thought and politics, both religious and secular. Though not limited to English or British developments, the essay is most attentive to the English 'utopian' heritage (which Kiernan's senior colleague in the Historians' Group, Leslie Morton, had come to make his own).[10] Kiernan first highlights both the fourteenth-century democratic priest, John Ball, and early-modern churchman and visionary, Thomas More. Then, under the heading of 'indigenous English socialism', a term borrowed from the Christian socialist, R.H. Tawney, he introduces the nineteenth-century utopian socialists, Robert Owen and William Morris, who confronted the 'progress' of the Industrial Revolution with their own visions of alternative social orders. Finally, he offers a set of reflections on the socialist experience of this century. As 'the prophetic memory', socialism is here conceived as the ancient but persistent vision of freedom from the tyranny of the monopolization of wealth and power: 'From the point of view of socialism, it is a question of depriving a limited number of men of a "freedom" based on a bloated power over the community's economic life, in order to liberate the growth of countless others, both as individuals and as members of a meaningful community.'

'Herbert Norman's Cambridge' is included in this collection (Chapter 8) in order to chronicle further the formative experiences of the contemporary British socialist tradition. This memoir – or what might today be called a piece of 'oral history' – of the Cambridge student left in the 1930s is written by one who was himself a central participant. Kiernan spent the years 1931 to 1938 at Cambridge, first as an undergraduate reading history at Trinity and then as a research scholar and Fellow of the College. He had joined the Communist party in 1934 and among his closest friends of those years were John Cornford and James Klugmann (the leading figures of Cambridge student Communism), and Herbert Norman.[11] These were dramatic times; with the world economic depression, the rise of fascism and the threat of a second world war (increasingly confirmed by the events of the Spanish Civil War). Yet, however dark the world appeared, to these young men and women there seemed the possibility of radical change through working-class revolution, a process to which they believed they could contribute by means of political and intellectual commitment and solidarity.

Still, however much these writings flow into the narrative stream of the struggle for 'the rights of the free-born Briton' they are also classically Kiernanesque. Even in those which are most evidently pursued as history from the bottom up, Kiernan never fails to be objectively critical regarding the limits and inherent contradictions of the popular movements he is considering. For example, in 'The Covenanters' he appreciates the historical significance of their efforts – 'Most of the resisters came from a downtrodden mass exploited since time out of mind by superiors against whom they had never attempted to rise. For them to rise up now and challenge authority was an immense feat in itself' – and recognizes that their immersion in Calvinist theology was their first 'introduction to the world of intellect'. Yet he is compelled to observe that their experience and their ideology inhibited the emergence of a struggle to reform the social order:

> In a slippery world, as treacherous as one of their upland bogs, their treaty with God, a perpetual bond never to be broken, was a comforting certainty to which they could hold fast. Neighbourhood sentiment might be strong, but Scots villagers had no such organization of their own as the commune of old Russia, or Vietnam, with fixed rights of cultivation and a traditional leadership. Only an unearthly vision, a pole star invisible to others, could lend them the sense of fraternity they needed. Devotion to their image of the Kirk may be seen as the false consciousness of a class, a coming together in defence of ideals instead of interests. Covenanters had a deep sensation of being wronged and oppressed, but they turned their indignation against an imaginary oppressor, a giant or monster called Erastianism, casting a still more horrid shadow of Popery and Idolatry. Rejection of bishops was an unconscious rejection of the social order.

Such critical assessments are not at all reserved for 'pre-working-class' movements as we see in the essay 'Labour and the Literate in Nineteenth-Century Britain' (Chapter 7). Here he pursues a theme not unlike that of 'Wordsworth and the People', that is, the perceptions of the 'literati' of the labouring classes and, in particular, the experiences of those who sought, in political or cultural terms, a collaborative relationship with them. In sum, Kiernan records that the 'intellectuals' who did seek to 'surmount the barriers' separating labour and the literate were generally disappointed by their encounters. His own view is that the British working class has rarely ever been interested in turning the world upside down. It is true that he expresses a certain admiration for the struggles which E.P. Thompson narrates as 'the making of the English working class', culminating in the Chartist movement, the first working-class political party: 'It is indeed remarkable that out of a mass so "degraded" and "demoralized" [as the novelists and social commentators had written] a labour movement of such dimensions and vitality should have arisen.'[12] But whereas the Chartists and their forebears are to be admired, the late Victorian working class has retreated into 'labourism':

> Whatever their weaknesses, it appears that the first generations of the proletariat were capable of some vision of a world cleansed and renovated, and of the mighty put down from their seats . . . After mid century the labour movement was stiffening into 'labourism', content with what improvements could be got by trade unions, and relinquishing any design of transforming society.

Moreover, he later adds: 'Working-class withdrawal from the political arena and from the national culture went together'; though he equally admits that workers' self-enclosure in labourism not only insulated them from socialism but from the worst features of ruling-class ideology as well.[13]

Kiernan's conclusion to the article indicates that he sees socialist politics in almost Leninist fashion: 'it would seem that socialist consciousness has always been restricted to a very few, and that the bulk of the working class (as of every other, it may be) is inert except when activated by some direct material stimulus.' This picture of the late-nineteenth-century working class has been criticized by various labour historians. I would subscribe to their criticisms for although the working class was far from the socialist consciousness envisioned by Marx and Engels, working people did evidence a class consciousness which may even have entailed what James Young has referred to as 'socialism from below'.[14] The problem, I would argue – and I believe Kiernan would agree (I will explain why shortly) – has not been merely working-class 'labourism' but at least equally the incapacity of socialist intellectuals to comprehend and effectively articulate working-class aspirations.

Along with their objectively critical assessments of popular movements, these essays are also clearly Kiernanesque in their attentiveness to the political and ideological presence and determination of the rulers of the day. In 'Patterns of Protest in English History' – which is as much an examination of resistance from above by Britain's rulers in the name of law, order and property as it is of popular protest – Kiernan points out how 'direct action' from below was readily matched by those on high. That is, the State and its governors have been quick to respond with their own modes of direct action.[15] However, as Kiernan also shows with great respect for their ingenuity, when British ruling classes have been incapable of suppressing the challenges to the political and social order in one *direct* action they have not generally pursued a further escalation of hostilities but have rather sought to disarm or incorporate elements of the opposition and its demands in order to avoid an even greater crisis. This pattern of limited conflict and struggle has, he reflects, made English and British history seem 'exceptional' in comparison with Continental experience, leading him to the further observation that 'If our own ancient régime ever does come to an end, it may be through pressure of opinion stiffened by the cumulative effect of numerous small nibblings and scratchings. Before this happens, recourse by the other side to direct action, official or unofficial, must be expected in the future as in the past'.

In a review of the work of his fellow British Marxist historians, Kiernan has stated that

'History from below' . . . may have had all the more attraction because in England the people, or working class, has so signally failed, or rather has not tried, to take control in the present. One consequence has been a relative neglect of study of the dominant classes, their formation, culture, mode of consciousness, self-imaging, which all have their importance, along with external power and wealth.[16]

A prime example of his own pursuit of the elites or ruling classes is 'Evangelicalism and the French Revolution' (Chapter 3). This essay, first published in the inaugural issue of *Past & Present* in 1952, presents an original contribution to the debates which have taken place around the Halévy Thesis that Methodism provided an antidote to political revolution during the course of the social upheavals and dislocations of the Industrial Revolution. To these discussions both Eric Hobsbawm and Edward Thompson were later to offer their own distinct contributions; the former arguing that, contrary to the Halévy Thesis, Methodism and Radicalism advanced together, and the latter insisting that 'religious revivalism took over at the point where "political" or temporal aspirations met with defeat.'[17] Kiernan, however, in his concern for the agency of those on top, is led to consider the manner in which the upper classes of early-nineteenth-century England sought to harness the popular resurgence of religion against the threat of the spread of Jacobinsim and atheism which they saw emanating from Revolutionary France. He acknowledges at the outset that his examination of evangelicalism is one-sided in nature, stressing its service in 'support of order and stability'. Moreover, he fully accepts the fact that even as a 'conservative' force the revival of religious enthusiasm must be recognized as 'something "popular", originating from the people, like every genuine religious impulse'. Indeed, he states, Wesley himself was more a 'liberator' than a 'creator' of the movement to which he 'gave his name and imprint'.

Kiernan, then, advances no simple 'dominant ideology' thesis for, as he notes: '"New Birth" teachings embodied, in part and imperfectly, the early efforts of common people to adapt themselves to an altering environment'; and they were in fact received with hostile response by Church and State elites. Yet, he explains, this made them all the more effective when taken up by other upper-class voices equally eager to defend the social order: 'In religion as in politics, an idea which is to disarm discontents must at some time, in some sense, have seemed both to friend and foe an idea of rebellion. We are only held securely by fetters we have helped to forge ourselves; no-one else can tell the exact fit of our wrists and ankles.' Not easily taken up by the Church, it was not until Wilberforce articulated and created a movement which could bring together the 'two nations' in such a way as to equalize souls without levelling the classes that evangelicalism was to become an acceptable practice within the established order. Cutting two ways, Methodism was to be an effective ideology of the 'rising' middle classes: on the one hand critical of old aristocratic and clerical elites and, on the other, offering to the working classes and themselves a culture which inspired, but not towards revolution.

Whereas 'Wordsworth and the People' is to be read in terms of Kiernan's collaboration with his comrades in the recovery of a radical democratic tradition, 'Tennyson, King Arthur and Imperialism' (Chapter 6) should be read in relation to his own particular interest in the ruling classes. It is not that Tennyson is to be construed as merely a poetic reflection of the rulers of Victorian England: 'Because of the uncertainty and insecurity of his early social position, as well as personal morbidities and chronic pessimism, Tennyson could never be the confident spokesman of any class with a clearly focused political outlook.' Furthermore, Kiernan asserts – claiming it to be subtly registered in *Idylls of the King* – Tennyson must have had 'an uncomfortably low estimate ... of the ruling classes of his England'. Rather, what connects Tennyson and his work with Kiernan's 'history from above'[18] is, first, that in spite of the poet's antagonism towards the aristocracy and an increasingly plutocratic ruling class, and his personal ambition to be 'the voice of the people', Tennyson's desire for England was not change in the social order but in the *moral* order: 'not to get rid of those in power, but to invite them to turn over a new leaf. . . . His ideal was peace between classes, an end to "the feud of rich and poor".' Never failing to admire and appreciate the poetic and aesthetic value of Tennyson's verses, and ever sensitive to the doubts and contradictions evidenced within them, Kiernan proceeds to show how the poet turned to 'the past' as a means both to render contemporary sentiments 'more lucidly' and to afford himself a vantage point from which to judge the present. Yet he also illustrates how in contrast, for example, to William Morris, who also found a critical but 'democratic' standpoint in Celtic and medieval landscapes, Tennyson provided an idealization of aristocratic values and chivalry *and* a patriotic and noble historical mirror for England's empire-building – for which he has been entitled the 'bard of Empire'.

Kiernan, then, is no populist. However much he may appreciate their historical accomplishments and be prepared to admonish writers who under-estimate them, he remains persistently 'objective' about popular and working-class movements and apparently very much an 'elitist' on cultural and political questions. This requires further explanation. Kiernan's position is not that the arts, letters and political thought of the past were, or are, to be transmitted to, and passively received and preserved by a working class recently admitted to the ranks of the literate and educated. Rather it is that after a promising start the post-Chartist self-enclosure of the working class in the culture of labourism has, at great expense to both the further enrichment of the common culture and the advance of socialism within it, inhibited the working class from 'appropriating' and '*developing* the things belonging to the common stock'. But, of course, is this not the very same aspiration expressed by Antonio Gramsci in his vision of a truly democratic and socialist education?[19]

Moreover, even as he has been critical of working-class culture and politics (and admiring of the ingenuity and tenacity of the ruling classes) he has been equally critical of the intellectual 'class' including, if not especially, those who would seek an alliance with the common people and working class. This can readily be seen in the present volume in the essays on Wordsworth and 'Labour and the Literate', and it is equally characteristic of his many other writings on intellectuals and the 'literati'.[20] He faults intellectuals both for their theory – finding them no less subject to illusions than the common people themselves, though perhaps of a 'higher' order – and for their practice. For example, he recounts how Ernest Jones, the Chartist, called upon writers to join *with* and write *for* the people, but observes that most often they proceeded to 'write *about* the working classes . . . as sympathetic critics rather than allies.'[21] And, as we know, this was a positive development in comparison with the perennial service of intellectuals as managers of polity and society on behalf of the ruling classes. Then, there has been the equally unfortunate tendency in the face of popular apathy, if not antipathy, to their courtings, for intellectuals to envision themselves standing in for 'the people' or the working class in the making of socialism, with all the anti-democratic dangers involved. As much as Kiernan might be characterized as an elitist, his conception of socialism is much too democratic to permit him to subscribe to a political strategy in which intellectuals serve as a proxy for the agency of the working class.

Critical of the culture and politics of the common people and censorious of intellectuals' practices, Kiernan's perspective is apparently pessimistic. However, without simply resorting to Gramsci's favourite aphorism, 'Pessimism of the intellect, optimism of the will', I would insist that even if Kiernan's remarks occasionally incline towards cynicism, his own writings contradict both cynicism and any insurmountable pessimism. For a start, along with a certain humour and romanticism – often expressed in rich metaphor and allusion – Kiernan is capable of a most pointed anger, as we encounter in 'On Treason' (Chapter 9). In this essay, originally published in 1987 in the *London Review of Books*, Kiernan defends the commitments of his generation of young Communists in the 1930s and the war against fascism, in the face of renewed efforts to blacken that experience through commercial and political exploitation of the 'Cambridge spies'.[22] Noting past and present 'treacheries' of the right, he vehemently challenges the patriotic rhetoric and political and economic schemes of the Thatcher government. Outraged by the equation of Toryism with the 'national interest' he writes: 'Morally, the "treason" of the thirties cannot for a moment be compared with the morass of crooked dealing, profit-gorging, deception, looting of national resources and indifference to national welfare, that make up the world of Thatcherism.'

Another aspect of Kiernan's work which takes us beyond a one-dimensional pessimism or fatalism is his insistence on 'seeing things historically'. The absence of historical consciousness has been debilitating for both the intellectual left and the working class:

> Socialism and humanism alike stand in need of a rational consciousness of the past, still silently at work in the present. Any country where ordinary folk could be got to think seriously about their past would have a better chance of a brighter future; fortunately for our governors, a serious concern with history is a slow outgrowth of culture, and does not come of its own accord to men and women, few of whom retain much recollection of things done or suffered in even their own bygone years.[23]

Confident about the intimacy of history and politics, his own studies and essays are clearly intended as interventions in contemporary debates. In the preface to *The Lords of Human Kind* he states that 'A Marxist would not think history worth much study if he were not convinced that there are serious lessons to be learned from it, and he is used to being reproached with making it too didactic.'[24] Moreover, Marxism itself as *historical* materialism must, he has always insisted, become ever more responsive to the insights to be garnered from the dialogue between past and present; and Kiernan himself has not hesitated to point out particular inadequacies in Marxist and socialist thought which need to be addressed in the engagement with history.[25] In 'Socialism, the Prophetic Memory' he writes:

> Marxism always disclaimed any necessitarian belief in revolution coming of its own accord, but it was led by its 'scientific' logic into some undervaluing, not of the factor of human will, but of the ideas and ideals, the emotional wants left by religion and many other things of the past, which are needed to create the will to socialism.

Most persistently perhaps he has called for a greater sensitivity to religion and religious experience. Marx and Engels have not infrequently been misrepresented on the question of religion, Kiernan notes; but in any case, he says, they gave too much weight to the 'wastebasket theory of history' which assumes that historical development would naturally lead to the demise of religion, and 'to this day Marxism has scarcely corrected this underestimation, or made sufficient allowance in its general theory for the energy and tenacity of religion . . . one of the determining forces in human history.'[26]

Kiernan's own upbringing, like that of other British Marxist historians, was in Protestant Nonconformism, and he has never failed to appreciate both its influence in his own movement towards socialism and, in history, its role in dissent and opposition.[27] He wrote in a review of Eric Hobsbawm's *The Age of Revolution* that

> However subservient to State and ruling class Protestantism might become, it could never entirely lose its original character of *protest* – against supernatural pretensions of fellow-mortals, against thought-control and the blanketing out of human intelligence, against religion as a boundless, endless opium-dream.[28]

Radical religion, dissent and Nonconformism have been, of course, an important theme in the writings of Christopher Hill and E.P. Thompson, and, as we see in the essays on the Covenanters and evangelicalism included here, for Kiernan as well. Indeed, in the concluding lines to 'The Covenanters' we are presented with one of the most direct calls for intellectuals of the left to reflect on popular religious experience:

> The Covenanters may be charged with misleading their class. . . . Yet if their gospel was too other-worldly to cope with hardships like hunger, the simply bread-and-butter movements of our day have proved equally incapable of lifting men's minds to anything so ideal, so distant, so necessary as socialism. How to reconcile the two visions, pushed so far apart by our society and its maladies, is what Marxists hitherto have been as far as anyone else from discovering.[29]

In fact Kiernan's own explorations remind us that for all of the subsequent antagonism and conflict between Western socialism and Christianity, socialism itself is an 'offspring of Christianity', and thus he can propose in his article on 'Religion' in *A Dictionary of Marxist Thought* that 'It may indeed be said that, like Marx at the outset of his intellectual life, Marxism has found in the historical scrutiny of religion one of its most stimulating tasks.'[30] Kiernan has also felt compelled to disclaim Marxism's long practice of eschewing the discourse of morality, ethics, justice and rights, though ever insistent that they be studied 'not in the abstract but in the setting of history'.[31] Thinking no doubt of studies from the bottom up then being conducted by his fellow British Marxist historians, as well as his own, he offered the following argument in 'Notes on Marxism in 1968', which Thompson was to elaborate as a central tenet in his critique of Althusserian structuralism a decade later: 'Every social struggle or movement of resistance has also been a moral issue, over which individuals took risks for the sake of their fellows. Resistance to oppression has not only speeded technical progress, but has built mankind's moral reserves, its accumulation of moral capital.'[32]

Along with religion and morality Kiernan has long demanded that Marxism be attuned to the arts which, he says, also 'had a share in inventing' the idea of socialism. In particular among the arts, he stresses literature, of which he has himself long been an active student, as the articles on Shakespeare, Wordsworth and Tennyson, and the literary references in other essays included here illustrate.[33] Noteworthy in this context is the well-grounded statement by Margot Heinemann, herself a prominent student of Shakespeare and his contemporaries, and also a comrade of the former members of the Historians' Group, that 'Much of the most distinguished Marxist literary commentary of recent years has indeed come from people who are primarily or partly historians – among them A.L. Morton, Victor Kiernan, E.P. Thompson, Jack Lindsay, and Christopher Hill . . .'.[34] This should not be too surprising since, on the one hand, there is a long record of Marxist historiographical interest in literature commencing with the 'old man' himself as Professor Prawer so comprehensively reveals in *Karl Marx and World Literature* and, on the other, there is an even longer tradition, as Fred Inglis reminds us, wherein 'the English intellectual tries to explain his ideas or to interpret those of others by resituating them in his literature.'[35] Kiernan's concern, nevertheless, is that Marxists learn to draw upon the creative expressiveness and values and aspirations articulated in literature, most especially, it should be noted, in *poetry*.

In 'Wordsworth and the People' Kiernan emphatically declares: 'There will not be another great poet who has not learned much from Marx. Marxism also has much to learn, that it has not yet learned, from poetry.' In a historical and biographical fashion the 'lesson' to be derived from Wordsworth's experience, as I have shown above, relates to his unfulfilled desire to transcend the divide between poet and people, reflecting on Kiernan's part, as Bill Schwarz contends, a central concern of the Historians' Group regarding their own 'isolation' from the working class in the 1950s.[36] Indeed, Thompson later made this question of Wordsworth's experience a subtext of *The Making of the English Working Class* which is revealed in the closing paragraphs of the book when he brought the Romantic poets and radical artisans together as 'parallel' oppositions to the rise of 'Acquisitive Man'. The tragedy he ponders was that 'In the failure of the two traditions to come to a point of junction, something was lost. How much we cannot be sure, for we are among the losers.'[37] Kiernan himself issued a warning derived from the personal histories of the Romantic poets: 'An artist who does not feel the People as a force positively on his side may soon come to feel them as something against him.'

In a postscript to 'Wordsworth and the People' written in 1973 (which is included here with the essay), Kiernan recalls the challenge but acknowledges that the relationship has become ever more problematic. He then proceeds to highlight the values in Wordsworth's poetry which should have special resonance today. In particular he refers to a stress on 'individual autonomy' in the midst of non-democratic and anonymous corporate and collective institutions (capitalist and socialist) and a preservationist concern for the environment. Also relevant here, Kiernan has mused in an article on 'The Socialism of Antonio Gramsci' that the English amongst all Europeans are the richest in poetry and history but, sadly, 'the most indifferent to both';[38] and in 'Labour and the Literate' he signals the tragic element in this state of affairs: 'Without memory of yesterday there can indeed be no vision of tomorrow and in this light history is indispensable to progress.'

To comprehend fully the character of Kiernan's pessimism it is essential to understand his tragic vision of history. Without underestimating the sense of loss and fatality, it should be recognized that his conception of tragedy is also imbued with an awareness, an expectation, of historical movement and so it also involves a sense of hope and possibility. In his own words: 'if tragic drama ends on a note of acceptance, of turning away from past to future, this only epitomizes human experience that through storms and stresses, the strife of wills and its unguessable outcomes, new beginnings are at last reached.'[39] He finds this tragic vision of history most brilliantly expressed in the works of Marx and Engels – 'Early Marxism adopted a panoramic vista of the past as tragic as its outlook on the future was optimistic; later Marxism has not yet found a convincing alternative'[40] – and, of course, in Shakespeare. In 'Notes on Marxism in 1968' he writes: 'the development of a theory of tragedy, and a special theory of Shakespearean tragedy, is among the grandest problems of historical Marxism.'[41]

Kiernan himself has been eager to develop a Marxian theory of Shakespearean tragedy. In the years immediately following the Second World War, as a Fellow of Trinity College once again, he produced a book-length manuscript on the subject (to which he has now returned). Moreover, his books *State and Society in Europe, 1550-1650* and *The Duel in European History*[42] clearly indicate his intimacy with the works of the great playwright, and their incorporation in his history writing. The essay included in the present volume, 'Human Relations in Shakespeare' (Chapter 4), well represents what might be termed the 'dialectical' character of Kiernan's tragic vision of history. As much as he celebrates Shakespeare's dramatic renderings of the impermanence and demise of the feudal epoch – and the rule of aristocrat and monarch – he finds within the plays an appreciation of the liberation of human relations associated with what we might now refer to as the making of the modern world, or the transition to capitalism: 'In a season of change one artist will fasten chiefly on what is bad in the situation, decline and decay, another on what is good, birth and growth. Shakespeare belongs emphatically to the second sort.' But this was written in the early 1960s and is likely to present Kiernan's historical vision in too 'optimistic' a light. A better way of seeing it today is suggested in Margot Heinemann's 'Shakespearean Contradictions and Social Change':

Shakespearean tragedy and tragic history implies a double view. We reduce it if we present it as wholly somber, showing history *only* as a meaningless cycle and human beings only as helpless or grotesque, doomed by fate. There is no need to replace this view by its opposite: that the endings (even in *Lear* or *Troilus*) must always be felt as 'optimistic', or even that tragedy is not an art for socialists. In the last quarter of the twentieth century, Marxists of all people must feel acutely the contrast between what men *could* make of history and life and what they *do*. This is truly a *tragic* sense of futility and waste – and not less because so much of the suffering is avoidable.[43]

Again we are returned to the issue of the *making* of history which must always be a central one for those of us who aspire to more democratic, egalitarian and libertarian social orders. Kiernan has long called for a 'reformation' of both Marxism and socialism reinvigorated by new ideas to be realized in the mirror of history. This again poses a question for Kiernan: in the light of the current debates about the future of Western socialism and the place of class struggle and working-class agency within it, does he align himself with those 'post-modern' socialists who contend that the working class – if it ever was so central – has been superseded by the 'new social movements' of environmentalism, peace, and feminism as the primary agents of progressive social change and the making of radical democracy and/or socialism?[44]

In 'Notes on the Intelligentsia' (1969) Kiernan wrote that 'The barrier fortresses of class power remain, and will not fall down for any blowing of trumpets, intellectual or other. Class struggle remains as necessary as Marxism has always said.' In those pages, and elsewhere since, he has insisted that 'the working class remains indispensable to any thorough-going change' both for the vigour and fortitude it would instill in the socialist movement and for the sake of ensuring that its victories entailed the maximization of democracy.[45] Yet, at the same time, he has said that 'There is no chosen class, any more than a chosen people', and he looks ahead with some hope to the emergence of a broad progressive alliance of workers, intellectuals, women and young people. Moreover, he has stated that 'socialism in Europe has been allowed to appear too closely linked to a single class' and, further, that Marx and Engels clearly underestimated the potential inclination towards socialism in sectors of the middle class.[46] The history of religion and art, he observes, shows how 'creations of the mind' are capable of transcending their historical circumstances and – more than Marxism has allowed – the same potential exists for socialism.[47]

The formation of a socialist alliance constructed around the working class and sectors of the middle class remains, however, problematic. In one of his most pessimistic articles, 'After Empire' Kiernan acknowledged: 'Socialism cannot be built without the working class, which is not interested in it; it cannot be built against the middle classes, which are hostile to it.'[48] Ever ambivalent – though never indifferent – he allows that the 'true nature of classes remains mysterious' and, thus, from the 'autonomy which the working class has preserved, negative as it may often seem, fresh beginnings can always be looked for hopefully.'[49] All of which, it seems to me, points again to the

'Wordsworthian' dilemma of surmounting the divide between poet and 'people'. And here I am led to withdraw, or recant, my accusation of Leninism directed at Kiernan's political thought, for his sympathies and inclinations are, as I have implied throughout this essay, actually much more often Gramscian with reference to the responsibility of left and socialist intellectuals to articulate the aspirations, ideals, and vision of socialism out of a 'dialogue' with 'the people'.[50] Indeed, *there* is the challenge – as it has always been – for radical democratic and socialist intellectuals. Kiernan himself proposed it thirty years ago in his review of Raymond Williams's *Culture and Society* when, for all his criticism of both Williams's book and the 'tradition' of cultural criticism delineated in it, he asserted that 'if the Tradition meant more than mere self-complacency it was because England had a record never long interrupted of popular resistance to society as it was, and of writers ready to put the feelings of the people into language.'[51] We could do no better than to emulate that long and honourable tradition.

## Notes

1. See my introductory essay, 'V.G. Kiernan: Seeing Things Historically', in the first volume of Kiernan's collected essays, *History, Classes and Nation-States*, Oxford 1988, pp. 1–28, for a general discussion of his work. For a complete bibliography of his writings to 1977, see the special issue of *New Edinburgh Review*, 'History and Humanism', prepared in his honour: nos 38–39, summer–autumn 1977, pp. 77–9.

2. A selection of other British studies by Kiernan will be included in the next projected volume of his collected essays, *Europe, Britain and the World*.

3. For example, see David Simpson, 'Literary Criticism and the Return to History', *Critical Inquiry*, vol. 14, summer 1988, pp. 721–47, and Jerome McGann, ed., *Historical Studies and Literary Criticism*, Madison, WI 1985.

4. See Harvey J. Kaye, 'The Use and Abuse of the Past: The New Right and the Crisis of History', R. Miliband, L. Panitch and J. Saville, eds, *Socialist Register 1987*, London 1987, pp. 332–64, and Patrick Wright, *On Living in an Old Country*, London 1985.

5. For example, the conference held in London in July 1988, 'Back to the Future', selected papers of which are due to be published in book form.

6. On the British Marxist historical tradition, see Harvey J. Kaye, *The British Marxist Historians*, Oxford 1984, and Raphael Samuel, 'British Marxist Historians, 1880–1980', *New Left Review* 120 March–April 1980, pp. 21–96. Also, on the work of particular historians, see the essays in Geoff Eley and William Hunt, eds, *Reviving the English Revolution*, London 1988 for Christopher Hill; Harvey J. Kaye, 'George Rudé, Social Historian', in H.J. Kaye, ed., *The Face of the Crowd: Collected Essays of George Rudé*, London 1988, pp. 1–42; and Perry Anderson, *Arguments within English Marxism*, London 1980, and the essays in Harvey J. Kaye and Keith McClelland, eds, *E.P. Thompson: Critical Debates*, Oxford, forthcoming, for E.P. Thompson.

7. Walter Benjamin, 'Theses on the Philosophy of History' in Hannah Arendt, ed., *Illuminations*, London 1970, p. 262.

8. John Saville, ed., *Democracy and the Labour Movement*, London 1954, p. 8.

9. V.G. Kiernan, 'Wordsworth Revisited', *The New Reasoner* 7 winter 1958–9, pp. 62–74.

10. See Maurice Cornforth, 'A.L. Morton – Portrait of a Marxist Historian', in M. Cornforth, ed., *Rebels and their Causes*, London 1978, pp. 7–20, and A.L. Morton's *The English Utopia*, London 1952, among a variety of other works.

11. Kiernan refers to those friends in the course of the essay. (Kiernan left the Communist

party in 1959, frustrated by its failure to reform itself after the crises and tragedies of 1956.)

12. See E.P. Thompson, *The Making of the English Working Class*, London 1963 and Dorothy Thompson, *The Chartists*, London 1984.

13. The concept of 'labourism' is derived from the work of his long-time friend and comrade, John Saville. See Saville's 'Ideology of Labourism' in R. Benewick, et al., eds, *Knowledge and Belief in Politics*, London 1973, and more recently his books *1848: The British State and Chartism*, Cambridge 1987, and *The British Labour Movement*, London 1988.

14. James Young, *Socialism and the English Working Class, 1883–1939*, London 1988; and, for the USA, see the writings of David Montgomery, for example, *Workers' Control in America*, Cambridge, Mass. 1979 and *The Fall of the House of Labor*, Cambridge, Mass 1987.

15. See also, for example, J. Saville, *1848: The British State and Chartism*.

16. V.G. Kiernan, 'Problems of Marxist History', *New Left Review* 161, January–February 1987, p. 117.

17. Eric Hobsbawm, 'Methodism and the Threat of Revolution in Britain', 1957, reprinted in his *Labouring Men*, London 1964, and Thompson, pp. 411–17.

18. We should be careful here, for 'history from the bottom up' is supposed to have been more a 'perspective' than a 'content' or subject. Thus even Kiernan's work is pursued as history from the bottom up in so far as it is pursued as a perspective.

19. V.G. Kiernan, 'After Empire', *New Edinburgh Review*, no. 37, Spring 1977, p. 30 (my italics). On the relation between Kiernan's view of culture and that of Gramsci, see Kiernan's essay, 'The Socialism of Antonio Gramsci' in Ken Coates, ed., *Essays on Socialist Humanism*, Nottingham 1972, esp. pp. 75–8.

20. For examples in addition to the chapters of the present volume, see Kiernan's essays 'Gramsci and Marxism', in his *History, Classes and Nation-States*, ed., H.J. Kaye, pp. 66–101, and 'Intellectuals in History', *Winchester Research Papers in the Humanities*, Winchester 1979.

21. 'Labour and the Literate' in the present collection.

22. Philby, Maclean, Blunt and Burgess. See also his review of David Caute's *The Fellow Travellers*, 1972 in the *Times Literary Supplement*, 16 February 1973.

23. Kiernan, 'The Socialism of Antonio Gramsci', p. 75.

24. V.G. Kiernan, *The Lords of Humankind*, Harmondsworth 1972 (Penguin Books edn), p. xiv. Unfortunately, all subsequent editions of the book – by other publishers – have omitted this important prefatory essay.

25. Regarding Marxism's failure adequately to address 'nationalism', see Kiernan's essays in his *History, Classes and Nation-States*.

26. V.G. Kiernan, 'Revolution and Reaction, 1789–1848 (a review of Eric Hobsbawm's *The Age of Revolution*)' in *New Left Review* 19, March–April 1963, p. 75. Also, see Kiernan's contributions to T.B. Bottomore, et al., eds, *A Dictionary of Marxist Thought*, Oxford 1983; in particular 'Christianity', 'Hinduism', and 'Religion'.

27. H.J. Kaye, 'V.G. Kiernan: Seeing Things Historically', pp. 3, 26; and *The British Marxist Historians*, pp. 10, 103. Also see Samuel, pp. 49–55.

28. Kiernan, 'Revolution and Reaction' p. 76. Also see his review of Christopher Hill's *Century of Revolution* in *New Left Review* 11 September–October 1961, pp. 62–6 on Protestantism and popular protest.

29. See on this issue David McLellan, *Marxism and Religion*, London 1987.

30. V.G. Kiernan, 'Religion' in T.B. Bottomore, et al., eds, *A Dictionary of Marxist Thought*, p. 416.

31. V.G. Kiernan, 'Notes on Marxism in 1968' in R. Miliband and J. Saville, eds, *Socialist Register 1968*, London 1968, pp. 207–8. Recent work on this is to be welcomed but Kiernan's call for historical specificity is not always heeded. For a prime example of such work, see Stephen Lukes, *Marxism and Morality*, Oxford 1986.

32. Ibid., p. 207. For E.P. Thompson's argument, see *The Poverty of Theory*, London 1978, esp. pp. 171–6.

33. Kiernan has remarked that 'A historian without strong literary interests is like a man without a shadow' (in a personal letter to the editor, 11 September 1986).

34. Margot Heinemann, 'How the Words Got on the Page' in G. Eley and W. Hunt, eds, *Reviving the English Revolution*, p. 73. For an example of Heinemann's own historical literary criticism, see her *Puritanism and Theatre*, Cambridge 1980. Also included in the volume *Reviving*

*the English Revolution*, is Kiernan's essay 'Milton in Heaven', pp. 161–80.

35. S.S. Prawer, *Karl Marx and World Literature*, Oxford 1978 and Fred Inglis, *Radical Earnestness*, Oxford 1982, p. 21.

36. Bill Schwarz, '"The People" in History: The Communist Party Historians' Group, 1946–56', in R. Johnson, et al., eds, *Making Histories*, London 1982, esp. pp. 76–7.

37. Thompson, *The Making of the English Working Class*, p. 915. It should also be noted that Thompson himself has been working for many years on a book on Blake and Wordsworth. See his articles 'Disenchantment or Default? A Lay Sermon' in C. Cruise O'Brien and W. Dean Vanech, eds, *Power and Consciousness*, London 1969, pp. 149–81 and 'London', in M. Philips, ed., *Interpreting Blake*, Cambridge 1978, pp. 5–31. Also, with reference to the British Marxist historians' interest in and commitment to poets and poetry, see Christopher Hill's masterpiece *Milton and the English Revolution*, London 1977 and the pamphlet by a senior figure of the Historians' Group, the classicist and professor of Greek, George Thomson, *Marxism and Poetry*, London 1945; reprinted 1980.

38. V.G. Kiernan, 'The Socialism of Antonio Gramsci', p. 75.

39. Kiernan, 'Gramsci and Marxism', p. 93.

40. Kiernan, 'Problems of Marxist History', p. 118.

41. Kiernan, 'Notes on Marxism in 1968', p. 198.

42. V.G. Kiernan, *State and Society in Europe, 1550–1650*, Oxford 1980 and *The Duel in English History*, Oxford 1988.

43. Margot Heinemann, 'Shakespearean Contradictions and Social Change', in *Science and Society*, vol. XLI, spring 1977, p. 16.

44. For a critical assessment of this current, see Ellen M. Wood, *The Retreat from Class*, London 1985.

45. V.G. Kiernan, 'Notes on the Intelligentsia', in R. Miliband and J. Saville, eds, *Socialist Register 1969*, London 1969, pp. 81, 76.

46. Ibid., and 'Socialism, the Prophetic Memory' in the present volume.

47. Kiernan, 'Notes on Marxism in 1968', p. 208.

48. Kiernan, 'After Empire', p. 33.

49. V.G. Kiernan, 'Labour and the Literate' in the present volume and 'Working Class and Nation in Nineteenth-century Britain', in H.J. Kaye, ed., *History, Classes and Nation-States*, p. 198.

50. On this, see my essay, 'Political Theory and History: Antonio Gramsci and the British Marxist Historians', *Italian Quarterly*, nos. 97–98 summer–fall 1984, pp. 145–66.

51. V.G. Kiernan, 'Review of Raymond Williams' *Culture and Society* (1958)', *The New Reasoner* 9, summer 1959, p. 79.

# 1

# Patterns of Protest in English History

'Direct action' is a phrase that has come rapidly into circulation in recent years. What it connotes is hard to define, since the boundaries that it crosses depend on what happens to be law, and on more quickly fluctuating opinion and convention. It may manifest itself in any shape from boycott to bomb; it may rely on moral coercion, like one of Gandhi's fasts or a suicide in Japan on an opponent's doorstep, or on physical force, which may be employed against buildings or other property, or against life or limb. Its extremest and most socially acceptable form is war. It may be concerned with political objectives, or with others, but here again the dividing-line is a fluid one, and political behaviour is influenced by habits belonging to other departments of life. For example, the English upper class clung less tenaciously than any on the Continent to the privilege of the duel, that vestigial right of blue blood to ignore the law; and it was also less prone than most to poke its sword into affairs of State.

There has always been direct action of one sort or another in practice, but as a principle, a deliberate procedure, it could only emerge in a society long familiar with other, more 'constitutional' methods, and as an expression of dissatisfaction with them. In Tsarist Russia, or in Asia at large, malcontents took to plotting, assassination and insurrection as naturally as M. Jourdain talked prose, because they knew of no other way to express their feelings. It was in the English-speaking world that direct action as a concept originated and found a name, like so many political things before it that have passed into currency everywhere. It was talked of in the USA before 1914, and in Britain before the end of 1918, and again in 1926 during the General Strike. A decade later it was afloat in India, in the wake of the Congress civil disobedience movements, and it was there that it had a first dramatic baptism of fire and blood in the Direct Action Day proclaimed by the Muslim League on 16 August 1946. Lately, other languages in and out of Europe have been either borrowing the English phrase, or making literal translations of it.[1]

In Britain or America it would have been more exact to call it *directer* action, for in reality their political life always directly involved large numbers in the management of national or local affairs, gradually transforming their people into that peculiarly English entity, the *public.* 'Of all societies since the Roman Republic', Morley could assert, '. . . England has been the most emphatically and essentially political', by virtue of its mode of 'government by deliberative bodies, representing opposed principles and conflicting interests.'[2] In medieval times, a ruling class formed by the Conquest, in a country just small enough to be managed by consensus of those strong enough to have a voice, acquired an exceptionally clear sense of itself as a collective body or estate. Violence was, as elsewhere, undeniably endemic – forcible self-help in the shape of private conflicts between barons, risings of baronage against Crown, struggles of towns against overlords, of peasantry against landowners; while interdicts to enforce rights of Church against State might be called an early version of non-violent non-cooperation. But all such contests had, in a higher degree than in most other regions, more or less of an institutional character, or took place within a framework of law or custom. Complexities of feudal property and obligation were too great for the most turbulent baron to rely on the right of the sword pure and simple, as a robber-knight beyond the Rhine might do. The Magna Carta came about in 1215 because King John's arbitrary demands for contributions upset 'the carefully balanced medieval society with its strong corporate sense and strict counterpoise of privilege and responsibilities',[3] and because, as in many later reform struggles, a 'moderate' or 'constitutional' leadership was able to profit by the pressure of more extreme factions on the government. In sum, the result was a surprisingly wide-ranging survey and definition of the rights of all entitled to claim them. Even peasants could find in manorial custom something like the warrant that the barons at Runnymede claimed in feudal prescription. In the peasant revolt of 1381, a rational, purposeful character can be seen, instead of a mere *jacquerie*, and despite its defeat it may have helped to avert a return to serfdom.[4] In 1450, the rebels, who were led by Jack Cade and came mainly from Kent, were 'a body of peasants with a very strong leaven of gentry, shopkeepers and craftsmen': also with a distinct political attitude, a reasoned case finding much support in London, on the eve of the Wars of the Roses, against weak and bad government.[5] It is another feature of all these pre-capitalist movements that diverse classes or sections of them were able to make common cause.

A century later, *A Mirror for Magistrates,* that compendium of Tudor statecraft, despite its bias towards authority could not withold a grudging tribute to Cade.[6] Sixteenth-century thinking had the same pragmatic quality as Chinese, and like it recognized that in the last resort a bad government lost the mandate of heaven and deserved to be overthrown; conversely, anyone who tried to overthrow the government and failed deserved to lose his head. Absolute monarchy as represented by the Tudors was relatively easy-going, because it rested less on armed strength than on support (as in other countries) of urban opinion, and on the special support of the chief propertied groups, more effectively organized or self-organizing than elsewhere. With the coming of the Reformation and its great social and economic changes, there was bound to be a moving apart, a friction between the interests that were pushing these on and benefiting by them, and a mass of opinion resentful of change or fearful of losing by it. Resistance inflamed by Catholic conservatism might drift in several directions. It broke out most formidably in the Pilgrimage of Grace in Yorkshire and Lincolnshire in 1536. This must have contained ingredients of feudal insubordination, antipathy to the new centralizing regime. But it can also be considered, it has been argued with reference to Lincolnshire, as an attempt by those who guided the elemental mass not to overturn the government but only to alter some of its policies. At a time when parliament could not yet be 'the effective conflict-resolving mechanism of the society', riots and manifestos, or seizure of a country town, might be the means by which a region, with a strong regional life of its own, expressed its disgust at maladministration. They were kept nevertheless within 'a framework of form and convention which aimed at limiting the disruptive effects of the movement, and the amount of damage which might result, particularly to the landed governing class.'[7] No wonder a plain man like Bishop Latimer might express, in his sermon against the rebels, some bewilderment as to what was really happening: 'They rise with the king, and fight against the king in his ministers and officers; they rise with the Church, and fight against the Church;. . . they rise for the Commonwealth, and fight against it . . . Lo, what false pretence can the devil send against us.'[8] He may really have been watching a primitive rehearsal of His Majesty's Opposition.

Something similar may be said of the peasant movement in Norfolk in 1549, led by Ket, which like Cade's in Kent a hundred years before had a sober and public-spirited complexion. A 'keen sense of order . . . permeated the whole undertaking', the occupation of Mousehold was 'a sort of vast sit-down strike'.[9] Though peasants might riot against sporadic enclosures, and had chronic minor grievances, there was no such issue to bind them together and alienate them from the State as the maintenance or reintroduction of serfdom that provoked the great agrarian revolts abroad. Ket was appealing to the government against bad local magistrates and landowners; he organized a substitute county administration – not altogether unlike the councils of action of 1926 – and demonstration only turned into rebellion when the authorities set out to crush it by force.

Outbreaks more fundamentally hostile to the new England that was taking shape were confined now to peripheral areas. There was a Western Rising in 1549 against the new Prayer Book, of rustics led by priests, in Cornwall, still part of the Celtic-speaking fringe of Britain, and Devon. In 1569 the feudal and Catholic Northern Rebellion took place, drawing its strength from the hills and moors of the north country. Subsequently, resistance of this type dwindled to the level of conspiracy, managed by Jesuits and other professional agents, with Guy Fawkes's plot to mark its dead end. Such plottings encountered an increasingly superior technique of counter-espionage, and were fatally compromised by their foreign connections and reliance on foreign backing, as other movements in Britain in later times have been. They were compromised also, perhaps, by a feeling already astir that the strategy of secret plans, disguises, deceptions, was somehow un-English, or alien to a land where some freedom of open debate, however restricted, always had a place; that it was only fit for 'priests, and cowards, and men cautelous', as Brutus says in a great speech that may be felt to embody a national distaste.[10] Possibly sensitive to this, when Essex made his rash attempt in London near the end of Elizabeth's life, appealing to the newer religious minority of Puritans, he went about it in an ostentatiously open, amateurish fashion.

England reached the seventeenth century with a well-formed conviction, proclaimed by Lord Chief Justice Coke long before W.S. Gilbert's Lord Chancellor, that

> The Law is the high embodiment
> Of everything that's excellent.

Respect for law was equally respect for property, whose guardianship was its chief duty, and collaboration among the propertied classes had developed sufficiently to enable Parliament to survive when most similar bodies, like the States-General or Cortes, were fading out. Yet in Coke's day, complex shifts in class interests and relations were preparing a long civil war. Any such social ferment may dissipate itself in mere froth or anarchy, if there is no strong containing channel, as the Wars of the Fronde in contemporary France largely did. Voltaire was to contrast the frivolity of these with English orderliness: like many Frenchmen, he saw history and politics very much in terms of Anglo-Gallic antitheses. 'The English displayed in their civil disturbances as it were a sullen fury and a reasoned frenzy.'[11] Who was on which side might depend a great deal on the still very active and still largely personal politics of each county, but there was enough sense of national destiny to resolve all these into a meaningful confrontation. Religion played an indispensable part in this, and in helping to nerve men for the venture into the unknown that armed rebellion in a land of settled government implies. The paradoxical outcome was that this land of law and lawyers carried out far the most successful revolution of all the many that were essayed in seventeenth-century Europe, as in 1215 it had carried out the most orderly feudal resistance of any in medieval Europe. England was undergoing not a collapse of authority but a collision between two rival authorities. Even the left-wing movement that emerged in defiance of both had a discipline and a rational programme of its own; whereas the only plebeian intervention in the Thirty Years War in progress in Germany was an occasional wild tumult.

Once the left movement failed, or could only take such action as the rising of the Fifth Monarchy men against Cromwell in 1657 (the religious forlorn hope of the revolution still pressing forward when all the rest was receding), Commonwealth politics sank into sterility. Among the Royalists especially there was again a labyrinthine weaving of futile plots, an efflorescence of secret cyphers; again, perhaps, uncongenial to the English temperament, if only on account of its impracticality, if less so to the clerical temperament: one of the most laborious spinners and weavers was a Dr John Barwick, D.D.[12] Nothing better came of it than the miserably bungled rising headed by Penruddock in 1655. In 1660, under cover of the Restoration, the divided ruling class moved quietly together again, broadened by coalition with other leading forms of wealth, and with a composite character, and therefore an adaptability and durability which a thoroughbred class is always liable to lack. Again the Fifth Monarchy men, buoyed by millenarian fantasy, rose in vain. More weighty attempts to upset the new balance could come only a quarter-century later, and then only in far-off regions and under the leadership of outsiders, Monmouth in the south-west and Argyle in Scotland, and their risings in 1685 were soon quelled. When James II sought to upset the balance from the opposite quarter, he was able to make a fight only still further away from Westminster, on the banks of the Boyne. From the wild Highlands, his son and grandson could levy war against the Crown as late as 1715 and 1745; but their dependence on this outlandish 'colonial' base only promoted English solidarity, much as Castilian loyalty was always cemented by the perpetual disloyalty of Basques and Catalans.

The Glorious Revolution of 1688 was glorious, for respectable opinion and Whig tradition, because the common people had nothing to do with it, except cheer. It was made for them, as the Reformation had been, by their superiors, men entitled by rank and wealth to take action on the country's behalf. Monmouth's ambitions had led him, very reprehensibly, to recruit peasants and miners. After their taste of Ironsides and Levellers, men of property had no intention of ever again allowing the people to partake in politics. On the other hand, their rival factions, Whig and Tory (the latter in particular as being normally the weaker), were prepared at times to conjure up for their own purposes that caricature of the people, the mob. A crowd running amok might be destructive, but it presented no real threat of subversion. It could be used by one party against the other, and later on, when a genuine left began to reappear, against this; hence the long history of the 'Tory mob', whose ancestry can be traced back to feudal demagogy, while its descendants come down to the age of fascism.

To the peaceable citizen, a mob was a recurrent bugbear, and the Riot Act was passed in 1716 to keep it under watch and ward. It was, moreover, 'a creature of very mysterious existence', as Dickens called it in his novel about the Gordon riots in London in 1780, published in 1841 amid forebodings of Chartist outbreaks.[13] In fact, a true 'mob' is seldom, if ever, merely criminal, but is rather a multitude of individuals making a convulsive effort to merge themselves into something bigger, to find a momentary unity and purpose in a society meaningless to them, to achieve a fugitive sense of power and of participation in events.[14] Hence it requires some ideal, or creed, however cloudy, and eighteenth-century Britain found it most readily in some sectarian delusion, residue of the religious fervour of the revolutionary age. This happened in the Sacheverell riots in London in 1710 under High Church watchwords, and in the Gordon riots, anti-Catholic and probably with an anti-Irish but also an anti-aristocratic colouring. Pathetically, the disinherited were seeking to identify themselves with their stepmotherly England, to protect her against imaginary foes; and the populace of a capital city, whether London or Stamboul, always feels a special responsibility for the national welfare. But in 1780 there seems also to have been a hint of a permissive attitude on the part of men in high places, who counted on the disturbances to clear the way for designs of their own.[15] An analogous situation brought about the Porteous riots of 1736 in Edinburgh, flavoured by national resentment against the Union of 1707 with England, lingering on among plebeians long after their betters had succumbed to English gold; and those in Edinburgh and Glasgow in 1779, forerunners of the Gordon riots, when anti-Popery feeling compelled the exclusion of Scotland from a Roman Catholic Relief Bill.

Town mobs must have been swelled by recent incomers, disgruntled or demoralized, from the countryside. The coalition of 1660, inaugurating the age of agrarian capitalism and nascent industrialism, was made at the expense of the English peasantry; the mass of this, isolated by want of any urban ally as it had not been in the past, was being gradually reduced to the status of landless labourers. It may be remarkable that the peasants submitted so tamely to their fate; but it came on them slowly, and they were already divided, the luckier ones rising to the farmers or English kulaks. There was, moreover, to nip any resistance in the bud, the immediate presence of the local landlord, still in decentralized England very much a feudal lord in relation to his own rustics. If the last Kaiser boasted of never having read the constitution, many a justice of the peace could have boasted that he never read the laws. A dwarfish class war went on for generations in the running fight between poachers and game-keepers: direct action by labourers to get some of the wages denied to them by landlords eager to protect the sacred rights of property with spring-guns and mantraps. At a later date, in rural districts with manufactures this could link up with higher kinds of struggle. 'The Luddites are now principally engaged in politics and poaching', a Derbyshire magistrate reported in 1817.[16]

In the Highlands, when Anglicized chiefs set about getting rid of their clansmen to make room for sheep, the peasants faced a more sudden and sweeping attack than in England, and there was some spirited resistance, particularly in Ross: in 1792, about 1820,[17] and even down to 1843. Elsewhere, in Sutherland notably, there was far less than might have been expected in a land of warlike memories. Emigration offered an escape, and sermons by the landlords' retinue of clergymen are said to have provided effective opium. In Ireland, under the changing surface of politics, the peasantry always kept alive the embers of resistance. Their fate differed from that either of the English, reduced to helots, or the Highlanders, turned off altogether; they were rackrented tenants under foreign or semi-foreign landlords, of alien faith. In all these contexts, the importance of religion, whether as stimulant or as soporific, stands out.

That Britain got through the world's first industrial revolution, slow and piecemeal though this was compared with later ones, without a major upheaval, is a remarkable fact, and a tribute to the firmness and flexibility of its institutions. Religion played its part here too. Still potent in all countries, here it possessed an exceptional range and diversity, enabling it to adapt itself to novel predicaments in a manner impossible to the petrified orthodoxy of most of the others. Methodism, mawkishly emotional, served, on the whole, to carry sufferers away from reality, to stifle social protest. In the older Nonconformist tradition, sparks of another spirit still smouldered, that of the armed sects and saints of Commonwealth days, and this entered in some degree into the combustion of the whole period of change. With the Elect it had seldom gone against the grain to rise up 'without tarrying for the magistrate'. The old radical Zachariah in Mark Rutherford's novel always had a hankering to rise up against the tyrant, and he was a keen Old Testament-reader as well as a predestinarian. 'There is a people, even in these days of Ahab, whose feet may yet be on the necks of their enemies.'[18] Another plank of the good old cause still afloat in radical minds was the argument that the glorious British Constitution was in fact a Norman yoke, a slavery imposed on Englishmen by the Conquest, which they must get rid of in order to regain their lost liberty.[19]

From 1793 to 1815 there was almost continual war, and this armed the government with special powers and patriotic appeal, assets without which the fairly smooth course of the industrial revolution might not have been feasible. But the war atmosphere and familiarity with military matters could also work the other way, by stimulating thoughts of resistance; Luddites attacking mills and destroying machinery might be armed with musket and pistol and carry out their operations in regular military style.[20] Direct action in England in these decades took a great many forms, from food riots to murder, and it was the same in Glasgow and the industrial west of Scotland.[21] In the growing mill towns, violence was often turned against blacklegs. Mrs Gaskell depicted in *Mary Barton* the waylaying and beating up by strikers of poor weavers flocking into Manchester from the countryside to take their jobs;[22] poor Irish and Highlanders were flocking likewise into Glasgow.

E.P. Thompson makes it clear that not all the plots heard of in the first two decades of the nineteenth century were imagined or concocted by police spies, as has been maintained by historians convinced that 'any determined revolutionary activity can be ruled out without examination as un-English'.[23] Sundry 'un-English' things have in reality been very English indeed, and sometimes have only ceased to be so under the same pressures that have made sundry things 'unAmerican'. If conspiracy had come to have an unpleasant flavour, it took on a different function in the planning of Luddite raids, aimed at immediate practical objectives. A relish for the conspiratorial may have crept into the raw new factory working class, with its Celtic and Catholic tributary streams, and brought into trade unionism those secret-society rituals that Disraeli, himself an exotic, described with gusto in *Sybil*.[24] They may have helped to infuse into it the close fraternity that the old small manufacturing communities bred more naturally.

But if this proletariat stood at first outside the body politic and its traditions, so did the usurping factory system that employed it; whereas the Luddites represented a very old class, an artisanate resisting the demon of industrialism in the name of time-honoured custom. They belonged therefore to the same moral world as the Kent or Norfolk peasants of old days, or the parliamentarians opposing Stuart innovation. 'Ned Ludd was the defender of ancient right, the upholder of a last constitution', the old legislation, now being rapidly dismantled for the benefit of the millowners, on apprenticeship and wages and protection of labour.[25] Modern experience seems to show that workers everywhere have been readier to fight against the establishment of industrial capitalism than for its abolition, once firmly established. It may be a fundamental difficulty for socialism that, since it is avowedly a new thing, men cannot walk into it backwards, eyes fixed on familiar landmarks of the past, as they walked into many earlier revolutionary changes. Moreover, the 'croppers' or shearmen who were prominent followers of 'General Ludd' were among 'the aristocracy of the woollen workers',[26] and a better-off class may be likelier to resort to force to avoid deprivation of social status, as well as income, than a worse-off class trying to raise itself from the bottom.

After the wars, the middle-class movement for parliamentary reform was free to revive, and soon began to draw in working-class discontent behind it. Here could be found an alternative ground for a fight in defence of ancient right, or, parliament being obviously old and warped, its renewal. Parliament's survival through the ages lent it a venerable aura, freshened by its survival through the wars: an England led by it had, after all, defied the conqueror of Europe, now its captive. Leaders of the reform agitation could both welcome the support of the working class, old and new, and feel that they were doing good service by leading it into the constitutional path. They were gaining strength fast enough to be unafraid of mobilizing the masses, in the spirit of Cobbett's maxim that history is not made by cloistered debate but by the hurly-burly of the streets. It was the authorities that decided to go one better, at Peterloo in 1819, in the spirit of Napoleon's maxim about a whiff of grapeshot keeping the streets clear. The decision emerged from very complex processes of thought and feeling, involving all kinds of men in office, high and low, central and local;[27] but, in sum, it was the ruling class collectively that was resorting to direct action, and this action was one of a long series of similar acts of authority in modern Britain and its Empire. They have been exploratory moves, experiments to test whether an opposition can be crippled by one hard blow. If the blow miscarries, as it did at Peterloo, British ruling-class instinct is not to go on launching heavier ones, but to step back, to find new ground, to try something else; to refrain from pushing things to extremes, for fear of coming off the loser, or with only a pyrrhic victory. Napoleon might have called it the instinct of a nation of shopkeepers, accustomed to settle everything by haggling; the shop-keepers might have reminded him that his own instincts had landed him at St Helena.

On its own dunghill, the countryside, the ruling class was far less ready for compromise, as appeared when the long-suffering farm labourers at last caught the infection of revolt and embarked on their own desperate course of machine-breaking and rick-burning, the 'Captain Swing' rising of 1830. Farm drudges *must* be kept half-starved and docile if the gentry were to live in luxury, and the mutineers were hunted down ruthlessly; 1,976 arrested, 19 executed, 481 transported.[28] Still, this unexpected turning of the worm was unnerving, and the landed oligarchy was far less able to cope with the big towns which erupted into rioting in 1831 as the agitation for the Reform Bill intensified – Bristol, for instance, in October, under the eye of the old poet Crabbe, who as a young man had watched the Gordon riots.[29] At such times of excitement, it would seem that some subtle change of temperature, some hint of a relaxed attitude to order in respectable quarters, is enough to give a lower class the signal that the hour has struck. A lawless populace then constitutes the battering-ram that opens the breach for those above it. It is by such a combin-ation of pressures that all 'peaceful' reforms, like that of 1832, came about. Under it, the landowners, themselves already a capitalist class, of the bastard agrarian type, were ready to take the industrial bourgeoisie into partnership and, as Macaulay had appealed to them in the House to do, 'save property, divided against itself'.[30]

Property was saved at the expense of the propertyless, as in 1660 at the expense of the peasantry. Between 1832 and 1848 the working class, cheated of any part of the reward, went on struggling by itself for the vote and – more threateningly – for a parliament drastically remodelled and made responsive to the popular will. Chartism occupied a halfway period in political evolution, and was more preoccupied with the choice between physical force and peaceful suasion than any other British movement before or since. Indignation at middle-class betrayal, and the obvious effectiveness of recent rioting, gave an initial impetus to thoughts of action. Drilling and arming had started before the Reform Act, with tacit middle-class approval, and went on sporadically afterwards without it. Members of the National Union of the Working Classes brought out a cheap edition of Colonel Macerone's *Instructions* for street warfare: 'The pamphlet was common enough in middle-class hands.'[31] There was a climax in 1839, when a lively expectation of rebellion spread, and Harney, an admirer of Marat and Robespierre, was proposing that the country should elect a new parliament without waiting to be given votes, and that a million armed men should march on London to install it. It does not appear that the physical-force men had made any large-scale preparations for any such move. One of them, John Taylor, had five old brass cannons buried somewhere, ready for a resurrection-day. 'Poor men! How little they know of physical force!', wrote General Napier, commanding in the north, himself humanely anxious not to have to resort to it.[32] The brass cannons remained silent, and despite much inflamed talk at mass meetings nothing graver happened than the Bull Ring riots at Birmingham.

After this, revolution was a diminishing prospect, though both friend and foe were slow to recognize the fact. Fiery talk went on. Often, no doubt, it was only rhetoric, serving to mark individuals out as men of spirit and determination, or to break down apathy and bring in recruits; or it might be a mere blowing-off of steam, or alcoholic vapours. But ordinary Chartists had no commitment to non-violence as a principle, and many who rejected revolution as a national programme were quite ready to engage in impromptu local affrays or scuffles.[33] Ernest Jones's thinking probably expressed the view of most of those given to thinking; for example, in his poem 'The Factory Town' (one of the best that the movement produced):

> Fear ye not your masters' power,
>     Men are strong when men unite;
> Fear ye not one stormy hour:
>     *Banded millions need not fight.*[34]

His general teaching was that Chartists should not be the first to strike a blow, but they were entitled to strike in self-defence.[35] How they could do this, if attacked as at Peterloo, without making organized preparations beforehand which would be taken to brand them as aggressors, was not clear – as in similar contexts it never has been.

While Chartism rumbled, respectable citizens with uneasy recollections of disorders they had lately winked at were frequently perturbed, though their picture of the mob remained confused and contradictory. In Kingsley's *Alton Locke*, the hero watches a tumult of starving farm labourers with sympathy, but soon notices plundering and discovers 'how large a portion of rascality shelters itself under the wing of every crowd'; he sees, too, how hastily it runs away at the first approach of the yeomanry.[36] Belief in the mingled folly, ferocity and cowardice of all crowds was rubbed deeper into the middle-class mind by every fresh commentator on Shakespeare, as it continues to be to this day. All the same, English political habits provided a safety-valve for unruly passions, in the mimic warfare of election days; passions not seldom shared by the candidates, who might be hereditary rivals for first place in the county and were not squeamish about how they got the better of each other. Crabbe had another brush with Demos soon after becoming rector of Trowbridge in 1814. 'A riotous, tumultuous, and most appalling mob' besieged his house, to prevent his going to the poll – though in fact it let him pass unmolested.[37] Rowdy election humours furnished novelists with a stock theme. In Eliot's *Felix Holt*, we hear a landowner's agent bribing miners to indulge in some rough play: 'No pommelling – no striking first. There you have the law and the constable against you. A little rolling in the dust and knocking hats off, a little pelting with soft things. . . .'[38] On the great day, party strife degenerates, according to rule, into a farcical drunken turmoil.[39] For the voteless plebeian, such an occasion had the charm of a saturnalia, when he was temporarily licensed to work off his feelings against the quality with insults, or something better. If the contest depicted in Tressell's *The Ragged-Trousered Philanthropists* was at all typical, brawling was still use and wont among enfranchised workers at the end of the century, and kept them harmlessly giving each other, instead of their bosses, black eyes or bloody noses.

Patterns of protest are always partly drawn by the weapons used against them. England's governing class drew some discretion from its lack of armed resources. It had no conscript army, and its professional army, besides being limited and largely required overseas, was recruited from the humblest classes, and might be tempted to fraternize with them.[40] To a great extent, property had to look to its own defence. West Riding manufacturers fortified their mills with an armed garrison, a cannon, a barrel of vitriol.[41] Landowners were well accustomed to self-help. In the winter of 1819 when Northumberland miners and west-of-Scotland weavers were showing 'a spirit of alarming insubordination', Scott and his fellow-lairds on the Borders set on foot 'a legion or brigade upon a large scale, to be called the Buccleuch Legion'.[42] In 1830, Wellington exhorted gentry and magistrates to collect and arm their grooms, huntsmen and footmen, and ride forth against the miscreants. In Norfolk, Lord Suffield 'enrolled his own private army of a hundred men',[43] very much like a feudal landlord in Bengal.

Private enterprise like this, seldom met with in more bureaucratic countries, was growing archaic as industrialism advanced, and had the demerit of turning things too nakedly into a class war, a battle of haves against have-nots. Use of the yeomanry was only a degree less provocative, as at Peterloo where the

Manchester and Salford corps seems to have taken the field bent on teaching the workers a lesson.[44] The new England of the manufacturers, personified by Peel, was working out a new system, a regular modern police. Dublin was the first area to be experimented on, in 1808; London followed in 1829, and the rest of Britain after it, while on the rest of Ireland in 1829 was bestowed the Royal Irish Constabulary. This was a paramilitary force, akin to the gendarmerie in France or the Guardia Civil in Spain, and similarly hated. Otherwise the new police were not given firearms, and this made a vital difference. They were not designed to court popularity, but rather to harass and intimidate, and were in fact for a long time detested. Chartist threats were sometimes a reprisal against their strong-arm methods.[45] Mayhew's costermongers, all keen Chartists, 'could not understand why Chartist leaders exhorted them to peace and quietness', and they hated their new shepherds. 'I am assured that in case of a political riot every "coster" would seize his policeman.'[46] Still, their having only truncheons kept retaliation within bounds, while in the long run their duties, like those of the State, would gradually expand to include all sorts of neutral or even benevolent functions. They enabled government to withdraw from property its rights of private warfare, and to interpose what could pass for an impartial shield between the jarring classes. It became easier besides to tolerate public meetings, as a country like contemporary Spain could not. 'The people have a right to meet', Lord John Russell declared in a speech at Liverpool in 1838; and it formed one of the great British discoveries that the more freedom the public was given to air its views, the more moderate and 'responsible' these became.

'While the English Chartists were debating the right to use physical force, those of Wales took to arms.'[47] Wales shared the preference of the Celtic borderlands, as of most unsophisticated peoples, for direct methods.[48] Chartism was brought to Newport in 1838 by Henry Vincent, an adherent of the force school, and after the rejection of the national petition in 1839 plans for a rising were promptly put in hand. Its miserable failure and its death-roll must have had a disheartening effect on all later thoughts of insurrection. But it was closely followed by a more authentically Welsh trial of direct action, the Rebecca Riots of 1843–4 in Carmarthenshire. These were concerned with tangible grievances that meant more to hill farmers than votes or debates at Westminster, with the new turnpike toll bars as the last straw. Toll bars were pulled down at night by bands of mounted men disguised as women, whose leader was always called 'Rebecca' as the commander of any Luddite operation had been called 'General Ludd': an illustration of the fondness of the folk-mind for eponymous heroes – 'Captain Swing' was another – which suggests a possible family tree for Robin Hood. The element of mummery afforded a rough disguise; it was also a psychological aid to illicit activity, in the same way as Ku-Klux-Klan cowls or hippy costumes, and it could make a special appeal to a hill people stuffed with old-time poetry. (Many Luddites came likewise from small upland villages.) Religion, if the name 'Rebecca' was taken as is usually supposed from the Old Testament, was once again nerving men to defy man-made law. Toll-bar keepers, unlike their toll bars, were seldom injured. Authority showed less restraint, and suppressed 'Rebecca' with some bloodshed; but her aims were largely achieved all the same (by contrast with those of Newport), as such limited aims often have been.

Little Welsh national feeling seems to have been in evidence.[49] It was very different with the agitations in Ireland. These went through two phases, the campaign for Catholic emancipation won in 1829, roughly analogous with the one that ended in Britain in 1832, and then the broader movement for repeal of the union with England, which may be compared with – and drew support from, and failed along with – the Chartist movement. In point of tactics, to Irish peasants as to Welsh (or to London costers) it seemed plain sense to utilize whatever methods came to hand for making things hot for the enemy. Tom Moore heard at Mallow during his 1823 tour of 'a strong feeling among the lower orders, that if they persevere in their present harassing and violent system, the Church must give in.'[50] But in the political leadership O'Connell stood firmly, despite the challenge of Young Ireland, for legalism, and under British prompting the Pope forbade any clerical encouragement of sedition.[51] In 1845–6 famine followed by mass emigration came to prostrate the country, luckily for the government before the tocsins of 1848 were set ringing round Europe.

1848 came and went, and the British Constitution floated securely, a water-tight ark, on the flood-waters engulfing Europe. Dramatic events abroad were bound to react on British politics, for the whole Continent was in some ways a single political whole. The defeat and bloodthirsty suppression of the Paris workers in June 1848 must have had a chilling effect on any Chartists spoiling for a fight. In the longer term, conflict abroad might foster partial reform in Britain. Just as 1830 in Paris must have helped to bring about 1832 in London, 1848 in Paris added point to Carlyle's jeremiads, kept up ever since his *French Revolution* in 1837 – his sermons to the ruling class about the need to read the signs of the times. Kingsley pointed the moral in his 1850 pamphlet about London's sweated tailoring workers, when he ended by predicting that increasing misery must sooner or later produce an explosion: 'the boiler will be stretched to bursting pitch, till some jar, some slight crisis, suddenly directs the imprisoned forces to one point, and then –

> What then?
> Look at France, and see.'[52]

Collective thinking is always a matter of images or symbols more than of logic, and industrialism, familiarity with mechanical processes, and imagery inspired by them, could help to give Englishmen a livelier sense of social realities than philosophers in agrarian Germany ruminating on 'organic' theories of the State.

As a rule, however, when John Bull cast his eye across the Channel he compared himself with his neighbours, greatly to his own advantage. National characters develop by interaction and repulsion. Planted between skipping Frenchmen and lurching Irishmen, he had long been coming to pride himself on his own solid, sturdy common sense and ballast. Laureates and leader-writers dwelt on the frivolity of the Gallic weathercock, 'the red fool-fury of the Seine',[53] as a warning against such fretful impatience at home. Whatever its brutalities, capitalism fitted in with and strengthened a rational quality already English, of which the word 'businesslike' was highly typical, and businesslike habits of handling affairs, from the House with its Speaker down to the share-holders' or club-members' meeting with its chairman, made bawling and brawling look childish. In Prussia a powerful bureaucracy was moulding a rationality of its own, but of another species. In England the notion of 'the King's Peace' had always had a flavour of voluntary acceptance, distinct from the Continental ideal of order imposed from above; or if Englishmen thought of order, it came naturally to them to talk of 'law and order' together.

This included, increasingly, the factor of progress. In Russia Zhelyabov the terrorist was complaining that history was frightfully slow, and must be given a shove forward; in Britain it seemed to be moving quickly enough. Even the sensation of travel by railway, faster than human beings had ever gone before, gave a sort of physical corroboration to the sense of progress. This could not be kept confined to miles per hour or tons per year, but must have its place in the political sphere as well: the masses should be admitted by safe degrees into the sacred parliamentary enclosure, at least into its outskirts. A liberal like Brougham drew from 1848 the lesson that universal suffrage would be fatal among erratic foreigners, but would be far less risky in England; indeed it would be a good thing to give votes straight away to 'the best and by far the most independent of the lower orders, the Artisans.'[54]

In the meantime, comfort could be found in the fact that bad as many things might be in Britain, abroad they were manifestly worse. Strong nations tyran-nized over weak, and respectable England was always ready to sympathize with national (not class) revolt, in Italy or Poland or Hungary, though not in Ireland or India. Patriotic risings there supplied some of the glamour that British politics lacked, and a vicarious sense of participation in heroic events (which the middle classes could also enjoy by reading Carlyle's *Cromwell*, published in 1845). A few individuals did participate, like Byron going to Greece; the host of volunteers of 1914 supposed themselves to be going to Belgium on the same errand. On the whole, feeling was content to express itself in enthusiastic welcomes to famous exiles – an Espartero, a Kossuth, a Garibaldi. Literate workers, who in Chartist days read Byron and Shelley, were drawn into these demonstrations, common ground for them and those above them. Occasionally indignation could find a legitimate vent on foreigners of the stamp of Marshal Hainau, roughly handled by the draymen of Barclay's brewery in September

1850 after his pacification of Hungary. Later on when international socialism dawned, this sentiment would take on another aspect, less palatable to official opinion.

By and large, England remained an unmilitary country, and this helped to foster peaceful political habits. Its one European war between 1815 and 1914, the Crimean, was fought in the aftermath of the Chartist peril, and helped to divert restless feelings outward; so did the Indian Mutiny in 1857, and the outburst of Gallophobia that led to the Volunteer movement of the years from 1859. Colonial troubles like the Mutiny taught Britain's rulers some lessons, and indirectly promoted better treatment of common people at home. If Coercion Acts were obviously proper for Irishmen, they must by the same token be improper for Englishmen. And they were the less needed because Englishmen, contemplating their Empire through the school-spectacles given them, could see there a grand vindication of the law-abiding virtues. The Pax Britannica was the extension of the Queen's Peace to dark continents that knew nothing but despotism or anarchy; the high seas were being added to the Queen's high road, as cherished phrases about 'Britannia policing the seas' emphasized. In the regions growing into dominions, democracy was coming effortlessly, and this helped to ensure its coming to Britain; though not the transforming democracy that Chartism had dreamed of.

Victorian Britain's self-complacent picture of a sober nation satisfied with a regulated growth of its liberties contained of course a good deal of wishful thinking. Behind it persisted much uncertainty and many forebodings; they found one expression in the spreading mood of religious doubt. In a nation so deeply divided, it was hard to make out how far the masses were coming to accept the picture. But the philosophy of parliamentarism, the settlement of sectional quarrels by compromise, could not be without an influence on them; ideas and modes of behaviour, like fashions of dress, seep down by a thousand crannies from one social level to another. For those still discontented, steam transport made it easier to choose another way out, a negative form of direct action, emigration. This was an important relief for all European countries: it came easiest to Britain, with its large colonies of settlement and its community of language with America, least easily to insular France. All this helped to bring it about that the barricade, a central fact of political life on the Continent, was almost unknown in Britain. It is noteworthy also that Britain had to borrow another, much newer French word, sabotage,[55] even if wooden clogs were as common in Lancashire mills as sabots in French. Luddism had become a mere memory, though it had a belated recrudescence in the 'Sheffield outrages' of 1866, when William Broadhead of the sawgrinders' union hired men to blow up a factory with new machinery and to make murderous attacks on inter-lopers; it is tempting to see in them a side-effect of the Volunteer mania and sabre-rattling of the 1860s. Of political terrorism, the thought scarcely spread beyond the trickle of foreign refugees who brought it.

Strict adherence to legality as a principle took hold more quickly at the top of the popular movement than at the bottom, where the plain man's faith in his fists lingered. Muscular energy of an elemental sort might overflow at times into assaults on Irish immigrants, precursors of the – happily few – race riots of the next century. But fists themselves were coming under rule and regulation, which made hitting below the belt one of the deadlier sins. It was indeed in the fantasy-realm of sport that the ideal Victorian pattern of society came nearest to fulfilment. Nothing could be more characteristic of England than the growing cult of sport, the mimic warfare of the playing field, presided over by codes of conduct like the 'laws' of cricket, and by impartial umpires, flesh-and-blood symbols of the impartial State. Most English of all was the Gentlemen v. Players match, first played at Lords in 1806 and annually from 1819. The Football Association was founded in 1863. Sport brought with it the notion of 'fair play', spreading far beyond its own arena and bringing the expectation – made up as in all such cases of some truth and more illusion – that sooner or later everyone would get his due.

How the gentlemen were likely to play the game when alarmed for their moneybags was illustrated by the events of 'Bloody Sunday', or 13 November 1887, when the police, with soldiers in support, were turned loose on a mass meeting of unemployed and pro-Ireland demonstrators in Trafalgar Square.[56] A vigorous labour movement was on the march again, tinged now with socialism. This operation was the Peterloo probe again, with truncheon instead of sabre. Its effectiveness must remain uncertain, as unemployment and discontent receded for some years, and the new imperialism helped to muffle them. English socialism was too confined to a few intellectuals to revive seriously, in the climate of the later nineteenth century, the Chartist debate about force and its place in political philosophy. William Morris, a very realistic idealist, did face the problem, and expected force to be necessary to give capitalism the final blow;[57] but that lay too far in the future for any close scrutiny.

For James Connolly, as an Irish socialist, the problem was not one that could be evaded. In Ireland, the agrarian struggle continued the old instinctive use of attacks on property, including now cattle-maiming. It also threw up, in 1880, that Irish contribution to world politics, the boycott, a form of non-violent coercion that as practised in its native land, against the obnoxious individual, may be supposed to have borrowed from the Catholic practice of excommunication (though it had an English analogy in 'sending to Coventry'). The official Irish political movement was playing the parliamentary game, but with an Irish difference, inventing the tactics of obstruction in order to strangle Westminster with its own red tape. But the extremist wing, Sinn Fein, made force so much the touchstone of patriotism that (as Connolly protested in an article in 1899) Ireland was unique in having a 'physical force party' agreed on nothing except the rightfulness of violence, erecting into a principle what revolutionaries everywhere else looked on merely as a weapon. Socialists neither extolled nor repudiated force in itself, he declared, but would stick to peaceful methods so long as the other side did so.[58] Like Ernest Jones before him, Connolly was not altogether meeting the practical dilemma. That a ruling class will at some stage abandon lawful procedures is certain; at that stage it will already be prepared for action, while its antagonists will not be, unless they have got ready in advance.

Paradoxically, the nearest to a mass political rising in Ireland was the Ulster rebellion of 1914, not against Britain but against separation from Britain. The alacrity with which British Toryism supported it was a revelation of how at bottom a ruling class always thinks of law and order as meant for its subjects, not for itself. The affair took place against the unsettling background of a warlike Europe long committed to the colonial rivalries and arms race about to explode in the Great War. In that period a mystique of force was not confined to Sinn Feiners. A year after Connolly wrote his article, a group of English Liberals deplored the spectacle 'of force and aggression becoming not only too often employed as means towards good or tolerable ends, but actually worshipped and glorified as ends in themselves.'[59] Strident imperialist propaganda was accompanied during the Boer War years (1899–1902) by a reappearance of Tory mobs, breaking up anti-war meetings. They included a good many students, whose patriotic zeal was loudly applauded by the press. Pro-Boer speakers sometimes came close to the fate of the anti-war MP lynched at the close of Galsworthy's play The Mob.[60] From this time on there was also the rivalry with Germany, setting Volunteers polishing their buttons with fresh enthusiasm.

In those years, with labour militancy reviving once more, there were further experiments at nipping it in the bud by short, sharp treatment. Liberals were in office after 1906, and, as often happens with Liberals everywhere, were anxious to prove that they could keep order; especially the fire-eating young Winston Churchill at the Home Office, who brought artillery into Sidney Street to deal with a few anarchists, and during a railway strike 'despatched the military hither and thither as though Armageddon was upon us'.[61] Now and then, down to 1911 at Liverpool and in Wales at Llanelli, strikers were fired on. This approach was then dropped, as likely to do more harm than good, but many lesser degrees of brutality were complained of. Doubtless some of the rough handling of strikers and demonstrators was due to bellicose local police chiefs or their men, but it fitted into a definite enough programme. On the workers' side, similar tactics might be made use of on the spur of the moment. An Anglican clergyman who stumped the country as an anti-socialist open-air speaker found that he usually got a fair hearing. But once in Attercliffe, that Faubourg St Antoine of Sheffield, 'a gang of hooligans tried to run the lorry from which I was speaking down a steep hill. . . . At Leeds an anarchist tried to stab me in the back, and at Norwich, which is the roughest place I know of, I was knocked off the platform.'[62]

Systematic defiance of law and order came not from Labour, whose leadership was increasingly committed to parliamentarism, but from the 'Women's Social and Political Union', founded by Mrs Pankhurst, a barrister's widow, in 1903. Women – like the peoples of the Celtic fringe – respresented a partially distinct race, indifferent to rules and conventions they have had no part in framing; and, being most of the time restricted to a narrow family circle, natural antinomians when outside it. Many working-class women were used to being knocked about by their husbands, and to be knocked about by a policeman came to much the same thing. Male rather than conservative prejudice hardened the government's heart against the Suffragettes, whose own politics were unpredictable: Mrs Pankhurst was later a Tory, one of her daughters an ardent socialist. It is a pity that since women got votes they have tailed behind man-made organizations, as the enfranchised workers for long tailed behind the Liberal party.

During the Great War, when men of other armies mutinied or deserted or went home, British troops, like the Germans and Turkish, went on to the bitter end with extraordinary stolidity. Still, the vibrations of the four-year cannonade were enough to shake the willing suspension of disbelief in its rulers even of the British people. Unsettlement might have been more far-reaching but for events in Ireland, not only terrible but to most Englishmen incomprehensible, and ending in a bloody civil war. Elsewhere the mood of revolt was strongest on the 'Red Clyde'. Here in 1919, the centenary of Peterloo, it was authority that took the law into its own hands, as so often before. In the 'battle of George Square' at Glasgow, a big meeting of strikers was attacked and broken up by the police.[63] This was on 31 January; on 10 April the move, appropriately intensified, was repeated at Amritsar, when a large concourse of Indian nationalists was fired on and several hundreds killed, on the same principle of getting in the first blow and frightening the public by a severe example. In Britain resentment found an outlet in the 'Hands off Russia' campaign, which cautious Labour leaders were willing to sponsor as a substitute for struggle on issues nearer home.[64] In the summer of 1920 when the founding conference of the Communist party was held, a fresh occasion arose for thinking out the basic question of ends and means, but it was, as before, left hanging in the air, most delegates probably content with the guiding-line offered by one of them: 'that the aim of the Communist party was the minimum not the maximum of violence.'[65]

Again in 1926 the General Strike revealed an astonishing capacity for orderly action and initiative, but anything that might have come of it was lost for want of any national leadership worth the name. Subsequently the spread of fascism abroad, the disappearance of one constitutional regime after another, gave parliamentarism in Britain a new lease of life, even with the 'National Government' in charge of it. Fascist brutalism, moreover, deterred the left wing from anything that might seem to resemble it, except in a strictly defensive spirit as in the East-End resistance to Mosley's Blackshirts. Even students adhered to strict political discipline; they thought in terms of 'mobilizing the broad masses', and direct action was no part of their vocabulary. Like nineteenth-century radicalism, Communism identified itself with armed action abroad, and found its battlefield in Spain. At home, the most authentically British development of the 1930s was the hunger-march, a form of class confrontation still within the boundaries of moral force. It was not altogether unlike the march of the Manchester 'Blanketeers' in 1817. It had an affinity with Gandhi's new tactics of civil disobedience in India. On the whole, after the storm aroused by the Amritsar massacre, the British government – unlike the French or Dutch – was not trying to shoot its way out of its colonial troubles, and Gandhi's non-violence was designed to encounter an opponent of this elastic, compromise-seeking type. Now, as before, a comparatively battle-free Empire helped to limit strife at home.

Since the Second World War, with its further transforming effects, loss of Empire has helped to make for a more natural attitude, liberation from the old musclebound posture of imperial dignity. Political effervescence of less orthodox types has once again been more obvious in the Celtic marches than in the phlegmatic Anglo-Saxony. On Christmas Day in 1951 the Stone of Scone was purloined from Westminster Abbey by four Scottish students, and later some letter-boxes were blown up because of their cypher 'Elizabeth II'. This was too nostalgically romantic to bloom for long; but Welsh nationalists more recently have graduated towards schemes for blowing up bigger things than letter-boxes. Of most significance in the past few years has been the student movement. Direct action – often in the shape of war – has always had more attraction for youth than for age, but it is only in universities that youth comes to form a separate estate, and one readier than a labour movement to acquire a cosmopolitan outlook and responsiveness. The guerrilla tactics that have come naturally to it have resembled in their unconventionality those of the Suffragettes.

There have been symptoms of an infection spreading to older groups as well. Early in 1971, a 'Resistance Movement' to prevent obliteration of villages by a third London airport was heard of, and the rector of Dunton promised his blessing to anyone taking up arms to defend his home – as we have all been taught from childhood that we ought to do. There is today an impatience with old-fashioned procedures which, even to the extent of their genuineness, are exceedingly roundabout, with no such straightforward means of expression as some countries possess in the referendum. Democracy of this kind comes to feel, like the interminable Chancery suit in *Bleak House*, 'a slow, expensive, British, constitutional kind of thing.'[66] In our sprawling amalgam of capitalism and bureaucracy and State socialism, parliament begins to seem hardly better as a 'conflict-resolver' than in Tudor days. Faith in old ways of achieving progress, whether on liberal or on Marxist terms, by slow, patient sapping and mining, gives way to a search for short cuts, a desire for action here and now, aimed at small immediate goals instead of complete transformation of a system grown so vast and complex that to transform it all seems hardly possible. Thus the inevitability of gradualness presents itself in a new guise, no longer tied to rigid observance of a parliamentary rule-book or timetable. If our ancient regime ever does come to an end, it may be through pressure of opinion stiffened by the cumulative effect of numerous small nibblings and scratchings. Before this happens, recourse by the other side to direct action, official or unofficial, must be expected in the future as in the past.

## Notes

1. Welsh and Irish, whose political terminology is of English formation, seem to have no equivalents of their own. German and Swedish also use the English words. In French, Spanish, Portuguese, Italian, Russian, Chinese and Japanese they have found a literal translation. More popular in America before 1914 was the anarchist phrase 'the propaganda of the deed', akin to that of the Spanish anarchists' *propaganda por los hechos*. I am indebted for this information to colleagues in the history and language departments of Edinburgh University.

2. J. Morley, *On Compromise*, Thinker's Library edn, London 1933, pp. 61–2.

3. J.C. Dickinson, *The Great Charter*, London 1955, p. 10.

4. R. Hilton, review article in the *New Statesman*, 28 August 1970.

5. H.M. Lyle, *The Rebellion of Jack Cade, 1450*, London 1950, pp. 19,21.

6. Ibid., p. 22.

7. M.E. James, 'Obedience and Dissent in Henrician England: the Lincolnshire Rebellion 1536', *Past & Present*, 1970, no. 48, p. 7.

8. *Sermons by Hugh Latimer*, Everyman edn, London 1906, p. 26.

9. S.T. Bindoff, *Ket's Rebellion 1549*, London 1949, pp. 16, 19.

10. W. Shakespeare, *Julius Caesar*, act 2, scene I.

11. *The Age of Louis XIV*, Everyman edn, London 1926, ch. 4. Cf. Balzac, *Le Lys dans la vallée*, 1835: 'Les Anglais offrent ainsi comme une image de leur île, où la loi régit tout, où tout est uniforme dans chaque sphère, où l'exercice des vertus semble être le jeu nécessaire de rouages qui marchent à heure fixe'. Nelson edn, Paris 1939, p. 252.

12. See *The Life of the Reverend Dr. John Barwick, DD*, by his brother Peter, trans. from Latin, 1724: there is a specimen cypher on pp. 408–9. Cf. M. Achley, John Wildman, *Plotter and Post-master*, 1947.

13. Charles Dickens, *Barnaby Rudge*, ch. 52.

14. Something like this struck some foreign observers of riots in Calcutta in 1970.

15. See D. Marshall, *Eighteenth-Century England*, London 1962, p. 477–80.

16. E.P. Thompson, *The Making of the English Working Class*, London 1963, p. 602.

17. Cf. T.J. Johnston, *The History of the Working Classes in Scotland*, Glasgow, p. 195: 'for years afterwards no stranger's life was safe, even gaugers being stripped naked and hunted from the district.'

18. 'Mark Rutherford', *The Revolution in Tanner's Lane*, 1893, ch. I.

19. See C. Hill, 'The Norman Yoke', in J. Saville, ed., *Democracy and the Labour Movement*, London 1954.

20. See Thompson, pp. 557–8, 578, & passim.

21. Johnston, p. 305.

22. Mrs Gaskell, *Mary Barton*, 1848, ch. 15.

23. Thompson, p. 486; cf. p. 553: 'Luddism was *a quasi-insurrectionary movement . . .*'

24. Benjamin Disraeli, *Sybil, or the Two Nations*, 1845, book 4, ch. 4.

25. Thompson, p. 530.

26. Ibid., p. 522.

27. See two recent studies: J. Marlow, *The Peterloo Massacre*, London 1969, which is very critical of the authorities' conduct; and R. Walmsley, *Peterloo: The Case Re-opened*, Manchester 1969, which is very sympathetic towards it.

28. E.J. Hobsbawm and G. Rudé, *Captain Swing*, London 1969, p. 262; cf. p. 263: 'From no other protest movement of the kind – from neither Luddites nor Chartists, nor trade unionists – was such a bitter price exacted.'

29. See *The Life of George Crabbe, by his Son*, 1834, chs 3, 10.

30. 2 March 1831; see G.O. Trevelyan, *Life and Letters of Lord Macaulay*, 1876, ch. 4. Macaulay's next sentence was: 'Save the multitude, endangered by its own ungovernable passions.'

31. P. Hollis, *The Pauper Press: A Study in Working-Class Radicalism of the 1830s*, London 1970, p. 41.

32. M. Beer, *A History of British Socialism*, London 1929, vol. 2, pp. 73–4.

33. I. Prothero, 'Chartism in London', *Past & Present*, 1969, no. 44, p. 81.

34. Y.V. Kovalev, ed., *Anthology of Chartist Literature*, Moscow 1956, p. 147. The poem belongs to 1847.

35. See J. Saville, *Ernest Jones, Chartist*, 1952, p. 22. Cf. his words after his arrest in 1848: 'In your agitation maintain peace, law and order, respect life and property, but do not – oh! do not be political cowards.' (Kovalev, p. 360). He wrote an account of the peasant revolt of 1381, which he saw, too pessimistically, as ending in mere failure and ruin, as a result of the rebels growing reckless and drunken (ibid., pp. 347 ff.); he may have feared that the same fate would befall an armed rising of workers.

36. Charles Kingsley, *Alton Locke*, 1850, ch. 28.

37. *The Life of George Crabbe*, ch. 9.

38. George Eliot, *Felix Holt, the Radical*, 1866, ch. II.

39. Ibid., ch. 31, 33. Cf. Dickens, *The Pickwick Papers*, 1837, ch. 13; A. Trollope, *Can You Forgive Her?*, 1864–5, ch. 44; 'Mark Rutherford', *The Revolution in Tanner's Lane*, ch. 25.

40. A. Swinson and D. Scott, eds, *The Memoirs of Private Waterfield*, London 1968, show that soldiers could be on friendly terms with ordinary folk in Yorkshire – where Waterfield's regiment had been sent to quell riots – in 1843 (see pp. 15–16).

41. Thompson, p. 560.

42. J.G. Lockhart, *The Life of Sir Walter Scott*, 1838, ch. 46.

43. Hobsbawm and Rudé, p. 255.

44. Marlow, pp. 97–8.

45. Hollis, p. 253. Cf. Disraeli, *Sybil*, book 6, ch. 3:

'If the Capitalists will give up their redcoats,
I would be a moral force man tomorrow.'
'And the new police', said Mick. 'A pretty go, when a fellow in a blue coat fetches you the devil's own con on your head, and you get moral force for a plaster.'

46. *Mayhew's London*, selections from H. Mayhew, *London Labour and the London Poor*, 1851, P. Quennell, ed., n.d., pp. 52–3.

47. A. Jenkin, *The Nations of Britain since the Industrial Revolution*, Our History Series no. 54, London 1970, pp. 6–7.

48. Cf. Beer, vol. 2, p. 93: 'The simple, emotional, and enthusiastic nature of the Welsh working men . . . expects sensational deeds in any popular agitation.'

49. Sir R. Coupland, *Welsh and Scottish Nationalism: A Study*, 1954, pp. 180–3.

50. P. Quennell, ed., *The Journal of Thomas Moore 1818–41*, 1964, p. 85.

51. In February 1848; see C. Woodham-Smith, *The Great Hunger. Ireland 1845–9*, London 1962, p. 342.

52. 'Parson Lot', *Cheap Clothes and Nasty*.

53. Tennyson, *In Memoriam*, 1850, cxxvi.

54. *Letter to the Marquess of Lansdowne, KG, on the Late Revolution in France*, 3rd edn, 1848, p. 165.

55. 'Barricade' dates from 1588 in Paris; 'sabotage' from about 1870. See C.T. Onions, *The Oxford Dictionary of English Etymology*.

56. See D. Torr, *Tom Mann and his Times*, London 1956, ch. 15.

57. See for example William Morris, *Signs of Change*, 1888, p. 116.

58. 'Physical Force in Irish Politics', in J. Connolly, *Socialism and Nationalism*, Dublin 1948, pp. 53–5.

59. F.W. Hirst, et al., *Liberalism and the Empire*, 1900, p. vi.

60. Produced in March 1914; the play deals with mob hysteria of the Boer War type, though Galsworthy invents an imaginary colonial war as background.

61. A.G. Gardiner, *The Pillars of Society*, 1916 edn, p. 154.

62. A. Goldring, *Some Reminiscences of an Unclerical Cleric*, 1926, pp. 144–6. When he spoke in Hyde Park, he says rather self-importantly, 'every bully and swell mobsman in London seemed to have been engaged by the Socialists to break up the meeting.'

63. See W. Gallacher, *Revolt on the Clyde* 1936, ch. 10: 'Police made a savage and totally unexpected assault on the rear of the meeting, smashing right and left with their batons, utterly regardless of whom or what they hit.'

64. This point is discussed by Mrs T. Brotherstone in a study of the period now in progress.

65. Cited in J. Klugmann, *History of the Communist Party of Great Britain*, vol. I, London 1968, p. 39.

66. Dickens, *Bleak House*, 1853, ch. 2. In a BBC talk on 28 May 1972, E.J. Hobsbawm argued interestingly the case against terroristic tactics as futile.

# 2

# The Covenanters: A Problem of Creed and Class

Part of the function of both religion and nationalism has been to provide substitutes for class consciousness among the poorer, with a resultant benefit to the richer. In this process of displacement, complex workings of both social psychology and political manipulation have been involved, for whose study Scotland offers special attractions. As a nation it was a peculiar hybrid. On a Celtic people, Gaelic-speaking in much of the Lowlands as well as Highlands until well on in the middle ages, were superimposed urban settlements and a feudal ruling class, originally brought in from Norman England by the first Celtic kings to strengthen their hold. An amalgam of feudal with tribal characterized all the Celtic fringes of the British Isles, and lent them a character of their own in feudal Europe, and Scotland particularly as their only independent monarchy.

As heads of clans, as well as lords, the dominant landowning class had a patriarchal status, which could make the peasant think himself bound in duty to submit to them, and pride himself on being distantly related to them. 'This gave a deceptively friendly air to a relationship which was dictatorial and could be tyrannical.'[1] Government being weak, taxation minimal, it was the landlord, not the tax-collector as in early modern France, who was the real oppressor, and ought to have been the target of popular discontent. Tenurial conditions in the sixteenth and seventeenth centuries were worsening for the cultivator, usually a tenant at will with no security, or no more than a one-year lease could give him. On top of this, and going on as in France into the eighteenth century, were feudal obligations which meant that the farmer was 'at the beck and call of his master continually and always at times when work on his own holding was imperative'[2] English visitors over many years were astonished and repelled by the misery of Scottish life and housing. Most Scots, one of themselves wrote

40

in the 1640s, were 'by continual custom, born slaves and bondmen, their ordinary food pease and beans.'[3]

With the Reformation some stirrings of protest broke in on this feudal limbo. An early nineteenth-century critic of Calvinism, writing when the alarums of 1789 were still fresh in mind, accused it of spreading everywhere a 'restless and revolutionary spirit', and Scottish Calvinists of being 'infected with as vile a spirit of insubordination as any of their brethren on the Continent.'[4] Opponents at the time did not find it hard to accuse the Kirk of aiming at a theocracy. 'The Ministers sought to establish a democracy in this land and to become *tribuni plebis* themselves', James VI declared.[5] Popular support could be gained by talk of devoting old ecclesiastical revenues to poor relief, all over Christendom one of the purposes for which Church endowments had been intended. A right was claimed by the Kirk of punishing, not merely reproving, offences against morals, and these included cheating with false measures and 'oppression of the poor by exactions'.[6]

On the other hand, in this economic sphere the Kirk was restrained by the fact that, the urban middle classes being as yet weak, Reformation was dependent on support by the nobles with axes of their own to grind, and in possession of most of the old Church lands and income. There could be no thought of summoning the poor to rise up against noble exactions, and by offering its own ineffectual protection the Kirk helped to divert them away from self-help. Calvinism might be politically revolutionary, but it was very rarely associated with social revolt by the poor. Whatever dream of social renovation the Kirk, or rather its more idealistic minority, set out with, was soon being rarified into a dual programme of doctrinal purity and moral purgation. After four decades of this treatment it could not help recognizing the state of the country as one of thoroughgoing alienation of rich and poor, instead of the interweaving of a feudal society in equilibrium: 'little care and reverence of inferiours to their superiours; as suchlyke of superiours in discharging their dewtie to the inferiours . . .'[7]

In the past anything like a jacquerie had been 'virtually unknown in Scotland'[8], and Reformation had no such effect as in Germany where its first breath brought the upheaval of the Peasants' War. Enough of old inertia survived to keep Scotland almost the only country in Europe free of peasant revolt, and this in spite of its being a country inured to war and civil broils, full of men with military experience. Opportunities of service abroad as mercenaries drew away many who might have made trouble at home. Others turned their backs on insoluble problems by giving themselves up to drunkenness and whatever other consolations they could afford. Calvinism seems to have polarized the village between the lax immorality the Kirk was perpetually denouncing, and the humourless gravity of the pious, as though reprobate and elect were each coming out in their natural colours. Such cleavage was one more obstacle to any united action by the poor, and would make the serious-minded, who should have been their vanguard, all the more inclined to turn away from worldly grievances to higher, spiritual things.

For these men and women there was much nourishment in the doctrine they heard from the pulpit. It could lift hungry scratchers of soil owned by others above the penury of their lot. Calvinism with its strong doctrinal fabric, built on infinities and eternities, could be a shelter from the perplexities of daily life. It had the appeal to a backward country, somewhat as Marxism has had for the Third World, of offering an all-embracing scheme, whose main propositions could be understood by anyone and give him a confident sense of understanding the universe, while its subtleties conferred on those able to grasp them the pride of intellectual achievement. By the puritan elite of the Scottish masses their faith came to be hugged with a dogged tenacity only comprehensible if it is recognized as a replacement for the frustrated social reform which the Reformation had seemed at first to promise. Like all such historical substitutions it came to be invested with an unreasoning emotional intensity.

With it there was growing attachment to the Kirk, a good deal as an institution round which inchoate national sentiment could gather. National consciousness was an ingredient in the Reformation from the outset, as in all other countries. It showed from the later sixteenth century in scholarly interest in Scottish history, while printings of the old tales of Wallace and Bruce met the popular taste, as they still did in the early nineteenth century.[9] This Scottish identity was all the more keenly felt because after 1603 and the union of crowns with England its survival seemed more and more in jeopardy. Scotland's kings became absentees; its parliament or Estates had no such weight or standing as England's; the Kirk might well appear the most authentic national institution, and its annual general assembly the country's most representative gathering.

The 'National Covenant' signed in 1638 by thousands of all classes, as a pledge to protect Kirk and creed against Charles I's interference, was a compendium modelled on an earlier one of 1580. 'Covenants' or 'bands' were a feature of the Reformation; they had antecedents in the 'bands' (bonds) entered into by feudal factions, but now one of the high contracting parties was God. 'Full of formal legalism',[10] and ambiguously worded so as to be 'all things to all men', the document had a vigorously nationalist flavour, supplying 'national conceit with a theological foundation' by playing on the idea, already time-honoured, of Scots being a chosen people, the equivalent in this age of the Hebrews in antiquity.[11] A poor country sinking into dependence needed a myth so magnificent to bolster its self-respect. (Welshmen too liked to fancy that they were part of the original chosen people, speaking a language akin to the first human speech, Hebrew.) A much less welcome sequel in 1643 was the Solemn League and Covenant with the parliamentary party in England, which to Englishmen was only a grand title for a military alliance against the royalists, but which left many Scots obsessed with a quixotic belief in their mission to presbyterianize England. From this 'enormous mistake'[12] they failed to move forward to any more common-sense programme; in the civil wars they floundered from side to side, becoming more and more deeply divided in the process. In the end defence of country and creed, first championed by the higher classes, largely though not exclusively from self-interest, would descend to the lower, to a plebeian mass which had failed and continued to fail to comprehend its own interests.

Elimination of bishops gave a fuller share of control of the Kirk to laymen of the propertied classes, serving as elders; this was regulated by the 'Form of Presbyterial Church-Government' adopted in 1645. It sought for the Kirk a balancing or moderating role; care of the poor had its place in the schedule of duties of pastors and parish officers. The 1647 'Catechism' in its elaborate commentary on the ten commandments equated society and family, in true feudal-clan style, by extending the fifth commandment to cover relations between all 'superiors' – who clearly seem to include employers – and 'inferiors', and dilating on their mutual responsibilities. The eighth is made a peg for numerous social maxims; hard work is inculcated, but injury to others, for instance by 'unjust enclosures' of common lands, is condemned. Theologically the catechism derived from the *Westminster Confession* painfully hammered out in 1647 by a joint Scottish and English commission. It represents the most elaborate edifice of Calvinist – perhaps of Christian – thinking ever reared, at the moment when this extraordinary system of ideas was about to begin crumbling under its own weight, and fading away everywhere except in backwaters like Scotland or New England.

Among some nobles who signed the 1638 'Covenant', like Montrose, fears had been expressed almost from the start that if the Crown were too seriously weakened the masses might take the bit between their teeth, and go on to sweep aristocracy away into the bargain.[11] There was similar anxiety in the Kirk over the spread of conventicles, or irregular prayer-meetings, since even before 1638.[12] By the strait-laced they were suspected of being tainted with sectarian ideas akin to those of the Brownists, or the Family of Love, which had disturbed conservative repose in England and elsewhere, and might be said to hover – as did so much religion in England during those years – on the borderline between doctrinal and social heterodoxy. In Scotland there is very little sign of any of the consequences so much feared, even when the country came under the rule of an English government committed to independency and wide toleration. In the spring of 1652 Edinburgh witnessed a mushrooming of sects hitherto unknown there – Brownist, Antinomian, Familist – and baptizing of Anabaptists in the water of Leith;[15] a stream with hardly enough water to baptize a child, as shallow as this current of religious novelty proved to be, even in the urban areas to which it was limited.

A Cromwellian soldier in Berwickshire spoke pityingly of a peasantry huddled in its hovels, evicted at the landlord's whim.[16] During the occupation the authorities showed much 'concern for social justice'.[17] It was their cue, as an observer noted, to detach 'the poor Commoners' from thraldom both to the aristocracy and to the clergy: it would be a good idea, he thought, to station good English preachers in the chief towns, to draw people away from 'their Pharisaical and rigid Presbyterian Teachers'.[18] At Edinburgh orders were issued for street-cleaning, and throwing of dirt out of windows was banned.[19] Such interference with cherished custom might have been enough to antagonize the capital, but Colonel Robert Lilburne, in command in Scotland in 1653, had cause everywhere to lament 'the spirit of the generality of people here, who have a deadly antipathy against us.'[20] In May 1654 union with England was imposed, and helped to ensure 'firm and good government', with more impartial justice than Scotland had ever known. Yet it made no dent on old clannish prejudice. 'Cromwell was in Scottish eyes almost another Edward I.'[21] Nationalism has been at least as often an obstructive as a progressive force. In a not dissimilar fashion women through the ages have submitted to ill-usage from their lords and masters, and often taken part with them against outsiders. Molière has a scene of a wife indignant at a stranger who interposes against the husband who is beating her.

Scotland was capable neither of reforming itself nor of accepting reform from outside. It was cutting off its nose to spite its face when it hailed the Restoration in 1660 with loud satisfaction. The hated union was dissolved, and good rule from London was exchanged for bad rule from London. 'The enemies of God', in the language of a stern Covenanter, were regaining power 'with the favour and the fawnings of the foolish Nation.'[22] It must be said in mitigation that there had been too little time before 1660 to permit economic recovery from the damage done by the wars. English occupation and the contacts it brought had done something, all the same, to widen horizons and stimulate the improving bourgeois outlook. In the towns some impatience of perpetual clerical squabbling had begun to be shown, and a turning away towards more mundane concerns. There was little public protest at the suppression of the ministers' assembly in 1653; and the despotic attitude of the bigots, when they were in the saddle, led to 'a strong reaction against the Covenants and even against presbyterianism.'[23] On the whole the decades following 1660 were a time of economic and cultural growth.

By the Kirk too the Restoration was welcomed uncritically, among both the 'Resolutioners' who had taken the Stewart side against Cromwell in 1650 and their 'Remonstrant' or 'Protestor' opponents. When it speedily proved that return to monarchy meant return to Episcopacy, regarded once more by royalists as an indispensable prop to the throne, moderates made the best of it; the more readily because Presbyterianism was not being subverted, but only placed under supervision of bishops, and church services were scarcely affected. But the need to obtain 'collation', or confirmation of their ministerial posts by the patron (now restored to his right of presentation) and the bishop, was more than the intransigent could bear; and in 1662 nearly three hundred, a considerable proportion of the total, were ejected from their pulpits.

They were giving a fresh display of the curious semi-republicanism Scotland had nurtured since the Reformation, or even earlier. It was riddled with contradictions, reflecting all the unclarity of an era of change and confusion. These unyielding men 'were not prepared to admit that lay rulers had the right to control the religion of their subjects.'[24] But the Kirk, meddling in politics, had often ignored its own precept of the Two Kingdoms, the spiritual and temporal each supreme in its own sphere. Moreover the zealots demanded action by government against everyone's religion but their own; in their eyes an essential part of the duty imposed on all good Scots by the Covenants was 'the extirpation of Popery, Prelacy, Superstition, Heresie, Schisme, Profanenesse'.[25] They were as far as could be from advocating freedom and toleration: theirs was the tribal insistence on all brethren facing the same way. A 'free people', they might eloquently declare, should be ruled by civil law, 'not by military force and cruelty',[26] but clearly only the strictest Presbyterians, a dwindling minority, were entitled to this right.

Fidelity to the Covenants was their watchword. Veneration of these compacts with heaven as immutable requirements of the faith, never to be relegated to the past as they were by the conformists, served as a bond of unity, in default of any more rational one, but unity in essence negative. A 'Covenanting' movement quickly took the form of illicit services, or conventicles, often held privately, but more defiantly as field-preachings, combined with non-attendance at churches occupied by conforming or intruded ministers. Such behaviour necessarily had an anti-English hue, which lost nothing by the fact that some of the new 'curates' were English, and hence doubly detested. Patriotic feeling must have helped to win sympathy, if not support, for the Covenanters. Their goal was salvation for the whole Scottish community, not for individuals merely; in this, theology can be seen as a chrysalis of nationalism. It was a counterweight to the isolation of the predestined soul, and of the tenant farmer, as much at the mercy of the landlord's caprice as his soul of God's.

Dislike of the new ecclesiastical order was widespread, but regional variations were strongly marked. It is easier from some points of view to see the Scotland of that time as a congeries of regions rather than of classes; the region formed an intermediate stage between the clan, with its denial of class, and the nation, within which classes are free to take shape. Conventicles were scarcely known north of the Tay; they were most numerous in the south-west. This had a rehearsal in earlier events. During the 1630s several of the group of pastors most resentful of Episcopal encroachments came from there. It was there too that unofficial prayer-meetings spread most readily after 1638, with the encouragement of some outstanding ministers. It was there again that 'Protestors' were most numerous, and from there that the 'Whiggamore raid' of

Kirk stalwarts marched to Edinburgh in 1648, starting the party nickname of 'Whig' on its long career. All this betokened no disposition to approve of the Cromwellian presence. A list of prisoners captured by an English force at Dumfries in 1651 is a long one.[27]

Among the ejected pastors nearly all those of Galloway could be counted, besides more than two-thirds of those attached to the synods of Ayr and Glasgow. It was in districts off the high road of history that zealotry was likeliest to persist, provided that they were not too torpid for Reformation teaching to have sunk into men's minds. Geography was one simple reason for the obduracy of the south-west. Fife and the Lothians were too close under the eye of a government whose military strength was fortified by civil war experience, with a standing army now come to stay. Gatherings there were usually domestic, and tended towards a pietistic withdrawal from the iniquity of the times. Ayrshire, Dumfriesshire, and the neighbouring Borders were rich in trackless moors, bogs, hills, where unlawful meetings could avoid detection or baffle pursuit, as smugglers and cattle-reivers had done in times still not quite gone by. Paden's Hill in the midst of the Cheviot Hills, even today not easily explored, is only one of several secluded haunts on which the name of the celebrated preacher Alexander Peden came to be bestowed. Galloway in the far south-west – the county of Wigtownshire and the county or 'Stewartry' of Kirkcudbrightshire – was not easy of access by land; John Knox had once taken refuge there. But unlike the landlocked Borders it was washed by sea and Solway Firth, and its bays and inlets and little ports assisted small-scale local trade. The nearness of Ulster, where Peden could find sanctuary at need in a Scottish settlement planted by the sword, with a Presbyterian fervour kept in constant heat by confrontation with popery, must have reinforced the intransigence of the south-west.

Regional feeling requires some measure of social solidarity, always largely illusory but sometimes favoured by circumstances. In most of Scotland landownership was concentrated in not many hands; in the south-west with its scattered patches of cultivation there were many survivors of the class of 'bonnet lairds', or 'small working landowners',[28] who formed a link between those above and below them. Trade helped to make for a gradation of ranks, up to a nobility itself not very wealthy. Cattle-rearing was a staple in Ayrshire and Lanarkshire, with export of herds to England, but still more in Galloway. Drovers and shepherds with their knowledge of hill and moorland could be useful guides or scouts, and might be of more independent temper than the ploughman. Bible-readers in country like this may have been more responsive than most others to the pastoral imagery of scripture.

After 1660 the growing ascendancy of the government was likely in all areas to bring about a widening rift within Scotland's too numerous and penurious nobility between families content with a provincial status, and others which chose to associate themselves with the court: individuals ambitious of treading a wider stage, and able to catch the royal or ministerial eye, who might also be men who had overspent themselves and needed a financial blood-transfusion which the government alone could supply. A convenient means by which it could do so was furnished by the fines imposed on suspects or opponents. Of the plunder represented by forfeited lands, half went (or was supposed to go) to the Crown, half to the commissioners empowered to act for it. A vulture aristocracy was continuing its predatory mode of subsistence in new guise.

One magnate of the south-west, the Earl of Annandale, was among those – 'bankrupt in estate as well as in morals'[29] – who escaped ruin by getting large subsidies from this source: in the last years of persecution he was one of its strenuous agents. But in that old-fashioned corner of Scotland most of the prominent families were still rooted in the local soil, and it was they, accustomed until not many years since to rule the roost without much reference to Edinburgh, who had the most tangible interest in preservation of regional autonomy. Over a Kirk free from official control they would have the greatest share of influence. Some were, besides, unquestionably sincere in their Presbyterian principles. There was an 'ultra-protestant' tradition among them;[30] this as well as dislike of the monarchy's centralizing policies enlisted their support for the Covenant. In the reforming assembly of the Kirk at Glasgow in 1638 the earls of Galloway, Dumfries, Wigtown, and Cassilis all took part, and for several years there prevailed an unwonted 'unanimity of the Galloway baronage'.[31]

In the previous century the French wars of religion had turned into a defence by the Huguenots of provincial and municipal self-rule in their southern strongholds, far away from Paris. In Scotland now the old type of feudal insubordination, chronic to the end of the sixteenth century, was no longer practical politics. Noblemen could not summon their vassals to take up arms; and when the common folk rose they 'acted for the first time on their own initiative'.[32] But in less dramatic ways local notables were ready enough to display their disapproval of government proceedings.

Foremost among them was the head of the Kennedy clan, John, sixth Earl of Cassilis. Such a man might well be shocked into better ways by memories of ancestral crime, like the Borgia who became Saint Alexander, for his two predecessors, one of them known as the 'king of Carrick', had been among the worst feudal ruffians of their times. The present holder of the title was one of three Scots laymen deputed to attend the Westminster assembly. He was one of only two in the parliament of 1661 who spoke against the royal supremacy in church affairs, and paid the penalty by being declared incapable of any public office. After his death in 1666 his son followed the same course, and his was the solitary protest in parliament against the 'Black Act' of 1670 which made field-preaching a capital crime.[33]

Another who fell foul of authority was John Maclellan, third Baron Kirkcudbright, like the second lord a staunch Presbyterian who had stood against both king and Cromwell. His fortune was crippled by costs of raising troops during the wars, and wiped out after the Restoration by fines for resisting the intrusion of a curate into the church at Kirkcudbright. In 1663 he was arrested for alleged sympathy with a riot there, in which women took a prominent part, and next year he died. The fourth Viscount Kenmure was an ardent royalist in the civil wars, and the sixth was to lose his life in 1715 as a Jacobite rebel; in between, a distant relative who succeeded to the title in 1663 went very much the other way. Like Cassilis, and the Earl of Galloway, not hitherto in the same camp, he was among those stripped of offices and jurisdictions for refusing the oath under the Test Act of 1681, when the accession of the Catholic heir, James, was approaching; he was deprived of his hereditary bailliary of Tongland.

Such men could use their positions as magistrates, and their local influence, to extend some covert protection to their humbler neighbours. To act in such a manner as the people's guardians was in line with the kind of 'populism' which had a place in feudal societies. They would be the more desirous of putting a check on the arbitrary conduct of officials and soldiery because their own estates suffered, if only indirectly, from the depredations. In 1667 a complaint by two noblemen and Sheriff Agnew about army extortion obliged the government to set up an enquiry. A few years later, when attitudes had hardened further, a petition to the king was ignored, and a deputation of western 'noblemen and gentlemen' wanting to protest to the privy council at Edinburgh about grievances like the quartering of troops on their districts was unceremoniously turned away.

From the first the government tried to get all landowners to cooperate with it. Some did, for fear of trouble or in hope of enhancing their own power by acting as its myrmidons. Many must have had mixed or wavering feelings. They might not be sorry to see tenants banging their heads against a brick wall, instead of combining against *them*. On the other hand it may sometimes have struck them, as it did the more apprehensive of the Covenanting nobility after 1638, that defiance of government might one day turn into defiance of rent-collectors. Yet, again, neighbourhood feeling was pervasive, the same common dislike of pressure from outside which sometimes drew or dragged French seigneurs into anti-tax riots. In 1678 even those well-disposed towards Presbyterianism made haste to assure the Council that they had no complicity in the scuffles with soldiers which were breaking out;[34] but they were clearly unwilling to accept the duty it wanted to thrust on them of keeping their plebeians in order.

Landlord authority being so extensive, the official assumption that they could do this if they chose was not unnatural: and without a good deal of malingering on their part it is hard to see how Covenanting could have held out so long. Trying to break down the obstacle, the government was no respecter of persons. Refractory nobles, not peasants, had always been its stumbling-block in the past. In 1682 Kenmure was ordered out of his mansion by Claverhouse to make room for a garrison.[35] There were financial motives too for striking at men of property. Tenants paid their rents mostly in kind; they could be laid under contribution chiefly by having soldiers billeted on them, but cash had to be looked for higher up. It was complained in 1666 that ninety-one persons in the Stewartry had been mulcted in a total of £47,860, and many gentry and other families ruined.[36] There is some ground for the statement that after the 1679 rising 'The Galloway gentlemen were the first sacrifices.'[37] Thirty-five estates in Galloway and Dumfriesshire were forfeited, either because their owners were suspected of disloyalty or as a warning to the rest of their class that they would not be allowed to stay neutral.

Among the zealots there were no doubt carpings at the reluctance of the bulk of the upper classes to come forward more boldly. All the same, their temporizing attitude may be supposed to have softened the bitterness which tenants as individuals must often have felt, and might come to feel collectively. Still more of a blurring of class relations may be ascribed to the part in the movement played by women of all classes, from highest to lowest. All women had grievances of their own against the social order, which could not yet find articulate expression, but could only merge themselves in a response to a more general summons. A Duchess of Hamilton did her best in the 1660s to shield Covenanters from prosecution. The Duke of Rothes, for some time the government's chief manager in Scotland, and among many other things chief collector of fines, had a conventicling wife. In 1672, while the Earl of Wigtoun was a member of the privy council, his lady was heavily fined for attending conventicles. When Claverhouse was man-hunting in Wigtownshire ten years later he reported that lairds were outwardly conforming, but allowing disaffected persons to haunt their houses, and having their children baptized by 'outed' ministers; when challenged, they laid the blame on their wives. He meant to put a stop to this comedy, he added grimly.[38] Kenmure married the widow of a laird, John Bell, shot by the military in 1685. At the bottom of the scale there was often a fierce devotion to Kirk and Covenants among servant-women, and wives of peasants, like Cuddie Headrigg's mother in *Old Mortality*, who could find in the exaltation of the cause and its perils a release from the harsh, narrow existence to which they were condemned.

Ousted ministers who took to field-preaching were another link between the classes. Ejected preachers and tenants always liable to eviction were fellow-sufferers, and the latter could appreciate the sacrifice of security their pastors had made. Some of these were of humble birth, and knew the hardships of the poor, and were now sharing them again; but as scholars, whose high standing came from their learning, they would prefer to rise above vulgar bread-and-butter questions and soar into the empyrean of divinity. A fair number of others had gentry connections; since the earlier days of the Kirk the ministry had become, in terms of financial rewards, a respectable profession. Manses were always likely to be occupied by members of nearby families, and in Galloway their abandonment by nearly all their occupants must have owed much to local ties. Birth entitled men who accompanied their flocks into the hill to added respect; while many of those foisted into their places were taxed with both low origins and – unjustly, it would seem[39] – with scanty attainments.

Covenanters were always divided between more moderate and more extreme, and it may be further supposed that ministers with landed connections were likelier to belong to the first, as well as to be even more immune than the rest to any social incendiarism. John Welsh, the leading moderate, was the son of a Nithsdale laird, though reported to have led a very wild life on the Borders before his conversion; a change that might be said to epitomize the evolution of the Border valleys from clan forays to a more spiritual sort of independence. Peden is described as an Ayrshire peasant proprietor's son, of bonnet-laird descent. James Renwick, in religion an extremist, was a weaver's son. Besides differences over ecclesiastical principle, however, there was another – as among Chartists later – about whether physical force could rightly be resorted to. Richard Cameron, who gave his name to the movement in its last years and was killed fighting, came from a town tradesman's family. But within the rural orbit individuals from higher ranks, traditionally involved in the faction-fighting that had been Scotland's politics, might be readier than others to draw the sword. Donald Cargill's father was a small laird and lawyer. Laymen would be more thoroughgoing than preachers. Two of the men, in another part of the country, who brought fiercer persecution on the Covenanters by murdering Archbishop Sharp in 1679, were lairds.

Age was another differential. Welsh came from an earlier, more unsettled Scotland. Peden was thirty-four at the Restoration, Renwick only twenty-six when he was executed in 1688 just before the Revolution: his whole brief life belonged to the time of persecution. But youth did not correspond with an advance towards appreciation of social issues. It may sometimes indeed have been the other way about. We are told that Samuel Rutherford, inducted at Anworth in 1627, showed sympathy with the common people's plight, for instance by remonstrating with a laird who in true feudal style raised his rents to defray the cost of his son's wedding.[40] Such an attitude preserved something of the Reformation clergy's concern with the state of the poor, which had some partial revival in the early 1640s. Doubtless conscientious ministers expected or hoped that study of the catechism would make landlords more benevolent, as well as tenants and labourers more docile. But their desire, all the more natural under stress of persecution, was to unite well-fed and hungry on the rock of scripture, not to divide them over the affairs of this transient world.

It is going too far to say that their following came 'almost entirely from the peasantry and small tenant farmers.'[41] Any peasant movement regularly requires some admixture of other elements, for leaven or stiffening, as has been observed of agrarian revolts in China. Lists of names of those who fell under official displeasure do not usually specify their occupations, but there is a sprinkling of others than cultivators, a few described as 'merchants', or relatives of lairds, but mostly of modest callings, such as smiths, tailors, weavers, down to servants.[42] Many of these must have had family links with the ploughmen and it was very common for small farmers to have other employments besides. They were all close enough in each district for mutual trust. There were occasional informers, but if there had been many the government would have found its work far easier. Their faith and its hazards were a relief from the isolation of their separate lives, as tenants competing for farms, or simply as shepherds alone in the hills, as well as from the dreary monotony which must have been painfully felt by the mentally more alert.

In a slippery world, as treacherous as one of their upland bogs, their treaty with God, a perpetual bond never to be broken, was a comforting certainty to which they could hold fast. Neighbourhood sentiment might be strong, but Scots villagers had no such organization of their own as the commune of old Russia, or Vietnam, with fixed rights of cultivation and a traditional leadership. Only an unearthly vision, a pole star invisible to others, could lend them the sense of fraternity they needed. Devotion to their image of the Kirk may be seen as the false consciousness of a class, a coming together in defence of ideals instead of interests. Covenanters had a deep sensation of being wronged and oppressed, but they turned their indignation against an imaginary oppressor, a giant or monster called Erastianism, casting a still more horrid shadow of popery and idolatry. Rejection of bishops was an unconscious rejection of the social order.

Their cause had some able controversialists, in exile, like the author of *Jus Populi Vindicatum*, whose treatise followed those of the old Huguenot writers in denying royal absolutism and asserting the right of resistance to abuse of the authority created by 'a voluntary compact, and consent of the Subjects'.[43] But learnedly lengthy treatises like this, or *A Hind let loose*,[44] were far removed from the realities and miseries of rural life. Their philosophy could not go beyond a tacit assumption that godly rule and fulfilment of the Covenants would make all well for all good Scots, besides putting a stop to 'the present overflowing and abounding of Idolatry, Superstition, Sodomy, Adultery, Uncleannesse, Drunkennesse, Atheisme . . .'[45]

To help to imprison Covenanters in their infatuation there was the grip of Calvinist dogma. In Scotland this creed could perform the negative task of sweeping away an older cult, and much that went with it, but it was far less capable of anything positive, because the social and economic foundations necessary for progress were not present, as they were in England or Holland. A theology can lend impetus to social drives, but cannot initiate them. In Scotland it remained a thing in itself, historically purposeless, except as unconscious symbol of rejection – rejection of life itself, it might often seem to the profane, or at any rate a hindrance instead of help to any useful new thinking. Religious excitement dammed up by the want of rational purpose turned into irrational obsession.

For men who could only turn their back on their world and dream of rising above it, instead of striving to alter it, such a doctrine might be appropriate enough. It is a salient difference between them, and the irregular sects of the previous decades, in Scotland and far more in England, that instead of unorthodox beliefs mingled with social aspirations they took their stand on unswerving orthodoxy. In the England of the Commonwealth the sects were a retreat into religious emotionalism after the defeat of the Levellers, the failure of revolutionary hopes, by groups of disoriented individuals who had no external links to sustain them. Covenanters were men on whom hope of revolution had not even dawned, the rearguard of an idealized past instead of the forlorn hope of an ideal future. For them all truth was already written. They combined with their afflatus a hard Calvinist intellectuality. As faithful adherents of a cause not long since subscribed to by the entire nation, they could feel that they were no mere sect; while their regional base gave them a cohesion which the sectaries had to win from outbursts of collective excitement. Repression and censorship made it harder for any novel thinking to filter into the beleaguered south-west. Here was another reason for the movement – or rather *stand-still* – being countenanced by sections of the propertied classes; its creed offered no threat to them, as the notions of break-away sectaries might.

Most of the resisters came from a downtrodden mass exploited since time out of mind by superiors against whom they had never attempted to rise. For them to rise up now and challenge authority was an immense feat in itself. They could only achieve it by having another, higher authority to look to; by virtue of firm conviction that God, through accredited representatives and the words of scripture, commanded them so to act. They were exchanging one obedience for another. As for the meaning of what they were bidden to do, God's intentions were inscrutable. For men and women haunted by fear of damnation, to defy earthly penalties by joining in prayer on a wild moor might be the most potent reassurance. Scottish Calvinism has been reproached with seeing God only as 'King and Judge', instead of father. 'The Scottish theologian had not emerged from the sphere of feudalism.'[46] If so, it would seem that feudalism in Scotland in its later phases had very little of a paternal character.

Just as defence of the Covenants was the first independent act of these hard-handed toilers, their first entry into public affairs, this theology was their intro-duction to the world of intellect. Through the two things together the old servile abasement of the Scottish peasantry before birth and rank, its pathetic eagerness to claim kinship however remote with them, was being replaced by respect for moral and mental qualities; here at least they were taking a stride forward, with more meaning for some of their descendants in a far-off future than for their own prospects. Well versed in the niceties of the catechism, and in scripture, they could be keen dissecters of abstruse sermons, each listener with his favourite predilections. Very often the thinking faculty has been exercised and developed on more arid matter. Even the meanest, Bishop Burnet lamented, were ready with Biblical texts to justify a veto on royal interference in religion: they were 'vain of their knowledge, much conceited of themselves, and were full of a most entangled scrupulosity.'[47] They were sons of a legalistic, if often lawless, nation, and of an era in which codification of law was going ahead; theirs was a religion of controversy and dialectic.

Protestantism and the English Bible had helped to banish Gaelic speech,[48] and were held on to all the more firmly as the induction into a new era. But Galloway had been the last Lowland area to lose its old tongue, and something of a Celtic temperament was still left. All theology, however academic, is a refinement of very primitive belief, and the south-western hills made a natural setting for what was semi-magical or fetishistic in the obsessive loyalty to the Covenants. Prayer-meetings in such surroundings, with nerves highly strung by danger, must have fostered stirrings of feeling more elemental than the ordered pattern of Calvinist doctrine. It was still the age of witchcraft and witch-hunting, and there was an appetite for the marvellous. Supernatural gifts, of prophecy especially, were attributed to Peden. Some who fought at Rullion Green in 1666 were convinced that their enemies, the ogre Dalziell of the Binns most of all, were protected by a pact with Satan against any but silver bullets.[49]

Covenanting was an early trial of passive resistance, or civil disobedience. At Urr near Dalbeattie when a new man, John Lyon, appeared in the pulpit 'The parishioners immediately began to manifest their antipathy to the "curate", by general abstention from his services, and indirect obstruction of his work.' Like most others of his species he was believed to aid the dragoons with information, and sometimes even accompany them on their raids.[50] Retaliation in kind was rare, even in hours of tumult; 'mob violence was never more leniently exercised against defenceless men.'[51] But one of the most interesting features of the agitation was its devising something very like the boycott method hit on by the Irish peasantry two centuries later.

Within a few years intruded ministers were driven to represent to the government that after their expenses of removal to this unruly quarter they were meeting with ill will, and finding their stipends grudgingly and irregularly paid.[52] Refusal to listen to their sermons was followed by refusal to work for them. It was a trenchant weapon out here, as Captain Boycott was to learn in the wilds of county Mayo. In 1680 the authorities were still having to promise protection to incumbents from 'the fury of some blind zealots', thanks to which 'even the necessaries of life, and the help of servants and mechanics are denied unto them for their money.'[53] Similar tactics might have been resorted to, there and in Scotland at large, against exorbitant rents and other burdens; a peasantry can do much to baffle landlord greed without going to the length of revolt. But for this a degree of unity is required which in seventeenth-century Scotland only the celestial trumpet could arouse.

From armed revolt the Covenanters were withheld at most times by their preachers, but also by the contradictoriness of their whole outlook, that of a movement disoriented from the real needs of its class, with no tangible aims to fight for, however much it might alarm the government into brutal repression. It was clearly believed that there was a threat of revolution in the west country: men would not imperil themselves so deeply for any lesser stake, and it could not be forgotten in London that the 'Great Rebellion' had been inaugurated in Scotland. In official eyes Covenanters were dangerous 'fanatics':[54] this word, coined in the previous century with the meaning 'mad', 'possessed', was now acquiring its modern sense. It was to be used incessantly by nineteenth-century imperialists of opponents like the Jehadists and dervishes of the North-West Frontier or the Sudan, with whom Covenanters had indeed some affinity.

Stevenson travelling with his donkey was haunted by thoughts of the Camisard rebels who, just after the time of the Covenanters, fought for years 'a war of wild beasts' in the Cevennes, built up 'an organization, arsenals, a military and religious hierarchy', and made their deeds the talk of Europe.[55] They were Protestants resisting Catholics, instead of erring fellow-Protestants; and they were poor country-folk left in the lurch by Huguenot citizens and gentry, to find leadership of their own. They were resentful of royal taxes as well as bigotry. By contrast the Covenanters' position was more complex and confusing, since apart from the fines imposed on them they were victims materially less of government than of their own gentry, to some of whom they owed a measure of protection. It was only in passive resistance that they could stand together.

They were not pacifists, and more and more as time went on their meetings were guarded by armed men; but except in immediate self-defence they only twice took up arms, and then only in an unplanned, unprepared reaction to molestation. They might then have made use of their hills to wage a guerrilla resistance, emulating Wallace's men who once ambushed the English by Loch Trool in the heart of Galloway, rolling rocks down on to their heads. Instead, on each occasion they marched out to confront their enemy in the open, in 1666 making for Edinburgh, in 1679 briefly occupying Glasgow. A rebellion must advance, it is true, but it must first consolidate its base, and be sure of support awaiting it outside. No such support was forthcoming. In these risings there was a gleam of the same unquestioning faith in God's readiness to stand by His true servants, a sense of the impiety of any distrust of this, of any hanging back, which had some part at least in hurrying the Scots army to destruction at Dunbar in 1650. No men of action comparable in talent with the leading preachers came forward to take command.

After their first defeat the government felt safe in reducing its forces and issuing the Indulgences of 1669 and 1672, which allowed vagrant ministers to come to terms, and preach in church instead of under the sky. Its aim was to split the ranks and isolate the irreconcilable, and it had some success. But the hard core remained strong enough to provoke in 1678 an extreme measure of coercion. A 'Highland Host' of freebooters (not all in fact were Highlanders) was let loose. It was an equivalent of the *dragonnades* by means of which Charles II's cousin and exemplar, Louis XIV, was trying to break the spirit of his Huguenot subjects. Fifteen hundred men were quartered on the Cassilis estates, so impoverishing the owner that a good part of them had to be sold. Memories of this occupation by ruffians licensed, as Defoe wrote in 1717, to commit 'rapine, violence, robbery and wickedness', were still vivid enough in 1745 to keep Ayrshire and Galloway even more anti-Jacobite than the rest of the Lowlands.[56]

Goaded into revolt again in 1679, the Covenanters won a first engagement at Drumclog, but then wasted their time listening to wrangles between the more and less inflexible of their ministers, until a few weeks later they were crushed at Bothwell Bridge near Hamilton. Led by Welsh, the moderates would have been content with freedom of conscience; those whose spokesman was Donald Cargill rejected any compromise with episcopacy, or reconciliation with the 'indulged' ministers who had made their peace. Next year the 'Sanquhar declaration' by the militants amounted to a withdrawal of allegiance, and in September Cargill followed it up by formally excommunicating the king and all his accomplices. This was going much too far to be countenanced by any men of respectable position. Moreover the obstinate stand of the remnant 'cut against feudal and clannish dependence'; and Cameron was reported to have predicted before his death in 1680 that when these troubles were over the hour would be at hand for nobility and gentry to disappear.[57] Towards the end landowners, in Wigtownshire particularly, were showing willingness to collaborate with the government.

Persecution intensified into what were remembered as 'the killing times'. With scarcely any ordained ministers left the survivors could no longer function as a regular church, but they maintained a loose organization, as 'Societies United in Correspondence' – the first 'corresponding societies' in modern political history – holding their meetings in more remote, inaccessible spots, ready to defend themselves if interrupted. Fantasy could swell their slender numbers with reinforcements from on high, where they believed Providence to be giving its closest attention to their barren hills. Their dreams, kindled by Old Testament reading, were of 'divine thunderclaps, irresistible legions, lethal swords of the Spirit . . .'[58] Short of miracles, little more was left, as for Wordsworth in his years of embitterment against an evil government, than to feed on the day of vengeance yet to come; and that day was receding beyond the boundaries of time. A rude epitaph in Glasgow cathedral, denouncing the executioners of nine martyrs there, ends:

They'll know at resurrection day
To murder saints was no sweet play.

Yet in the end they were still capable of an astonishing burst of energy. When William landed in England in 1688, and in November James II had to withdraw his troops from Scotland, they flocked together in arms, and 'for some months the Cameronians were masters of the south of the kingdom.'[59] That winter they marched across the Lowlands unopposed, ejecting Episcopalian clergymen. In 1689, with Claverhouse raising the Highlands against William, they were invited to form a regiment; there were debates and scruples, but a sufficient number agreed to enlist. Their spirited defence of Dunkeld nullified the Jacobite victory at Killiecrankie, and saved the situation. They were proving that they could fight as well as Cromwell's Ironsides, given proper leadership and the concrete task of defeating counterrevolution.

Thus in a sense the cause had triumphed, but only illusorily; these Covenanters were emerging from their lair into a Scotland where they were strangers, and where there could be little place for them. Shut up in their hills they could have no notion of how the world was changing round them. Theirs was the 'enthusiasm' of a class which had received a powerful injection of ideas without a practical outlet, a class not yet reduced to the condition of wage labourers, as their descendants would soon be, but with only a spurious independence, idealized into dedication to independence for Kirk and country. They were at the same time stragglers of a fading social order, feudal and oppressive but with a rough and ready spirit of brotherhood.

Early in 1690 the Cameronian regiment was removed to Flanders, one of several from Scotland to take part in the wars of William and Marlborough against the French. In 1706 there were still three hundred armed men, described as Covenanters, ready to march into Dumfries and burn a copy of the unpopular treaty under which next year Scotland was drawn into another and longer-lasting union with England. Once more they were a rearguard destined to defeat. But their instinct was true; for many years to come the poor had good reason to detest the Union. Incorporation into capitalist England accelerated tendencies towards unrestricted profit-making, achieved – as in England from an earlier date – by a combination of feudal power with capitalist appetite.

Already in 1695 the Scottish parliament had passed Acts to abolish the old practice of joint cultivation known as run-rig, doubtless primitive and inefficient, and to speed up consolidation of holdings and division of common lands, guided of course by the golden rule that to him that hath, more shall be given. In the south-west one stimulus was the growth of Glasgow, by 1715 as Scott noted in *Rob Roy* the commercial metropolis of Ayrshire and Dumfriesshire as well as its own environs. In Galloway large-scale enclosures began about 1720, with increased export of cattle to England since the Union making it profitable to substitute cattle-rearing for cultivation.[60] This made it necessary to get rid of many small farmers there and in neighbouring areas. Their removal was defended with the argument that the Galloway people were 'very lazy', and mismanaged the land.[61] This may have been in a way true. Shiftlessness in workaday life, indifference to comfort or neatness, might well go, as it did in the Highlands, with a martial spirit, a readiness for adventure, all the more so because in the conditions of the Scottish countryside labour was likely to be so unrewarding. Such men as the Covenanters could not walk, like ordinary beings, but could only soar; they were better capable of exalted and sacrificial moods than of grappling with humdrum daily tasks.

The class from which most of them had come was now being brought down from the clouds to face economic reality; and the exhausting fight for the now-defunct Covenants may have made it less easy, or more impossible, for this class to rally together now. There was much bitterness, and in 1724 some hundreds of families turned adrift were pulling down stone walls built by the enclosers in parts of Dumfriesshire and Kirkcudbrightshire; but these 'Levellers', as they were nicknamed, were soon quelled by dragoons sent from Edinburgh. An account of Galloway dating from about 1730 speaks of bare-footed peasants leading a 'coarse and dirty' existence in 'most miserable hovels', many for want of bed or mattress sleeping on the ground.[62] They had always been poverty-stricken, but a statement that few could read suggests a falling back since the days of the Bible-conning rebels.

Compensations for lost independence were in store for Scotland, or for some Scots, opportunities to be grasped by enterprising individuals from all ranks. Protestantism could not be the midwife to a social revolution the country was unready for, but it could in some ways deputize for an absent or feeble national development by forging a national character or mentality in many respects 'bourgeois', even while the framework of society was still feudal. Thanks to this historical detour there was being moulded in advance of economics a nation many of whose members were ready, as soon as circumstances detached them from their past, for a new, modern life. Opportunity beckoned most enticingly of all from an expanding empire; though for the poor, removal to the colonies might be an eviction from Scotland resembling eviction from their farms. A symbolic anticipation may be found in the story of the Covenanter transported to Jamaica and sold into plantation slavery, who was half-killed by his master for refusing to work on Sunday, but then by faithful service won his confidence and the hatred of the blacks over whom he was made overseer, and who tried to poison him.[68] To strain at the Sabbatarian gnat while swallowing the camel of nigger-driving was quite in harmony with the Covenanting bent for abstractions, as well as with Scottish peasant attachment to any master, however bad.

As for the Cameronian regiment, in more pedestrian phrase the 64th Foot, its part in the suppression of a Highland regiment's mutiny at Edinburgh in 1778 might be called a long-delayed tit for tat for the Highland Host of exactly a century before. But like so many other Scottish troops it was quickly found work in the empire; it was in at the crushing of the Indian Mutiny, and went on to assist in the conquest of Zululand. A vestigial link with the heroic past was always preserved, in an annual church service before which pickets were placed round the building and an officer with a lantern made a search for lurking enemies, as if a conventicle were meeting once more to sing its psalms in the hills.

The Kirk as remodelled after 1688 was not one that would hinder the rich from becoming richer and the poor poorer. Elimination of bishops left the Presbyterian organization again, as it had been earlier, 'admirably adapted to be an instrument of the aristocracy and gentry.'[64] Patronage, abolished in 1690, was restored in 1712, though enveloped in much complexity and uncertainty. More important, the elders, who were coming to hold office for life, were drawn from the propertied classes, oftener by cooption than by election. Covenanters and their heirs could scarcely think of trying to democratize the system; in their fieriest days they had not pretended to believe in majority rule, for the majority would always be recalcitrant to the rule of the saints.

Social control became the Kirk's primary function, and it enjoyed great though informal power of coercion through its control of poor relief and its ability to get any individual it disapproved of refused a tenancy or a job. Lay elders were often also magistrates; to a remarkable extent 'the instruments of economic, social and political power were delegated to the Kirk.'[65] This facilitated the further squeezing of the masses on which the Scottish Enlightenment, the eighteenth-century flowering of upper-class culture, depended. Capitalist farming led to agricultural improvements, but it was only after about 1780 that they made a significant contribution to national wealth.[66] Until then landowning income was being improved, as usual in a feudal society trying to catch up quickly – Peter the Great's Russia, for instance – by the privileged taking more from the unprivileged.

As always since the Reformation, the rural masses seem to have been oddly divided into puritanical and libertine, many soberly pious, many others having to be incessantly disciplined and dragooned. It would not be surprising to find that the demoralized now were those who had sunk into wage-servitude or pauperism, and the virtuous those still struggling, by austere abstention from cakes and ale, to keep their footing. Their struggle went with fidelity to everything traditional in religious practice and belief, like the old clinging to the lifeline of the Covenants. From this conservatism the better-off were moving away; religious divergence reflected a widening social gap. Arminianism, a Calvinist writer complained, was creeping into Scotland by 1750, chiefly among the higher classes, and many of the clergy shunned themes like predestination in their sermons, though the masses were still tenaciously attached to them.[67] Horrific doctrines like Calvin's, an Anglican divine wrote with strong distaste, are only suited to the vulgar, who relish coarse, pungent stimulants.[68] A poor man might not always feel certain of his own salvation, but he would suffer from few doubts about his landlord's or the government exciseman's damnation. Arminian sentimentality, redemption for all, would rob him of his revenge, the social revolution to begin on the day of judgment.

Among Scots still stuck in the old ruts, theology as fantasy-solution for material grievances, or means of rising above them, is well brought out by a report from a parish in Elgin in the 1790s – while France was having its terrestrial revolution – that almost the sole pleasure of the inhabitants was 'conversing about some of the abstrusest doctrines of Calvinism . . . varied by occasional reflections on the degeneracy and oppressions of the age.'[69] Twenty years later still an agricultural description of Ayrshire regretted that the distinction chiefly coveted by the peasantry was not skill with the plough but 'an extensive acquaintance with the mysterious, abstruse and disputed points of systematic divinity'.[70] Only removal to a fresh environment would enable them to apply the mental dexterity thus acquired to more useful avocations.

All classes in their various ways felt a lingering dislike of the Union, and either smouldering Scottishness or political opportunism might bring them together now and then, as, most explosively, in the affair of the Porteous riots at Edinburgh in 1736. Patriotism of this sort was the successor to older regional loyalties, and likewise helped to keep social friction within bounds. It was felt most strongly, though inarticulately, by the poor, who got least from the Union. But national consciousness can regress, as well as evolve, and turn back to more elementary symbols. On the Half-Moon battery of Edinburgh castle the guns had come to be known as the Seven Sisters, a name originally bestowed on some cannon made in the castle foundry which saw action against the English at Flodden. When they were carried off to London in 1716 to be melted down for scrap, it 'was like to break all the old women's hearts in town.'[71]

Among more important monuments, or badges of Scottish identity, the Kirk stood easily first, with all its rights intact after the Union except religious monopoly, and it was not always subservient to London. It was the people's church, but not under the people's control. Its managers, a pamphleteer of the next century wrote, the elders who flocked to Edinburgh for the annual Assembly, were not 'Cameronian, plaided, blue bonneted men from the muirs and upland pastures', but lairds, provosts, lawyers.[72] All the more was the common man anxious that it should be held fast to creed and catechism, as the true Scottish inheritance, now being abandoned by the anglicizing gentry with their taste for heathenish philosophy. Lurking bitterness against the higher classes, xenophobia against England, could thus go together.

Among the more modern-minded, old-fashioned Calvinism might be harder and harder to salvage, but as time went by the Covenanters could be looked back on as religion's most selfless paladins, and as part of what the Kirk stood for in cherished national tradition. A poet of the early nineteenth century extolled them as men who

Perish'd that Scotland might be free.[73]

A painter depicted the drama of a Covenanter hiding in a hole in the rocks, about to be seized by unpitying soldiers.[74] Memorials, grand or humble, littered the country. Like so much else in later-day Scottish patriotism, many tributes were no more than conventional tinsel. Christopher North brought into one of his dialogues a piece of fustian rhetoric about a maiden martyr drowned on the sands;[75] one might prefer Aytoun's honester Tory jibe about a tuneless hymn sounding as if 'composed by the Reverend Saunders Peden in an hour of paroxysms on the moors'.[76] But Scott, repelled by the Covenanters as bigots and mutineers, despite his Toryism was fascinated by them as well.

A law-abiding admirer was careful to except from his praise the two armed risings, putting them on the same bad level as the Radical disturbance in Scotland in 1820, fresh evidence that attempts to cure public ills by force only make them worse.[77] But Scottish Chartists were fond of seeing themselves as heirs of the Covenanters. So was Keir Hardie, the Scottish socialist. One more turn of the wheel brought 1914, when their legend as patriots was invoked in recruiting propaganda because 'Nothing stirs the enthusiasm of Scotsmen more than the story of the trials and triumphs of the Covenanters.'[78] Since then, if the man in the street has been forgetting them, Scottish historians have not, and lately these have been joined by Marxists, compelled to think more about such corners of the past now that the present has come to look so intractable.

What's Hecuba to him, or Covenants to a Galloway peasant? All men in action are actors, playing parts often genuine enough but always with some admixture of the histrionic, through which inner impulses of diverse character find expression. They have habitually turned earlier ailments and aspirations into a sort of anagram, or pictorial language supplied by ideas floating in the air of their time and place. In retrospect, or from an outsider's viewpoint, incongruities between the two planes will always be evident. As collective and perpetual obligations binding on all, the Covenants are reminiscent of the feudal oath of fealty that bound lord and vassal together. Speaking of the oddly familiar, even peremptory Presbyterian style of addressing the Almighty (foreigners were often struck by the rude familiarity of Scotsmen talking to their superiors, even to their sovereign while he still dwelt among them) Notestein cites an account of a pastor's prayer for God's aid when the movement was nearing final defeat:

'And if', said he, 'Thou wilt not be our secondary, we will not fight for Thee at all, for it is not our cause but Thy cause; and if Thou wilt not fight for our cause and Thy own cause, we are not obliged to fight for it.'[79]

This is very much what clansmen or feudal tenants, called out to serve their lord in war, must have felt when he was not seen fighting in their ranks; and it sounds curiously as if, close to despair, some Covenanters were catching a glimpse of reality through the Maya-veil of theology.

They were men of a decaying social order who got into a blind alley and spent their energies there. History teems with examples of high gifts futilely expended, and the cumulative wastage, like that of stifled individual talents, must have been very great, and one of the causes of mankind's faltering progress. Within a generation of 1688 a British government would understand that a challenge like that of the Covenanters could be ignored; whether they listened to sermons in their pews or on their hillsides mattered very little. Both sides had been fighting an atavistic war of the past. It may still be said that without that long-drawn wrestling match, that 'last weird battle in the west', rulers would have been slower to learn the lesson. If so, there is substance in Froude's tribute to the Covenanters as the men who forced open the door for David Hume, Adam Smith, and the steam engine.[80] It was not a compliment that any of their ghosts can have relished; but if valid it is a notable illustration of how history makes use of mortals' toils to bring about results quite other than what they tried to achieve.

In a more general view, it may be permissible to think of a conservation of moral energy, thanks to which its loss is never total. Whatever their narrowness of outlook, one chronicler of the Covenanters wrote, they embodied certain vital qualities in the national life.[81] By showing that nameless poor men could stand up against tyrannical authority they were giving proof of something that would be the keystone of Burns's poetry. In the Scottish consciousness they may have come to symbolize an uneasy sensation of a riddle left unsolved, a primitive virtue lost in the scramble, a promised land foregone for the fleshpots of England and India. They were the uncompromising opposite of everything that modern Scotland drifted into being, gaining a good share of the world and perhaps losing its soul.

Some part of their moral make-up must be discoverable in all mankind's idealists. There must be, running through human nature, something aloof from the common satisfactions which content most people at most times, and justify Marxism in its materialist theory of history, its equivalent of the Newtonian law of gravity. It is something that comes to life in individuals and minorities, and turns them into dissenters. But if history can in some measure be made by men and women like the Covenanters, it may also be marred by them. The chosen few are liable to plunge in odd directions, and to tilt at windmills. The Covenanters may be charged with misleading their class, debarring it from a practical grapple with its ills, by engaging its emotions for generations on behalf of martyrs suffering for a chimera. Yet if their gospel was too other-worldly to cope with hardships like hunger, the simply bread-and-butter movements of our day have proved equally incapable of lifting men's minds to anything so ideal, so distant, so necessary, as socialism. How to reconcile the two visions, pushed so far apart by our society and its maladies, is what Marxists hitherto have been as far as anyone else from discovering.

# Notes

1. C.V. Wedgwood, *The King's Peace 1637–1641*, 1955; London edn, 1966, p. 53.

2. J.E. Handley, *Scottish Farming in the Eighteenth Century*, London 1953, pp. 88–90.

3. Patrick Gordon, cited by Andrew Lang, *A History of Scotland*, 3rd edn, Edinburgh 1924, vol. 3, p. 151.

4. James Nichols, *Calvinism and Arminianism*, London 1824, pp. xli, 205.

5. *Basilikon Doron*, 1603, cited by Lang, vol. 2, pp. 438–9.

6. T.I. Rae, *Scotland in the Time of Shakespeare*, Cornell University, 1965, p. 21.

7. A. Peterkin, ed., '*The Booke of the Universall Kirk of Scotland*', Edinburgh 1838, pp. 434–5.

8. William Ferguson, *Scotland's Relations with England: a Survey to 1707*, Edinburgh 1977, p. 120.

9. Rae, p. 30; Anon. (?James Myles), *Chapters in the Life of a Dundee Factory Boy*, Dundee 1887, p. 27.

10. J.M. Reid, *Kirk and Nation. The Story of the Reformed Church of Scotland*, London 1960, pp. 68–9.

11. Gordon Donaldson, *Scotland, the Making of the Kingdom, James V–James VII*, 1965; Edinburgh edn 1978, pp. 315–6.

12. Reid, p. 75.

13. David Stevenson, *The Scottish Revolution 1637–1644. The Triumph of the Covenanters*, Newton Abbot 1973, pp. 224–6.

14. Ibid., p. 200.

15. James Grant, *Old and New Edinburgh*, London n.d., vol. 3, p. 90.

16. Lang, vol. 3, p. 204.

17. Ferguson, p. 138. Cf. Sir R. Coupland, *Welsh and Scottish Nationalism*, London 1954, pp. 88–90.

18. C.H. Firth, ed., *Scotland and the Commonwealth (1651-53)*, Edinburgh 1895, pp. 339–40 (a report from Dundee, 14 Nov. 1651).

19. Ibid., pp. 347–8.

20. Ibid., p. lii.

21. W. Notestein, *The Scot in History*, London 1946, p. 145.

22. Anon. (Alexander Shields), *A Hind let loose, or An Historical Representation of the Testimonies of the Church of Scotland*, s.l. 1687, p. 97.

23. Donaldson, p. 365. Cf. W.L. Mathieson, *Scotland the Union. A History of Scotland from 1695 to 1747*, Glasgow 1905, pp. 16–18.

24. Reid, p. 76.

25. Anon. (Sir James Stewart), *Jus Populi Vindicatum, or The People's Right, to defend themselves and their Convenanted Religion, vindicated*, s.l. 1669, pp. 3–4.

26. Ibid., p. 5.

27. Firth, pp. 321–2.

28. W. Thompson, 'From Reformation to Union', in T. Dickson, ed., *Scottish Capitalism*, London 1980, p. 75. See also the same writer's 'The Kirk and the Cameronians', in M. Cornforth, ed., *Rebels and their Causes*, London 1978.

29. J.K. Hewison, *The Covenanters. A History of the Church in Scotland from the Reformation to the Revolution*, Glasgow 1908, vol. 2, p. 119.

30. Donaldson, p. 338.

31. A.S. Morton, *Galloway and the Covenanters*, Paisley 1914, p. 79.

32. Donaldson, p. 317.

33. For details of these and other magnates, see Sir R. Douglas, *The Scottish Peerage*, ed. Sir J.B.

Paul. Much scattered information will be found in P.H. M'Kerlie, *History of the Lands and their Owners in Galloway*, 5 vols, Edinburgh 1870–9. On some lurid episodes of the Cassilis past, see C.H. Dick, *Highways and Byways in Galloway and Carrick*, London 1916, ch. 27.

34. I.B. Cowan, *The Scottish Covenanters 1660–1688*, London 1976, p. 93.
35. Morton, pp. 199–200.
36. Ibid., pp. 118–9.
37. Ibid., p. 173.
38. Ibid., p. 197.
39. Donaldson, pp. 367–8.
40. James Barr, *The Scottish Covenanters*, Glasgow 1946, p. 173.
41. Cowan, p. 157.
42. Some lists are given by Morton, pp. 223 ff; cf. Barr, p. 228.
43. P. 144; cf. pp. 471–2, etc.
44. *Jus Populi* runs to 472 pages, *A Hind* to 742.
45. *Jus Populi*, p. 438.
46. Alexander Webster, *Theology in Scotland*, London 1915, p. 95.
47. Notestein, pp. 158–9.
48. Ibid., pp. 159–60.
49. Morton, p. 272. Nine witches were strangled and burned at Dumfries in 1659; Dick, p. 3. On witches in Covenanting areas and in Scottish Calvinist thinking, see Christina Larner, *Enemies of God. The Witch-hunt in Scotland*, London 1981, pp. 32, 163 ff., 172, 199, etc.
50. D. Frew, *The Parish of Urr . . . . A History*, Dalbeattie 1909, pp. 30–1.
51. Lang, vol. 3, pp. 418–9.
52. Morton, p. 108.
53. Ibid., pp. 176–7, 185.
54. Ibid., p. 148.
55. 'The Country of the Camisards', in *Travels with a Donkey*, 1879. See also Charles Tylor, *The Camisards*, London 1893.
56. James Fergusson, *John Fergusson 1727–1750*, London 1948, p. 99.
57. Angus Calder, *Revolutionary Empire*, London 1981, p. 278.
58. Hewison, vol. 2, p. 327.
59. Sir Herbert Maxwell, ed., *The Lowland Scots Regiments*, Glasgow 1918, pp. 243–4.
60. Handley, p. 199.
61. Ibid., p. 200n.
62. James Murray, *Life in Scotland a Hundred Years Ago*, Paisley 1900, pp. 64–7.
63. Morton, pp. 444–5. He relates the story without seeing any incongruity in it.
64. Donaldson, p. 321.
65. K. Burgess, 'Scotland and the First British Empire, 1707–1770s', in Dickson, *Scottish Capitalism*, p. 119.
66. T. Dickson and T. Clarke. 'The Making of a Class Society', ibid., p. 147; Cowan, pp. 156–7. On the Scottish agrarian background, see also T.M. Devine and D. Dickson, eds, *Ireland and Scotland 1600–1850*, Edinburgh 1983, chs 3, 8, 13, 19; on religion and the economy, ch. 17.
67. Nichols, p. xxix.
68. Rev. A. O'Callaghan, *The Bible Society against the Church and State*, London 1817, pp. 8–9.
69. Murray, pp. 91–2. Dumfriesshire, however, was regarded in 1797 as a hearth of radicalism, and there was a tumult at Wigtown: S. Mullay, *Scotland's Forgotten Massacre*, Edinburgh 1979, pp. 11, 48.
70. David Daiches, *The Paradox of Scottish Culture: The Eighteenth-Century Experience*, London 1964, p. 7.
71. D.H. Caldwell, *The Scottish Armoury*, Edinburgh 1979, p. 32.
72. *Our Zion: or, Presbyterian Popery, By Ane of That Ilk*, Edinburgh 1840, p. 9.
73. Morton, pp. 308–9. Fred Kaplan, discussing Carlyle's early religious environment, notes that 'The tradition of the Covenanters was strong in Annandale' (*Thomas Carlyle, A Biography*, Cambridge 1983, p. 21). In 1844 Lord Cockburn commented on the respect still felt for their memory (*Circuit Journeys*, ed. Kelso, 1983, p. 157).
74. W.F. Douglas, 'The Recusant's Concealment Discovered'.
75. C. North, *Noctes Ambrosianae*, Dec, 1829.

76. W.E. Aytoun, *Stories and Verse* (1845), ed. W.L. Renwick, Edinburgh 1964, p. 29.
77. Barr, p. 207.
78. Morton, pp. 6, 21.
79. Notestein, p. 166.
80. Cited by Hewison, vol. 2, p. 542.
81. Ibid., vol. 2, p. 484.

# 3

# Evangelicalism and the French Revolution

The religious revival in England which was part of the transformation of eighteenth century into nineteenth century, was perhaps the most significant that has occurred in Europe in times recent enough for the historian to be able to approach them familiarly. This makes it a useful basis of enquiry into the connections between religious and other social trends. It invites attention also because it recapitulated some features of the earlier, more important, revivals in the sixteenth century, and may throw a retrospective light on these.

In the form of Wesleyan and Calvinist Methodism, the revival began a little before 1740, in the dawn of the Industrial Revolution. Underlying it through the next hundred years were the complex social shifts brought about by economic change. In the middle of this period there was a sudden acceleration, a broadening of a sectarian cult into something like a national faith. It may be permissible to say that in general, as in this case, religious impulses begin at the lower social levels, in response to changes to which the mass of people are more sensitive, because more directly exposed, than those above them; and that the latter move from hostility to acceptance only when an external shock comes to emphasize the dangers of internal discontent. Jacobinism, which abolished the Christian calendar in France, helped to establish the Victorian sabbath in England.

The following remarks are concerned with the moment, about 1800, when religious enthusiasm was recognized as a possible support of order and stability. In other words they are mainly concerned with only one, and a negative, aspect of the movement. On this side many of its affinities are with the 'Counter-Reformation type' of religious revival, that namely of which the social function is to help in preserving an essentially static social order. As a whole this revival is an heir of the Reformation, a descendant of English Puritanism, and like them is associated with the emergence of a new social pattern out of an old one.

But even for an understanding of the conservatism of 1800, the revival must be seen as something 'popular', originating from the people, like every genuine religious impulse. Wesley, a staunch conservative of High Church leanings, gave his name and imprint, and an organization, to something he had liberated rather than created: it created itself, in some ways in spite of him. 'New Birth' teachings embodied, in part and imperfectly, the early efforts of common people to adapt themselves to an altering environment. They were an inchoate mode of social thought, a groping towards a new birth of society. They had been derided or denounced by those in Church and State who were satisfied with things' as they were, and unwilling to recognize that the times were changing. When occasion arose for revivalism to be enlisted by the friends of order, these facts were positively useful. In religion as in politics, an idea which is to disarm discontents must at some time, in some sense, have seemed both to friend and foe an idea of rebellion. We are only held securely by fetters we have helped to forge ourselves; no-one else can tell the exact fit of our wrists and ankles.

Panic inspired by the French Revolution did not and could not of itself conjure up any religious revival. It could at best shake upper-class free-thinkers into a more active persecution of lower-class ones. Even in the good old days Warburton had thought that atheists should be banished.[1] In the frenzy inspired by Jacobinisn and the outbreak of war in 1793, when atheism was supposed to have produced revolution by parthenogenesis, the upper classes underwent a sharp revulsion from their former scepticism. 'Most fortunately for the interest of religion and morality, or of their prudential substitutes at least, the name of Jacobin was everywhere associated with that of Atheist or Infidel.'[2] Officially, Englishmen 'panted for an opportunity to take the lead in restoring erring man to his allegiance to the Heavenly Sovereign.'[3] Patriotic drums were beaten, reform was condemned as sedition. Loyalty, conservatism, Christianity, became identical. 'Those who are hostile to the British constitution, are almost always equally hostile to the Christian revelation.'[4]

But the established Church, as a whole, was in no position to meet new needs. It had stood still: aristocratic at the top, pauperised at the bottom, worm-eaten with patronage and pluralism, angry and astonished at the collapse of the Catholic Church in France. Among eighteen thousand Anglican clergymen a severe censor was able by 1799 to detect some hundreds of 'zealous and lively men.'[5] But these obscure parochial stirrings were not enough. Bishop Beilby Porteus of London (with great tact or greater simplicity) observed that 'a wicked and profligate clergyman is a monster in nature, of which I will not suppose the existence'; but the 'present awful situation of the country', he cried in alarm, demanded much more.[6] Indeed, the very conservatives had ceased to pay much attention to the Church, or at any rate to invest in it; subscriptions to Queen Anne's Bounty (for the augmentation of small livings) came in very sluggishly.[7]

It was not that the argument in favour of religion as indispensable to social order failed to make itself heard. It failed to convince, because it was too utilitarian and rational. In eighteenth-century England, as in parts of Renaissance Europe before social tensions became explosive, an unchallenged upper class had ceased to feel much need of heaven, had come to reply on use and wont, and to justify itself by common sense, for which religion was little more than another name. Much had been heard in the age of Paley of the 'reasonableness of Christianity'. But a public creed only looks 'reasonable' (this question is very little affected by the logic of its doctrines in themselves) so long as the prevailing relations between man and man are accepted as reasonable. And when an upper class appeals to common sense, others follow its example. Reason was now divided against itself. Burke, with tremendous passion, appealed to men's good sense; but so did Thomas Paine.

In Anglican practice, as in a good deal of later medieval Catholicism, dogma had been supplanted by ethics – ethics as understood by the powers that were – and formal observances; theology had ebbed away into 'natural religion'. Bishops as well as Unitarians could be regarded as not much better than Socinians or Pelagians. 'So ethical, so heathen-like', complained an Evangelical clergyman of the (very rare) sermons preached by most Bishops.[8] While the interests of the Optimates were accepted as equivalent to those of the nation at large, sermons could be strung together from moral platitudes. Within a stable social framework good and evil need no elaborate definition. We all know that the poor must not steal from the rich. When social harmony was disturbed, as after 1789, the weaknesses of 'mere moral preaching,' or what Scotsmen called 'a blether of cold morality', made themselves felt. Dogmatic religion, by contrast, has the merit of standing above and beyond the realm of political wrangling.

Two conceptions of religion were living in England side by side, and the French Revolution compelled a choice between them. One was of religion as the formulary of an established society, its statement of faith in itself; the other as a catastrophic conversion of the individual, a miraculous shaking-off of secret burdens. One was fixed on this world, the other on the next. From a certain point of view victory for the latter would mean regression, as the resurrection of ancient dogmas by the Reformation had done. In a different sense it would mean advance, at least to the point of recognition that society had changed, and under its old rulers and guides could no longer pretend fully to understand itself or its problems.

For religion to promote social stability it was necessary, now as in Counter-Reformation Europe, that upper and lower classes should find common ground, that they should believe the same things. At any rate a proportion of the upper classes should join heartily in belief, and the rest should make a better pretence of dong so. This could not come about 'reasonably', since there was no basis of social agreement. It was time for cold logic to give way to warm emotion, morality to mystery – as in the sixteenth century when social upheaval turned humanist speculation into Protestant and neo-Catholic dogmatics.

In such an adjustment, very broadly speaking, the poor tacitly recognize the worldly position of the rich, and the rich accept the spiritual position of the poor, while by accepting the religious critique of society they help to prevent this from evolving into a political critique. In the present case, orthodoxy might denounce disbelief and point out its horrid consequences at Paris, but it was not well equipped to say what ought to be believed; dust lay thick on the Thirty-nine Articles. It could not invent items of faith on the spur of the moment; whereas in the revivalist movement astir since 1740 these already existed. They had seemed antiquated, not to say barbarous, to the polished mind of before 1789. But what had seemed modern before 1789 was now antediluvian. If high and low were to join in worship, it must be the worship of the poor.

The rich would not accept this solution with any alacrity. 'It was of incalculable benefit to the nation', thought an Anglican writer in later years, 'that such a power as Methodism existed just at the time when otherwise the revolutionary torrent would have swept away multitudes in its course.'[9] Methodism, indeed, was going on its humble way in the 1790s, despite some internal friction after Wesley's death in 1791. So was the new spirit it had helped to kindle in the Old Dissenting bodies, and in the small Evangelical movement within the Church. Yet, modest though these movements were, only from them could salvation come. At the time, conservatives in Church and State very decidedly failed to see matters in this light. They suspected hot-gospellers from plough and loom of nourishing the same ambitions now as in the dreadful, never-forgotten days of the Levellers. As before during the American Revolution, episcopal thunders did not spare the Old Dissenters either; 'the most fearful denunciations were published concerning them, as ignorant, factious schismatics, guilty of heresy and treason.'[10] Many upper-class converts to the Revival would have to be compelled to come in from the highways and byways; to be dragooned into belief, if less ungently than by the Inquisition once upon a time in Spain. There would thus be an element in it of the lower orders triumphing over the higher, and enjoying at least a meta-physical conquest.

To bring the respectable round to this point required both hard experience and able advocacy. The distance they had to travel may be seen by comparison of Burke's *Reflections* (1790) with Wilberforce's *Practical View* (1797)[11] – both addressed to the upper classes, and both immediately applauded by them.

Burke undertook to defend the Church with all her wrinkles. He invoked, not a creed, but a dignified clerical corporation, tempering the moral discipline of the ruling class and striking awe into inferiors. Fully admitting that the mass of mankind had no part in the splendid 'partnership' of his State except as degraded menials, he had to call in religion to 'consecrate' it.[12] Religion interested him only in relation to the State, and he failed to see that what he was saying really amounted to what the 'infidels' had been saying (with their eighteenth-century one-sidedness) for a long time – that religion was an invention of those in power to control those out of power.

There is a symbolical touch in the story of Burke on his deathbed reading Wilberforce's new book.[13] It was time for another man to take over his mission. Wilberforce could undertake it because he saw it in different terms. He was as much alive as any wealthy man to the perils threatening property, and he was willing to state his political case bluntly – 'to suggest inferior motives to readers, who might be less disposed to listen to considerations of a higher order.'[14] But he had been a moderate reformer in politics, and was still a humanitarian, who consented reluctantly to Pitt's policy of war and repression; he remained always a Tory of the left. His religion was perfectly genuine: he had been 'converted' before 1789, though it required the Revolution to make a religious propagandist of him. England was changing before 1789, and in such times of change there are individuals in the upper classes who are as sensitive to the psychological stresses as the lower classes are to the economic, and who likewise turn to religion for support. A man like Wilberforce needed religion also to give him a sense of union with the mass of his fellow-men which he could not achieve in any directer form, especially in the dark years when even agitation against the slave trade savoured of sedition, and languished. What was emotionally necessary to him, he could recommend to others as politically necessary. He had no novel ideas; his mind fused together Wesley's conviction that man's soul was in danger, and Burke's that society was in danger. His book came out, appropriately, at the crisis of the great naval mutinies.

England's distemper, he wrote, 'should be considered rather as a moral than a political malady.'[15] The root evil is selfishness, wearing diverse shapes in the various walks of life, but at bottom everywhere the same.[16] All ranks being vicious in the same degree (neither Burke nor Robespierre would have admitted this), only Christianity can keep the social fabric from falling to pieces. 'Moderating the insolence of power, she renders the inequalities of the social state less galling to the lower orders, whom also she instructs, in their turn, to be diligent, humble, patient' – and so on and so forth.[17] This passage, the kind of stuff that enraged Hazlitt and Cobbett, occurs in one of the two sections of the book that he particularly asked his friend Pitt to read.[18] The other section deals with the essentials of Christian doctrine.

To suppose, as lukewarm 'nominal Christians' did, that Christianity was no more than religion in general, and religion no more than morality, was 'a great and desperate error'.[19] He outlined the 'Gospel scheme' of salvation – grace, faith, justification – and insisted that these were the true tenets, too long neglected, of the Church of England.[20] Fallen man, corrupt in every fibre, could be snatched from damnation by nothing except 'the sufferings and atoning death of a crucified Saviour'.[21] No other form of religion, moreover, was 'at all suited to make impressions upon the lower orders, by strongly interesting the passions of the human mind.'[22] But – and here was a link with the political side of the case – true or 'vital' religion could not be simulated, and a Church system could not be kept up in this new age by worldlings only bent on 'retaining the common people in subjection'.[23]

Thus Wilberforce did not appear to set up religion for the sake of the State: religion made its own infinite demands, and wholesome political consequences followed merely as a by-product. Whereas Burke had put the religious horse squarely before the political cart, Wilberforce concealed the horse behind the cart. Or, more properly, he transformed the characters of both. All the gorgeous panoply of Burke's State disappears; the crown is replaced by the bowler hat, Louis XIV turns into Louis Philippe. This in itself was a sort of abdication. It was, in its own way, a *radical* solution that Wilberforce put forward, for his religion was, in contemporary terms, the despised creed of the Methodists, the hedge-priests, the lower orders.[24] Wesley had begun his mission in the shadow of the Forty-five and of economic unrest. Wilberforce proposed the same remedy to meet a greater crisis.

To bring the 'two nations' closer together was clearly the most urgent task, and nothing stronger could be found to link them than the mystical cable of theology. Evangelicalism did not concern itself with the nicer subtleties of theology (a discipline capable, like mathematics, of aesthetic qualities – but the Revival cared little for art); in so far as it dealt with these matters, it inclined towards Calvinism, towards the Methodism of Whitefield rather than of Wesley. Most of its spokesmen, particularly the laymen, were very moderate Calvinists, quite unlike the furious zealots of Lady Huntingdon's Connexion.[25] Wilberforce, like Wesley, was a practical man, for whom decrees of absolute reprobation had little charm; one of his favourite divines was Baxter. He and his friends kept to the broad highway of Reformation doctrine, wishing to bring serious men of all Protestant denominations together, not to divide them.[26] On one point they did not moderate their zeal: they believed in hellfire, and Wilberforce himself affirmed his faith in the real and dreadful existence of the Evil One.[27]

Hell burns brightly in times when men's hatred of each other is rancorous and extreme; it lends a local habitation to the images of fear and cruelty lurking in their souls. Moreover, it is no respecter of persons. 'Vital religion' had the great merit, in face of egalitarian ideas, of throwing into relief the equality of souls without disturbing the inequality of ranks. All men were not equally good, as Rousseau had made people think, but they were all equally bad. Fraternity lay in an equal share of Adam's guilt, not of the rights of man. Original sin, therefore, was a dogma of crucial importance. Bishop Porteus, who had an acute sense of 'the present awful situation of this country', dwelt on it in his charge to the clergy of 1789–99. 'It will not be sufficient to amuse your hearers with ingenious moral essays . . . This will be a feeble and ineffectual effort . . . You must show them to themselves . . . you must convince them that they are frail, corrupt, and fallen creatures' – and so convince them also of 'the extreme, the contemptible insignificance of every thing this world has to offer.'[28]

Men as individuals are more readily persuaded of their depravity when collectively they are faced by dilemmas that seem insoluble. Conviction was deepened by a dawning consciousness of many social evils; by the despair that in some minds had succeeded to the transcendent hopes of 1789; by social disharmony, for men feel guilty when they hate one another; most palpably, by the long disasters of the wars. An Old Testament feeling was taking root of divine wrath visited on a chosen but erring nation; a nation chosen, that is, to save Europe and civilisation from France. There was an outpouring of mystical and prophetical interpretations of the great events of the day, which seemed to defy human understanding.[29]

Hence the call for a national reformation of manners. 'The great mass of the people are going headlong to the devil for their sins; the nation, because of its transgressions, is absolutely verging towards destruction.'[30] Implicit in such sweeping judgements was a denial of any peculiar blame attaching to griping landlord or brutal mill-owner. National contrition and expiation were not to be directed along very realistic lines. While war kept reaction in power, much reforming zeal meandered into pettifogging channels like the Society for the Prevention of Vice.[31] Sabbatarianism played a prominent part here, and acquired an irrational, because displaced energy. Sabbath-observance supplied an element of the mystical, akin to the miracles and rituals of the Counter-Reformation; and it was another substitute for equality.[32] If the rich could not be accused of grinding the faces of the poor, they could be accused of sabbath-breaking. They in turn could find it in their hearts to plead guilty of it, and their critics to accept this as true contrition. When Jane Austen, describing the deplorable Mr Elliot of *Persuasion*, chose to accuse him of travelling on Sunday, she was obeying the Evangelical formula: the spirit of the age had breathed on a corner of *her* crystal mirror. An article in the *Evangelical Magazine* of 1805 impartially condemns two parallel offences of this kind. A set of Irishmen from the back lanes of London had been brought before the Lord Mayor for attending a Sunday night *hop* (or dance), and resisting arrest. On the same day the Marquis of A—— gave a splendid dinner, followed by dramatic recitations and an evening party at which the beautiful Lady H—— sang 'and obligingly exhibited all her wonted fascinations of attitude.' These vipers in high life were not, indeed, arrested.

Along with theology and the sabbath, the Bible was being extracted from its eighteenth-century cobwebs, an achievement largely due to that remarkable organisation, the British and Foreign Bible Society.

In May 1803 war broke out again between England and France. In the same month Wilberforce and others were consulted about the plan of a new Bible society, and heartily approved.[33] In the winter of that year Napoleon was reviewing his troops at Boulogne. On 3 March 1804, a public meeting at the London Tavern agreed on the inauguration of the British and Foreign Bible Society. In May Lord Teignmouth, whose name was suggested by Porteus, accepted the Presidency.[34] Clearly these dates have a meaning. England faced its greatest ordeal since 1588, and popular discontent was still rife. Certainly friends of order who helped to sponsor the scriptures hoped that they would have a sound effect on the public mind. Copies were soon reported to have reached the navy, where not long since *The Age of Reason* had been circulating.[35]

On the other hand, the plan itself arose quite naturally out of a need felt by 'serious' clergymen in Wales for a better supply of Welsh Bibles, which were in widespread demand, and it was a Baptist, the Rev. J. Hughes, who started the idea of broadening the scheme to cover all Britain and the world.[36] The true revivalists were carried forward by a real and potent emotion, by the inspiration of a task which, to everyone's surprise, was able to bring together churchmen, dissenters, and even Quakers, people hitherto denizens of an almost unknown world of their own.[37]

Success was not very rapid until about 1809, when local auxiliary associations began to take shape on a permanent basis.[38] In these, all the motives that went into the Revival could co-operate; as is well illustrated by the 1814 Report of the Auxiliary Society of Southwark,[39] an area infested in 1792 by a Society of the Friends of the People.[40] This body had twelve subsidiaries, with 650 active members, and was subsidised by Jews and Catholics as well as Protestants, though it felt obliged to decline subscriptions from 'abandoned females'. Collateral agencies were supplying bread, fuel, and clothing, and keeping up 'a constant investigation of the state of the poor'; and a point was made of drawing the poor themselves into the work of circulating Bibles, and so of allowing them to be 'partakers in the privileges of the Rich'.

Defence of the plenary inspiration of Scripture gave the sects a common task and spirit, such as the Evangelicals were anxious to promote. Adam Clarke dealt exhaustively with the vexed question of whether the Ark was big enough to accommodate all its passengers and their provisions for a year, and was able (following Bishop Wilkins) to allow his wolves a liberal diet of one sheep per head every six days.[41] Scriptural redoubts and entrenchments thus erected were to prove in various ways an obstacle to progress in the next decades. Charles Darwin was to find the ubiquitous Moses lying in wait for him, as he had not lain in wait for Erasmus Darwin. It struck Blanco White that the theological atmosphere in England was vastly less free and progressive than in the German universities, and he was disgusted by the ranting tone of the Bible Society set.[42]

But doctrine was not enough. One weakness of Burke's philosophy had been that it stood still: it offered only self-complacency to the rich, resignation to the poor. Wilberforce offered them a measure of honest, practical cooperation, even if the immediate objects he set forth were far removed from the nation's most pressing needs. He was able to bestir himself, and make others do the same, and in the heat and bustle of a useful life he confirmed the unity of his politico-moral convictions. A Christian was a pilgrim, 'travelling on business through a strange country.'[43] None the less he *had* business, and that was to be useful in his generation; 'not to meditate, but to act.'[44] Wilberforce enlisted those who, like himself, feared upheaval but felt that it could not be averted by police methods only, or longed for something more idealistic than the existing order.

Wesley, who in early days had been suspected of Romish tendencies, was often compared with Loyola. And Loyola had preached the philosophy of action against the Spanish quietists of his day. The practical movements Wilberforce helped to organize are reminiscent of phases (some of the *best*, not the worst phases) of Counter-Reformation history, and the resemblance is not accidental: in both cases a social order incapable of radical change, but suffering from acute tensions, was seeking moral renovation or outlets for idealism. The crusade against the slave trade is strikingly like the agitation in sixteenth-century Spain against colonial misrule.[45] One leading feature of the Revival, affecting all the sects, was the growth of interest in missionary work, and the Evangelicals, like the Jesuits from their first days, threw themselves with ardour into promoting missions. These activities, thousands of miles away from home, recaptured for the body politic its good conscience, its moral faith in itself, in spite of sedition trials, famine wages, and French victories.

Another main task of the Counter-Reformation had been to stimulate the flow of charity, and thus soften the harshness of an unjust society. Wilberforce understood like Wesley, or Loyola long before, that professions of Christian brotherhood must be supported by brotherly aid. He called for 'a vigorous principle of enlarged and active charity',[46] set the example himself, and tried to induce ministers to add public assistance to police coercion.[47] Before long England was priding itself on a flow of charitable funds on a scale never before approached.

About 1800, it has been said, Evangelicalism crystallized from a tendency into a party.[48] Morals and politics, that is, were now brought into alliance by the Clapham Sect.[49] Circumstances helped its progress. The character of the wars was changing; middle-of-the-road men could be heard again;[50] anti-slave trade agitation recovered, and in 1807 came Wilberforce's triumph, the abolition. A more respectable tone crept into public life; Pitt's last hours were reported as edifying, and statesmen like Harrowby and Perceval were quite 'serious.' All Protestant bodies except the Unitarians, tainted with Jacobinism, were expanding. 'Society' began to look very different from what it was when Wilberforce first entered the House of Commons and found only one openly religious man in it.[51] By 1813 things had gone so far that the Duke of Kent

found himself patron of the London Society for Promoting Christianity among
the Jews. Moreover, the Church was now worth subsidising. In 1804 Parliament
gave it the first of a series of grants, and from about 1808 private benefactions
to Queen Anne's Bounty began to rise sharply.[52] The new funds strengthened
the Evangelical wing.

Meanwhile the party of the unreformed and unrepentant High Church
looked on in disgust; a fact heartening to the godly, because it reassured them
that they were working for God and not for Mammon. In 1810 the Bible
Society was severely criticized by Dr Wordsworth, chaplain to the Archbishop
of Canterbury, who had to be answered by Teignmouth himself.[53] With
Hibernian exuberance the Master of the College of Kilkenny, refusing to be
'stunned with the holy declamation' of 'spiritual Jacobins', depicted the society
as a 'formidable confederation', a 'strange and portentous comet' hanging over
the world, ominous of 'convulsion and dissolution.' To invite peasants to read
Scripture themselves, unguided, was to overthrow, in the end, all respect for law
and order.[54]

Such indignation was not unreal. The Bible, after all, without careful
commentary, cannot be relied on to promote undiluted conservatism. And the
strength of the Revival's appeal lay precisely in its omission to identify itself too
obviously with sublunary dispensations. True, Wilberforce was ready to
endorse measures of repression in the 1790s, and again between 1815 and 1820.
Methodism likewise backed the government against radicalism after 1815.[55] A
celebrated definition of religion is called to mind by De Quincey's curious
statement that his opium-eating habits were shared by Wilberforce, Dean
Milner, Erskine, and Sidmouth's brother, as well as by Coleridge and by a mass
of pauperized work people in Lancashire.[56] Yet as a rule the Evangelicals went
on a path of their own. Simeon of Cambridge, paying his respects to the British
Constitution, was not being very fulsome when he observed that the condition
of Britain was very different 'from that of the Roman Empire in the time of
Nero.'[57] In the midst of the wars the *Evangelical Magazine* devoted immense
space to overseas mission reports, but scarcely any to war propaganda in any
direct form. It could even give Napoleon credit for his religious toleration,[58] a
policy which – as amongst Protestants – it supported at home.[59]

Religious revival was in truth a double-edged weapon. The dogma of
original sin and the depravity of human nature, for instance, has had in all its
periods of influence a dual significance fitting it to stand at the conflux of dual
forces. It contains a censure on the powers that be, including the absentee
prelates and selfish aristocrats of 1800, as well as a dissuasive from popular
rebellion. Luther and Calvin, two of its foremost champions, struggled from
the first on two fronts, against papalism and against Anabaptism.

There were as many shades in the Revival as social groups affected by it,
stretching all the way from the house where Samuel Butler's Theobald Pontifex
was growing up through Clapham Common to the rebel artisans of Tanner's

Lane. After about 1800 there was a strong admixture of pretence. But for various classes it had an urgent meaning, and for the nation as a whole it helped to express the mood of a people moving forward, planlessly and painfully, into the uncharted future of the machine age. How extreme was the moral tension of the age is measured also by the greatness of English poetry then. Squalid and humdrum as it looked by comparison, the Industrial Revolution was a greater innovation in world history than the French Revolution, and moved on a more shadowy road. Moving forward with it, the English looked back for reassurance to the God of their forefathers, the God of Abraham and Isaac, of Cromwell and Bunyan. But it was the mood, however confused, of an expanding and not a stagnating economy. Economic advance, underlying the eddies of politics and ideas, kept revivalism from belonging fundamentally to the type of sixteenth-century Spanish religion.

Hazlitt and Hunt, Sydney Smith and Bentham, as well as Kilkenny and Barchester, lamented the 'torrent of fanaticism' deluging the country. But the radicals stood alone, quarrelling among themselves, and in any case they wanted reform without revolution; and the uprooted masses could not borrow a programme from the Revolution that established capitalism in France. In England the advance was from an earlier to a more mature stage of capitalism; politically the way forward was towards 1832. Evangelicalism brought together the developing sections of the middle classes, gave them an independent outlook, relieved their fears of the more elemental forms of mass unrest, showed how a respectable working class could be led by a respectable middle class. In fact it prepared the ground for nineteenth-century English liberalism. The dream of a national reformation of morals was followed, after the war years, by the Benthamite renovation of Church and State.

## Notes

1. W. Warburton, *The Alliance between Church and State*, 4th edn, London 1766, p. 304.
2. S.T. Coleridge. *Aids to Reflection*, 1825, Bohn Library 1913. p. 253.
3. Rev. A. O'Callaghan, *The Bible Society against the Church and State*, London 1817, p. 4.
4. Beilby Porteus, Bishop of London, *A Charge delivered to the Clergy of the Diocese of London, in the years 1798 and 1799*, London 1799, p. 15.
5. Rev. D. Simpson, *A Plea for Religion and the Sacred Writings*, 1797, 2nd edn 1799, reissued with notes etc., by Rev. John Gaulter, Liverpool 1812, 318 n. Rev. J.H. Overton, *The Evangelical Revival in the Eighteenth Century*, London 1886, p. 85, describes the Evangelical clergy as by 1800 'a very numerous and influential body'. Rev. T. Timpson, *British Ecclesiastical History, including the Religion of the Druids*, 2nd edn, London 1847, p. 518, quotes an estimate of five hundred Evangelical clergymen in 1795.
6. Porteus, p. 31. In February 1799 Porteus began a Lent series of lectures on Scripture at St. John's Church (*Evangelical Magazine*, VII, p. 130).
7. E.g., Porteus, pp. 4–7.
8. Simpson, pp. 136–141.
9. Overton, p. 141.
10. Timpson, p. 449. Cf. R.W. Dale, *History of English Congregationalism*, London 1907,

pp. 563–80. On the parallel state of affairs in Scotland, see H.W. Meikle, *Scotland and the French Revolution*, Glasgow 1912, ch. X.

11. W. Wilberforce, *A Practical View of the Prevailing Religious System of Professed Christians in the Higher and Middle Classes in this Country, Contrasted with Real Christianity*, 2nd edn, London 1797.

12. Edmund Burke, *Reflections on the Revolution in France*, Everyman Library, 1910, pp. 157 and 94.

13. R. Coupland, *Wilberforce*, Oxford 1923, p. 244.

14. W. Wilberforce, *A Practical View*, p. 422.

15. Ibid., p. 415.

16. Ibid., p. 399.

17. Ibid., p. 40; cf. Hannah More, *Christian Morals*, London 1813, vol. I, p. 155.

18. Coupland, pp. 243–4. The two sections were ch. VI, and ch. IV, section vi.

19. Wilberforce, p. 248.

20. Ibid., pp. 62–3.

21. Ibid., ch. II, and p. 125.

22. Ibid., p. 409.

23. Ibid., pp. 407–8.

24. Cf. William, Hazlitt, *On the Causes of Methodism*: 'Vital Christianity is no other than an attempt to lower all religion to the level of the lowest of the capacities of the people.' Cf. also Hazlitt's picture of Wilberforce, in the essay on him in *The Spirit of the Age*, 1825, as a 'Mr Facing-both-ways'. Coupland, pp. 422 ff., points out Hazlitt's unfairness in some respects.

25. On Lady Huntingdon's Connexion, see Timpson, *British Ecclesiastical History*, book VIII, ch. xvii. The *Evangelical Magazine*, IV, pp. 152 ff. has a description of it in 1796. On the 'Calvinistic controversy', which had attained a most venomous intensity, see Overton, pp. 191–9, and R. Southey, *The Life of Wesley*, 2nd edn, London, 1820, ch XXV, and notes XXIX–XXXI.

26. See, e.g., A. Clarke, *The Doctrine of Salvation by Faith Proved*, 1815, 2nd edn, London 1819; cf. Overton, ch. X, 'The Doctrines of the Revival', and Southey, ch. XX, 'Wesley's Doctrines and Opinions'.

27. Wilberforce, *A Practical View*, pp. 42–4.

28. Porteus, pp. 31 and 22–5. Cf. C. Simeon, *The Danger of Neglecting the Great Sacrifice*, (an Assize sermon) Cambridge 1797, and *Horae Homileticae*, No. 922, *Vileness and Impotency of the Natural Man*.

29. E.g., Simpson, pp. 192 ff., 236 ff., and editor's note, p. 235; More, vol. I, p. 47; Porteus, p. 42; *Evangelical Magazine*, IV, 1797, pp. 98 ff., 303.

30. Simpson, p. 147; cf. p. 313.

31. The society was formed in 1802, replacing an earlier one of 1787.

32. *Evangelical Magazine*, XIII, 1805, pp. 237–8.

33. Rev. J. Owen, *The History of the Origin and First Ten Years of the British and Foreign Bible Society*, London 1816, vol. 1, pp. 17–8.

34. Ibid., pp. 67–9.

35. *Evangelical Magazine*, X, XI, 1813, pp. 390–1. There was also a 'Naval and Military Bible Society', a forerunner of which had existed from 1780.

36. Owen, pp. 2 ff., 17.

37. Ibid., pp. 37–44, describing the inaugural meeting and the author's own feelings on that occasion. Quakers had already been active against the slave trade. A body of 'Evangelical Friends' formed itself within their society (Timpson, pp. 545–6).

38. Owen, pp. 172, 423–4.

39. *The Formation, Progress, and Effects of Bible Associations as detailed by the Committee of the Southwark Auxiliary Bible Society*, London 1814.

40. H.W.C. Davis, *The Age of Grey and Peel*, Oxford 1929, p. 78.

41. Cited in Simpson, pp. 266 ff., note by editor.

42. See J.H. Thom, *The Life of the Rev. Joseph Blanco White*, London 1845. 'No country in the world suffers more from false notions of religion than England' (letter to J.S. Mill, 1835; vol. II, pp. 137–8). 'Even the most bigoted Germans do not venture to support Theories which in England are still regarded as the Basis of Christianity' (1838; vol. III, p. 16).

43. Wilberforce, *A Practical View* p. 300.

44. Ibid., p. 344.

45. See L. Hanke, *The Spanish Struggle for Justice in the Conquest of America*, Philadelphia 1949.

46. Wilberforce, *A Practical View*, p. 337; cf. More, vol. I, p. 190.

47. E.g., in 1800; see Coupland p. 264. Cf. the charitable appeal in the *Evangelical Magazine*, VIII, 1880. p. 540.

48. Halévy, *Histoire du Peuple Anglais au XIXe siècle*, Paris 1913, vol. I, p. 410.

49. On the Clapham Sect, see Coupland, pp. 248 ff.; Halévy, p. 412.

50. The *Edinburgh Review* was founded in 1802.

51. C. Oman, *Britain against Napoleon*, London 1943, p. 321. Pitt, who had shocked serious men by duelling, 'highly interested the religious world' by the edifying accounts published on his last hours. (Simpson, pp. 405–6, note by editor). Men like Byron, of course, in less responsible positions that Pitt's, were inclined to lag behind. See a review in the *Evangelical Magazine*, XIII, 1805, pp. 131–2, of 'The Fashionable World Displayed', a severe satire on aristocratic morals by the Rev. John Owen.

52. This becomes clear from a study of the annual detail of benefactions given in C. Hodgson, *An Account of the Augmentation of Small Livings*, London 1826.

53. Owen, pp. 469 ff.

54. O'Callaghan, pp. 5–9, 44, 59.

55. Davis, p. 143. Southey (p. 565) was hoping about this time that Methodism might still find its true place as an 'auxiliary institution' of the Church, like a confraternity within the Roman Catholic Church.

56. Thomas De Quincey, *Confessions of an English Opium Eater*, preface of 1821.

57. Simeon, *Horae Homileticae* (skeleton sermons on the scriptures), vol. IX, 1820, No. 945, 'Duty to Civil Governors'. In No. 997, 'The Benefit Arising from Attention to the Poor', Simeon neglects to point out any political benefit. He thinks sickness the only grave trial of the poor. 'The Poor in a time of health are happy; because their minds and habits are fitted to their state.'

58. *Evangelical Magazine*, XIII, 1805, p. 89; cf. X, 1802, pp. 36–7.

59. Ibid., XIX, 1811, pp. 276 ff.; XX, 1812, pp. 356–62. On the Act of 1812, see Halévy, pp. 404–9. Note the argument against intolerance in the *New Theological Repository*, Liverpool 1800, vol. I, pp. 35–48.

# 4

# Human Relationships in Shakespeare

Elizabethan drama grew in a no man's land between the two historical epochs that we call the feudal and the capitalist. All around it old habits and ways were crumbling, new ones beginning to take shape, in a medley of fragmentary relics and experiments. In the medieval society that was falling to pieces the individual had been enclosed, snugly though crampingly, inside a narrow framework of institutions and beliefs, like an apprentice safe and warm in his airless cupboard–bed in one of the old houses of the Hansa merchants still to be seen in Bergen. Now the snug crib which was also a prison was releasing or ejecting him into a strange environment where he must learn to find his way about, among others groping likewise.

Life was thus both exhilarating and frightening. The epoch of free competition was coming in, the world was an oyster waiting for anyone's sword to open it. Competition was at its most venomous among the jarring factions at court, where the shortest cuts to fortune lay – and where the theatre had close links: Lear's

> . . . packs and sects of great ones
> That ebb and flow by th' moon.
>
> (*King Lear* V. 3. 18–19)

Many risks had to be run, not only at court. Lieutenant Bardolph came to the gallows while still struggling to get his oyster open. Men had been haunted ever since the Renaissance by the thought of 'blind Fortune' and her wheel, emblem of the instability of all earthly affairs; it was fed by the separation of man from man as the old social order faded, the dissolution of accustomed ties and mutual duties. Success might come to some, the most unblushingly egotistic, but it was likely to be paid for by the isolation which makes one of

Shakespeare's most successful men, Henry IV, feel in the weariness of
disillusion and insecurity that no one who could foresee his future would ever
want to live through it.

To see how disturbing and unnerving this climate was, to the same Englishmen who in more sanguine moods could identify themselves in fantasy with
Marlowe's world-conqueror

> And ride in triumph through Persepolis,
>
> (I *Tamburlaine*, II. 5. 758)

one has only to read Burton's *Anatomy of Melancholy*. This indispensable though
unintended commentary on Shakespeare depicts a whole generation grown
morbid, anxiety-ridden; at bottom because, then as now, an old society and its
morality were dying and a new one coming to birth. When men feel so
unfathomably uneasy it is always because they have lost touch with one
another.

> . . . O, what's become
> Of the true hearty love was wont to be
> 'Mongst neighbours in old time,
>
> (II. 2. 222–4)

laments a pessimist in Middleton's *Women Beware Women*. Needless to say, there
was the usual quota of illusion here: the times, like *Punch*, have never been quite
as good as they used to be.

Dramatic art had a sudden flowering in many parts of Europe, where the
change from medieval to modern was in progress, all the way from the Globe
to Hungary. Between the theatre in England and in Spain the resemblances are
astonishing. Men's heightened consciousness of themselves and of one another
found a natural outlet in drama, the social art of all arts. They went to the
theatre first of all no doubt in search of entertainment, and a casual remark of
Burton's indicates how popular it was in London: in all lands people have hit on
some favourite way of shaking off their troubles – Italians sleep them off, Danes
drink, 'our countrymen go to Plays'.[1] But it is not fanciful to suppose that in
this hectic, disoriented society, especially in dizzily growing London where
newcomers poured in from every province, men went to the theatre also as a
place where they might learn something about life and their fellow-creatures.

In a season of change one artist will fasten chiefly on what is bad in the
situation, decline and decay, another on what is good, birth and growth.
Shakespeare belongs emphatically to the second sort. It is hard to resist the
temptation to read a symbolic meaning into the words of a speaker in one of
the late romances, which sound so full of prophecy and vision –

Thou met'st with things dying, I with things new-born
(*The Winter's Tale*, III. 3. 108)

Most of his rivals in the theatre belong as unmistakably to the first sort. These literary men were descendants of the humanist scholars of the Renaissance, brilliant talents whose fate it was to float unattached, except precariously to rich patrons, in a Europe whose ordinary people they had no contact with. Humanism meant belief in man; but this was harder to hold on to than disbelief in God, when it was not strengthened by faith in men's ability to live and work together, to co-operate fruitfully with one another. As a result the humanism we associate with Erasmus and the educationalists had been a vulnerable and short-lived growth. Elizabethan playwrights were similarly unattached, though writing for a popular audience was itself an attempt to escape from this situation. Struggling to make a living by their pens, they were forerunners of all artists in modern society, and peculiarly exposed to the uprooting influences of the age. Not seldom they had to fall back on private patronage, if they could find any. They have an air of being chronically on bad terms with an audience that seemed to them tasteless and ungrateful; Ben Jonson cannot help falling foul of it even in the preface to a masque.[2] An artist is always inclined to judge the human race by the calibre of his own public. Shakespeare was more tolerant than Jonson of both. Part of the reason may be that he had roots in Stratford, one of the little towns where something of an older neighbourliness lingered on, as well as in feverish London. Another part of it must be that he was actor and theatre-man as well as writer, professionally involved like Molière with a company, a group of men dependent for success on one another's efforts and on their team spirit.

Over a great part of Elizabethan and especially Jacobean drama hangs a cloud of gloom and embitterment. Its preoccupations are with death and with madness, the two things that separate the human being most totally from the rest of humanity. Its characters tend to be hard, distinct, unmingling entities, repelling like billiard-balls, imparting to one another only a mechanical kind of movement. Most typical among the bad ones are the 'Machiavels', self-proclaimed villains emancipated from all bonds of conventional virtue. Machiavelli's conception of human beings as unfused particles, each completely self-contained and self-centred, had a creepy fascination for the men of this century, and it did become, in less melodramatic forms than on the stage, the philosophy of life of many of them. Shakespeare himself has his Richard III and Iago, and, rather less inhuman, his Edmund. Marlowe brings on the ghost of Machiavelli as prologue to one of his plays (*The Jew of Malta*). At the opposite pole the same acceptance of isolation as the bedrock of the human condition found expression in a cult of stoicism, the lofty individual rising above society, rejecting its laws as meaningless and making higher laws for his own unfettered self. Chapman especially always seems to be trying to strip his hero down to an inmost core, to find out what he is made of, like a philosopher stripping away from matter its form, colour, taste, in search of ultimate reality, and in the end finding that matter has disappeared.

Contemporaries appear to have thought of Shakespeare and his poetry as 'sweet'; an epithet which may not at first sound very appropriate, but which ceases to surprise as soon as we compare him with almost any of the other playwrights. The difference between one of his plays and one of theirs – between a *Twelfth Night* and a *Chaste Maid in Cheapside*, to take two at random – is the difference between a living earth, a landscape with a warm sunshine of human feeling playing over it, and a frozen moon. Among his characters the self-enclosed natures, moving about among their fellow men without any emotional need of them, stand out the more remarkably by their fewness. Iago alone is completely alienated from humanity; Falstaff, Hotspur, Henry IV and Prince Hal, however self-sufficient, crave at least for the applause of those about them. Collectively Shakespeare's men and women may be described, as Iago with a possible touch of envy describes Othello, as 'of a free and open nature'. They move freely and unhesitantly in a world not foreign to them because they have an assured knowledge of its inhabitants and an assured place among them; whereas the other denizens of the Elizabethan stage seem often to live by the rule of Dickens's lawyer 'Foxy': Always suspect everybody'. Shakespeare is making fun of this over-wordly wisdom when he puts it into Pistol's mouth:

> Trust none;
> For oaths are straws, men's faiths are wafer-cakes.
> (*Henry V*, II. 3. 50–51)

A kind of diffused kinship among all human beings, or the suggestion at least that there ought to be such a kinship, pervades a play of his in a way difficult to define but impossible to miss. We might venture to call it, in Dr Johnson's language, *clubbability.* One sign of it is the rich flow of humour, compared with the narrow trickle in most of the other plays. Another is that conversation among these people is really conversation, not declamation. They continue to interest us because they are willing to be interested in one another. Instead of being turned in on themselves they have an outgoing quality, an ability to feel with and associate themselves with something outside them: another person, a cause, an ideal, a nation. In the comedies, where women reign, the enchanting heroines overflow with a golden readiness of fellow-feeling for the world and everything in it, a readiness to be amused by it, to help it, to scold or reform it. In the tragedies the great figures come to find themselves isolated, Timon last and most absolutely, and that is indeed their tragic destiny; but they are not at all solitary by disposition. They have a gift of spinning threads out of themselves in many directions, of linking themselves with other men and women and with the ideas of their time. Only Julius Caesar tries to play the part of a self-conscious superman, to be like 'the northern star' with 'no fellow in the firmament'; and Caesar is a sick old man, his rhetoric pathetic as well as magnificent. Cato the arch-stoic, much admired by both Chapman (in *Caesar and Pompey*) and Ben Jonson (in *Catiline*), only comes in for a mention from Shakespeare as the father of Portia – which Cato himself might have thought was damning him with very faint praise.

Shakespeare criticism, growing up in days of fully-fledged individualism, was apt to fix its attention on characters as separate units, 'portraits', each a work of art in itself. Some of Shakespeare's own words show him thinking rather of the individual as the sum of his relationships, actual or possible, with his fellows. Brutus has to see himself in the mirror of Cassius's mind before his duty becomes clear to him. Achilles has to look at himself in that of Ulysses, who goes on to argue at some length:

> That no man is the lord of anything . . .
> Till he communicate his parts to others;
> Nor doth he of himself know them for aught . . .
>
> (*Troilus and Cressida*, III. 3. 115-19)

Shakespeare was concerned with men in combination, interacting, entering into one another's lives, becoming part of one another. Macbeth would have been a very different man, and Lady Macbeth a very different woman – or things slumbering under the surface of their minds would never have woken into life – with any other wife or husband. We think often of Shakespeare's characters, seldom those of the other playwrights, in pairs; and Beatrice and Benedick, Brutus and Cassius, Goneril and Regan, signify when brought into contact much more than a simple arithmetical addition.

His finest speeches are likely to grow directly out of men's feelings for one another; those of the other dramatists are likelier to be inspired by men's feelings about themselves, or by sensations or speculations concerned with impersonal things, fate or death or heaven. These others knew how to emulate 'Marlowe's mighty line' and write 'the style of gods' (or to borrow from Scott about his own work, 'the big Bow-wow stuff'); what lay more out of their reach was the kind of brief and unadorned but extraordinarily poignant phrase that multiplies towards the climax of any Shakespearian tragedy. When Antony learns that his follies have at last driven one of his oldest followers over into the enemy camp:

> . . . Call for Enobarbus,
> He shall not hear thee,
>
> (*Antony and Cleopatra*, IV. 5. 7-8)

the words have a crushing impact, a blank finality as of a door closed for ever. They fall so on our ears because they fall so on Anthony's. There is an opposite effect, of something imperishable, in Brutus's promise to mourn his dead friend:

> I shall find time, Cassius, I shall find time.
>
> *(Julius Caesar*, V. 3. 103)

This intense simplicity, in which the plainest words are transfigured like a group of plain notes in a symphonic development when it is a Beethoven who is writing, is made possible only by the intense strength of the human relations that generate it.

Shakespeare's paramount interest in what human beings mean to each other was not at all the same thing as that 'slavery to the confined interlocking of personal relationships, intricate as clockwork',[3] that a critic has complained of in present-day English drama. He was not concerned to count the yawns of a husband and wife coexisting in a corner of suburbia, or to chronicle the mannerisms of acquaintances who after getting on each other's nerves for twenty years remain at the end just what they were to begin with. Real contact, a real meeting of selves, depends on mutual knowledge, which comes only out of activity, out of joint doing and striving by individuals working with – or against – one another. Shakespeare's folk acquire such knowledge because they live venturously together on a planet where many things are as untried as the daffodils 'that come before the swallow dares'.

It is on public life that this proclivity of theirs and his has its most practical bearing. Historical progress is regulated not alone by the pace of objective development but also by the capacity of those who desire progress to form coherent leagues, to pool their energies in furthering it. Modern history is the history of the political party. But this political faculty is conditioned in any society by its members' ability to form stable relationships in private life. It is a cardinal error to suppose that the requisite aptitudes are natural rights of man, and come to him by instinct. They are the fruits of long, painful evolution, and they have matured variously under diverse social conditions, as anyone transplanted to a fresh environment, trying to join in activity with people of a different inheritance, quickly learns. And if such aptitudes are lost, as they may easily be in a period of rapid change, much else will be lost with them. History like Nature produces nothing out of nothing, and a new society struggling to grow can only draw upon the moral, or psychological, as well as the economic resources bequeathed to it by its past.

We can see Shakespeare as one of the men of that age who were trying to salvage the consciousness of a social whole made up of its human parts; to preserve and adapt, that is, the talents humanity had acquired for combining and cooperating otherwise than by blind compulsion. In other quarters more artificial frameworks were being offered, to take the place of the old one. Patriotism and religion provided the two most obvious means of lessening men's distance from one another. In an age of religious wars, and of wars needed for the promotion of capitalism, the two often went together, and a great deal of humbug and worse went with both. Shakespeare did his share of patriotic tub-thumping when he wrote *Henry V*, where his idealizing of the English army as a 'band of brothers' is illuminating: it was a lost brotherhood (part reality, part myth) that Englishmen were trying to regain. Where Shakespeare was more truly himself he was looking for more vital relations between men, and men and women, to infuse a new spirit into the common-weal. For the same reason his profoundly humanistic outlook made him profoundly unreligious; he was not interested, as some of the dramatists were, in ropes to link human beings together that had to be slung over the pulley of a remote heaven.

The society fading away had for its metaphysical counterpart the 'Chain of Being' that united everything in the universe, angel and man and dust, in one ordered hierarchy. This was too static a notion, and too blatantly feudal, to retain much force, though it went on and on being repeated. Shakespeare was in search of fresh and living, instead of fossilized, connections. His quest was part of the all-round emancipation of the individual that was unfolding; but if he wanted a community enlivened by free choice and opportunity, he did not want one in which the individual would be 'set free' by being turned loose in a moral wilderness, abandoned to mere egotism and the survival of the most rapacious. Like poets in many epochs he put the contrast of old and new sometimes into the form of two contrasting generations. In *Hamlet* all the older people are warped and dehumanized by habits of mind that have grown petrified; nearly all the younger people share at least an impulsive, spontaneous quickness to feel, and to feel for others more than for themselves. Art, and drama in particular, is an active agent in the formation of new states of mind and of society. Shakespeare can be thought of in all his work as a preserver, modernizer, transmitter of the values of an older time for the benefit of a later one. All cultural values are delicate, and do not easily survive the trans-mutations they must undergo; those that arise directly out of men's relationships are the most fragile of all, most in need of a Shakespeare's genius for *psychochemistry*.

To try to reduce any part of Shakespeare to statistics invites his own question:

> . . . Will you with counters sum
> The past-proportion of his infinite?
>
> (*Troilus and Cressida*, II. 2. 28–29)

Reduction to cold figures of his world of life and movement can scarcely avoid travestying it; no tabulation can catch unique qualities, and nothing is more remarkable in Shakespeare than his way of making each chief relationship among his characters something unique. What there is between Hamlet and Horatio can be classified as 'friendship', but it is quite unlike anything that might grow between either of them and anyone else, or between any other pair. Any attempt at cataloguing must, besides, be biased by personal feeling as to what is more or less significant. In spite of these difficulties (and many more) there may be something to be gained from an experiment in putting Shakespeare's treatment of relationships into figures and columns, as a basis for comparing one part of his work with another in this respect, and his work with that of other Elizabethans.

His plays abound, needless to say, in fathers and sons, husbands and wives, friends, confederates, neighbours, and so on. Among each of these sorts of relationship there are some that stand out and impress us by a special vitality or colouring; something that makes them, as well as the individuals concerned in them, memorable. They may be referred to for convenience as 'positive relationships'; they are connections that engender some active, working force, able to alter the human beings who take part in them, and through them to alter the lives of others also. A play rich in this kind of ingredient is *Julius Caesar*. Here we may distinguish a 'positive relationship' between, first and foremost, Brutus and Cassius; another uniting these men and the whole band of conspirators; a third between Brutus and Portia. Then there is the binding force between Caesar and Anthony. There is besides some genuine feeling between Caesar and Brutus; between Caesar and his wife Calpurnia; between Brutus and his attendants and subordinate followers; and between Cassius and the friend after whose supposed death he commits suicide, Titinius.

All these possess the electric spark; but clearly they are not all on the same level of emotional or dramatic importance. The first three among them may be singled out as of the highest significance. In a second class may be placed the next tie, that between Caesar and Antony. All the remaining four, striking or touching as each of them is at certain moments, seem to fall into a third class, of inferior weight, because they do not affect leading figures in the plot, or do not affect them vitally. Collectively 'positive relationships' such as these last do much to add depth and tone to the Shakespearian background; but for purposes of discussion it is the first and second classes that matter most. The same three-fold classification may be applied to family or other relationships, whether of a 'positive' character or not. Thus, to take a mixed set of married couples, none of which have this character, Henry VIII and Katherine are clearly entitled by their dramatic importance to be put in the first class; Hotspur and Lady Percy may be assigned to the second rank, and so may Capulet and Lady Capulet, whereas Montagu and Lady Montagu must be relegated to the third.

Working on these lines we may count altogether, in Shakespeare's thirty-seven plays, a total of one hundred and forty-nine 'positive relationships'. Of these twenty-four appear to belong to the first class of importance, and thirty-five to the second; making a total for the two groups, the ones chiefly to be considered, of fifty-nine out of the one hundred and forty-nine. It may be noted that very frequently the leading relationships have originated before the start of the play, though they may go on evolving during its course. Only eight out of the fifty-nine come about in the course of the plays they occur in; or, discounting previous marriages and other family connections, eight out of thirty-four. This helps us to feel that we are looking at bona fide beings at one critical point of their lives, instead of at puppets called into life only for a couple of hours. In general their relationships are healthy as well as lifelike; they are oftener good than bad in their influence. Of thirty-nine out of the fifty-nine it may be said that they unite good people, and encourage goodness; of only four that they tend on both sides to the promotion of evil.

Of the one hundred and forty-nine relationships taken all together, the lowest average number to be found is in the ten histories, only 2.7 per play; the highest in the four romances, 5.5. There is thus a notable increase of numbers as between Shakespeare's early and late work. Twelve comedies show an intermediate average of 3.6. By way of comparison it may be remarked that Marlowe's seven plays, considered in the same manner, show fourteen analogous relationships, an average of only two, and with only four in the first class. In twenty-one of Shakespeare's thirty-seven plays, all of them except *Titus Andronicus* and *Timon of Athens* histories or early comedies there are none of the first class. Taking the fifty-nine of the first and second classes, there are thirteen plays with none; nine with one; three with two; six with three; five with four (*Julius Caesar, King Lear, Anthony and Cleopatra, The Winter's Tale, The Tempest*); one with six (*Hamlet*). When the plays are arranged in their more or less accepted chronological sequence, five of the fifty-nine fall into the first third, twenty-seven into the middle third, twenty-seven into the last. But within each group and period we can perhaps distinguish plays where Shakespeare seems interested primarily in relationships, for example *As You Like It*, from those where his attention is fixed rather on situations, as in *A Midsummer Night's Dream*, or on problems, as in *All's Well That Ends Well*. The group of three late comedies and 'problem plays' (*Twelfth Night, Measure for Measure, All's Well That Ends Well*) contains only three out of the fifty-nine; whereas the previous three plays (*Julius Caesar, Troilus and Cressida, Hamlet*) contain thirteen, the richest vein in the whole collection.

The broadest dividing line to be observed is between relationships in which the individual finds himself entangled willy-nilly, and those initiated or at least accepted by his free choice. A society of feudal cast, in Europe then as in Asia now, provides husband or wife just as nature provides all other relatives. Love, in its modern romantic guise, breaks out from this ready-made circle; so does friendship, or loyalty to others besides friends, for example to a sovereign, when this loyalty is more than conventional or unavoidable. Various of Shakespeare's lovers turn into married couples; in what follows, marriages that have grown visibly and recently out of mutual love, like those of Romeo and Juliet or Othello and Desdemona, are treated as cases of love instead of matrimony. Of the fifty-nine most interesting relationships, then, twenty-five, or fewer than half, fall into the linked categories of marriage and other family ties (thirteen out of twenty-four however in the first class; in the third or lowest, about a third). Love contributes six relationships out of twenty-four in the first class and two out of thirty-five in the second; friendship, in a wide sense, three and fourteen; other loyalties, usually between ruler and subject or master and man, two and seven.

All the strains and tensions of an age of change set up vibrations inside the family, which is indeed the historian's most sensitive seismograph for detecting them. There was much to disturb the harmony of the Elizabethan family: disagreements over religion, politics, morality, and the financial jealousies that always become more obtrusive when 'the time is out of joint'. Hardships of younger sons condemned to poverty by the custom of primogeniture have been a stock theme of all the literature of western Europe. Property may be a bone of contention also between heads of families and impatient heirs. A play ascribed to Massinger, *The Old Law*, turns on an edict for the execution of all women at the age of sixty and men at eighty. Most of the sons and daughters, not realizing that it is a trick on the part of their ruler, are undisguisedly delighted; Cleanthes, who discourses virtuously on the bond between parent and child, looks a very odd young prig among them. This is satire, but it underlines a portrayal of the family by Massinger and others that forms part of their prevailingly gloomy picture of life.

Shakespeare's own view of it is far from rosy. But he, much more clearly than the others, can be said to have two families in mind: a traditional one, aristocratic or coloured by aristocratic prejudice, and an ideal one, the family as it might be – as it will be, he leaves us convinced, when his amiable young lovers have had time to grow up and to reclaim other husbands, wives, and parents by their example. The old family has been turning into a cage; Juliet complains of the 'bondage' it keeps her in. But the cage is crumbling. If England in the later histories, respectable England outside the taverns of Eastcheap, is becoming a grey sort of place, this is a good deal because the archaic household and its allegiances are crumbling, along with the feudal order of which they are an intrinsic part. In the rebellion that ends at Shrewsbury the loyalties of the Percies to their own clan ought to be the strongest binding force; instead uncle, brother, son are each led by his own interests or passions: Northumberland leaves son and brother in the lurch, Worcester deceives his nephew, Hotspur's recklessness takes no account of any wishes but his own. Shakespeare could not bring the desiccated family of the past back to life, but he never gave up the search for a 'new model', which led him further and further as time went on into the realm of inspired fantasy.

He has five married couples prominent enough to be put in the first class, and fourteen in the second, out of a total of thirty-five or about one per play. On the whole they represent the old unregenerate style of matrimony, now sinking into lifeless routine – the 'dull, stale, tired bed' (*King Lear* I. 2. 13) that Edmund derides – if not into something worse; and as we go on through the plays marriage as an institution is not improving, but deteriorating. In them all, only a single marriage of any long standing impresses us as really authentic and wholesome, that of Brutus and Portia. Of the other seventeen leading instances (deducting Petruchio and his Katherine as mainly farcical) seven may be accounted tolerable or trivial; ten must be classed as, in point either of the relations between the couple or of their influence on each other, bad or very bad. We can discern more or less of genuine affection on both sides in only five of these nineteen cases; on one side alone in three; in eleven, on neither. (In eighteen extant plays attributed in whole or part to Massinger there is affection on both sides in four out of twelve comparable ménages.) More often than not there is temporary or chronic dissension, not brought about by external factors solely. Two marriages end in divorce or long, wilful separation; two in husband killing wife. Three of the wives commit or attempt or instigate murder. They are, to give them their due, seldom unfaithful; this is something that Shakespeare could not easily bring himself to accuse women of, whereas in much of Elizabethan drama – as in the Restoration comedy that was growing out of it long before the Restoration – it is taken for granted.

There is broadly the same story about other family ties. The seven of these involving parents, children and siblings are represented in all (if we neglect a few infants and other shadows) sixty-five times; twenty-two times in the first class and forty-three in the second, an average for the two combined of two per play. Out of these sixty-five, fourteen may be dismissed as of no more than conventional interest; of the remaining fifty-one only nineteen qualify as 'positive relationships' in the sense indicated above. Estrangements befall no fewer than thirty-nine of the pairs (or groups), often of a serious nature; serious enough fifteen times to drive relatives to kill or desires to kill one another. It is true that twenty-two of the quarrels end in reconciliations, even if some of these (with Shakespeare as with the other playwrights, when happy endings have to be arranged) are not very convincing. Father and son appear fifty-six times, but no more than five times in the first class, and in only two of these cases is their relationship really attractive. Hotspur shows little respect or liking for his father, who deserves little better from him. Henry IV suspects his son of wanting him dead and out of the way, or even it would seem of contemplating his murder. Shakespeare's mothers are not ardently maternal, especially towards their daughters. Brothers find a great many reasons for falling out with one another. Between sisters things are worse still. The happiest relationship, by a long margin, is between brother and sister. But while there is not on the whole much positive affection or good will within the existing family, there are many sighs over their absence. These regrets help to persuade us that men's feelings for one another *ought* to be filled with warmth and life, even if 'in this harsh world' we can think of no other answer than Hamlet's to his mother's chilling platitude about how common it is for us to lose and forget our nearest and dearest: 'Ay, madam, it is common.'

In the comedies, where the new voluntary ties replace the stereotyped ones of the histories, Shakespeare likes to relieve his people of family connections, except that the heroines must have parents or guardians to make trouble for them. Their detachment from kith and kin, accentuated by foreign settings and (as in Molière) outlandish names, seems meant not to isolate them, but on the contrary to allow their feelings and affections to sprout freely and follow their own bent. Love holds the first place here. To revitalize marriage, and with it the family, Shakespeare advocated freedom for young men and women to choose their own partners in life. He was doing so from very early days –

> For what is wedlock forced but a hell,
> An age of discord and continual strife?

(I *Henry VI*, V. 5. 62-63)

The idea of such freedom has been in all societies of feudal mould a perennial expression of longing for a better life, betterment of the family and, by poetical implication, of mankind altogether. It inspired operas in medieval China, and Molière, as well as Shakespeare. It has glowed most brightly in times of transition like his, when windows open on to long vistas; it can then be a truly revolutionary impulse, a factor in a revolutionary transformation of society.

Shakespeare's point of view was close to that of the more humanistic Puritans, men like the young Milton who must have acquired it partly from reading his plays. It was in other words the point of view of the most enlightened and liberal section of the middle class then growing up – and growing up for a revolutionary trial of strength against the ancien régime – of which Shakespeare himself was a member. His 'freedom' here too is a new morality, not a discharge from morality. The choice once made is irrevocable. Heroines are at liberty to break with their parents, but not with their husbands, and equally Troilus declares that once a man has made his 'election' there can be no repenting of his bargain. Florizel promises Perdita to be 'constant': it is one of Shakespeare's great words, and embodies one of his great beliefs, to which he clung all the more closely as his world grew more harsh and storm-beaten. In his mind it went with that inner integrity of the individual which makes a firm alliance between him and others possible. This is the quality that Hamlet prized in Horatio, and that Cressida lacked: having no trust in herself or in the life about her, she was unable to be faithful to Troilus's trust in her. It went too with the antithesis Shakespeare was never tired of making between sincerity

and pretence, between what a man really is and what he wants to be thought, or
what he seems to be –

> Out on thee! Seeming! I will write against it.
>                 (*Much Ado About Nothing*, IV. 1. 55)

For European countries struggling to shake off the fetters of the past,
romantic love had the same excitement of novelty then as in Asia today, and the
recurrent Elizabethan image of love as a voyage of discovery was appropriate
enough. But the atmosphere of Elizabethan London, tainted by the practice of
mercenary or forced marriages, by prostitution flourishing on social distress, by
puritanism reacting against aristocratic licence was not one in which romanticism
could breathe easily. Of this there is plenty of evidence in Shakespeare's
own works, and his ability to suck up into his imagination all that was good
and new in the age, and distil it into feelings like those of Beatrice and
Benedick, or Perdita and Florizel, was an outstanding part of his achievement.
Even for him it cannot have been easy. He has eighty-six cases of love, with
fifteen in the first class and twenty-one in the second. In eleven of these thirty-
six, love is felt by one party only and not returned. Among the remaining
twenty-five there are many strains and stresses; only fourteen of the couples
end happily, and about half of the others have their own shortcomings to
blame. Only eight of the twenty-five, or one-third, qualify as 'positive
relationships', and three of these eight belong to the world-beyond-the-world
of the romances. In the eighteen Massinger plays, it may be added, we find
fifty-three cases of love, a higher frequency than Shakespeare's; but in as many
as thirty-three of them, or eighteen out of the thirty more important ones, love
is unrequited, and often amounts to no more than an unwelcome pestering of
A by B.

Love in Shakespeare is a social, not an isolating force. Beatrice and Benedick
are brought together initially by a trick played on them by their friends, but,
much more seriously, by the impulse that moves them both to defend someone
else against injustice. Love in other words is part of life, bringing with it
concern and responsibility for others as well, not a substitute for social life as it
becomes in later romantic literature. With the other playwrights it was
becoming a substitute already. And with them love was not always, as it always
was for Shakespeare, an individualized, personal bond: it was less a matter of
free choice, more a survival in new guise from the kingdom of necessity, a mere
freak or fatality. They fell back on sexual attraction as writers always do when
they can think of no other means of bringing characters together and setting
them in movement, because their society contains too little else that can bring
human beings close to one another. Love made use of in this way, as a sort of
magical force or conjuring trick, could not be woven into any pattern of real
life; it was felt as part of the incalculability of everything in that age of disinte-

gration. On the stage it was liable to grow freakish, unnatural, theatrical. One of its modes, and one of a number which did not interest Shakespeare, was incest. His lovers, it is worth noticing, seldom fall in love at first sight: this happens only half a dozen times among his thirty-six leading cases, only three times where there is love on both sides. In fifteen of them the lover or lovers are already head over heels when the play begins, so that we can allow them the benefit of the doubt and suppose them to have given some careful thought to what they are doing.

There are forty-one friendships in Shakespeare, and thirty-nine ties of loyalty; the two things tend more and more to merge, as he searches for a new moral cement to take the place of crumbling feudal affiliations. Only five of the total of eighty can be assigned to the highest class, twenty-four to the second. Friendship like love did not grow easily in the Elizabethan soil. 'Our age calls, erroneously, friendship but a name', says Farneze in Massinger's *Bashful Lover*, one of a pair of friends who set a worthy example by risking their lives for each other after a lost battle. Marlowe has only two 'positive' instances of friendship, one of them criminal. It is revealing both of him and of his failure to turn the Faust myth into real drama that he embarks Faustus on his terrific adventure all alone, without human aid or counsel. His 'friends' Valdes and Cornelius, Wagner whom he makes his heir, the scholar whom he calls his 'sweet chamber-fellow' – all these are left remote spectators of his fate. Shakespeare would not have chosen this theme, but if he had he would have handled it very differently.

Friendships always meant much to him, as witness an early, touchingly ludicrous image in *King John* about hairs stuck together by a teardrop 'in sociable grief',

> Like true, inseparable, faithful loves,
> Sticking together in calamity.

> (III. 4. 65–67)

And his friends, unlike many of those drawn by the other playwrights, lend small support to Dr Johnson's dictum that friendships are usually partnerships in folly or confederacies in vice. But they suffer in the comedies from a tinge of mawkishness, of self-conscious sentimentality, as in Antonio's devotion to Bassanio in Venice, or the other Antonio's to Sebastian in Illyria. Both these men insist on running themselves into danger without much rhyme or reason, and their choice of friends looks fanciful and unmeaning. In the mature plays friendship is more realistic, bringing men together in face of the problems of a real world: a world where they do well to choose their friends carefully and then 'grapple them to their souls with hoops of steel'. Words which from Polonius are a fossilized wisdom of the past possess a meaning that Hamlet learns through living experience. When the shock of his mother's marriage and knowledge of his father's murder drives him into self-isolation, he behaves somewhat like a 'Machiavel', or a Timon, solitary and embittered and distrustful. But this in him is so unnatural that he can only keep it up be pretending to others, and half-pretending to himself, to be mad; and it paralyses his faculty of action. Unable to trust anyone else, he at once discovers to his chagrin that he is unable to trust himself, or even to take himself and his grand mission seriously. It is through his recovered confidence in Horatio that he recovers faith in his world and what has to be performed in it, and with this the ability to prepare calmly for action.

An American radical, G.C. LeRoy, wrote lately of the 'new thinness of personal relationships' in the USA of today, and of the impediment it represents to any banding together of citizens against reactionary pressures.[4] A similar 'thinness' is to be looked for in the twilight of every social cycle, and we are in the same phase of ours as the Elizabethans of theirs. In their day as in ours moreover the individual was dwarfed and overshadowed by a towering political authority. It made use of spying and delation, terrorism and corruption, and politics included the suborning of great men's followers by their rivals, or by the government. Shakespeare was acutely aware of this growth of the State, a force in his eyes necessary perhaps, terrible certainly. What Ulysses says about secret intelligence work as an instrument of the omniscient and therefore omnipotent State has no conceivable relevance to the affairs of a Greek camp, but very much to those of Tudor statecraft: it is Burleigh and Walsingham all over. Under such conditions there can be no combining for political action without strong mutual trust, or what we may call a willing suspension of disbelief in our fellow men. Machiavelli the Florentine, his hero Cesare Borgia, and the 'Machiavels' of the theatre were all political failures, in spite of their boasted realism, because trust was a thing not dreamed of in their philosophy.

Shakespeare would be one of the great political poets if he had written nothing besides *Julius Caesar*, and his masterwork there is the evocation of a group of men united by a truly Roman blend of private friendship and devotion to a public cause. When one of them is asked whether he means to betray a dangerous confidence, and replies briefly

> You speak to Casca, and to such a man
> That is no fleering tell-tale,

> (I. 3. 116–17)

we feel as sure of him as his hearer does. Every man can rely on all the others to go without flinching 'as far as who goes farthest'. Brutus and Cassius call each other 'brother', and all the conspirators are, more genuinely than Henry V and his army of freebooters, a 'band of brothers'; much more than the Percies, they are all one family. There is a striking contrast to be observed between their plot and the *Conspiracy of Byron* in Chapman, where the hero has no party and no programme and goes to work on his own just as the hero of the popular revenge type of play usually did. There is an equally sharp contrast with Chapman's Romans in his *Caesar and Pompey*, stonily statuesque personages with none of that mutual faith and regard that Shakespeare's conspirators are brimful of; and again, at the opposite pole, with the demoralized Romans in Ben Jonson's *Sejanus*, where evil bestrides the narrow world far more tyrannically than Shakespeare's mightiest Julius ever did, and goes unchallenged.

Brutus and his friends also fail, because their heroic qualities are not shared by the common people. They are 'noble Romans' in rank as well as in temper; and for Shakespeare human qualities above the level of the pedestrian, and with them the capacity for vital relationships, are still aristocratic, not yet the common property of mankind. English history in the half-century after his death, with the revolution and the New Model army and the rest, is from this standpoint the history of a partial democratizing of these virtues, a widening of the moral franchise; a complex process in which Shakespeare's plays are themselves one ingredient.

It has been often enough or too often said that Shakespeare had a horror of anarchy, of social disorder; what really horrified him was not any breakdown of 'order' in the policeman's understanding of the word, but something more fundamental, the destruction of men's faith in one another that is always liable to accompany the break-up of an old social pattern whether authority remains intact or not. He was always struggling to banish the chilling distrust that invaded his England in the later histories and the following plays. Disloyalty and ingratitude are two of the sins he condemns most eloquently, and if he so habitually censures men by comparing them with brute beasts, what he has against the animals is, surely, their incapability of fellow-feeling. Tragic emotion in his plays springs, more generally than in those of other Elizabethans, from a sense of men's best feelings for one another being alienated or violated. Estrangement is one of his great themes; something that could not be said of Marlowe, in spite of his taking Dido and Aeneas for a subject. Of Shakespeare's fifty-nine leading 'positive relationships', twenty-four in all are disturbed by failings of the individuals concerned, only six by external accident alone. The quarrel of Brutus and Cassius is the classic 'quarrel scene' of all literature because it combines perfectly the malign pressure of circumstances with the inner weaknesses that they bring out. And because the better selves of the two men rise superior to their weaknesses and reunite them, though to die together, the play ends tragically but triumphantly.

When Brutus tried to repel Portia's sympathy or risked a breach with Cassius he was coming close to the edge of a moral gulf. In the tragedies this goes further. Lear capriciously throws away attachments and loyalties, to recover which he has to pay a fearful price. For Macbeth there is no recovery.

He becomes odious to himself because he has cut himself off from humanity, and isolation and suspicion push him into indiscriminate crime, but to us he never becomes odious, or never altogether a lost soul, because he can still feel excruciatingly, what Iago and the 'Machiavels' would never feel, the value of all that he has sacrificed to win the crown,

> As honour, love, obedience, troops of friends.
>
> *(Macbeth* V. 3. 25)

Macduff's lament over the murder of his wife and children by Macbeth –

> I cannot but remember such things were,
> That were most precious to me
>
> (IV. 3. 222-23)

– might have been spoken by the murderer himself.

Shakespeare's tragic climaxes are apocalyptic, because the human bonds that hold together his world of imagination are so close-knit and vital that their disruption seems portentous, far more than that of any 'social order' in the abstract. The hero's life is enmeshed with the lives of others, his fate implies the ruin or transformation of everything round him. The world breaks up, but at the same time it is, in a new way, reunited; its virtues and loyalties are liberated from what has warped or divided them, and death reconciles as well as destroying. Hamlet's dying response to the appeal of the dying Laertes –

> Exchange forgiveness with me, noble Hamlet
>
> *(Hamlet* V. 2. 321)

– is in the same accent as the last words we hear between Prince Henry and Hotspur, Antony and Brutus, Edgar and Edmund. Tragedy is not softened, by any means, but it is saved by this note of communion from ending in simple negation. In the other playwrights there is no such knitting-together, no such density of human feeling to be disrupted. Their tragic sense is concentrated on the life and fortune of a particular man or woman coming to an end; it is allied to the besetting horror of death as the extinction of individual existence which haunts the plays of Ford and Tourneur and Webster, as it haunts men in all crumbling societies where the cold winds of time blow in through every crack and chink. Shakespeare's firm attachment to the universe of man, mankind as one whole, and the freedom from religious glooms that it helped to give him, preserved him from these other men's nightmare. 'Take any shape but that! . . .' To his great characters death comes in a very different shape, and they die thinking not of their own annihilation but of one another, and of the life that is to go on.

## Notes

1. Burton, *Anatomy of Melancholy*, Bohn edn, vol. II. p. 213.
2. Ben Jonson, *Masque at Lord Haddington's Marriage*, 1608.
3. L. Kitchin, *Twentieth Century*, February 1961, p. 172.
4. G.C. LeRoy, *Monthly Review*, September 1962, pp. 268–9.

# ══ 5 ══
# Wordsworth and the People

> My heart was all
> Given to the People, and my love was theirs.
> (*The Prelude*, Book IX)

Wordsworth devoted the greater part of his life to the study of political and social questions, and Marx a great part of his to the study of poetry. For both men the French Revolution and the Industrial Revolution were supreme facts; and of the other chief ingredients of Marxism the poetry of the Romantic age is at least as important as the German metaphysics. Marx himself was once a young romantic poet, and if later on he and his friends were notably silent about the nature of their ideals, it was because they took these for granted and could confine themselves rigorously to building the road across chaos to the new world that the poets had seen in the distance. Today it may be time for Marxism to defend not only the economists of that age against their erring successors, but its writers, as men of revolutionary hopes and therefore in bad colour now, though in good company, with Milton.[1]

That in modern society intellectual and artist are separated from any genuine contact with their fellow men has come to be a matter of course. Only in epochs of great and volcanic energy is a high enough temperature generated to melt down this stony isolation, even partially. For the Romantics of Europe the fall of the Bastille was a wonderful event, above all because it made it seem possible for men like them to be brought back into the circle of humanity, as if returning to Eden. Of the English Romantic poets Wordsworth was the only important one who saw the Revolution as it were face to face; he experienced longer and more urgently than any of the others the problem of the relation between artist and people, art and life, individual and mass. 'Society has parted man from man';[2] he searched for a means of overcoming this morbid division, and his task was at bottom the same as that of finding a bridge between himself and the world of men. He failed; but if it is true that he has meant little to modern poets,[3] most of these have perhaps not even attempted what he failed in; and his work in the years round 1800 may still be, both for example and for warning, one of our chief starting-points for a new literature.[4]

In Wordsworth's *Descriptive Sketches*,[5] written in 1791 and 1792 on the ban
of the Loire, can be found a surprising number of what were to be tl
dominant themes of his later work. Prominent among them was that or
freedom, always to remain, though in diverse forms, one of his leading
thoughts. Ages ago man was 'entirely free, alone and wild', 'none restraining,
and by none restrained', unless by God. Even now, 'traces of primeval Man', of a
bygone society not divided into classes, could be found in remote valleys like
those of Switzerland, or of Cumberland. There, the argument implied, men felt
no need of any government and ran no risk of misgovernment; all they wanted
was to be left alone. There was another side to the picture, however, in the
cutting poverty of the free mountain folk, poverty in which Wordsworth saw
reflected 'the general sorrows of the human race'. His early pessimism was
much more than a youthful pose; he was never to shake it off for very long. And
this thought led directly to the conclusion of the poem, in which he saw the
Revolution arming for battle against the leagued despots of Europe and prayed
for the triumph of the good cause. He believed in the Revolution because he
felt that it promised to bring freedom down from the mountains, where she
had been hiding like a timid chamois, onto the fertile plains. France had made
the grand discovery that 'Freedom spreads her power Beyond the cottage-
hearth, the cottage-door'.

Poverty could thus be abolished, for most of mankind were only poor
because they were enslaved. In Wordsworth's later account of these days in *The
Prelude*, the most poignant moment is the one where his friend Beaupuy points
to the starving country girl and exclaims "'Tis against *that* Which we are
fighting."[6] Wordsworth was haunted all his life by the image of an outcast,
suffering woman. It occurs first in the earliest of his poems that reached publi-
cation, 'An Evening Walk' of his college days – a sick woman dragging herself
along the Lakeland roads with her starving infants: a single painful episode in
an idyllic poem.[7] It reappears in *Descriptive Sketches*, and in all the succeeding
long poems, including *The Borderers*, as well as many short ones, down to 1800;
it has other reincarnations after that, especially in *The White Doe of Rylstone*, and
finally it dwindles away into those chocolate-box martyrs, the Russian fugitive
and the Egyptian princess. In this figure we have a key to Wordsworth's social
problem, that of poverty, as in the idea of freedom we have a key to his political
thinking. The Revolution brought the two together.

His politics in the period after his unpublished 'Apology for the French
Revolution' of 1793 can be seen most clearly in two letters to Matthews in
1794, when they were planning a political journal.[8] His views were very radical
indeed: he thought, though reluctantly, that things might soon become so bad
as to make even the terrible event of a revolution in England welcome; not
agitation, but a villainous government, was driving the country towards it. He
was above all outraged by what in his eyes was the monstrous wickedness of the

government in going to war with France; war, indeed, seemed to him the characteristic crime of States. He was doubly isolated. He wanted France to win, as she did; he was revolted by the Terror, the Jacobin dictatorship of the crisis; at home those in power seemed to him eager to imitate so far as they could the crimes though not the virtues of the Revolution, and to degrade law into 'A tool of Murder'.[9] The middle-class progressive movement towards parliamentary reform was blocked; abstract radical theorizing among Godwinian intellectuals was no substitute for healthy activity. Wordsworth, a practical countryman, always wanted to come to grips with something concrete. He was growing disgusted with his own sort of people, as well as with his country; he 'Fed on the day of vengeance yet to come'.[10]

Hence his turning away from the educated classes to the 'common people', towards whom history was, at it were, forcing him all through his years as a great poet. The impulse had stirred in him earlier than this time. In his first vacation from Cambridge he had looked at his plain rustic neighbours with a new sense of 'love and knowledge', a new 'human-heartedness', and it was then he had his nocturnal meeting with the old soldier whose 'ghastly figure', 'solemn and sublime' in its simplicity, was to throw a long shadow over his poetry.[11] In France he had loved 'the People', but a foreign people, and in part a figment of political rhetoric. Now he wanted to know his fellow beings as they really were.

How far he could get on this new road would depend on many things beside his own resources. He began, necessarily, with remnants of an older, pre-1789 way of looking at things, in which the philosopher or sage (or 'intellectual', as we say) virtuously dedicated himself to the happiness of his less fortunate fellows. In phrases like 'the labours of benevolence', 'the labours of the sage', 'Heroes of Truth',[12] we can see that attitude peeping out. From it to a real enrolment of the intellectual in a progressive mass movement was to be a very long-drawn historical process, far from completed a century and a half later. He found no organized movement to gravitate towards; and he was living near the end of the pre-Copernican epoch in political thought – with the Revolution, action had for the time left theory far behind – and had no serviceable analysis of classes or the State to help him. A radical error lurked in him from the beginning: he was turning to the common people, not so much in search of a force capable of carrying to success the lofty hopes fostered and disappointed since 1789, as in search of a consolation in the sight of humble virtue for the 'Ambition, folly, madness' of the world's rulers. He wanted to satisfy himself that 'real worth', 'genuine knowledge', 'true power of mind', could be found in the labouring poor, in spite of an unjust society, and that the basic human qualities could thus survive in an iron age in the common people who – he agreed with Robespierre – were free of the corruptions of their superiors.[13]

These ideas must have been growing in his mind for a considerable time before he came to systematize them in the *Preface* of 1800. In *The Prelude* he associated them with, for instance, his walk on Salisbury Plain in 1793, when he felt again a fresh stirring of his poetic energy.[14] This was the decisive moment in the moulding of his next long poem, 'Guilt and Sorrow'.[15] It is a very impressive, though it may not be a dazzling poem. It moves firmly, with a strong cumulative effect; Wordsworth was never to achieve greater success along this line, or rather was never again to undertake anything quite like it. It owes its firmness of outline, and the solidity of its two chief characters, to the fact that the sufferings of these two homeless outcasts are rooted in the reality of social injustice. As before, Wordsworth keeps his two problems of government and poverty close together, under the shadow of his prime evil, unjust war. In 'An Evening Walk' the poor woman's husband was a soldier, far away 'on Bunker's charnel hill'. Here the man is a sailor, press-ganged and made to serve for years as 'Death's minister'; maddened by ill-usage, and so hurried into the crime of murder. His fellow vagrant is the daughter of a poor man ruined by oppression, the widow of an artisan ruined by war and unemployment and driven by hunger into the army, where he perished. She too has been forced by misery into crime.[16]

Wordsworth comes closest here to reaching, but does not quite reach, a recognition of State and Law as things not foreign and extrinsic to society, but integral parts of an unjust social order. His band of gypsies are happy because they have no chiefs or separate property among them, but they too stand outside society and can do nothing to remedy it – they are free men astray and soiled in a bad world. War is an unexplained evil; and in later years, when Wordsworth came to accept the war with France, he came to accept the British government with it. At present, though this is a radical and 'progressive' poem, Wordsworth has not succeeded in making it a revolutionary one. Its atmosphere belongs to Dostoyevsky rather than to Gorky, or even to Tolstoy. At the bottom of these forlorn creatures a fundamental goodness remains, a light glimmers in the darkness. They, unlike their rulers, have sinned involuntarily, and it is better, the sailor tells the brutal peasants, to suffer than to inflict injuries. Wordsworth feels overpoweringly the guilt of society, but he is not strengthened by any active movement towards setting it right. It seems irremediable, and because of this transfers itself to its own victims, who become its scapegoats. The sailor's obsessive memory of his own crime is what the poem succeeds most vividly in presenting. Haunted and paralysed by this sense of guilt, the sufferers of the social order are powerless against what has ruined them. It ends in that turning away from earth to heaven, later to become the fatal habit of Wordsworth's thinking.

In September 1795 he went to live with his sister Dorothy at Racedown in Dorset; from there he moved in July 1797 to Alfoxden in Somerset, in September 1798 to Germany, and finally in December 1799 to Grasmere. This 'healing time of his spirit'[17] has been much dwelt on by biographers, and he has been given much credit for shaking off his revolutionary nonsense and settling down sensibly like a middle-class poet to write middle-class poetry. This is misleading in several ways. He was not exactly retiring to the countryside, for he had already been spending nearly all his time there. In the region he was moving to in 1795 he would be likely to see a good deal more of the poverty and distress that beset his thoughts than he had been seeing in Penrith. 'The peasants are miserably poor,' wrote Dorothy in one of her first letters from Racedown.[18] The works he now set about writing (*The Borderers*, 1795 to 1796, and *The Ruined Cottage*, a slower growth) were still of an extremely gloomy cast, and continued the wrestling with his problems where 'Guilt and Sorrow' had left off. He was not throwing down his shield and flying from the battlefield like Horace at Philippi; he was only turning away from a 'fretful stir unprofitable', which included the uproar of war propaganda as well as vexation at his own unavailing efforts to find an active part to play. He still hated the government and the condition of society, though it may be with less of urgency in his opposition as the war changed its character. The Revolution was over, France was out of danger after the Basle treaties of 1795, and on both sides the Anglo-French contest was falling back into its old rut, the quarrelling of two empires over markets and slave-plantations.

Wordsworth's opposition did, in the years 1795 to 1800, acquire more of a passive and negative character. In these five years he was to turn over many new leaves in English literature, and produce much work of high value. Other parts of his output were to be less good. He was losing as well as gaining, declining as well as advancing; and what he lost politically through being out of touch with any movement was of ill omen for his poetical future.

He began – simplifying his task for the moment and complicating it for the future – by separating his 'political' from his 'social' problem. *The Borderers* is an intellectual study of politics, based on Wordsworth's understanding (necessarily limited and fragmentary) of the French Revolution; more exactly, a study of the psychology of action, and particularly – in the character of Oswald – the psychology of terrorism. In it he moved towards a conviction that the troubles of mankind were insoluble by *action*, which was more likely than not to lead to worse than failure. 'Action is transitory,' its consequences incalculable. A tragic fatality seemed to overshadow even 'the motion of a muscle this way or that', as it had overshadowed the sailor's crime in 'Guilt and Sorrow'.[19] Here, growing upon Wordsworth's mind, was the mode of thinking of the isolated spectator of events, to whom the possibility seemed remote of any activity being both good and successful. 'The world is poisoned at the heart.'[20]

*The Ruined Cottage* is removed from the world of action altogether. A cottage-weaver, reduced to misery by unemployment following bad harvests and war, deserts his wife and infants and joins the army; she dies slowly of a broken heart and of want. Wordsworth tells this story, taking many of its touches from the life of the people around him, with profound sympathy, and the quality of the poetry is very high. It is so partly because Wordsworth takes a more limited canvas than in the woman's story in the earlier poem. His new heroine Margaret is a stationary figure, not a wanderer over the earth; she is a passive victim of misfortunes that squeeze her life out inch by inch. She has no contact with other victims, though it is a time of mass distress that the poem refers to; this is a step back from even the half-formed idea in *Descriptive Sketches*, that in 'life's long deserts' it is better to be joined with others in the 'mighty caravan of pain: Hope, strength and courage social suffering brings.' The writer is now looking at his theme more from outside, as a fine painting of human grief. War is attributed to the will of heaven, rather than to iniquity. Attention has moved from the social to the individual; and Wordsworth's inability to see any remedy for the ills he describes is taking shape in the philo-sophical narrator of the story, the old pedlar. As the poem gradually grew and unfolded like a plant, this part of it expanded, until by March 1798 Dorothy could speak of the pedlar having come to play the *largest* part in it.[21] This throws a long shadow forward; for the pedlar of 1798 was to grow into the wanderer of *The Excursion*, and he already embodied the negative, quietist tendency in Wordsworth's mind – much as Coleridge's later decrepit self was prefigured by the reformed churchgoer at the end of the 'Ancient Mariner'. Through the pedlar, Wordsworth was groping for moral instead of political solutions; he was trying to extract from 'mournful thoughts' and sights 'A power to virtue friendly', and coming closer to the quagmire of resignation that was one day to swallow him up.

He was not satisfied; he went on for years and years tormenting himself over this poem, trying to cobble it into something more convincing. He had now written a good deal since 1793, but had got nothing into a shape for publi-cation, which was a symptom of his frustrated condition. Now, in 1798, came the change marked by the first volume of *Lyrical Ballads*. For him the short poem was a novelty, and always remained something of a condescension, a bagatelle; but it allowed him to express feelings as they arose, to strike sparks where he could not kindle a bonfire, and thus to recover himself now as a poet with something to say to the public. He had Coleridge to admire and stimulate him, and in some ways this was, as it has often been called, his springtime and rebirth. Spring was in his thoughts, his powers were expanding, he heard the 'mighty sum of things' speaking to him in fresh tones. 'Never did fifty things at once Appear so lovely, never, never.'[22]

In preparation for the giant life-work now floating before his eyes, he felt again the need to learn more of himself (he was soon to begin *The Prelude*), and more of his fellows. These two studies were still closely related. He was going in search of the People again, not hiding from them; the voice of nature included the voice of simple, natural man. But as before there was loss as well as gain. Neither Coleridge nor Dorothy, nor the 'wise passiveness' they were helping to foster in him, could be an altogether reliable guide for such a man. In the prologue to 'Peter Bell' (summer 1798) it is possible to read a dual meaning into the poet's return from his imaginary voyaging among the stars to 'the dear green Earth' where alone he could feel 'I am a man', and his rejection of 'the realm of Faery' in favour of the humdrum tale of a potter beating a donkey. He was banishing fantasy and choosing reality as the theme of his poetry; but fantasy was beginning to include the limbo of political strife and faction, as Wordsworth thought of it in those moods when he turned away too indiscriminately from 'the sages' books' to the running brooks.[23] 'Reality' was thus in danger of impoverishment.

However lovely the face of nature might seem, the subjects that attracted him were often far from lovely. Fewer than half of the 1798 *Lyrical Ballads* leave a cheerful impression. Nearly half are concerned with Wordsworth's own feelings and interests – those of a young romantic suffering chronically from bad nerves, indigestion, headaches, fevers, insomnia, irregular hours; not of a sober, well-disciplined moralist. He was seeing himself anew, in new relations with his environment; but it is noteworthy that he succeeded much better in his more personal poems, with which six of the eight successful new poems of the volume[24] may be classed, than in the others. In these latter there was a distinct falling off, instead of an advance, in point of imaginative realism, and it corresponded with a loosening of the framework of ideas in which his pictures of humanity were set. Compared with the characters in 'Guilt and Sorrow', those of the *Ballads* tend to be flat and dull, or else melodramatic and unconvincing.[25] There is a practically complete absence of normal human beings; Wordsworth is alone with his sister in a circle of children, ancients, beggars, imbeciles. Only in these poems, not about himself, did he make much use of the new and soon famous style that may fairly be labelled the *idiot style.*

Prominent among their characters is a bevy of unfortunate females, whose hard lot wrings few tears from the reader: the deserted Red Indian woman; the mad mother (not too mad to assure us that she is legally married); the erring penitent of 'The Thorn' (very little removed from the 'super-tragic' mourners whom Wordsworth remembered with amusement in his juvenile efforts);[26] Goody Blake, the doddering old spinner; and the two unbearable gossips of 'The Idiot Boy'. Then we have Simon Lee limping tediously on his swollen ankles in front of the final quatrain of a poem that has no need of him, and the old man of 'Animal Tranquillity and Decay'. It is a set of bad poems, offering an unappetizing picture of the deserving poor. 'The Thorn' was composed 'with great rapidity', and 'The Idiot Boy' 'almost extempore'; what is more surprising is that the latter was written 'with exceeding delight and pleasure', and its author continued to read it with the same complacency.[27] Evidently he believed himself to have accomplished something significant in enlarging the circle of poetry to include such waifs and strays, when he seemed to others to be making a caricature of life. Social injustice – as if he was now left bewildered and helpless by it – had descended to the farcical level of Goody Blake's tale where her oppressor, the grasping farmer, is punished, not by a combination of the labouring poor against him, but by an old woman's curse; a 'true' story told by Wordsworth in the manner of one relating an edifying though improbable anecdote to a Sunday-school class.[28]

Extravagance of subject in these poems is only exaggerated by ultra-literal diction. In 'Guilt and Sorrow' and *The Ruined Cottage* the language had been quite simple enough; in 'Michael' it was to be so in perfection. Wordsworth's theory of diction, a *democratic* one, grew out of his political radicalism.[29] But there was in the sectarian lengths to which he pushed it at this stage an element of compensation for what was missing – any practical remedy or protest against 'what man has made of man';[30] and with it a touch of self-mortification, as of one wilfully refusing to stand well with his public. Having discarded the 'artificial' life of the city in favour of the cottage, he was proposing to revive English poetry by ridding it of artificial conventions. But this was in any case a negative reform, and no reform of diction could take the place of a regeneration of the social order.

The theory which he fancied to be broad and liberating was in fact narrow and restrictive. He had been clinging to his trust 'In what we may become';[31] but to limit poetry to the everyday language of ordinary men and thereby to their everyday thoughts would condemn him to see people and things as fixed and unchanging – as, ultimately, all existence was to seem to him. This was to fall into the same arid 'realism' that he complained of in Crabbe.[32] He was incurring this danger because he had turned away from the people in arms to the people in rags, squalor and helplessness, and now he was inclined to project into them his own sensations of gloom and defeat, blind to the power that was still in them of struggling against their fate. Tempted to seek the bedrock of their own experience in himself in solitary abstraction, he was looking for it in the poor also as detached individuals, the *disjecta membra* of humanity, and coming to seek in them a refuge instead of a source of energy. Contemplating a very old man, alive only by the faintest flicker, he was fascinated by the thought of an absolute immobility, a Nirvana of thought. In the dim recesses of an idiot boy's mind, and the mother's near-animal affection, he could find an impregnable shelter from life at the very moment when he supposed himself to be grappling most closely with life – 'Thou art the thing itself!' It was often in future to happen to Wordsworth to be furthest from 'reality' at the point where he believed himself nearest.

There are other children in these and the later *Ballads*, seeming to symbolize new beginnings, though quite often it is the memory of dead children that he is thinking of. From these young minds he felt that he could and must learn; and so too from common humanity at large. But he was losing sight too completely of the people as a collective thing, and what he needed most was something that could not be learned – though many valuable smaller lessons could – from fragmentary talk with wayfarers on the roads of Somerset or Cumberland,[33] any more than from the peasant pilgrims Tolstoy talked with on the road to

Kiev. It had to be learned with, not from, the people, and on the high road of history. Failing to see that 'real life' must be rooted in a collective life, and one still in development, he fell into the error he denounced in mechanistic science: 'we murder to dissect'.[34] When he came to write his own history he missed much of what had gone to make him, because he lacked an understanding of the process of history in the wider sense; in the same way now he was failing to see how many of the qualities he admired in the poor were the outcome of an active, purposeful social existence and centuries of social conflict – which might be said also of their vocabulary. He was losing sight even of any close links between individuals, except those of the family, which he was coming to see as the only shelter in a bleak world.[35]

If previously Wordsworth had thought of an educated elite guiding an inert popular mass, he was now involved in the converse error of wanting to merge himself in the mass, at the cost of ceasing to be himself; whereas the true task for such a man was to find ways of contributing his own special resources to a common struggle in alliance with the people. His new notion meant living among the poor, and like the poor, in a somewhat mechanical fashion, and thinking and writing only such things as a humble neighbour might think or say. It would mean, if persisted in, a sacrifice not merely of Wordsworth's worldly prospects, but of his inmost self and business in life, of the talent which is death to hide. He could only make the effort spasmodically, and while he did so there was bound to be an element of pastoral masquerade in his work, of the intellectual awkwardly bringing himself down to the level of the people. He dabbled at times in verse meant to be read by the poor themselves,[36] but he was not finding much to say to them. When Cobbett wrote in the *Political Register* for his 'Chopsticks', the same south of England labourers Wordsworth was now living among, he wrote a language a good deal less simple than that of some of the *Ballads*, without ever puzzling his head about the matter, and they understood him. Wordsworth's still sad music was leading him astray, by leading him towards those who suffered most, not those who had most to give to the future. An artist needs to hear drums as well as dirges. In the England of 1798 the drums of the future were indeed thickly muffled. The new factory proletariat was taking decades, even generations, to form out of the debris of an older society. It was still half a century before Marx and Engels would open the leaden casket of the industrial slums from which Wordsworth (and Cobbett not much less) recoiled in horror.

Usually Wordsworth was writing about the poor for his own class. There seems to have been floating in his mind the dream that was to visit Tolstoy and Gandhi of opening the eyes of the better-off classes and giving them a change of heart, so that they would stop despising and ill-treating the poor: they would become as little children, and society would be a happy family again as in the golden age gone by – if a poor and primitive family; humanity reduced to the ancient, indestructible core of its material.[37] In harmony with this was the concern for goodwill in private relations as forming the 'best portion of a good man's life'.[38] But belief in such a programme could not come easily to a man of Wordsworth's native shrewdness, and the effort and strain involved may be seen as one cause of the 'extremism' of the *Ballads*.

What the idea must mean in practice was of course reconciliation of jarring classes within the prevailing order for the benefit of its rulers. In 'Peter Bell' Wordsworth can be seen drifting towards the weir, though as yet the idea remained in an allegorical shape, not reasoned out as it was later. In this fable, moreover, he strained every nerve to keep within the limits of rational possibility – instead of throwing the responsibility on to providence – a change of heart in a villain guilty of callously ill-treating women and animals; in effect, in the terms of Wordsworth's symbolism, an oppressor of mankind. Peter's consciousness of guilt is powerfully developed, as in 'Guilt and Sorrow'; his conversion, with the aid of a donkey and a Methodist hymn, is ludicrously unconvincing – much more than if the means of grace were avowedly supernatural as in the parallel poem, 'The Ancient Mariner'. Wordsworth had bowdlerized the problem of reform into a silly parable. He turned away at present from this path, only to come back to it later. 'Peter Bell' was published in 1819, in the most reactionary period of Wordsworth's political life. In his respectable old age it was precisely with class harmony and conciliation that he came to be associated, as the public orator at Oxford did not fail to note when rewarding him with a degree.[39]

Wordsworth's quest for the People seemed to have petered out. There was, however, another 1798 poem, 'The Old Cumberland Beggar' (published 1800), that pointed another way. Here, refreshed by a breeze from his native hills, he wrote with restraint and effect, at once realistically and – because he saw the old man's existence as interwoven with that of the society around him – imaginatively. In the 'vast solitude' of extreme age, this beggar still seemed to him to play a useful part on the earth, through the charitable impulses he called forth in the cottagers, themselves poor enough, thus providing a moral cement for a rural community where he, like Scott's Bluegown, had a distinct place of his own, more as a pensioner than as a vagrant.

Here was an image, death and life intertwined in a way characteristic of him, that Wordsworth could fasten on to. The social and moral disintegration of the English countryside, with its capitalistic agriculture and pauperized labourers, was equally disintegrating to his poetry, where it engendered the unreal or dying creatures of the *Ballads*. At Goslar in the winter of 1798–9, living with Dorothy in complete solitude, he was turning his eyes back towards Lakeland, as an oasis where a decent human existence still went on, and he was making sketches for the first two books of *The Prelude*, on his boyhood days. Among the other 'German' poems that were to appear in volume II of the *Lyrical Ballads* (1800), the Lucy poems, as well as 'Lucy Gray' and 'To a Sexton', show him preoccupied with thoughts of death. In 'Hart-Leap Well', with its hill-country setting, he again gave an allegorical, but this time a much more sober, version of the world's cruelty, drawing a moral of non-violence, or brotherly love.

Writing at this period of the poisoned atmosphere of the times – 'This melancholy waste of hopes o'erthrown', fear or apathy or defection on all sides – Wordsworth thanked 'Nature' for his own ability to hold fast, with 'more than Roman confidence', to his faith in humanity.[40] When in December 1799 he settled at Dove Cottage, to live henceforward close to the source of his inspiration, it was not a question of getting back merely to the hills, considered as rock and bracken: what he was seeking was the 'natural' order of society that he associated with the hills, where he could see 'Man free, man working for himself',[41] and breathe freely. His return, decided on with many heart-searchings and hesitations, as *The Recluse* (Book I, 1800) shows, was a quest, not an escape. The sentimental tourist's notion of 'peace, rusticity, and happy poverty' in Grasmere[42] was not for Wordsworth, who was well aware that Lakeland poverty was not always happy. Dorothy's early Grasmere journal is full of accounts of tramps and beggars on the roads, outsiders from Ireland or Manchester; misery could be found among the native peasantry too, as when the Wordsworths and Coleridge, basking in the summer beauty of the waterside, were suddenly broken in on by the sight of an old, infirm, hungry man trying to get something to eat out of 'the dead unfeeling lake'.[43] None the less, there was still a core of the old rural order left; and poverty did not usually appear as man-made (which later was to encourage Wordsworth to view it as made by heaven). Here was little of a resident gentry; he had scarcely ever in youth seen a human being who claimed anything on the score of birth or rank,[44] social oppression was out of sight, and 'no people in the world are more impatient under it', a contemporary wrote.[45] Labourers were few, and lived with the farmers' families. Wordsworth could feel that there was at least no 'extreme penury', no suffering beyond what good neighbourship could relieve.[46] In Grasmere vale, with its forty or fifty scattered cottages, he and Dorothy found the old ways 'little adulterated' and the people 'kind-hearted, frank and manly, prompt to serve without servility.'[47] Unlike the pauperized masses of the south, a great many of them were still small independent farmers, rather hugging the chains of sentiment that bound them to a poor soil than hating their condition, and thus seeming to prove that for the spirit of man, poverty – which Wordsworth was accepting for himself too – was not the worst, or an unbearable, evil.

He loved the combination of individual pride and tenacious spirit of neighbourhood. It underlay his own conception of the combined independence and civic responsibility of the artist. These Lakeland small-holders, part farmer and part shepherd, had only of late years been emerging from a 'natural economy'. Each household was an almost self-sufficient unit, rooted in the thin soil like a gnarled tree – or like Wordsworth's genius – growing out of the rocks. Each household was drawn close about the spinning-wheel and loom that occupied all its free hours; the hum of the wheel had something sacred in Wordsworth's ear, which linked it with all the decencies of a stable family life.[48] Better than any other great poet he understood how the moral as well as the economic life of a free peasantry is bound up with the patrimonial acres that unite each individual with ancestors and descendants, form the repository of all his memories and emotions, and stand to him for history, art, and religion. Folk-art and popular imagination had been largely uprooted from the rest of England when the land was taken away from those who tilled it.

Like any other writer trying to overcome his isolation by finding a framework of living ideas wider than his own self, Wordsworth was identifying his outlook with that of a particular class, and supposing that he had achieved a 'universal' viewpoint. With this class of smallholders, among whom he had spent his early years, he shared many qualities, for instance a sense of humour more hearty than subtle.[49] In particular the shepherd of the high moorlands was a man through whose eyes he felt he could look at life; they had in common days made up of toil, hope, danger, and the 'majestic indolence' of freedom,[50] and perhaps he felt an analogy between shepherd and poet, as teacher of mankind. In the series of great years now opening before him he owed very much to the strength he drew from living side by side with a sturdy self-respecting race.[51] It gave him his rugged quality of endurance, as the Revolution had given him a soaring energy. He needed both, and under extreme adverse pressures his genius maintained itself for longer than that of most of the Romantic poets of Europe; because he was able, as *The Prelude* asserts over and over again, to maintain his faith in the common man and the qualities lurking in him.

The renewed integration of his mind found expression at once in the remaining *Ballads* of the 1800 volume. Hardly anything of the 'idiot' style survives here. There is less of the crudely painful; less of death; less of old age and more of childhood (though still not very much in between). More of the successful poems are concerned with things outside the poet. In general the literary quality is a good deal higher.[52] If there is a hint once more of something lost as well as gained, in the practically complete absence now of any reference to social injustice, at present this does not stand out; for Wordsworth has got away from his helpless weaklings to real men, men like old Michael of the 'stern and unbending mind'. This means also that he is throwing off his recent musings about conciliation between the classes. Lakeland knows only a rudimentary division of classes, and the shepherd fights his battles with storm and mist knowing and caring nothing about what educated folk may think of the poor. Wordsworth is grasping at the idea of rescuing the old peasant proprietorship, as the solution of England's problem of pauperism.

This is the point of his letter of January 1801, with a copy of the *Lyrical Ballads*, to Charles James Fox. He laments the 'rapid decay of the domestic affections among the lower orders of society', with the uprooting of the peasantry, and calls on the statesman to arrest this vicious process. (How, he does not explain; and it is a bad omen that he is calling on Fox to save the people, instead of on the people to save themselves.) He sends him the book exclusively on account of two poems, 'The Brothers' and 'Michael', written 'to shew that men who do not wear fine cloathes can feel deeply.'[53] These two long 'pastoral poems' are remarkable achievements, and the second in particular is Wordsworth's finest tribute to the old way of life. What is good in it, and what is painful, are realized with equal intensity, though it is the good that he wants to bring forward. He insists, as earlier in *Descriptive Sketches*, that these rude shepherds do acquire from long familiarity and force of association a genuine love, akin to his own, for the mountain scenery they live amidst. There is an austere simplicity, dignity, pathos in these beings, so different from the hysterical creatures of earlier *Ballads*. They live in a hard, bleak, masculine world where women and heaven have little part to play. Michael's cottage has never been 'gay', scarcely even 'cheerful'. When he inherited his acres they were mortgaged; until he was forty he had a hard struggle to free them of debt. Now, through a nephew's 'unforeseen misfortunes', he is crippled again, and the struggle must be faced anew. Such is the bitter inheritance he would hand on to his young son Luke, separated from him, as if symbolically, by so many years. Luke, infected and ruined by 'the dissolute city', never returns to take it up. Toiling to the end, dying in extreme age, Michael has no one to follow him, the land passes to a stranger, the plough turns up its grass.

'The Brothers' – a dialogue in the churchyard that was to become within a dozen years Wordsworth's spiritual home – likewise concerns the breaking up of a family, one that has clung to its patch of land for generations until at last the load of debt grew too heavy to bear. Lakeland was now exposed to the rough airs of a commercial age, and we read in a 1794 account: 'These small properties . . . can only be handed down, from father to son, by the utmost thrift, hard labour, and penurious living.'[54] Many of the younger sort were sucked away by the attractive power of the new towns. To Wordsworth this was a desertion of the post of freedom for the lure of sordid comfort.[55] He himself, preparing to undergo 'solitary and unremitting labour, a life of entire neglect perhaps' [56] for the sake of his creed, saw in the stern and unbending Michael a brother-spirit.

This lonely stoicism – this *surly virtue* – could not for long be a substitute for the 'soul-animating strains' of an active movement of progress. Lakeland was, at best, on the defensive. Moreover, while each dalesman waged his desperate struggle against circumstances, they were not as a body carrying on any fight against anything so tangible as a body of landlords. Such a fight might have drawn Wordsworth in on the right side, and his pen could have contributed to it. The need was not lacking. Although in these dales there might be little visible oppression, there were man-made evils which, as often in peasant regions, were hardly recognized as grievances, because they were matters of immemorial use and wont. Neither in the 'pastoral poems' nor in the letter to Fox did he speak of the vices of an archaic tenurial law in this old border country, still burdened with 'numerous and strong remains of vassalage', covered with customary manors demanding heriots, boon services, and worst of all those arbitrary *fines* on succession which did as much as anything to make it hard for families to cling to their little holdings.[57] Yet the poet's father had been legal agent to one of the worst of the manorial lords, and himself a victim of his master's injustice.

Lingering decline rather than a galloping consumption was to befall Lakeland. Cobbett found many of the old patriarchal ways still alive in 1832.[58] But whatever survived here could be only an odd fragment of the national life. Peasantry and cottage industry were vanishing before capitalism and the machine. Wordsworth, whose long span of years coincided exactly with the long-drawn extinction of the independent craftsmen, was writing gloomily in 1819 on the passing of his beloved spinning-wheel, and again in 1827 on this 'Venerable Art Torn from the Poor'.[59] Only by transformation into a new pattern could something of the good of the old days be preserved. Sucked into factory towns the once independent craftsmen could contribute a militant element to the battle for reform. Wordsworth, refusing to follow them, was left with more and more of the husk and less and less of the spirit. Insensibly his mountain fortress turned into a snug summer-house. His 'common man' grew all too uncommon, and he gradually came to attribute to bare hills, by a sort of imputed righteousness, the moral influences that he had known as the property of a simple social system; while conversely he grew to hate in towns their smoke rather than their slavery.[60]

Settling in Grasmere, he was still blaming 'an unjust state of society' for men's troubles,[61] but he was receding from the conception that had come to him in 1792 of expanding and organizing freedom, and marrying freedom to plenty. Now as before the Revolution he felt that a life worthy of human beings could be lived only in secluded valleys. Because his idea of freedom came back to this negative, primitive level – similar to the anarchism of Europe's surviving craftsmen-communities later in the century – he could have no idea of a State power taken over and used by the people, and he was unlikely to develop that of a constructive popular movement; which meant that in the end he must be drawn into a reactionary current. Such a phenomenon has been seen in various parts of Europe analogous to Wordsworth's. A democratic society is the last that will think of creating a democratic State.

It is to *The Excursion*, especially its later (1810–14) books, that we must look for the record of Wordsworth's decline. Hints of what was to come are thickly scattered over his work after 1800, when the initial recovery conferred by his return to Lakeland had worn off, and he was being left stranded between his two worlds, that of Michael and the hills and that of books, London, Napoleon. Michael was dead, and no other such towering, rock-hewn figure took his place. In 1802, once more oppressed with thoughts of decay and desertion 'And mighty Poets in their misery dead', Wordsworth's imagination caught for comfort at a much lesser figure, the Leechgatherer, endowed with no more than a passive tenacity of life. (It was his imagination, grappling with reality, that created all his significant figures – not his pocket-book jottings from reality. There was no Leechgatherer, as there had been a Simon Lee.) To live long was to live wretched, he reflected at the graveside of Burns.[62] Every living thing's heart was an 'impenetrable cell' of loneliness.[63] Death hung about his thoughts. The age he had been reserved to was a 'degenerate' one.[64]

From the renewal of war in 1803 until its end in 1815 his poetic moods were largely conditioned by the situation of Europe, since that of Lakeland was static. When he wrote of Toussaint, the black man born in slavery defying and morally defeating the master of Europe – or again in 1808 to 1809 when all Spain rose against the tyrant and he wrote *The Convention of Cintra* – Wordsworth could identify himself with struggling people far away; but enthusiasm for freedom and justice abroad could not for long take the place of struggle for freedom and justice at home.[65]

In 1804 and 1805, in a superb burst of energy, he completed *The Prelude*, ending it on a curiously mingled note of hope and pessimism. Free now to embark on his serious life-work, in 1806 he wrote, or put together, the first part of *The Excursion*, whose opening sections had been planned or sketched in 1804 and even earlier. It was not the poem he and Coleridge had dreamed of in 1798. Book I was the old *Ruined Cottage* of that year, in a new guise. This was followed in Book II and the beginning of Book III by the story of the Solitary, which as regards Wordsworth and the French Revolution is better autobiography than most of *The Prelude*. The Solitary was his old self, as the Wanderer (the former pedlar, grown into a 'venerable Sage') was his new – or rather they were moods still conflicting in him.[66] Thus he was throwing together the dual problems of his earlier years, of poverty and of freedom. They stand side by side in the Solitary's tremendous catalogue of evils –

> Wrongs unredressed, or insults unavenged
> And unavengeable, defeated pride,
> Prosperity subverted, maddening want . . . [67]

This disappointed revolutionary is a splendidly Byronic character: the finest ever invented, in fact – Byron could never make his heroes speak as this man does. But he is alone, frustrated, impotent; he can denounce oppression and misrule, but all he can *do* is to weep for an old pauper's death and console a child by telling him the old man is in heaven.[68] What Wordsworth himself could do was dwindling to little more.

By 1806 he was rationalizing the failure of the Revolution into one leading idea: the men of his generation had committed the sin of hubris by their 'proud and most presumptuous confidence In the transcendent wisdom of the age', when really they were no better than their fathers, nor their age wiser than any before it.[69] The answer to Wordsworth's view is that men in his day had in fact gone beyond all their predecessors, and with the help of science and industry got on to higher ground from which more of the universe past, present and to come was discernible. Wordsworth would not have admitted this: for him the sky was still 'unvoyageable',[70] when balloons had begun to rise into it. All he could see of that 'new and unforeseen creation', machine industry, was the 'vice, misery and disease' it produced.[71] He missed the good side because he had no faith in men's ability to control what they had created. He knew nothing of factory workers, and even when he had asserted most ardently the survival of virtue in the rustic poor, he had been thinking too much of passive resistance to life, too little of active control of circumstances. He saw industry turning more and more of the country into an arena of blind, brutish forces, men and machines almost equally inhuman, equally intractable to intelligence. Effort to remodel society seemed futile. The problems he was setting himself to wrestle with were more than ever insoluble. He could not even bring them really together. Margaret, the dead woman of Book I, and the embittered rebel of Book II, remained in separate worlds. Their troubles could not be cured separately; mass poverty and intellectual isolation could only be overcome with and through each other, in the process of social advance. The duality of Wordsworth's thinking ran through all his experience: self and mankind, people and law, soul and body, freedom and wealth, intuition and logic, Mary Hutchinson and Annette Vallon, the mountains of Cumberland and the Mountain of Paris: and from now on the dividing walls were to grow thicker and higher.[72]

Wordsworth could not turn away and luxuriate in 'world-excluding groves' and 'voluptuous unconcern'. Only now the idle hedonism he despised included any utopian kind of poetry made up 'to improve the scheme Of Man's Existence, and recast the world'.[73] His problems were really coming down to this: Life being what it was and must be, was it worth living, or should men give themselves up to despair? If fate could not be bent to their will, it must be a question of men bending to the will of fate. In Book IV (sketched, with a further part of Book III, in the same year, 1806) he groped towards an answer in terms of a philosophy just at the point of hardening into a religion: belief in providence was the one 'adequate support',[74] since the world as seen and felt by man was inexplicable. With this answer the debate hung fire, and Wordsworth was for long at a standstill. He had conjured up spirits he could not exorcise. Meanwhile he went on sinking into deeper abstractions from life. How far he was drifting away from any sense of identity (not of sympathy) with the people can be seen in his essay on them, addressed to an archdeacon, where he reviewed their educational needs with benevolent detachment.[75] Another essay was on epitaphs and immortality. In his poetry he reached the furthest degree of isolation, or mid channel between his former and his later self, in *The White Doe of Rylstone* (winter 1807–8), in which his quietism hardened into what Harper calls an 'almost oriental renunciation', and his poetry declined to what Jeffrey called, nearly as fairly, 'a state of low and maudlin imbecility'.[76]

From the North Pole all roads run south, and after his 1808 freezing-point (and the interlude of the Spanish war) Wordsworth could only begin sliding from despair of progress towards distrust of progress. For himself he was not only accepting his isolation but making a virtue of it; when he took up *The Excursion* again he was always pausing in the poem to congratulate himself on his cloistered seclusion from a world whose soil was 'rank with all unkindness',[77] and he could indulge the thought that 'in these disordered times' it might be well for a few men, 'from faction sacred' – impartial philosophers – to resume the life the ancient anchorites once led.[78] Inevitably, he carried the poem on by deepening its religious side. He wanted to fill the gap he had left between earth and heaven, and he filled it chiefly with a collection of stories from the Grasmere churchyard. The germ of this theme of the graves can be found near the beginning of 'The Brothers', where the village pastor remarks that he could make a 'strange round' of stories out of the graves he is looking at. Wordsworth had forgotten little in these years, but he had not learned enough. This second part of his poem bears some analogy with *Paradise Lost*, and its spiritual ascent and poetical descent from hell to heaven. If the first part stands like a sombre sphinx staring out across the nineteenth century, the second is a sand-heap half burying it. Yet even now, in these last few years remaining to his inspiration, Wordsworth is not less than Archangel ruined; his 'creeping' tale, to use his own simile, still catches every now and then 'The colours of the sun'.[79]

In its outward forms the poem he was writing was still of the people, democratic. Wordsworth did not shrink from proclaiming his belief in 'the aristocracy of nature'[80] by confronting the polite world with a philosophical poem (costing two guineas) whose Socrates was a retired Scots pedlar, like his creator an 'advocate of humble life'.[81] Yet the choice of 'nature's unambitious underwood'[82] for his main theme was bringing him round by a back door to reaction. Contenting himself with the kind of ideas that could be supposed intelligible to humble virtue, fatigued with the toil of searching for undiscoverable truth, he was coming to acquiesce in the necessity of ignorance. From here it was only a step to the obscurantist notion that 'the lowly class' whose station exempted them from doubts or questionings, as they pursued 'The narrow avenue of daily toil', were really the luckiest.[83] The 'lowly class' would have enough troubles without those of the intellect; such troubles as befell Margaret. On her fate Wordsworth had pondered for years, and it preyed on his mind the more morbidly because he could find no practical answer to it. Religious history is full of examples of how simply feeling sorry for the poor breeds reactionary attitudes. It was only 'natural wisdom', Wordsworth concluded, not to let the mind dwell too long on irremediable calamity.[84] The only remedy, and the only lesson a sage could teach, was resignation.

Margaret's cottage stood by itself on an 'open moorland',[85] out of sight of either landlord and merchant to oppress or fellow workers to defend. Wordsworth had not forgotten that there was 'misrule' on the earth, whose nations groaned under their 'unthinking masters'.[86] But by now these rulers had receded into an indistinct distance. Every breath of social conflict had been hermetically excluded. There was only heaven above, misery below, philosophy looking on. Wordsworth laid great store by

> . . . the line of comfort that divides
> Calamity, the chastisement of Heaven,
> From the injustice of our brother men;[87]

his Wanderer, journeying from village to village, had been wont to point out this line to poor men chafing under their misfortunes, and thus help to allay social discontent. From this it was easy to drop little by little into the habit of thinking of all human ills as due to providence, and losing sight of what was wrong with society. In order to cherish this comfort Wordsworth had to remove the towns from his field of vision (though by another contradiction he saw their wealth as necessary for beating Napoleon and keeping England great and free), and in effect most of the countryside too, because there also, as the Solitary insisted, conditions were deplorable. The 'old domestic morals' were 'Fled utterly! or only to be found In a few fortunate retreats like this'.[88] In Lakeland poverty could still be thought of as 'wholesome', because it kept temptation away and made men more sensible of their need of help from above,[89] while the 'true equality' of virtue was accessible to all; the rustic benefited from his few and simple wants also in learning from them 'patience and sublime content'.[90] This is a point of view congenial to landlords and bishops. There is a *facilis descensus* from praise of the poor to praise of poverty. But Lakeland's 'fortunate retreat' was itself shrinking and decaying. Wordsworth turned instinctively now, for its soul and centre, to the graveyard, an inmost sanctuary where history could not penetrate. Here were true peace, equality, fraternity, with no tombstone or monument to make one man different from another, and the justice of heaven. All that Wordsworth had once hoped for on earth now stood in his mind as 'the sublime attractions of the grave'.[91]

Hence the long collection of churchyard anecdotes. Like those of the old pauper in Book II, and of the lonely couple in the mountain cottage in Book V, they are mostly, as the Fenwick notes show, true stories. Some of them had been written years earlier, in the same Lyrical Ballad mood whose errors were now magnified into a system; the seeds of this melancholy harvest had long been sprouting in Wordsworth's mind.

In his case-book, as in the graveyard itself, the dead lie indiscriminately, but they can be arranged to illustrate four propositions.

First and foremost, a quiet country life is the best for moulding character. Half a dozen of the fifteen cases fall under this heading. The restless clergyman (Wordsworth's old crony, Mr Simpson) had resented his banishment to a small country cure, but it had preserved him from frivolity or vice. It shows how much the family bond had replaced all others for Wordsworth that he counts it to providence for righteousness, instead of complaining of the state of medical science, that this clergyman and his whole family all died within a few months, and thus were not separated for long. Then we have a model rustic, a fine sturdy intelligent young fellow, leader of the local volunteers. He was buried amid the patriotic regrets of the whole valley, which seems to make Wordsworth view the tale as a striking vindication of his main argument: for him now, little but death could bring men's hearts together in such a flow of feeling. Equally characteristic of him, though less edifying, is the case of the mining prospector, a rugged individualist who succeeded by years of lonely persistence, and then drank himself to death. A neighbour still alive, but soon to join the happy band, is a poor, aged, cheerful labourer, so close to nature as to be barely distinguishable from the animal kingdom – just rational enough to attend church.[92]

Secondly, with Heaven's grace the worst trials can be borne without repining. A man deaf from infancy, and a blind man, are the examples. Wordsworth has the archaic thought of God sending blindness as a parable to teach sublime truths.[93]

Thirdly, time and patience soften misfortunes, such as the loss of wife or child, or disappointment in love.[94]

Lastly, sin can be atoned for by suffering and repentance. We hear of a talented, strong-minded girl who, cramped and thwarted by her narrow rut, grew into a hard and avaricious woman. Wordsworth dwells, not on a pathetic waste of human promise, but on resignation achieved before death under stress of illness and unhappiness. A story – the longest of all – of a poor village Gretchen he tells with sympathy, tolerance, and delicacy; but it is all in the mode of a bygone age: the girl is to forgive her betrayer, turn her thoughts upward, lose her infant, and die of a broken heart. The whole affair is an instance of heaven's kindness – a good specimen of the sort of heart-rending cheerfulness that Wordsworth is working himself up to.[95]

Wordsworth was trying to answer great public questions from the data of private experience. He offered his stories as 'solid facts', 'plain pictures' of real human beings.[96] These beings were indeed too, too solid, with none of the 'visionary' character of such a figure as the Leechgatherer; Wordsworth's imagination breathed little life into them. He was seeing the people as a collection of halt, lame, or senile individuals, each creeping on his separate way and groaning in his separate key; victims of spiritual or physical infirmity who seem to stand in place of the social disorders that Wordsworth no longer wanted to think of – but that broke in on him again in the final Book in spite of himself. Compared with the eccentrics of the 1798 *Lyrical Ballads* they are flesh and blood folk; compared with the Michael of 1800 they are feeble, ailing creatures.

Wordsworth keeps them as far apart as possible, like a careful nurse separating children so that they can do one another no harm.[97] Deafness, blindness, old age reinforce his barriers. The prospector digs alone; the quarryman is never heard of at work with his fellows, but only in the inaccessible nook where his old wife spends her eventless days with her peaceful pious thoughts.[98] Wordsworth's rustics have become as solitary as himself, or the sole-sitting lady of the lake, or the shepherd whom his fancy calls up whenever he thinks of Greece, alone in the hills with his meditations and concocting Greek mythology out of them.[99] The one positive quality left in these characters is a dumb, tenacious, peasant endurance: even this, since the class as a whole is beginning to disintegrate, requires in its members more of a religious substitute for the old cement. They all die without any resentment against their fate; the reader, contemplating their patience, is to learn to feel ashamed of his own discontents.[100] Religious consolation for helpless suffering had been one more of the ideas floating loose in the *Descriptive Sketches* twenty years before.[101]

Wordsworth had not turned into a 'reactionary', but as a discouraged 'progressive' he had come near the brink, and would in fact tumble over before long. An artist who does not feel the people as a force positively on his side may soon come to feel them as something against him. The people need allies, not patrons; to gain allies they need strength. Wordsworth was too little conscious of their collective strength, too much of their individual weakness. The weakness, not the strength, of the people frightens an artist in such a position as his, by conjuring up in his fears a blind, anarchical monster incapable of rational purpose. Wordsworth in 1812 was in fear of social war breaking out in the towns.[102] Near the close of *The Excursion* he advocated universal education, as a universal right, but also as a means of counteracting the 'ignorance' that was breeding discontent,[103] a highly illiberal notion, exactly opposite to the principle of learning 'from the People'. Growing away from them, he was growing closer – there being no third direction in politics – to their masters.

As always, excessive concentration on the individual self had bred in him its counterpart, a morbid sense of the helpless frailty of the individual amid the 'deserts infinite' of time and space.[104] Deserts, an old image with him, were taking on a more sinister quality, as of barbarism menacing the little oasis of civilization. He saw them within the soul as well as all round it. A favourite adjective of his – *dread* – came to him instinctively now when he peered into the 'dark foundations' of man's nature, embedded in a gulf 'Fearfully low';[105] as low, we might add for him, as memories of guilty love, or the depths of the Faubourg St Antoine. In 1818 he would be waking the echoes of Keswick with warnings of the approach of 'A FEROCIOUS REVOLUTION'.[106] By then he only

wanted the people to lie peacefully in the graveyard where he had taken leave
of them, while he, hiding behind his mountains like a King of Prussia behind
his bodyguard of giants, continued to play the part of poet of nature.

At the end of *The Excursion* Wordsworth dodged all the problems he had
raised, culminating in the final book in the passionate denunciation of
industrial society (for which we may read capitalism), by going out on the lake
for a picnic with the charming clergyman and his family: not a bad forecast of
how the rest of his life was to be spent. He never continued the poem, as he had
intended: it had been too much for him. As an essay in consolation it is
laborious taskwork; as a monument to the pessimism of modern man it is
incomparable. It is also the funeral monument of Wordsworth's genius, to
which by now 'Night is than day more acceptable', sleep than waking, death
than sleep.[107] Its greatest passage of all has a frozen majesty as of fate answering
the Revolution –

> Amid the groves, under the shadowy hills,
> The generations are prepared; the pangs,
> The internal pangs, are ready; the dread strife
> Of poor humanity's afflicted will
> Struggling in vain with ruthless destiny.[108]

Settling in Grasmere, Wordsworth had still been hopeful of a 'milder day' to
come.[109] But he settled down to look at life through the eyes of a moribund
class and a decaying order, and his mind shared in their decline; he came to
resemble the sentinels in his poem, set 'between two armies' in the chill night
with nothing better than 'their own thoughts to comfort them'.[110] He no longer
saw life in the Revolutionary crucible, all its elements melting, running, re-
combining, and he no longer felt as if poetry were an active part in an
apocalyptic transformation of the world. Things cooled down into separate,
inert blocks, fundamentally because he came to see the structure of society as a
rigid hierarchy of classes. Human nature, having no warmth of action to
transform it, was unalterable; duty abstract and changeless; suffering irremediable.[111] No room was left for imagination as an active, working force. It
came down to merely laying a varnish of verse over a worm-eaten surface.
After 1814 scarcely anything but the deaths of those he had loved could rouse
his imagination again, because only death could knock holes in the walls round
him and let him see out.

It was not that he was turning into a bad man. In 1815 Haydon found him a
man he could 'worship as a purified spirit'.[112] At Rydal Mount bread and cheese
were kept ready for all who knocked. Nor was he habitually, after this date, the
frightened reactionary of 1818 and 1831; he mellowed into a cheerful,
loquacious, amiable, humane and reasonable householder, not averse to
cautious reforms. But the bread-and-cheese of charity was no diet for the muses,

nor timid reformism breath for the trumpets that sing to battle. Wordsworth suffered for intellectual, not moral, errors. An artist has to understand as much as to feel.

Though Wordsworth's finest work still lay ahead of him when he came to Grasmere, nearly all of it was to be about his own or the social past. Before long he was troubled with fears that the lease on which he held his poetic gift was running out, like a peasant's lease of his farm. He began writing a lament on the vanishing of something from his world: rainbow and rose came and went, but the 'celestial light' that had touched common things like a dream shone no more.[113] As so often happened with him, he stopped for several years – he could not find out what it was that he had lost. Then in 1806 in his deepening isolation he added the famous stanzas on childhood and a life before birth. Caught in the 'prison-house' of life he clung to half-imaginary memories of his earliest years, and saw them fading like a lost inheritance; he looked further back still, into an earlier existence, and credited to it the sensations that can only belong to man in an elaborated society. That he was weaving private myth out of public reality he might have guessed by recalling those lines in *Descriptive Sketches* on the tradition, still handed down in the Alps from father to son, of an ancient golden age free from labour and hardship. His prison-house was a divided society, the 'fen of stagnant waters'[114] that was his England; his poem achieved its immense power through its tragic sense of the loss and laying waste of human value by this captivity. His infancy, about which heaven lay, was the infancy of mankind, of which a relic lingered in the primitive democracy and fraternity of Grasmere. Not the individual child playing with its toys, but the human race grappling with its tasks, could claim those lofty and inextinguishable gifts, those 'truths' of an early unbroken social bond that men in later ages must 'toil' painfully to rediscover, and could hear the 'mighty waters' of history.

A poem that should have been a hymn to humanity and a splendid memorial of the Revolution turned into an enigma, almost a splendid absurdity, because Wordsworth could now only think of the mind's contact with other minds in social life as cramping and strangling, instead of moulding and fertilizing; because he could see no road forward out of a dismal present, but only a road receding into the mists of a bygone age. It was left to Shelley and Marx to rebuild his 'imperial palace' on new foundations, in the future instead of in the past.

Since Marx, the problems that baffled Wordsworth have begun to be, in principle, soluble. Any poetry that neglects to try and solve them will go wrong, not so much by being untrue, as by being irrelevant, and therefore in danger of being ridiculous. There will not be another great poet who has not learned much from Marx. Marxism also has much to learn, that it has not yet learned, from poetry.

## Postscript (1973)

That Marxism and poetry both stand in need of each other's aid seems to me, after nearly twenty years, more true than ever, but its fulfilment harder than ever. In 1954 I was writing as a member of a party; today as an independent Marxist I am more conscious of the obstacles – which Communist parties seemed to have found no means to overcome – in the way of any genuine coming together of writers or scholars with 'the people'. This pre-Marxist and less uncomplimentary name for 'the masses' links Wordsworth with the long tradition, much studied of late, of populism, still an active force in the newly developing lands. In the idea of 'the people' there have always lurked ambiguities and contradictions, many of which revealed themselves, as he might have recognized more clearly, in the French Revolution. But the 'masses', or the 'proletariat', of Marxist thinking have also turned out to be far less simple and comprehensible than we used to suppose.

Since 1955, when my essay was written, the Cultural Revolution has sought to unite thinking individual and mass mind in a newer, more organic fashion, and this accounts for much of its appeal to the West, particularly to the student movement it helped to generate. Whatever the political value of that grand upheaval, however, it would not seem to have had much value for the arts, or 'culture' in any traditional sense; rather it seems to have called on artists and intellectuals to become good Chinese by ceasing to care about being themselves. Wordsworth's 'peasant' style would have been highly acceptable to Mao, but not that of *The Prelude*, nor the themes Wordsworth treated in either medium. There is peril for the writer in being cut off from popular feeling, but there is at least an equal artistic risk of being sucked too deeply into a movement, of being reduced to the role of propagandist, first for a cause, then for a party, finally for a leader. An intellectual who seeks to lose himself in the mass is too much like the mystic who craves to lose himself in the world-spirit, to be a lump of salt dissolving in the ocean.

In England in the 1790s there was more than my essay allowed for of a radical 'movement', and Wordsworth's retreat from London was in one way an instinctive flight from its demands on him. It could not be easy for him to find a congenial place in any movement, because of his autarchic temperament, his impatience of routine, his loafing propensity; the same qualities, bred by a boyhood in the hills and by a nascent sense of destinies of his own, that prevented him from working hard at college, or choosing any profession. (The one he had a hankering for – the army – was the one which would have imposed on him the most constraint, the discipline he could not impose on himself.) But for these qualities we should not have had his poetry, but they made also for the self-absorption that was to startle so many who knew him, and would later help to drag him into Toryism. It would then be his ironic nemesis to have to worry his head over petty official papers and the distribution of stamps in Westmorland.

Ideally a poet should be a man of action too. The French Revolution, while it charged Wordsworth's mind with so much electric fire, also left him with haunting doubts of the validity of action as a means to change the world. As a means to preserve it, he could come to believe in action in its conventional, respectable form of war; it is characteristic of the freakish logic of history which transposed so many of his convictions into their opposites that from the condemnation of war in his early poems he arrived at the doctrine of 'Carnage is God's daughter'. But for Wordsworth in his own person, as for any writer, to *act* should mean action through the practice of his art. For this he required an audience, one both sympathetic and critical, and responsive on both a literary and a social plane. His isolation from 'the people', which in the end reduced him to a tinkling cymbal, began as isolation from any such reading public. He could not write for a peasantry, even if he tried briefly to borrow its language. He could for a while, like Shelley, by withdrawing into solitude write for a half- or more than half-imaginary audience of ardent young listeners, men and women worthy of his highest inspiration. It was for them, with Coleridge as their fittingly elusive representative, that *The Prelude* was written but it is one of the astonishing facts of literary history that he was to die with his greatest poem still unknown. Appropriately enough it came out at last, in 1850, close after another thunder-clap of European revolution, and partly no doubt for that reason struck readers as desperately radical.

That Wordsworth was able to write so splendidly for ten years, and this poem above all, is more notable than his subsequent decay. Unpolitical admirers, among them his latest and excellent biographer Mrs Moorman,[115] have continued to think of his genius as awakened and sustained by withdrawal to the peaceful countryside. Clearly this leaves the later decay more inexplicable, but even for the years of inspiration it fails to do justice to what 'nature' meant to Wordsworth. As a portrayer of scenery he was far from being a pioneer; he marks the culmination of a long English development of landscape verse and painting. His innovation, and what made him great then and gives him meaning now, was his attempt to trace interacting influences of nature and society on man's being. He was not withdrawing to the countryside in order to shut his eyes to the human condition, like many 'nature poets' before and since, but to seek a fresh comprehension of it. His success was, indeed, limited. Racedown belonged to the same county of Dorset as Tolpuddle and its martyrs of the next generation. Wordsworth would not have guessed at this banding together of miserable farm labourers against their tyrants. He knew too little about a class which had a smaller place in France, hardly any in Lakeland, and it must be said that he made too little effort to learn about it. His was the same humanitarian sympathy for the unresisting poor as for the suffering animals that appear in the *Lyrical Ballads* beside his human waifs and strays. Peter Bell's donkey never takes it into its head to kick its brutal master. Fellow-feeling with the waifs and strays came all the easier because Wordsworth himself, having thrown off the shackles of convention and respectability, was a kind of outcast. It has been remarked of Orwell and his tramps and destitutes that such figures, unlike the working class as a mass, find a ready response in the romantic middle-class mind by virtue of being unattached atoms, 'casual, masterless, integral, spontaneous men'.[116]

Removal to Cumberland meant withdrawal to a quite different social climate, a fortress protected by mountains and by their inhabitants, like himself sturdy individualists but with strong social ties. When William and Dorothy set up house at Grasmere in 1799 they were founding a miniature utopia, a settlement in the wilderness such as Coleridge and Southey had been planning to found in America. Wordsworth was hitting on the right place for it on his own doorstep, in his native hills which he felt a sort of shame at having ever abandoned, like old Michael's son, for the distractions of the busy world. Here he had the freedom and solitude necessary to him, and could still have hope and confidence in mankind, even if now this was a somewhat disembodied or symbolic mankind, a race of past or future more than of the present. He had belonged to the left, and would later belong to the right; in his great years his mind was close to the centre of a vortex of conflicting currents, and it was this vital involvement in Britain's, and still more in Europe's, contradictions, this state of being neither partisan nor indifferent looker-on, that lifted his genius to the heights.

Irreconcilable things outside forced him to postpone from year to year his grand philosophical poem: he was only able to write this, or begin it with *The Excursion*, when he was clear of his maelstrom, a party spokesman once more. Writing *The Prelude* he was driven inward, to search within himself for clues to the mysteries of man's private and social self. There was egotism in his laborious tracking of his own mental growth, but he was at the same time finding a fresh identity between himself and his 'people', humanity on the long pilgrimage of which his own secret history seemed to him an illustration. In what was healthy in himself he could proclaim the work of nature allied with a right social order, whose blessings he still thought could be extended to all, and mankind thus regenerated. The poetry of *The Prelude* stands as proof that he was not altogether wrong.

Wordsworth's dalesmen as he saw them were, like his leechgatherer, in part figments of his imagination; they were in any case a 'reactionary' class, in the sense in which Marxism has – often too hastily – used the word of an obsolete social group impeding the march of history by its unwillingness to disappear. In this light his later desire to preserve England's landed aristocracy might be called a morbidly logical replacement of his earlier desire to keep its peasant proprietors and shepherds on their farms. It had some affinity with his choice of a Scots pedlar, a straggler from his old poems of common folk, to expound the conservative philosophy of *The Excursion*, and this combination of demo-

cratic facade and reactionary core entitles him to count as a forerunner of
Tory democracy. Another Scot of humble origin, Carlyle, was soon taking it up;
Disraeli would be a third recruit from far away. It has been pointed out that
radical embers were still aglow in him as late as 1809, and what in the end
pushed him into panic and reaction was the rioting of 1810 and similar
symptoms of mass unrest.[117] His fits of patriotic excitement about the long-
drawn war were intermittent: the menace on the home front, the newly
spawned English proletariat, frightened him more than Napoleon, because he
knew of no answer to it. His 'people' was turning into something alien, cut off
from all the old associations, a denizen of slum cellars instead of green hills, far
more unknowable than even the farm labourers of the south. If from now
onwards he was drifting further and further away from the people, it was he
who felt that he was being abandoned. His solitariness, which formerly helped
him to have faith in his fellow men, now helped to distort them into malignant,
inhuman shapes.

On a spring evening a year or two ago a knot of youngsters passing
Wordsworth's grave was to be heard grumbling comically about how he had
bored them at school. Yet ours is, for youth above all, an age of revolutionary
change, and no writer has ever expressed more vividly than the young
Wordsworth the sensation of drawing breath in such times. Literary criticism, as
much accustomed as any other science to 'murder to dissect', must be credited
with robbing him of much of the political passion that belonged to his being, or
with failing to rediscover it after the long Victorian torpor. We may wonder
how different an image we should have of him, and how differently English
poetry might have evolved, if *The Prelude* had come out in those decades of
ferment to which the younger Romantics belonged, and *The Excursion* been
kept locked up instead. It has never come to be fully grasped as the finest
political poem ever written, of which it may be said that to be able to feel its
climactic passages with all their vibrations is to belong truly to European
history, to the onward-moving conflict of the centuries. Scarcely ever has
Toryism had better cause than in the long burial alive of this poem to
congratulate itself on a damaging blow at England's soul – to call it so for want
of a better word. It is typical of our situation that the richest of languages has
not yet found a better expression, 'cultural life' being the private domain of the
academies, 'spiritual life' of the churches.

There may at present be more prospect of Wordsworth the conservative
being reprieved by Wordsworth the conservationist. He could not rescue the
English peasantry, but he went on trying to save England's scenery, which we
today, stifling and suffocating in our monstrous heaps of concrete, are being
compelled to regard as one of the planet's precious and irreplaceable resources,
daily ravaged and looted for private profit. Wordsworth thought too readily of
the cures he found for his own spiritual ills, seclusion and 'wise passiveness' and
visionary moorlands, as cures for society too. In the longer run, two centuries

after the start of the Industrial Revolution, we can perceive more of practical social wisdom in the gospel he took over from the physicians and gave a fresh meaning, of the *vis medicatrix naturae*, nature's healing power. Even the bundle of reluctances that kept Wordsworth from winning college prizes and throwing himself into a career, while vaguely dedicating himself to a *mission*, takes on a novel aspect today. 'Getting and spending, we lay waste our powers', he complained to his contemporaries: in our more prosaic speech he was opting out of the rat-race, the pursuit of rewards and dignities to which the rest of the Wordsworth clan – a rising middle class in itself – devoted themselves so ardently.

When Wordsworth accused his generation of 'presumptuous confidence' in its own superior wisdom, he was condemning the illusions of 1789 in almost the same words as Metternich, but his charge lay also, and far more justly, against the power and ambition of a greedy and soulless capitalism; and the two things were, more than he ever understood, parts of the same historical process, the better and worse sides of the same penny. Turning his back on industrialism, he turned away from progress, but he repudiated also the capitalism in which Marx too was to find only present ill, though future good. The social patterns that Wordsworth fell back on in his own environment for bulwarks against its spirit of blind competition, its thirst for *getting on* at all costs, were primitive and archaic: the peasant eking out a bare living from his narrow plot, the family keeping itself, and keeping itself together, by cottage industry. He over-idealized them, especially cottage industry which he made a cult very much like Gandhi's of the spinning-wheel, failing to realize what crippling toil it often implied.

In a larger historical vista, none the less, these old-world modes of livelihood can be seen as enshrining values, transmuted and preserved in Wordsworth's poetry, that we today feel painfully the lack of. Marxism has concerned itself too exclusively with their 'reactionary' features. Already in 1955 I felt misgivings, some of them prompted by Wordsworth, about the collectivization of land being pushed on in Eastern Europe. Events since then have shown one Communist regime after another compelled to come to terms with a tenacious peasant individualism. This is not merely, though it may be largely, kulak selfishness and greed: as against the anonymity of big mechanized agriculture it has a kinship with the craftsman's satisfaction in work done by himself, or by his small group. In Western factories in the past few years the workman's impulse to make something himself has collided more and more with the juggernaut conveyor-belt that reduces him to a mere cog. A search has begun for less automatic methods of production, to restore autonomy to small working teams, and resurrect the old skill of the handicraftsman on a higher level. This is a dilemma confronting big industry, whether capitalist or socialist. Socialism simply as 'public ownership of the means of production' cannot put an end to the intricate problems of relationship between individual and collective, of which that between artist and people is another instance.

Wordsworth would have had need of an Ariadne's thread to guide him through the labyrinth of such a span of history as the one he lived through. The historian who tries to trace his poetic and political evolution has need of it equally. And both verse and virtue, such as the stoic endurance Wordsworth shared through long years of neglect with his dalesmen, though they can only grow in very special soil, once grown escape from their points of origin in history and take on a wider significance. All these questions about Wordsworth still seem to me worth studying, perhaps more than ever before, because as an English poet he is second only to Shakespeare, and because we have reached a time when what is authentic in his poetry both of revolution and of preservation has potent meanings, somehow to be reconciled.

# Notes

1. 'What Byron saw already – that Pope was a greater poet than Byron himself or any of his contemporaries – is now generally recognized. The Romantics are now under a cloud . . .' (S. Spender, *Shelley*, London 1952, p. 44.)

2. *The Prelude*, II, 219. This and all later quotations from this poem are from the text of 1805 edited by E. de Selincourt, 1933. All references to the long poems are to the book and the line.

3. D. Bush, in G.T. Dunklin, ed., *Wordsworth Centenary Studies*, Oxford 1951, p. 9.

4. With this work Blake's *Songs* might of course be coupled, and the resemblances and contrasts between these two poets are highly instructive.

5. Both the 1793 and the later versions are printed in the Oxford one-volume edition of Wordsworth, 1904. All passages referred to here occur in the earlier text, if not in both. The earlier text is often the less polished; but Coleridge was to say of it: 'Seldom, if ever, was the emergence of an original poetic genius above the literary horizon more evidently announced.' (*Biographia Literaria*, 1817, IV); cf. De Quincey's appreciation, in *Reminiscences of the English Lake Poets*, Everyman edn, pp. 129–30. G.M. Harper remarks that here already Wordsworth was describing common people with a novel freedom from condescension (*William Wordsworth, His Life, Works and Influence*, 1916, vol. I, p. 95).

6. *The Prelude*, IX, 509 ff. The French Revolution and Wordsworth's interpretations of it are among the relevant topics which there is only space to mention briefly in this essay. He was a sort of 'Girondin', but his 'Apology' of 1793 could be at least as well described as 'Jacobin' in temper. In general, he may be forgiven for not having fully understood an upheaval whose complex forces we are still trying to understand today, after a hundred and fifty years.

7. The 'Evening Walk' was a rewriting of the still earlier 'Vale of Esthwaite', and the picture of the forlorn woman was originally borrowed from a poem by Langhorne. (See H. Darbishire, *The Poet Wordsworth*, Oxford 1950, p 20; E. de Selincourt, *Wordsworthian and Other Studies*, Oxford 1947, pp. 15 ff.) For criticisms of the 'psychoanalytical' view that this theme was inspired by nothing more than a guilty conscience in Wordsworth himself, see W.L. Sperry, *Wordsworth's Anti-Climax*, 1935, p. 95; H. Sergeant, *The Cumberland Wordsworth*, London 1950, pp. 28 ff.

8. *The Early Letters of William and Dorothy Wordsworth, 1787-1805*, ed. E. de Selincourt, 1938, pp. 114, 119.

9. *The Prelude*, X, 648.

10. *The Prelude*, X, 275. 'Wordsworth, as the course of his life shows, had not a real confidence in himself. He was curiously compounded of timorousness and courage.' (Harper, vol. II, p. 323; he emphasizes that Wordsworth was 'the most political of all our great poets' except Milton; vol. I, p. ix.) This inner uncertainty in Wordsworth is to be connected with his isolation from any organized movement.

11. *The Prelude*, IV, 200 ff., 400 ff.

12. 'Lines left upon a Seat in a Yew-tree', *Lyrical Ballads*, I, and cancelled stanzas of 'Guilt and Sorrow'. (See Selincourt, *Wordsworthian and Other Studies*, pp. 27–9.)

13. *The Prelude*, XII, 71, 98–9. Cf. Robespierre: 'I bear witness . . . that in general there is no justice or goodness like that of the people . . . and that among the poor . . . are found honest and upright souls, and a good sense and energy that one might seek long and in vain among a class that looks down upon them.' (Speech of 22 August 1791; see J.M. Thompson, *Robespierre*, 1935, p. 168.)

14. *The Prelude*, XII, 312 ff.

15. According to Wordsworth's note on this poem (see *The Prose Works of Willam Wordsworth*, ed. A.B. Grosart, 1876, III, p. 10) the story of the 'Female Vagrant' forming the second part was taken from life. The poem was begun in 1791, completed in 1794, and re-worked later; for instance in Germany in 1799 Wordsworth was thinking of inserting another improbable coincidence (Selincourt, *The Early Letters*, p. 223). It was not published as a whole till 1842. With its range of ideas may be compared that of the *Religious Musings*, 1794, of Coleridge, whose development was in many ways parallel to Wordsworth's.

16. This version of 1798, as the 'Female Vagrant' stood in *Lyrical Ballads*, was later somewhat toned down.

17. J.C. Shairp, p. xvii.

18. Selincourt, *The Early Letters* p. 148. The passage goes on: 'their cottages are shapeless structures . . . indeed they are not at all beyond what might be expected in savage life'. In many parts of Dorset whole parishes were being engrossed into one or two hands, and this 'fatal blow' was reducing the small farmer to a labourer, considered by the wealthy farmer as 'a mere vassal'. (J. Claridge, *General View of the Agriculture in the County of Dorset . . .* 1793, pp. 22–3.)

19. See the lines from *The Borderers* which Wordsworth later prefixed to *The White Doe of Rylstone*.

20. *The Borderers*, p. 1036.

21. Selincourt, *The Early Letters*, pp. 176 ff., containing a draft of the poem in the form described here.

22. 'Expostulation and Reply', *Lyrical Ballads* I; 'Peter Bell', prologue.

23. 'The Idle Shepherd Boys', *Lyrical Ballads*, II, cf. 'A Poet's Epitaph', ibid.

24. 'Expostulation and Reply'; 'The Tables Turned'; 'Anecdote for Fathers'; 'Lines written at a small distance . . .; 'Lines written in early Spring'; 'Tintern Abbey'.

25. It is hard to agree that 'the prevailing notes are exultant and happy' (Darbyshire, p. 34). Wordsworth was soon finding fault with 'The Female Vagrant' (see Selincourt, *The Early Letters*, pp. 268 ff.); perhaps, though not ostensibly, for political reasons.

26. *The Prelude*, VIII, 531.

27. See notes to *Lyrical Ballads*, and Selincourt, *The Early Letters*, p. 295.

28. In the preface he tries to rationalize in psychological terms the effect of the curse.

29. The assumptions he was working on belonged to the medley of progressive ideas, 'mingled somewhat vaguely in the brain of the average English "Jacobin"', that are described by C. Brinton in *The Political Ideas of the English Romanticists*, 1926, p. 29 (cf. K. MacLean, *Agrarian Age: A Background for Wordsworth*, 1950, pp. 100–1). Cf. Hazlitt on Wordsworth in *The Spirit of the Age*, Bohn's standard Library, 1904, p. 152): 'the political changes of the day were the model on which he formed and conducted his poetical experiments'; and Stopford Brooke, *Theology in the English Poets*, 1874, pp. 166–7.

30. 'Lines written in early Spring'.

31. *The Prelude*, VIII, 806.

32. *The Life of George Crabbe*, by his son, World's Classics edn, 1932, p. 164, shows that Crabbe reciprocated the criticism.

33. *The Prelude*, XII, 161 ff.

34. 'The Tables Turned'.

35. Cf. 'Guilt and Sorrow', stanza LVII.

36. See Grosart, vol. I, p. 336. Literacy was widespread in Lakeland; and there was the example of Burns. L. Abercrombie (*The Art of Wordsworth*, Oxford 1952, p. 78) recalls that *We are Seven* was sold in the countryside as a broadsheet. Engels (*The Condition of the Working Class in England in 1844*, trans. by F.K. Wischnewetzky, 1892, pp. 239–40) believed that Shelley and Byron were read chiefly by the proletariat. Cf. Scott: 'I am persuaded both children and the lower class of

readers hate books which are written *down* to their capacity.' (Sir H. Grierson, *Sir Walter Scott, Bart.,* 1938, p. 272.)

37. Selincourt, *The Early Letters*, p. 295.

38. 'Tintern Abbey'.

39. See G.H. Healey, *Wordsworth's Pocket Notebook,* 1942, p. 65; cf. Lady Richardson's account of the celebration of his seventy-fourth birthday by all ranks (Grosart vol. III, p. 444). There is a heated condemnation of all the ideas of class struggle in Coleridge's *The Friend,* section I, essay 5.

40. *The Prelude,* II, 248 ff.; a passage suggested by a letter from Coleridge in 1799 (see note by Selincourt).

41. *The Prelude,* VIII, 152. The journal of the Scottish tour of 1803 shows much interest in society as well as scenery. The idea of retirement to cottage seclusion was an old one; cf. the 'Evening Walk', and a poem of 1794 to Mary Hutchinson (Selincourt, *Wordsworthian and Other Studies,* pp. 21–3).

42. Gray, quoted by W. Hutchinson, *History of the County of Cumberland,* 1794, p. 233n.

43. 'Poems on the Naming of Places', IV, *Lyrical Ballads,* II. Two of the first individuals in Grasmere who fixed his attention were a crippled workman and a paralytic (see *The Recluse,* appendix A in the edition of *The Excursion* by E. de Selincourt and H. Darbishire, Oxford 1949, pp. 329–30. All references to *The Excursion* are to this edition).

44. *The Prelude,* IX, 217 ff.

45. J. Housman, *A Topographical Description of Cumberland, Westmorland, Lancashire . . .,* 1800, pp. 103–5.

46. *The Recluse,* pp. 324–5.

47. Selincourt, *The Early Letters,* p. 236.

48. See e.g. 'Song for the Spinning-Wheel', 1812.

49. As, e.g. in 'The Waggoner', 1805.

50. *The Prelude,* VIII, 388; see this whole passage on shepherd life, and the long cancelled passage of *The Excursion* pp. 432 ff.

51. Even the woman begging on the roads in 'The Sailor's Mother', 1802 – drawn from life – had a bearing 'like a Roman matron's'.

52. Of forty-one poems altogether in volume II, twenty-five may be reckoned successful; but the improvement in quality is greater than this figure suggests.

53. Selincourt, *The Early Letters,* pp. 259–63; cf. p. 266, to Poole.

54. J. Bailey and G. Culley, *General View of the Agriculture of the County of Cumberland,* Board of Agriculture, 1794, p. 44. Cf. the story of Wordsworth's neighbours, the Greens (see the memoir by Dorothy, in E. de Selincourt, *Dorothy Wordsworth,* 1933, pp. 227 ff.) or that of the old woman of eighty-four in Portenscale who lived by spinning, scorned charity, and kept two guineas locked up for her funeral (Hutchinson, p. 158n). See also the Lakeland parish reports in Eden's *State of the Poor,* 1797, and on the effects of the price-fall here in the depression after 1815, *Agricultural State of the Kingdom,* Board of Agriculture, 1816, pp. 64–5.

55. Cf. 'Repentance', a poem of 1804 on a family 'frivolously' giving up its land: Wordsworth's note (Grosart, III, p. 58) shows that much of it was 'taken *verbatim* from the language' of the daleswoman concerned, Margaret Ashburner. Dorothy found it hard to get a servant, because 'the county is drained by the cotton works and the manufactories, and by the large towns whither they are tempted to go for great wages.' *The Letters of William and Dorothy Wordsworth, 1806–11,* E. de Selincourt ed. 1937, p. 26.

56. 'Advice to the Young', (Grosart, I, pp. 316–7); cf. in a letter of 1806 'a man of letters . . . ought to be severely frugal' (Selincourt, *Letters, 1806–11,* p. 60). Wordsworth may have thought of himself, as well as Milton, as 'almost single, uttering odious truth' *The Prelude,* III, 285).

57. Hutchinson, pp. 36–9; cf. Bailey and Culley, pp. II, 44 ff.; Housman, pp. 59–66. MacLean, p. 101, is one of the very few writers who have taken notice of this aspect of Lakeland. Elsewhere he points out the tendency of Wordsworth and the other 'rustic' poets 'to neglect the part the landlords and improvers had in creating distress' in the counties affected by the Agricultural Revolution (p. 38; cf. p. 95). The tale of injustice at the beginning of the 'Female Vagrant' had a Lakeland setting.

58. 'The land-owners are very numerous in Cumberland; the farms generally small . . . the people look very neat and clean.' (Cobbett, *Tour in Scotland and in the Four Northern Counties of England,* 1833, p. 245.)

59. Sonnets: 'Grief, thou hast lost . . .', 1819, and *To S.H.*, 1827; the note to the former (*Grosart*, III, p. 55) says 'I could write a treatise of lamentation upon the changes brought about among the cottages of Westmorland by the silence of the spinning wheel.' Wordsworth did not perhaps observe how immensely laborious the old cottage industry was. Wages in Kirkoswald parish, Cumberland, are 'very inconsiderable', we read: 'a woman must labour hard at her wheel 10 or 11 hours in the day, to earn 4d' (Eden, II, p. 84). In Cumwhitton parish none of the poor spent as much as 3d on a day's food (ibid., p. 74).

60. Mountains, he had written earlier, 'are good occasional society, but they will not do for constant companions' (Selincourt *The Early Letters*, p. 128). As Bowra says, the consolation he now found in a new attitude to nature could not solve his problems (C.M. Bowra, *The Romantic Imagination*, Oxford 1950, pp. 100–2). Cf. C Caudwell, *Illusion and Reality*, 1937, p. 98: 'Wordsworth's "Nature" is of course a Nature freed of wild beasts and danger by aeons of human work, a Nature in which the poet . . . lives on the products of industrialism . . .'.

61. Selincourt *The Early Letters*, p. 306. But there is no 'injustice' in volume II of the *Lyrical Ballads*.

62. 'At the Grave of Burns', 1803.

63. 'The Kitten and Falling Leaves', 1804.

64. *Grosart*, I, p. 322.

65. Wordsworth's interest in the affairs of Napoleonic Europe, and his new concept of nationalism, are not discussed here, for want of space, though they have a greater importance in his development.

66. On Mr Fawcett, the ostensible model for the Solitary, see Harper, vol. I, pp. 261–6. On the chronology of *The Excursion*, see Selincourt and Darbishire, pp. 369 ff.

67. *The Excursion* III, pp. 374–6. The passage originally belonged to 'The Tuft of Primrose', a lengthy sketch of 1808 (Selincourt and Darbishire, appendix C).

68. *The Excursion*, II, pp. 508–11; cf. III, pp. 983–6, on the futility of action. The Solitary began as a *political* figure only; his domestic misfortunes were a much later addition to Book III. (See notes, pp. 418–9.)

69. Ibid., II, pp. 235–6; IV, pp. 278 ff. and 418 ff. Pride was the 'false fruit' that had corrupted men (IV, pp. 289–93).

70. Ibid., V, p. 342.

71. Ibid., VIII, p. 90; VII, p. 854. Cf. H.L'A. Fausset, *The Lost Leader*, 1933, p. 205; by rejecting the Industrial Revolution altogether, 'he turned his back upon the ideas and forces which for good and evil were to determine human development during the next hundred years . . .'.

72. Hazlitt noticed in Wordsworth 'a total disunion and divorce of the faculties of the mind from those of the body' (*Lectures on the English Poets*, World's Classics edition, 1924, p. 203).

73. *The Excursion*, III, pp. 332 ff.

74. Ibid., IV, 10 ff.

75. *Grosart*, vol. I, pp. 335 ff., June 1808. In *The Excursion*, IX, p. 327, he was to appeal on behalf of the poor to 'the State's parental ear': *Grosart*, vol. I, p. 275, 1835.

76. Harper, vol. II, p. 155; A.B. Comparetti, *The White Doe of Rylstone*, 1940, pp. 253–4.

77. *The Excursion*, VI, 635.

78. Ibid., V, 29–36; the same idea pervades 'The Tuft of Primroses'.

79. Ibid., IV, 1122–26. Lamb called *The Excursion* 'a vast and magnificent poem' (letter to Southey, 20 October 1814, G. Peacock ed. *The Letters of Charles Lamb*, Everyman rev. edn, 1945, vol. I, p. 347); Keats thought it one of the three wonders of the age (letter to Haydon, 10 January 1818, M.B. Forman, ed. *The Letters of John Keats*, 4th edn, Oxford 1952, p. 78). Byron saw much talent wasted in it, like rain on rocks or sand (letter to Hunt, September–October 1815, R.G. Howarth ed. *The letters of George Gordon, 6th Lord Byron*, 1933, p. 134), and Hazlitt compared it neatly to Crusoe's canoe: 'noble materials thrown away' (Hazlitt, *Lectures on the English Poets*, pp. 240–1).

80. Wordsworth's note on I, p. 341.

81. *The Excursion*, II, 628. As Coleridge pointed out (*Biographia Literaria*, ch. XXII), this Socrates was a pedlar only in name. The 'democratic' character was becoming merely formal.

82. *The Excursion*, VI, 653.

83. Ibid., V, 593–601. (The Solitary makes a trenchant rejoinder to this rigmarole.) In the same vein is Wordsworth's note (*Grosart*, III, pp. 153–4) to *In the Firth of Clyde*, 1833.

84. *The Excursion*, I, 602.

85. Ibid., I, 26.

86. Ibid., I, 379–81.

87. Ibid., II, 72–4. The same distinction had been drawn in the *Apology* of 1793 (*Grosart* I, p. 8), but there the stress was on repelling human injustice.

88. *The Excursion*, VIII, 142–7; 236, 253–4.

89. Ibid., I, 306; IV, 786–9.

90. Ibid., IX, 248; IV, 818. Yet in practice Wordsworth saw that there were woeful differences between man and man, and vaguely attributed them to 'injustice' (IX, 253–4). Mary Lamb, reading *The Excursion*, felt 'it was doubtful whether a Liver in towns had a Soul to be Saved.' (*Pocock* p. 339; letter to Wordsworth, 9 August 1814).

91. *The Excursion*, IV, 238; cf. III, pp. 220–4, and 'George and Sarah Green', 1808, where the grave is seen to represent, in Wordsworth's instinctive thinking, escape from trouble into annihilation.

92. Of the four cases referred to here, the third belongs to Book VI, and the others to Book VII.

93. *The Excursion*, VII, 395–515. Cf. *The Prelude*, XI, p. 375, where God 'corrected' a fit of boyish impatience in him by killing his father – an idea revealing the streak of peasant superstition in Wordsworth. With these two cases compare the subjects of 'The Matron of Jedborough and her Husband' and 'The Blind Highland Boy', 1803.

94. Here may be placed the unhappy lover (VI, 95 ff.), the old Jacobite and Whig (VI, 392 ff.), and the bereaved family (VII, p. 632 ff.).

95. Also in Book VI are the prodigal son returning to die in his parents' arms, and the husband who dies of remorse after going astray under pressure of bad luck.

96. *The Excursion*, V, 637–8.

97. The treatment of the old man in Book II, and of Ellen in Book VI, brings about the death of both, but the cause is no more than a little rustic ill-nature.

98. *The Excursion*, V, 670 ff.; with his idyllic picture may be compared another that has survived of the same Betty, beating her drunken husband home from the Black Bull. (A.C. Gibson, quoted in G.S. Sandilands, *The Lakes, an Anthology of Lakeland Life and Landscape*, 1947, p. 144.)

99. *The Excursion*, IV, 846–7.

100. Ibid., VII, 1951–7.

101. Religion to Wordsworth was a 'natural' consolation. As Hale White points out, there is no theology in *The Excursion* (*An Examination of the Charge of Apostasy against Wordsworth*, 1898, pp. 36 ff.).

102. Harper, vol. II, p. 201, quoting Crabb Robinson. Southey was talking of 'the imminent danger in which our throats are at this moment from the Luddites' (letter to Capt. Southey, 17 June 1812, *Letters of Robert Southey*, ed. M.H. Fitzgerald, 1912, p. 202). So far as this goes, there is some point in the contention that Wordsworth's anti-popular attitude of 1818 was spontaneous (E.C. Batho, *The Later Wordsworth*, 1933, pp. 59–60). But his need of patronage from the Lowthers (Harper, vol. II, p. 204), was helping him along the same road, towards his place in 'The Black Book: or, Corruption Unmasked' of 1820 (I, p. 89).

103. *The Excursion*, IX, 293–335, 346.

104. Ibid., V, 1107; cf. 500–514.

105. Ibid., IV, 970; V, 296.

106. *Grosart*, I, p. 255.

107. *The Excursion*, III, 275–81.

108. Ibid., VI, 553–7.

109. 'Hart-Leap Well', *Lyrical Ballads*, II. The same phrase recurs in an allusion to this poem in a cancelled passage from *The Recluse*. (See notes on p. 319 of Selincourt and Darbishire's *The Excursion*.)

110. *The Excursion*, VI, 535–8. Both the absence of *action* from Wordsworth's philosophy, and the tendency of much of his best poetry towards a bare, grim, wintry austerity (noticed, e.g., by G.W. Knight, *The Starlit Dome*, 1941, pp. 4–5), are connected with the fact of his drawing his nourishment from a dying social order.

111. Ibid., IV, 71–6, 205–14.

112. B.R. Haydon, *Autobiography*, 13 April 1815, World's Classics edn, 1927, p. 278; cf. Southey: 'in every relation of life, and every point of view, he is a truly exemplary and admirable man' (letter to B. Barton, 19 December 1814, in Fitzgerald, p. 235). It was Wordsworth as a public man that Hazlitt attacked with savage irony in his article of December 1816 (A.R. Waller and A. Glover, eds, *Collected Works*, vol. III, 1902, pp. 157 ff.), and that Shelley called 'a beastly and pitiful wretch' (Harper, vol. II, p. 295).

113. Cf. Abercombie, p. 25: 'Perhaps the great Immortality Ode, the climax of his art, marks the turning-point in his psychological history.' It was begun in 1802 and finished in 1806.

114. Sonnet: 'London', 1802.

115. I may refer to my review of the first volume of Mrs Moorman's biography, and of two other new works on Wordsworth, in *The New Reasoner* 7, (winter 1958-9).

116. P. Thirlby, 'Orwell as a Liberal', in *Marxist Quarterly*, Oct. 1956, pp. 241-2.

117. F.M. Todd, *Politics and the Poet: A Study of Wordsworth* London 1957, pp. 132, 141, 151 ff.

# 6

# Tennyson, King Arthur and Imperialism

Tennyson was a great English poet, far the most richly gifted of the past century and a half, who failed to write great poems. If he ever, like the young Wordsworth, made 'rigorous inquisition' into his own qualifications, he might well have seemed to himself to be endowed with every requisite. He had extraordinary verbal felicity, a mastery of English words and sounds never surpassed and scarcely ever equalled, with an inexhaustible flow of imagery, and minutely delicate observation of nature. He had besides a keen interest in the widening horizons of knowledge. Concern for social and public questions came to him less spontaneously, at the prompting of friends and critics and, no doubt, of a wish to enrol more readers. But by 1835, when he was twenty-six, he was anxious, as his son and biographer Hallam records, to grapple with broad human issues. How to capture them in words and rhymes was another matter. His wrestlings with it were to beset him all his life, and made him curiously ready to resort to advisers for subjects. A story got about of Tennyson ruefully declaring: 'I have the best command of English since Shakespeare, only I have nothing to say.' Since long before his time the artistic impulse and the themes of art had been separate things, brought together in a variety of ways, often with the patron as matchmaker. In the nineteenth century the connection between them was becoming acutely uneasy. Poetry had outlived its old community functions, except at the humble level of weavers' or miners' songs, and fears were expressed that in a steam-driven world there was no room left for it. 'The genius of this time is wholly anti-poetic', Bulwer Lytton wrote in 1833.[1]

Many had no fault to find with this new age; others accepted it, as sensible men, because it had its good side, and nothing better was conceivable; but among the more imaginative there was a compulsive turning away in fantasy, in a variety of directions, from a society emotionally starved and bewildering.

Repelled by the squalid greed of what they had not yet learned to call capitalism, they were very apt to counterpose to its values, as a noble opposite, those of war. Rome and its army and empire were a staple of secondary education. Carlyle extolled violence; Ruskin, in his 1865 lecture (in *The Crown of Wild Olive*), preached a cult not unlike Nietzsche's of war as fountain of culture, mother of the arts, which could not draw breath in a money-grubbing environment. Some military men came to romanticize their profession as the upholder of true manhood against base materialism and effeminacy; T.E. Lawrence ended by shaking the dust of civilization off his feet and joining the air force.

In all this there lurked a fatal blindness, to the fact that capitalism, so far from being tamely pacific, would, as it evolved, bring far greater wars than ever seen on earth before, and that whatever their high-sounding pretences they would be wars for gold. This was so above all with imperial wars, and to Britain, far more than to any other country, war and its elevating devotion to duty meant empire-building. Writers were often in the lead of Victorian readiness to hug the empire as a balm for nagging dissatisfaction with the rat-race at home. Carlyle recommended a return to colonial slavery, Dickens had strongly authoritarian attitudes and close family connections with the colonies. Yet the record of the earlier, merchant-capital imperialism, the wars for spice trade and slave trade, ought to have been warning enough of how false was the antithesis of noble war and ignoble money-making.

Many rays of light were deflected onto British banners from the Roman eagles; many also from medieval shield and plumed helmet. Idealizing of war drew on the admiration for chivalry kindled by Scott and the rest of the feudal-izing romantics. Its first thought, like Spenser's, was of a gentle knight pricking on the plain, a plain in the Punjab or Kaffraria for example. In its most archaic, absurd form chivalry was a nostalgic daydream of aristocracy conscious of sinking into futility or derogation, the baron turning into the *bourgeois gentil-homme*. Of this the Eglinton Tournament in 1839 was the most melodramatic ebullition. More widely, it was a daydream of a heterogeneous middle class, never fully and frankly belonging to the industrial age, easily ashamed of 'low' connections with 'trade' instead of glorying in 'business' like Caleb Garth in *Middlemarch*. A good part of it, professional especially but drawing in more and more sons of prosperous businessmen, was turning into a caste of *bourgeois gentilhommes*, learning from genteel Oxbridge tutors to assimilate itself to the gentry. But historians were making their unwelcome appearance, and throwing a more realistic light on the Middle Ages and their chivalry. For English fancy a ready retreat was open from Middle Ages into Dark Ages, or Arthurian Britain filtered through the halo of chivalry, an unreal but captivating past where feudalism itself had found a magic mirror to reflect its features in knightly guise. There chivalry could live on, disembodied, in a Camelot 'never built at all, and therefore built for ever', as Tennyson wrote, in a setting very unlike the more autochthonous Celtic twilight frequented by Irish writers.

With Tennyson the struggle to transmute reality into art began with painful personal experiences. Tennyson's father was a clergyman embittered by being baulked of the inheritance which went to a younger brother instead, with a dangerously violent temper inflamed by drink. His large family grew up in a shabby-genteel condition, looked down on by their flourishing cousins. To kindle radical stirrings in a young writer some such private irritant may be useful – the Wordsworth family's grievance against the Earl of Lonsdale was another – but it cannot be relied on to keep a blaze going. In Wordsworth's case it was quickly fuelled by the French Revolution. Tennyson had a similar but much more limited phase. He got into a student set at Cambridge, the 'Apostles', who discussed very advanced ideas, and he took part with some of the members in a brief Spanish adventure on behalf of a Liberal conspiracy; one of them and all the Spaniards were caught and shot. In the same year 1830 there was the fall of Charles X in France, and then in England rioting farm labourers, of whom Tennyson saw something, and the agitation for the first Reform Bill.

All this ought to have been invigorating, but the chaotic family existence of his childhood and adolescence seems rather to have infected him with a lifelong dread of social disorder. He was capable of warm indignation at social evils, but those he attacked were too narrowly of the sort that individuals like himself on the fringes of the upper classes were exposed to; in particular, the mercenary and snobbish prejudices which prevented him for long years from marrying. Anti-aristocratic feeling of this kind may be at least as forcibly expressed by writers like him or Thackeray or Trollope, growing up on the edge of gentility, desiring entrance to the charmed circle, thinking how much worthier they are of a place in it than most of its occupants, as by men whose affiliation is with a consciously non-aristocratic middle class, men like Cobden or Bright. In Tennyson it outlasted his days of poverty and frustration. But he was not finding a way to transform personal resentment into a more generalized indictment of injustice. In a letter of 1847 he complains of the dullness of the English country gentry and their rustical conversation, but he only goes so far as to add: 'I wish they would be a little kinder to the poor.'[2] Here in a nutshell is his social doctrine: not to get rid of those in power, but to invite them to turn over a new leaf. Smouldering inner fires found their outlet not in opposition to the established order, but in religious or philosophical doubts and questionings, of the governance of heaven rather than of earth.

Already in the early 1830s, an old head on young shoulders, he was an advocate of slow, cautious, imperceptible progress. His ideal was peace between classes, an end to 'the feud of rich and poor'. To bring this about he could at times contemplate some vaguely grand transformation of society, and recognize that it must involve strain and upheaval.[3] But that 'the old order changeth' was easier to admit in the abstract, or on a stricken field in ancient Britain, than to come to terms with in his own time and place. Professionally, he achieved success with his poems published in 1842. A pension followed in 1845, marriage and the laureateship in 1850. He went on to make a fortune out of writing, handsomer probably than any other English poet ever achieved. It was a story of success that Samuel Smiles must have approved, but prosperity did not do away with all his uncomfortableness. There was madness, dipsomania, and drug addiction in his family; he himself suffered from hypochondria, and ailments with, it may be surmised, psychological causes, and was tormented by fear of blindness, and soothed his nerves with incessant smoking and a daily bottle of port.

On the literary plane, Tennyson's infirmity of nerves could be more beneficial, by keeping alive a restlessness, a sense of irreconcilabilities. He remained in old age what he had been in youth, a brilliantly accomplished versifier and often something far better, and an experimenter to the end. Poetically as well as politically, there was no such rapid ascent to glory, and then rapid and prolonged decline, as in Wordsworth's case.

Many traces of painful experience can be seen or guessed at in *Idylls of the King*, as well as in poems more transparently self-concerned; of long-delayed marriage, for instance, in Arthur's cry of longing for Guinevere, in 'The Coming'.

> What happiness to reign a lonely king,
> Vext – O ye stars that shudder over me,
> O earth that soundest hollow under me,
> Vext with waste dreams?

No one has more poignantly expressed the leaden forebodings that lie heavy on a nervous temperament, thrown much on its own resources. At Vivien's flattery Merlin – Tennyson's poetic doppelgänger – fell mute,

> So dark a forethought roll'd about his brain,
> As on a dull day in an Ocean cave
> The blind wave feeling round his long sea-hall
> In silence.

Few have found an image as keen as the one in 'Guinevere' where the very thin-skinned Tennyson speaks of the resentment stirred up in Modred by an affront which

> Rankled in him and ruffled all his heart,
> As the sharp wind that ruffles all day long
> A little bitter pool about a stone
> On the bare coast.

Because of the uncertainty and insecurity of his early social position, as well as personal morbidities and chronic pessimism, Tennyson could never be the confident spokesman of any class, with a clearly focused political outlook. His conservatism was not that of a stout, solid John Bull, but of an anxious, anchorless individual, who had grievances of his own against the social order, liked to think himself a progressive, but was held back by spectres of chaos which a neurotic fancy, legacy of a frightened childhood, too easily conjured up; dread of a relapse into dark-age barbarism which beset all propertied Europe in times of social dyspepsia like 1848.

Committed to poetry's social responsibility, he set out to be his country's public orator; more than that, to be the voice of the people, or such of the people as he had any comprehension of. It was one asset that he had in himself so much of the Victorian contradiction between energy and confidence, hesitancy and pessimism; but it was the doubts and perplexities that he entered into more readily. When he tried to be outspoken and positive he was too likely to be more a mouthpiece for what the man in the street was already thinking than an instructor, and more influenced than influencing. This sometimes landed him in attempts to revive poetry by injections of crude excitement which could only make its languor more obvious. It would be wrong all the same to think of the Laureate turning out such wares to order, like a bespoke shoemaker, or espousing accepted notions for the sake of his position. He had his own needs of the thrills of war or empire, like his hero or other self at the end of 'Maud', to rouse him from the spider webs and shadows of his inner landscape. Sounds of distant bugles could stir in him a stronger confidence in national and human destinies. Like most patriots, he had no liking for most of his countrymen, and he could think of them with most satisfaction far away in time or space, like Sir Richard Grenville's bulldog crew in the *Revenge* or the garrison of Lucknow, though as a rule the commander had more of his attention than the men. He could admire men of action the more because he was very little capable of it, and by putting himself into his heroes' shoes could rise above his customary inertness. Here too was justification for his art –[4]

> The song that nerves a nation's heart
> Is in itself a deed.

Compared with social anarchy, war could appear to him, as it has to so many others from Shakespeare down, a lesser evil, a controlled outlet for violence. An exceptionally humane man, he did not upset himself by thinking too realistically about mangled corpses. War was with him a mainly cerebral affair, fought with toy soldiers, lance and sabre not often smeared with real blood. Highly imaginative though he was, there was apt to be a certain want of practical or human realization in his flights. In a marvellous passage in 'Morte d'Arthur' Sir Bedivere 'swiftly strode' down from battlefield to shore:

> Dry clash'd his harness in the icy caves
> And barren chasms, and all to left and right
> The bare black cliff clang'd round him, as he based
> His feet on juts of slippery crag that rang
> Sharp-smitten with the dint of armed heels –
> And on a sudden, lo! the level lake,
> And the long glories of the winter moon.

As word-painting these lines, with the sudden modulation in the last two from harsh to liquid consonants and from short to long vowels, are incomparable; they recall the sound-painting that nineteenth-century musicians strove after in their tone poems. Yet anyone who has scrambled over wet slippery rocks knows that an iron-shod man in armour could not possibly stride downwards across them in that fashion – even without a wounded man on his back.

It was always possible, moreover, to think of England as on the defensive, a small nation surviving by quality and courage. 'Lucknow' is about the dogged British defence of the residency, not the savage British assault on the city. In the Wellington funeral ode the duke wins the day in India 'Against the myriads of Assaye'. In the patriotic tradition of the thin red line Englishmen were always, like Macaulay's Romans, facing fearful odds. The *Revenge* is swallowed up in the maw of a Spanish fleet, the three hundred of the Heavy Brigade are engulfed in 'Russian hordes'. Tennyson could with a better conscience repel the charge of militarism, as he does in an 'Epilogue' to 'The Charge of the Heavy Brigade', in the form of a dialogue with a reproachful young lady. Man must be ready to fight for the sake of 'true peace'.

England's combats might be righteous and unsought, but they were gaining for it the widest-ranging empire in history, for Tennyson a bastion against his haunting sense of mutability and impermanence. It was something tangible and vast, which could be admired from every point of view from commercial to moral, and was coming to be seen almost as God's final bequest to humanity, the labour of His eighth day. It had, of course, the warrant of Roman precedent, and of Virgil and Horace, whose poetry he had at his fingertips. His tribute to Virgil dwells mostly on peaceful themes, common humanity, but it does not fail to catch an undying echo of 'Imperial Rome' in the Mantuan's 'ocean-roll of rhythm'. Before the Caesars there was Alexander. A youthful sonnet in his honour began with the same words – 'Warrior of God' – as the epitaph decades later on Gordon.

His interest in the empire and its fortunes dawned betimes. About 1842 he was all for putting up with no nonsense from the Afghans,[5] and he contemplated a poem on the battle of Miani which won Sind in 1843. (Meredith's first poem was on the battle of Chilianwala in the Punjab in 1849). But his verses dealing directly with episodes of this kind were to be not very numerous, for so prolific a writer, and not very good. He found it simpler to put all such themes into disguised, mythic form. We may suspect him of doing this with his Ulysses, weary of ruling 'a savage race' who – strangely enough – know him not: they are his own islanders, but he sounds for all the world like a bored colonial official somewhere in the back of beyond. Tennyson's friend Spedding (of the Colonial Office) observed in him when still quite young an 'almost personal dislike of the present, whatever it may be.'[6] In *Idylls of the King* he made his most ambitious effort to render the feelings of the present more lucidly by transposing them into the past.

Poets were groping not only for subjects which might come home to men's business and bosoms in an unpoetical climate, but also for modes of expression worthy of them. Forced to justify its existence, only by great creations could poetry hope to survive; but these called for grand forms, which music, free to soar on wings instead of walking, was proving much better able to invent. Wordsworth was condemned to a lifetime of unrealizable aspiration by Coleridge's incitement to compose a majestic philosophical poem; Tennyson, equally consumed by his vocation, was tantalized by the mirage of an epic. As his reputation rose he was increasingly sensitive to the appeals of friends and admirers for some masterpiece to immortalize him, much as Brahms was harassed by summonses to come forward as the symphonic successor to Beethoven. The outcome, produced disjointedly at intervals during nearly twenty years, was the cycle of collected narratives about ancient Britain known as the *Idylls*. 'There is no doubt that he regarded this poem as his chief lifework.'[7] Its Saxon simplicity of diction was not long in being noticed; it may be that here more than usually he was trying to live up to his image of himself as poet of the people, in the spirit of the Wordsworth of *Lyrical Ballads*.

Clearly the central idea of the Arthurian legend, of benign ruler and highborn followers vowed to protect the weak and right wrongs – a social inversion of Robin Hood and his foresters – has had a tenacious attraction. Rabelais might burlesque the knights of the Round Table as tatterdemalions earning a pittance in the next world by ferrying devils across the Styx,[8] Cervantes might banish all knight errantry to the realm of farce; yet for centuries it went on casting a Celtic spell over the hard-headed Sassenach. Milton thought of King Arthur as the subject for his great work; Blake made a symbolic interpretation of the myth as a version of the fall, from Eden or innocence;[9] Scott, Matthew Arnold, Swinburne, William Morris, all wrote Arthurian poems. From early in the century interest was reinforced by study of mythology. G.S. Faber, whose work may have coloured Tennyson's 'Morte d'Arthur', conceived of the ancients as believing in a cycle of eras, each in turn relapsing into chaos.[10]

Tennyson grew up reading the stories. He was fascinated by Merlin, seeing in him a type of the spirit of poetry; thinking thus of poetry as a species of magic, potent to alter the world, as Shelley believed it could. At twenty-four he was meditating an epic or drama about Arthur, and it was about then that he wrote the splendid fragment 'Morte d'Arthur'. He published this with an awkward fiction of its being a relic of a long epic, all the rest destroyed, which revealed his mistrust of his darling project as too archaic and remote from the contemporary mind. Years later, on the point of bringing out the first Idylls, he declared that one would have to be 'crazed' to write an Arthurian epic in the mid nineteenth century.[11] By writing it in bits he could try it on his public by stages, as Byron had done with *Childe Harold* and *Don Juan*; and the breath of applause might fill his hesitant sails.

Only a third of the dozen tales have happy endings, and it is significant that their final dénouement was the first fragment to be written, a gloom-laden picture of two survivors, one dying, of two dead armies. Tennyson might have chosen to write of Hengist and Horsa bringing Saxondom into Britain; or (another theme that occurred to Milton) of Alfred valiantly defending their descendants against the Danes; or of William conquering England. Ancient Britain by contrast was a dying civilization, which appealed far more to his inner self, and could set many chords in readers' minds vibrating. Camelot is a candle in a naughty world, soon quenched, as the *Revenge* is overwhelmed by the mass of its enemies. In its remote shadows he could allow himself to see man and his world as he feared they really were. His villains, or evil-doers, like Milton's are far more vital than most of his virtuous men and women. But he was withdrawing into this far-off realm in order to deliver warnings to his countrymen from it, as well as in quest of affinities with his own self. For this purpose he had to import into it some incongruous migrants, ideals and idealists from his England, or his own corner of it, or this corner as he tried to see it, and it to see itself. They are marshalled by an Arthur turned into a Victorian gentleman, refined and rarified, but a muscular Christian too, a king on horseback; a type of the heroes like General Gordon who were building the empire, liberating its peoples supposedly from the darkness of bondage and superstition. Gazing at the empire, Tennyson could feel a simple certitude of rightness, a simplification of moral and political issues, unattainable in his own ever-complicated country. Of the realities of empire he knew as little as of ancient Britain; of the connection, for instance, between City usurers and the occupation of Egypt which he lauded. Arthur remains unnatural, unconvincing, because Victorian standards of behaviour, within the family notably, contained so much over-strained pretence and deceit; but also because the idea of the empire as benevolent and disinterested was more than half a figment of fancy, or deception.

As later when writing his historical plays, Tennyson took great pains to get up his subject, even to the point of learning some Welsh. His materials were gathered from a variety of sources, beginning with Malory and the *Mabinogion*. Likewise, the reflections on his own times, the new wine poured, often incongruously, into these old bottles, must be looked for in diverse quarters. He talked of the work as having many meanings. 'Every reader must find his own interpretation.' For him, its essential meaning was human endeavour ruined by temptation and sin; or 'the world-wide war of Sense and Soul, typified in individuals'.[12] It was an elastic enough formula. Soul and sense could modulate smoothly into the conflict of civilization and barbarism, which had a powerful hold on the European and above all the British mind. Empire meant in ideal terms the bringing of order and peaceful progress to lands beyond the pale. It would be strange if this notion did not find its way, however obliquely, into the *Idylls*. Three centuries earlier Camoens had written an epic on the expansion of Portugal in his own epoch. But he felt obliged to mix up history with classical mythology, and sculptors went on presenting captains and kings in Roman garb. In an age of telegraphs and newspapers, high events were far too heavily clogged with everyday associations to be treated without disguise in a long poem.

Tennyson's first musings produced a prose sketch and an allegorical framework in which Arthur stood for religious faith, the Round Table for 'liberal institutions', Modred the traitor for scepticism.[13] But more than two decades passed, like Wordsworth's long delays over *The Excursion*, before he was ready for these 'public' themes, or could work out a less unmanageable plan. When he had any scheme ready he was remarkably rapid in execution for a writer of such highly finished work. The *Idylls* were composed in two spells, the first from 1856, with a stay in Wales that year to encourage inspiration, to 1859, the second from 1868 to 1874. They were thus the performance of a man travelling from the age of forty-seven to sixty-five. Four narratives, one of them later divided into two, came out in 1859; taken in order of composition they stand in the final sequence of twelve as numbers 6, 3 and 4, 11, and 7. There was then another lengthy spell of hanging fire. His wife pressed for further progress with the grand design in which he seemed to have lost faith;[14] so in 1868 did Jowett, one of his chief mentors.[15] Four more were published in 1869 (in the sequence, numbers 9, 12, 8, 1); 'The Passing of Arthur' incorporated the fragment of many years earlier. 'The Holy Grail' was done in a fortnight, and was followed at once by 'The Coming of Arthur'. At the beginning of 1870 the poet was feeling 'extraordinarily happy' at the prospect of reaching his goal;[16] and the last three (10, 2, 5) were completed between 1871 and 1874, though one ('Balin and Balan') was kept unpublished until 1885.

By the bulk of the reading public in their own time the reception of the *Idylls* was enthusiastic, and set the seal on Tennyson's success, partly because of the factor discussed by Bagehot in his *Literary Studies*, the entry of lower middle-class elements seeking culture as a part of their certificate of naturalization in respectable society (though they could scarcely be more uncritical than Byron's largely upper-class admirers). More discriminating readers had reservations, much like those piled up against Tennyson later on; among them were the faithful FitzGerald, Elizabeth Browning, Hopkins, Meredith, Swinburne, Bridges. As narratives the poems suffer from Britain's failure to take on the semblance of a living, breathing country. Their actors declaim in an empty theatre. In style too, in the effort to rise to the height of his great argument, or to convince us and himself of its height, Tennyson often labours, as if loaded with cumbrous armour; and he is always addressing us from a distance, from a pulpit or stage, instead of buttonholing us and talking man to man as writers are expected to do nowadays.

Yet moments of true drama come often enough. At the end of 'Gareth and Lynette' there is a sudden release of tension when the dreaded black knight,

> High on a nightblack horse, in nightblack arms,
> With white breast-bone, and barren ribs of Death,

is discovered to be a 'blooming boy'. At the end of 'The Last Tournament' the reader is taken by surprise in a very different way, when Tristram is in the act of presenting his trophy of victory in the lists to his mistress, King Mark's wife Isolt:

> But, while he bow'd to kiss the jewell'd throat,
> Out of the dark, just as the lips had touch'd,
> Behind him rose a shadow and a shriek –
> 'Mark's way', said Mark, and clove him thro' the brain.

Amid much that today sounds unconvincing there are countless compelling touches, often of realistic imagery. Tennyson as well as Dickens knew what London roadways were like, and Merlin talks bitterly to Vivien of how unintelligible is virtue like Arthur's

> To things with every sense as false and foul
> As the poach'd filth that floods the middle street.

While Arthur looked sadly on at the last tournament

> . . . the laces of a helmet crack'd,
> And show'd him, like a vermin in its hole,
> Modred, a narrow face . . .

Tennyson's blending of ancient and modern is hinted at in the carvings on the gate of Camelot, stared at so long ago by the newcomer Gareth, where

> Were Arthur's wars in weird devices done,
> New things and old co-twisted, as if Time
> Were nothing.

But whatever the meanings, intended or unintended, of the *Idylls*, there can be no gainsaying the quality of their workmanship. They are doubtless curate's eggs, only good in parts, but not seldom superlatively good, stored with echoing phrase, dazzling simile, hypnotic description.

The years of the first group of Idylls belonged, on the national scene, to the reassuring lull following the defeat of Chartism in 1848 and its ensuing decay, the Crimean War from 1854 to 1856 helping to finish it off with a burst of jingo enthusiasm from which the working class was not immune. In the colonial field excitements multiplied. Apart from skirmishings with Kaffirs in South Africa and Maoris in New Zealand, there was the conquest of the Punjab in the later 1840s and of Lower Burma in 1854. During the years of composition of the first idylls there followed the second China War (1856–60), the attack on Persia (1857), and above all, during 1857 and 1858, the greatest of all European colonial conflicts until after the Second World War, the outbreak and suppression of the Indian Mutiny, which, his son records, 'stirred him to the depths.' A brother of his friend Jowett died in India, the second to do so, in 1858.[17]

This was, for Tennyson as for most Englishmen and many other Europeans, a fearful display of barbarism revolting against Christian civilization, a land only narrowly prevented from 'reeling back into the beast' like Arthur's Britain. He was shudderingly reminded of it by the disturbance in Jamaica at the end of 1865, when the blacks were accused of planning, and the whites headed by Governor Eyre actually resorted to, a reign of terror. In the grand division of opinion in England Tennyson was one of an array of eminent writers who took Eyre's side. He would have done well to recall the moral of his poem 'The Captain', about a naval commander whose brutality brings his ship to disaster: the guilt of anyone in authority who 'only rules by terror'. His preconceptions must have been sharpened by one of his sisters having married a lawyer who went to Jamaica as chief justice. He was one of numerous writers with family links with the empire; a brother went to Tasmania, one cousin was in the navy, another, who died in the West Indies, in the army. He himself visited Ireland a number of times, and developed towards it an attitude, as an Irish historian who has studied it says, of 'naive hostility which became increasingly racialist with age. . . . On Ireland his mind was one of angry, unhappy prejudice.'[18] So was his wife's; she considered the Irish 'a nest of traitors'.[19]

In 1866 came the Abyssinian expedition, Napier's march to Magdala on a rescue operation like so many Arthurian adventures, to liberate British captives of the half-crazy despot Theodore. A couple of years later Tennyson had as a visitor Theodore's young son Alamayu, in the custody of an English officer. In 1870 there was the repulse of the Fenian incursion into Canada from the USA, and the Red River fighting in the Canadian north-west. The next year Maori resistance was brought to an end; in 1874 the decisive campaign against the obdurate Ashanti kingdom took place. At home the agitation leading to the second Reform Act in 1867 was quite enough to flutter Tennyson, whose vivid fancy was always ready to magnify scuffles into cataclysms. On the Continent the Franco–Prussian war was followed by the Paris Commune, which threw all conservative Europe into a panic.

An epic must have a hero, and Victorian England believed, with help from Carlyle, as firmly in heroes and great men as in great works of art or engineering. Tennyson's Arthur is compounded from too many idealistic abstractions to be a convincing creature of flesh and blood. He is always a visionary, a stranger like Christ among his disciples. Somewhat like Tennyson himself, he has risen from obscure beginnings: his birth is shrouded in myth, and he has not inherited his throne but won it by prowess and a mysterious heaven-bestowed gift of leadership. He has no heir, no apparent interest in an heir; this is a childless realm altogether, built by one man, destined to perish with him. It is faintly illuminated by rays of Christianity lingering from Roman times, but the sudden advent of a highly religious and civilized reformer in the midst of primitive darkness is left as enigmatic as the white man's arrival must have been to Mohicans or Maoris. On this more workaday level, Tennyson may have owed something to his friend Carlyle's laudatory account of Dr Francia, dictator of Paraguay, as a solitary beacon of European enlightenment in the wilderness. On one side the *Idylls* are an encomium on monarchy, which in his own England the Laureate was doing much to refurbish. But Arthur is no constitutional monarch. In spite of Tennyson's early allegorizing idea of 'liberal institutions', there is no sign of the king sharing decision with anyone else. He sits at the table with the rest, but the others are all sworn to obedience as unquestioning as the Light Brigade's.

Since Roman times Britain has been in turmoil, like the dark continents, Africa and Asia, as beheld from Europe. With Arthur's coming recovery begins, 'a nobler time' for the land. Pacification may seem for a while fairly complete, and Arthur's sway extends from the south to the Orkneys, Gareth's homeland, though we hear of no navy. But robber barons still infest the country, as Lynette complains to Arthur himself, each lording it over the neighbourhood of his tower, and bridge and ford are 'beset by bandits'. 'Caitiffs' of all kinds abound – a Tennysonian archaism from the thirteenth century which could cover all undesirables.

Jeffrey and Borrow criticized Scott for resurrecting medieval chivalric bric-à-brac, as a covering for conservatism. In their own day the first inventors of the code of chivalry were useful to feudalism by giving their feudal patrons a better look. That trampling young conqueror the Black Prince took the motto 'Ich Dien', and *service* has been the apologia of American capitalism. All fantasy-spinning is liable to turn into a grotesque caricature of itself. Tennyson can be taken as preaching the need for a conscientious landed aristocracy, doing its paternalistic duty to its humble neighbours or dependants. Carlyle had been preaching something much like this, moral rearmament of the upper class as prophylactic against a French Revolution on this side of the Channel.

In his own Britain Tennyson never knew what to make of common people.

He was sorry for them, feared them, hoped they might be improved by education. In ancient Britain he could dismiss them to the wings, leaving the stage to their betters. We hear in 'The Coming' that they clamoured for a king, and Merlin presented them with Arthur, whom the 'great lords' rejected; but no idea of rousing commoners to resist oppressors could ever occur to Arthur, whose menials are 'thralls' or slaves. In Camelot itself we have a fugitive reference in 'Gareth and Lynette' to a 'healthful people' basking in their sovereign's protection, and in the 'Grail' a glimpse of them in the fields round about, in sight of the city's towers and grateful for royal guardianship against 'the heathen'. Their activity stretches no further than to turn out and applaud the knights at a tournament.

It is by warlike prowess that Arthur convinces admirers like Gareth of his right to be king. We see him in 'Lancelot and Elaine' wading in heathen blood, crimson from plume to spur, like a true crusader. He founds his Table as a substitute for Roman law and order, as he says in 'Guinevere', and to be 'a model for the mighty world' – as the British empire now was. In 'The Coming' he repulses the claims of an expiring Rome on Britain, not as a British nationalist or Fenian but simply because Rome is too feeble now to shelter the country from incursions; before Arthur comes to his aid Guinevere's father Leodogran, a harassed kinglet, is heard sighing over the disappearance of Roman power. Tennyson's unimpressive poem 'Boädicea', which belongs to 1859, carries evident overtones of the Indian Mutiny: it is a very unsympathetic presentation of rebellion, full of wild bawling and brawling and religious hysteria, and the threat of a ferocious revenge.

> . . . Boädicéa, standing loftily charioted,
> Mad and maddening all that heard her in her fierce volubility,
> Girt by half the tribes of Britain, near the colony Cámulodúne,
> Yell'd and shriek'd between her daughters o'er a wild confederacy.

Very likely Tennyson thought of the Rani of Jhansi, the Indian heroine of 1857, as a similar virago. Metrically, the poem is one of those he called 'Experiments', and the freely handled trochaic lines of eight feet labour, with imperfect success, to echo the pandemonium of revolt. On the other hand the Romans are depraved and decadent; another warning against ruling-class misbehaviour, in this case in a colonial setting.

An imperial dimension of the Arthurian story is visible throughout. Arthur's expanding kingdom is itself a small empire, subjugating or overawing less civilized areas and bringing them within the pale of Christian manners. In the same style modern Britain was carrying fire and sword, light and sweetness, into the dark places of Asia and Africa. It may even not be irrelevant that Arthur has an exceptionally fair complexion, as if to typify the white man (though Lancelot is raven-haired, as Tennyson was), and one of the latest-written

Idylls ('The Last Tournament') gives us a remarkably Nordic vignette of a victorious Arthur on his throne, with golden hair and 'steel-blue eyes'. In 'Geraint and Enid' he sets off to improve a neglected district, remove bad officials, break 'bandit holds', and even, less distinctly, extend agriculture, just as a commissioner in a newly annexed province of India might do. He reproaches himself with not having assumed direct control of this region sooner, instead of allowing it to become, in 'delegated hands', the 'common sewer' of the realm; very much as, in the same year 1856 when this was written, the Governor-General of India, Lord Dalhousie, annexed the ramshackle kingdom of Oudh, on the strength of Sleeman's highly coloured report on its lamentable condition.

Many casual touches in the *Idylls* suggest empire parallels. Those in power before Arthur behaved like 'wild beasts', we are told in 'The Coming', and rulers like them were still at large in Asia and Africa. Mark of Cornwall is refused membership of the Table, as a princely black sheep in India might be refused a coveted decoration. Like the British there, Arthur stops petty royalties from fighting among themselves, keeps the better of them as tributaries, takes their sons into his service, like those of King Lot of the Orkneys. Exalted by his vision of the grail, Galahad rides about overthrowing 'Pagan realms' and 'Pagan hordes', single-handed apparently, and 'Shattering all evil customs', very much like the long arm of modern Britain quelling Mad Mullahs or abolishing suttee. Among Gareth's opponents the 'Morning Star', waited on and armed by 'three fair girls', barefooted and bareheaded, has a markedly oriental look. He is derived from a knight of Malory, Sir Persant of Inde; in medieval romances longitudes and latitudes were often wildly mixed up. Balin has been banished from court for striking a servant, and must learn to control his hasty temper and cultivate courtesy to high and low; Tennyson might well be admonishing his countrymen in India, who with all their sterling qualities were much given to beating their servants, and very little to winning native goodwill. There is a far graver breach of the code of chivalry in 'The Last Tournament', when moral decay has gone far. Arthur is leading in person an expeditionary force against a malefactor in his fortress. In the days of his 'Coming' he had been able to halt bloodshed as soon as the enemy turned tail, but now his men run wild, and after breaking into the enemy stronghold go on killing indiscriminately,

> Till all the rafters rang with woman-yells,
> And all the pavement stream'd with massacre.

Such scenes disfigured the conclusion of many sieges by British and other colonial forces, and were looked on by professional soldiers as often inevitable, if regrettable. Multan in the Punjab in 1849, Delhi and Lucknow during the Mutiny, were among the sufferers.

Each nation which has in turn felt itself the strongest – Revolutionary

France, Victorian Britain, and in our day the USA – has wanted to impose its will on others, but to think of itself as their warden or rescuer. To Englishmen their long series of colonial wars might quite naturally seem to resemble the labours of Hercules, ridding the earth of its scourges. Theocritus's set of poems on the legends of Hercules were among Tennyson's models.[20] Arthurian myth fell neatly into the same pattern, and damsels in distress and their paladins lent a romantic appeal. Thanks to the Romantic revival, chivalric notions were in the air; a titular archbishop of Carthage helped to launch King Leopold's private fief in the Congo by proposing a new order of chivalry to serve in Africa. But links are not hard to find between the special Arthurian attraction for English writers in that age, and England's spreading dominion over palm and pine. On the more serious-minded among those who were building and guarding the empire, the *Idylls* may well have had a considerable influence.

Sir George Grey, a notable governor and enthusiast like Tennyson for imperial federation, noted in his collection of Maori legends a tale that reminded him of the finding of the child Arthur.[21] An Englishman teaching in a college in India wrote a book on the *Idylls*, and found them full of 'moral significance'.[22] A poetaster lauded Outram, 'the Bayard of India', as

> Prompt to redeem the helpless in distress,
> And for the weak his lance in rest to lay.[23]

Canon Tyndale-Biscoe, very much a devotee of the trinity of army–navy–empire, wanted the boys of his school in Kashmir to act like knights errant, always ready to spring to the aid of victims of injustice.[24] In the same spirit, Conan Doyle's explorer in Amazonia, Lord John Roxton, set himself to act as 'the flail of the lord' and wipe out a gang of murderous slavers.[25] Possibly Tennyson looked back on his own Spanish adventure as an exercise in knight errantry. In 1895 Sir G.C. Carter at Lagos criticized his subordinate, Captain R.L. Bower, who had bombarded the town of Oyo, as over-impetuous, too much inclined to pose as a knight errant.[26] The group of empire intellectuals active early in this century round Lord Milner, high commissioner in South Africa, had been connected with a new Round Table, 'an Arthurian dream of a new Camelot as the focus for a dedicated British Empire.'[27] In America Walt Whitman, a warm admirer of Tennyson, admired the *Idylls* pre-eminently.[28] Unlike his countryman Mark Twain, he was an imperialist himself. Some of Tennyson's large following in America may have recognized a popular counterpart to the *Idylls* in the swelling literature of the wild west, with its sheriffs and vigilantes battling against Indians, brigands, and other caitiffs of the New World.

Tennyson believed in God and immortality, not very positively in anything more of religion; but he deplored the decay of religious convictions as jeopardizing social bonds, and his England needed a crusading faith overseas, a

broad practical creed for men of action. He was with difficulty, and only by
ducal and royal persuasion, brought to include the Holy Grail among his quests,
and in the poem common sense struggles with mysticism and incense fumes.
With regard to sex he felt less objection to excess of virtue. All the knights were
pledged not to exceed the limits of monogamy, but some high-fliers, we hear in
'Merlin and Vivien', choose celibacy. Again, however, it may be worthwhile to
look outward from Britain to the empire, where, even after English women
became more generally available, it was often financially impossible for men to
marry before middle age, as it had been for Tennyson himself; so that the only
alternative to total abstinence was resort to prostitutes, or, at the peril of white
prestige and racial purity, to native concubines.

Gladstone's private philanthropy was the rescuing of fallen women, who
abounded in all big towns, a bleak reproach to the Victorian conscience. To his
friend Tennyson thinking of such human degradation brought painful doubts
about the condition of England. In the hall of the barbarous Earl Doorm, in
'Geraint and Enid', at sight of the captive Enid and their amorous lord

> Some, whose souls the old serpent long had drawn
> Down, as the worm draws in the wither'd leaf
> And makes it earth, hiss'd each at other's ear
> What shall not be recorded – women they,
> Women, or what had been those gracious things . . .

In women in high places a moral tone was an indispensable requisite of a
healthy society. All the Idylls of 1859 were studies of good and bad women, and
of the devastating influence of the bad. A lurking sensation of insecurity in a
class may show in the individual as a nagging fear of infidelity in the home.
Society in England, that is to say the propertied classes at their then stage of
evolution, could be stable only if women were prepared to accept the honorific
but cramping place allotted to them. In Tennyson's longer poem 'The Princess',
respectable ladies had been seeking liberation in one way, claiming freedom of
the mind and turning their back on men, an extravagance from which they had
to be reclaimed. In the *Idylls* bad women were bent on a different freedom, of
the body; to Tennyson a far more fatal deviation. In our time women have been
following both paths of emancipation, the second hitherto with rather greater
ardour and success.

As seducer of the wise Merlin, in the Idyll first written, Vivien is the
embodiment of sense working against soul. As agent of the rascally King Mark,
sent to Camelot in 'Balin and Balan' to make mischief, she resembles the
courtesans who had a place in the diplomatic practices of Tennyson's bête noire
Napoleon III, and Mark's licentious court is contrasted with the purity of
Arthur's as Napoleon's might be with Victoria's. She too can be viewed in an
empire setting as well, as a native siren with the voluptuous, insidious charms

that white men in torrid lands had to be on their guard against. She is an avowed pagan, and in 'Balin and Balan' prophesies revival of the 'old sun-worship' and overturning of Christianity. Yet against the moral chastity-belt of Victorian virtue she represents something like a real revolt of womanhood, escaping from her creator's control like a miniature female Satan. Unlike Guinevere, she suffers from no guilty conscience; she preaches the life of the senses, and dismisses all Arthurian idealism as mere humbug or folly.

> Old priest, who mumble worship in your quire –
> Old monk and nun, ye scorn the world's desire,
> Yet in your frosty cells ye feel the fire! . . .
> The fire of Heaven is lord of all things good,
> And starve not thou this fire within thy blood,
> But follow Vivien thro' the fiery flood!

It is not surprising that she startled some readers. There was a 'pagan' admixture in Tennyson himself, as there must be in every artist, and memories of his first love, and Rosa Baring's physical attractions, may have come back to life in Vivien, stirring some lingering regrets, and driving him to take refuge in his dualism of flesh and spirit.

That a hopeful kingdom should fall to pieces through the contagion of a queen's adultery was a central point of his Arthurian conception from the beginning. Guinevere was to be another Eve, bringing death back into the world. Arthur's knights at first 'worship' her, as their emblem of truth and purity, Balin declares. (Victoria, if not worshipped, became a genuine cult figure for Englishmen in the outposts of empire: her death was shattering.) But rumours are soon heard, and alarm husbands like Geraint. Later on her liaison with the always conscience-stricken Lancelot has a cruder parallel in that of the more scandalous Isolt, Mark's queen, with the burly sensualist Tristram. Demoralization is spreading among the elite, and must lead to national ruin.

In the dedication to the Queen of the 1859 Idylls the poet could strike his optimistic note, as one singing 'in the rich dawn of an ampler day' ushered in by science and industry. In the springtime of Camelot, when women were still 'pure' and 'shy', a future of perpetual brightness could seem to stretch before the knights, with the exhilaration of service in a great cause. But radiant beginnings were soon clouding over. Heroic values flourished best in the pristine days, amid the 'heathen wars' when Arthur was laying his foundations. As in 'Maud', peace and prosperity seem to breed decay, and an atmosphere of over-ripeness hangs over the scene. There is a reaction, voiced by Tristram in 'The Last Tournament', against Arthur's puritanism, as only 'the wholesome madness of an hour', usefully nerving men to great exertions while these were required, but the time has come for them to enjoy themselves. Simplicity gives way to over-sophistication – 'too much wit Makes the world rotten', the fool tells Tristram. The final tournament ends in disorder, and riotous festivities with women taking part.

In fact the moral stamina of Arthur's chosen few proves feeble enough; which hints at an uncomfortably low estimate by Tennyson, hard though he must have tried to repress it, of the ruling classes of his England. Modred as faction chief is a weasel of a villain, destitute of any greatness. His tactics consist of fomenting feuds within the Order and conspiring with the 'heathen'. In the closing catastrophe, the 'weird' battle in the western mists, he has 'the Heathen of the Northern Sea' for allies; they may be credited with some kinship with the French whom Tennyson was always expecting to see landing on England's shore.

In artistic design the *Idylls* are tragic, 'the great Arthurian tragedy' in his son's words.[29] Their completion left him preparing to devote the best of his remaining energies to a set of tragic dramas, mainly from English history. He was revealed in the *Idylls* as the poet of decay and change, penetrated by a sense of the unreliability of men and things which was always at odds with his longing, bred by a disturbed childhood, for reassurance.

With these forebodings and his fears of moral bankruptcy, all Tennyson's publications were in favour of a linking or fusion of the new bourgeoisie with the old aristocracy or gentry, or at any rate an amalgam of what seemed to him best in both. His nostalgias lay with the older class, his moral standards, like most of his readership, joined him to the newer. Belonging to the professional fringe of the gentry, he was well placed to aid in promoting communications between the two. He was doing so in one important way by recommending the empire, of which the new middle classes or their radical spokesmen were for long suspicious, as a joint investment. In the later decades of the century it was contributing greatly towards bringing the two propertied groups closer. But instead of being the sustainer of high resolve and rugged simplicity that he looked so expectantly to, it was a siren leading England astray, another Vivien learning the secret of a spell and using it as a fetter.

There was emerging, in short, the plutocracy whose greed and depravity Tennyson, along with other censors, contemplated with disgust. Not the best, but the worst, of two epochs was being combined. For him there could be no hope of a political or social order surviving for long after exhausting its moral capital. He could never shake off his fear of lost virtue bringing with it harsh penalties. Shakespeare's Henry IV in old age foresaw an England sinking into 'a wilderness again, Peopled with wolves';[30] and if we read into his words a premonition of the fate of the monarchy as it was in Shakespeare's day, and all that went with it, we may find in Tennyson's very similar language a warning that the death of property might be at hand. The 'red ruin' Arthur accuses Guinevere of bringing on the land is a compound of many evils, not all explained; but it must include something of 'the red fool fury' of revolutionary Paris which was Tennyson's grand political phobia.

His long, deep plunges into the past, and returns to his own day may be compared with those of other writers who took the time-machine back to Rome, like Kingsley in *Hypatia* and Pater in *Marius the Epicurean,* or into the Middle Ages like Bulwer Lytton in *Rienzi,* or into the Renaissance like George Eliot in *Romola,* and Browning, all in search of other vistas and of an observatory from which to survey their own epoch. The most revealing contrast is with William Morris and his pilgrimage into the far northland. Morris was fascinated by the sagas, and set about translating them, in the 1860s; in the early 1870s he made two visits to Iceland, as Tennyson visited Wales. He was profoundly impressed by 'the cold volcanic island and its fierce mythologies', finding there a secret 'strong enough to carry him out of his despair to the greatness of his last years.'[31] Like Tennyson going back beyond medieval chivalry to its fabulous Celtic ancestry, Morris was going back beyond the Saxon and Dane of an era coming under the scrutiny of historians eager to demonstrate the Saxon origins of the British Constitution, Cambridge University, and all other good things, to a mysterious Nordic twilight. There human grandeurs could be found enshrined in the sagas, as those of the Celtic mist could be found in the *Mabinogion.*

It was an opposite world, not of king and lord and lady of high degree, but a rough democracy of warrior farmers, leading a simple, rugged life where each man's fortunes rested on his own hardihood, his single courage and endurance, and on his own fate. Instead of a paternalist Arthur creating an aristocracy of merit to protect the helpless, what set Morris afire was the sturdy readiness of every man to protect himself, in a harsh endless feuding of individuals and groups, and of men against nature. In Morris's Iceland as in Tennyson's Britain, we are aware of the pressure of a writer's feeling about his own England; and we glimpse 'the imminence of his own participation in political life'.[32] In the Norse myth of the downfall of the gods he saw a presage of revolution, and after composing his version of the Volsunga saga between 1875 and 1876, a few years after the last Idylls were finished, he was ready to advance to revolutionary socialism. To Tennyson the collapse of the Christian firmament in ancient Britain was an omen not of a better but of a far worse future. He too was soon to participate in politics, by joining not a socialist party but that aristocracy of merit, the House of Lords.

What Tennyson accepted exultingly in the progress of his age was chiefly its less human side, its scientific soarings; in various other ways it was deeply and, despite personal success, increasingly uncongenial to him, as materialistic and without faith. His mind moved away from it in time, backward into the past, and in space, outward into other continents: in each case into spheres from which economic calculation could be banished. Camelot and empire were above vulgar thoughts of pelf, the money cares that so oppressed his own youth. For him the two spheres were complementary. In the first his poetic imagination could work, if not altogether freely, towards a tragic vision. From

Camelot he judged his own England, and found it wanting. From the vantage-point of empire he could admire and applaud his England, and reassure himself that beneath all appearances it was still inwardly sound. There the civilizing mission, dutifully performed, vindicated the rightness of English principles and English religion; and the story had a happy ending, or rather no ending, to satisfy his craving for political stability. Camelot's great hall had fallen, but the Residency at Lucknow stood, and would stand, like Horace's Rome,

> . . . dum Capitolium
> scandet cum tacita virgine pontifex.

Celebrating empire victories he could strike a note not tragic, but triumphalist.

In the epilogue to the *Idylls*, addressed to the Queen, Tennyson expressed a not very sanguine hope that England would get the better of its maladies – materialism, sloth, cowardice, impiety, libertine French ways; as if offering a cure for them, he blew the empire trumpet loudly, with indignant repudiation of those soulless Little Englanders who wanted to save money on defence by cutting Canada adrift. This elicited a response by a Canadian poetess,[33] and an assurance from Lord Dufferin, the governor-general, that it had made a fine impression in 'this most powerful and prosperous colony'.[34] Some years later a Canadian named Harper, drowned while endeavouring to save life, was commemorated by a statue at Ottawa of Sir Galahad, and a memoir by his friend the later prime minister, Mackenzie King, who held him up as a model of all the virtues and 'above all a Tennyson man'.[35]

Tennyson's youthful confidence in Europe had faded, leaving him with a stereotype of a continent sunk in dark despotism and blind revolutionism. By contrast, the empire could stand for orderly progress. Having for a while dreamed of a 'federation of the world', he was ready to content himself with imperial federation. He seems to have thought of the white settlements as healthy offshoots of a good old England, which might better preserve the old heritage because less infected by the germs now creeping through England's veins. He made friends with Sir Harry Parkes, premier of New South Wales, entertained him on a visit to England, and in 1890 hastened to congratulate him on his firm stand against the 'monster' of a strike movement[36] – a stand all the more praiseworthy because Parkes was English-born and came of a working-class family. Hallam Tennyson would one day be governor of South Australia, and then governor-general of Australia.

The very prosy song 'Hands all round!' (an 1882 adaptation of some juvenile verses) called for brotherly union between England and its colonies, and might be taken to imply at the same time the harmony of classes which ought to prevail at home. It gave this reserved man, a sufferer from childhood from an isolating estrangement, and ill at ease with all but intimates, a chance to indulge in a bout of hearty good fellowship. In a way his friendliness towards Canada or

Australia, peopled with emigrants mostly plebeian, was a democratic sentiment which found little scope at home; and the same might be said of his good will towards America. But in 'The Fleet', a fiery accusation of neglect of British naval strength, Tennyson displayed a less sentimental side of his thinking; if the country were hindered from importing food there would be mass hunger and social anarchy, 'the wild mob's million feet' trampling civilization down. An ode of 1886 for the opening of an Indian and colonial exhibition, winding up with another appeal for imperial solidarity, had as its refrain: 'Britons, hold your own!' To 'their own' another kingdom was being added that year, Upper Burma.

An admirer of Tennyson as bard of empire felt that he sometimes 'loved to dally too long in that strange, mystic atmosphere of bygone history', and to overlook heroes of the present in his preoccupation with those of antiquity.[37] During the years of the *Idylls* he was not, in fact, writing much about imperial achievements in the visible world, as opposed to his imaginary one. There was some recoil of public feeling after the Indian Mutiny. Possibly an uneasy awareness that Britons in India had not been blameless led him to bring into 'Aylmer's Field' an unpleasant 'Sahib', a retired officer from India with a train of dusky attendants, and lavish of 'oriental gifts'. He is fond of running 'a Malayan amuck against the times', and, unforgivably, extolling French progress; he is, in short, a nabob of the bad old days, not perhaps left so far behind as they ought to have been. But when the Idylls ended in 1873 the climax of European competition for colonies was at hand, and Tennyson's part in ensuring approval of Britain's renewed exertions must have been appreciable. No question of right or wrong is allowed into his lines on the occupation of Egypt in 1882, addressed to General Hamley; it may even seem deliberately excluded, since they start with a pretty picture of autumn in Sussex and end with another of stars paling in the dawn and the glory over Tel el Kebir. Their author was not a close enough student of military affairs to know that Hamley and his commander-in-chief, Wolseley, had the very worst opinion of each other.[38]

That the empire was an intensification, not negation, of capitalist greed, or that British privates in India were villainously treated, and British officers always grumbling about their pay and jockeying for promotion, as jealous of one another as any artists, were matters equally beyond Tennyson's ken. Nevertheless, misgivings crept in even here in his late years, and with them an uneasy feeling that Europe as a whole, or Christendom, was going the way of Camelot. He can hardly have been able to shut his eyes completely to the fact that the later stages of European expansion were not always so edifying. Machine-gun massacres did not lend themselves so well as earlier contests to romanticizing rhymes; and too many foreigners were taking a hand now, whose principles could not be anything like King Arthur's. In 'Columbus' the explorer is seen in despised old age, and is commended as a good Christian and spreader of light and knowledge, who has brought the world closer together; but Tennyson idealizes no less the old native America, as an abode of golden-age simplicity, and regrets the villainous behaviour of the Spanish intruders. An unpublished poem of his youth, 'Anacaona', had pictured a Haitian princess in her idyllic tropical glades just before the Spanish irruption.[39]

There is a sombre contradiction at the heart of imperialism, even if Tennyson cannot admit it of his own empire. 'Locksley Hall Sixty Years After' dwells on the ferocity of other conquerors of olden times, 'iron-hearted Assyrians' and Tamberlane's 'wild Moguls', adding an allusion to Christians throwing defeated fellow Christians into the flames. 'The Victim', a tale of the 1860s about human sacrifice to Thor and Odin, recalls both Arthur's resistance to heathen invaders and enormities of paganism in Tennyson's own day, notably those cults of human sacrifice in West Africa which were made a prime justification for European intervention. But if Dahomey is painted in 'The Dawn' as full of brutish savagery, so also is Europe, with its 'Christless frolic of kings'; the human race is still in its infancy, and the poet can only gaze longingly at what it may be a million years hence. In 'Kapiolani' (not much of a poem, though of some technical interest) it is left to a native chieftainess, a high-minded convert to Christianity, to deliver her Hawaii from the evils of idolatry. Clearly, Tennyson could no longer think so unquestioningly of the white man as fit to carry civilization into dark places. England itself might be gaining the whole world and losing its own soul. In the new 'Locksley Hall' it seems in danger of sinking 'back into the beast again'. Tennyson might be myopic at identifying social ills and cures, but he was at any rate no complacent optimist. His last poems show him sometimes struggling with despair. Already in 'Merlin and Vivien' thoughts hovering over

> The sad sea-sounding wastes of Lyonesse

can be seen drifting towards the Waste Land of our own inwardly crumbling world.

## Notes

1. Cited by D.J. Palmer, in D.J. Palmer, ed., *Tennyson*, London 1973, p. 36.
2. Hallam Tennyson, *Alfred Lord Tennyson, a Memoir. By his Son*, London 1897, vol. I, p. 243.
3. *In Memoriam*, 1850, pp. cv, cxii.
4. Epilogue to 'The Charge of the Heavy Brigade at Balaclava'.
5. Tennyson, *Alfred Lord Tennyson*, vol. I, p. 185 n. 2.
6. Ibid., vol. I, p. 154.
7. J.H. Fowler, *Idylls of the King*, annotated edn, London 1930, p. ix.
8. F. Rabelais, *Gargantua and Pantagruel*, Book 2, ch. 30.
9. H. Adams, *Blake and Yeats: the Contrary Vision*, Ithaca, NY 1954, pp. 58–9.
10. W.D. Paden, *Tennyson in Egypt. A Study of the Imagery of his Earlier Work*, New York 1971, pp. 75 ff.

11. C. Ricks, *Tennyson*, London 1972, p. 264.
12. Tennyson, *Alfred Lord Tennyson*, vol. II, pp. 127, 130.
13. Ibid., vol. II, pp. 122–6.
14. J.O. Hoge, ed., *The Letters of Emily Lady Tennyson*, State College, PA. 1974, p. 27.
15. Tennyson, *Alfred Lord Tennyson*, vol. II, p. 55.
16. Ibid., vol. II, p. 93.
17. Ibid., Vol. I, pp. 432–3, 435.
18. O.D. Edwards, 'Tennyson and Ireland', *New Edinburgh Review*, nos. 38–9, 1977, p. 50.
19. Hoge, p. 162 (a letter of 1861).
20. P. Turner, *Tennyson*, London 1976, pp. 164–5.
21. J. Milne, *The Romance of a Pro-Consul*, London 1911, p. 254.
22. H. Littledale, *Essays on Lord Tennyson's Idylls of the King*, London 1893, pp. 10–11.
23. A.J. Trotter, *The Bayard of India*, London 1909, p. ix.
24. *Tyndale-Biscoe of Kashmir. An Autobiography*, London, n.d., p. 240.
25. A. Conan Doyle, *The Lost World*, London, n.d., ch. 6.
26. J.A. Atanda, *The New Oyo Empire*, London 1973, p. 63.
27. H. Tinker, *Separate and Unequal. India and the Indians in the British Commonwealth 1920–1950*, London 1976, p. 24.
28. See Walt Whitman, *Democratic Vistas*.
29. Tennyson, *Alfred Lord Tennyson*, vol. II, p. 134.
30. W. Shakespeare, *Henry IV, Part II*, act 4, scene 5.
31. E.P. Thompson, *William Morris*, London 1977, pp. 181–2.
32. Ibid., pp. 186, 189.
33. W. Greswell, *Tennyson and our Imperial Heritage*, London 1892, p. 21.
34. Tennyson, *Alfred Lord Tennyson*, vol. II, p. 143.
35. H.S. Ferns and B. Ostry, *The Age of Mackenzie King*, London 1955, p. 92.
36. Tennyson, *Alfred Lord Tennyson*, vol. II, p. 382.
37. Greswell, p. 7.
38. J.H. Lehmann, *All Sir Garnet. A Life of Field-Marshal Lord Wolseley*, London 1964, pp. 303, 308.
39. Tennyson, *Alfred Lord Tennyson*, vol. I, pp. 56–8.

# 7

# Labour and the Literate in Nineteenth-Century Britain

Nineteenth-century Britain, drifting into a new and strange epoch, and uneasily aware of a widening gulf between the classes, has left a voluminous record of the impressions of the better-off about the mass of their fellow countrymen. They were for the most part gloomy, whether concerned with material or with moral conditions. A distinct part of the record is made up of the experiences of individuals who tried to surmount barriers and prejudices and to work actively with labour movements, hoping to provide these with ideas and guidance. As a rule they wanted to guide mass discontent into channels of gradual reform. A few saw it as a positive force which could transform society and put mankind on a new road. Of the two sorts, the gradualists sometimes met with disappointment; the revolutionisers, Chartist or socialist, far more frequently. Their frustration might be due to their own lack of clear practical ideas, or inability to win working-class confidence. But the same failure has befallen latter-day socialists with definite programmes. It has equally been the fate of individuals drawn from the working class itself. The uncrossable gap it seems has not been between class and class nearly so much as between idealistic groups and the bulk of any classes. Cobden and Bright, those middle-class revolutionisers, came to feel as deeply disillusioned with their own class as any worker socialist has been with his.

No review either of the impressions of the literate public, or of the experiences of literate individuals of whatever origin collaborating with the working class, can be more than fragmentary. The latter especially were often contradictory, and many opposite ones can be cited; the same men or women went through shifting moods, less or more hopeful, and no doubt age and fatigue brought despondency. Nevertheless, here too on the whole the gloomier note seems to prevail. There is moreover the objective fact that British society has not, after all, undergone a revolutionary change, though it has altered very greatly in very many ways; and today the mass of labour appears as little interested in any such transformation as it has ever been. It may almost seem as if a statistical law, the product of human existence from the beginning, forbids the great majority of human beings to respond to any but limited, short-term, tangible aims, and condemns the rest to be a perpetual small minority.

To the literate the ancient adage that there is as much difference between lettered and unlettered as between living and dead has often seemed a self-evident truth. Their efforts to guide and improve their fellows have often left them convinced that they were casting pearls before a swinish multitude. In the opening words of the *Essay on Satire* of Dryden's patron Lord Mulgrave:

> How dull, and how insensible a beast
> Is man, who yet would lord it o'er the rest?
> Philosophers and poets vainly strove
> In every age the lumpish mass to move.

Over Christendom there has always lain its archetypal image of the people's friend murdered by the people. A legion of the disappointed must have recalled it, as Macaulay was transparently doing when he consoled himself for the loss of his Edinburgh seat in 1847 by writing high-falutin' verses about his destiny from the cradle as a superior man, far above worldly success or the breath of popularity, one born to defy

> A sullen priesthood and a raving crowd
> Amidst the din of all things fell and vile,
> Hate's yell, and envy's hiss, and folly's bray.

He had in fact been a very unsatisfactory MP.[1]

In Wordsworth's youth all his love was 'given to the people', as he recalled in *The Prelude*. It was a mystic marriage gone through by many others, analogous with the Romantic proclivity for falling in love with women, and equally a leap in the dark. All the Romantic poets withdrew before long into seclusion or exile, whether they turned conservative or remained progressive; from an obscure conviction perhaps that the bustle of the streets and the writing of poetry could not go together, but also perhaps from an uneasy sense of failure to reach a meeting of minds with the people. Byron and Shelley did all the same find a popular audience; Chartist writings are full of echoes of them, and their influence, along with that of the theatre, may be felt in the high-flown rhetoric which labour agitators seem to have indulged in.

Hazlitt, always a staunch radical as well as the greatest of English journalists, was not without an appreciation of the common man. Writing 'On the Ignorance of the Learned' he declared that 'more *home* truths are to be learnt from listening to a noisy debate in an alehouse than from attending to a formal one in the House of Commons . . . the mass of society have common sense, which the learned in all ages want.' But he was too much a pessimist, early youth once gone by, to put his faith in any popular movement (he died two years before the first Reform Act). He concluded that men are only brought together by interest and prejudice, and to be kept together must be approached on their worse side; he saw reformers drifting apart into opinionated, quarrelling cliques.[2] For his own moral reinforcement he turned abroad, giving a dogged loyalty to revolutionary France and then, much less wholesomely, to Napoleon, as champion of the people and apotheosis of the career open to talent.

Industrialism was marking off the working classes from the rest more rigidly, and making 'people' a far less attractive word: it was beauty turning into beast, instead of the other way round. England like China in those days was a country increasingly urbanized yet still governed by landlords and the habits of mind their sway had formed. Trollope contrasted docile farm labourers with rowdy brickfield workers,[3] and it was men like these, or the semi-nomad navvies, on the fringes of orderly life, that the better-off were likely to encounter at times and shy away from. But it was the remote, unknown mass of labour in the industrial towns of the north that bulked largest and most frighteningly in the upper-class imagination; the distance between the classes was geographical as well as social. The southern yokel might be boorish, Gissing wrote, but at least he belonged to an old pattern, represented 'an immemorial subordination', unlike the northern workman 'just emerged from barbarism', with a 'frank brutality' of mind and manner native to his 'primitive state'.[4] Gissing was not exceptional as a literary man, one of the aristocracy of mental labour, in suffering from a general distaste for humanity, which the airs and graces of 'refinement' could divert like the perfumes of Versailles and its unwashed courtiers, leaving it to concentrate itself on the workers.

Mutterings or tumults in the factory districts were the more alarming because of an uneasy sensation that industrialism had made the country unbalanced, unstable, vulnerable as Lord Melbourne wrote to Queen Victoria on 17 August 1842 to all 'the wild and extravagant opinions which are naturally generated in an advanced and speculative state of society.' That the rich ought to be less rich and the poor less poor was clearly one such opinion. Half a century later it was remarked that most of those who talked about the proletariat without first-hand knowledge of it were apt to suppose, mistakenly, that 'working men must be men of extreme and revolutionary opinions.'[5] Their jumping to this conclusion suggests guilty consciences; at an earlier date it may not have been so wide of the mark. Another symptom of ignorance was that pictures of the working class were strongly coloured by impressions of foreign lands. It was a long time before the shadow of the French Revolution, above all, ceased to fall darkly across the English mind. With Melbourne that 'extraordinary shock . . . loomed ever at the back of his consciousness.'[6] When the revolutions of 1848 broke out the dismayed reformer Brougham quoted lurid reports of drunken Paris mobs fighting over their loot, and added that at Messina things had been worse still: 'there is no doubt whatever that sixty Neapolitans were roasted and devoured by those infernal furies, those worse than barbarous cannibals.'[7] A more sober commentator, James Mill, was horrified by a socialistic speech of Attwood during the 1831 agitation, as opening up prospects 'worse than the overwhelming deluge of Huns and Tartars'. His son, John Stuart, endorsed a foreign observer's view of British workers as skilled at their tasks, but 'in conduct the most disorderly, debauched, and unruly, and least resectable and trustworthy of any nation', only kept in hand by 'iron discipline.'[8]

It was a fact moreover that a large proportion of the new working class was of alien origin and speech, Irish in Lancashire and Highland in Glasgow. Engels's well-known description of the 'Milesians' is not much less horrific than Carlyle's. There must have seemed further risk of Irishmen in England picking up subversive ideas which might filter back to their already trouble-some homeland. It was partly in order to strike awe into Ireland that the queen wrote to her ministers on 23 June 1843, when there were riots in South Wales, calling for 'measures of the greatest severity . . . to suppress the revolutionary spirit.'

There was an ominous likeness to 1789 in the fact that religion seemed to have lost its virtue as the time-honoured harmonizer of classes and bridle of discontent. Side by side with Methodism there was a plebeian rationalism which rejected the doctrine preached, for instance, at Edinburgh on the General Thanksgiving day in 1798, that the Christian is to study scripture 'with a child-like, with an humble and teachable disposition', and learn from it 'that the powers that be are ordained of God'.[9] Here too rural and industrial labour stood in contrast. The worthy pastor in John Galt's *Annals of the Parish* (1821) was happy to find the bumpkins in his flock in 1795 'uncontaminated by that seditious infection which fevered the minds of the sedentary weavers, and working like flatulence in the stomachs of the cotton-spinners, sent up into their heads a vain and diseased fume of infidel philosophy'. In the industrial slums of Lancashire it was rather indifference that prevailed. Religious ignorance among 'these degraded beings', wrote P. Gaskell, 'is truly astonishing . . . often there is no belief in the superintending care of a Beneficent Creator'. Even the pious minority were mostly Dissenters, and all dissent implied a degree of frowardness, while some sectaries were positively disaffected. Browning's long poem 'Christmas Eve and Easter Day' vividly expresses the educated man's inability, in spite of Christian duty, to feel any fellowship with the botched, the sickly, the stupid, of a working-class chapel in 1849.

Religion in danger, family in danger. Gaskell's survey of the working class, some years before Engels's, might rather be termed an indictment of a class 'filled with immorality . . . ingratitude, ignorance, and vice, in every conceivable form in which it can develop itself'. At bottom these miscreants were suffering, he argued, not from shortage of money but from break-up of family life. Cottage industry had 'fostered the establishment of parental authority and domestic discipline' whereas now the family was 'a body of distinct individuals', all earning 'and considering themselves as lodgers merely'. This disintegration was 'the most powerfully demoralizing' consequence of the factory system, and he clearly saw in it a menace to order as well as to morals: 'Politically speaking, the common people may be a dead letter, whilst their homes exhibit private independence and social enjoyment.' Conversely they may carry political weight 'whilst their homes exhibit social disorganization and moral worthless-ness'. There may well be some truth in this; the disruption of old social and familial patterns may have been liberating and stimulating for the labour movement, whereas later on, as industrial life settled down to more normal standards, the patriarchal family could rebuild itself, and fit better with cautious reformism than with the daring hopes of earlier years.

Any inclination of the workers to meddle with politics, the preserve of their superiors, Gaskell like most others reckoned among their bad proclivities – 'the pursuit of debasing pleasures, if they can be so called; viz. in the beer-shop, the gin-vault, or the political club'.[10] Drunkenness was a very frequent charge – though high society was at least as alcoholic – and was thought to go with inflammatory politics. One of Harriet Martineau's edifying stories, *Cousin Marshall* (1832), opens on a Sunday morning scene of workmen sprawling in the street where they have sunk down at the end of the previous night's debauch. Some shrewd heads must have seen in this kind of thing an insurance against any proletarian uprising worth the name.

Even a man like the economist T.R. Edmonds, whose ideal was a sort of socialist society, felt that any changes brought about by the working class itself must be impractical and self-defeating: 'The establishment of the social system should be the work of the thinking and richer classes, for only to them would the bulk of the population pay attention.'[11] It is indeed remarkable that out of a mass so 'degraded' and 'demoralized' a labour movement of such dimensions and vitality should have arisen. On the economic side, Galt noted how skilled were 'weavers and cotton-mill folk', as early as 1803, 'in the way of committees and associating together'. Ideas of political reform or socialism came from outside. Between the two appeals there was an oscillation of interest. They converged most closely in the hopeful early years of Chartism, inaugurated in 1837 and 1838 and accompanied by campaigning for more factory legislation and shorter hours. Mill could speak of Chartism in 1845 as 'the revolt of nearly all the active talent, and a great part of the physical force, of the working classes, against their whole relation to society'.[12]

During these stormy years some national as well as many local leaders arose from the ranks. To rise like this required a fair equipment of education, often self-education, which was bound to alter them and make them in some

measure strangers to their own class. Discords among them partly reflected a
diversity of social elements within the working class, and the superior mental
mobility of the craftsman compared with the mill-hand. William Lovett was a
skilled artisan who helped to organise the London Working Men's Association
and launch the Charter, but after a painful spell in prison during 1839 and 1840
he was regarded as a traitor to the cause when he argued that the first require-
ment was self-education and self-improvement by the workers. Another of this
type who came to grief was Thomas Cooper, son of a dyer and wretchedly poor
in boyhood, but a prodigy at picking up learning. He came out of prison
in 1845 more inclined than before to rely on peaceful methods, quarrelled
with O'Connor over this and other issues, and in 1846 was denounced
at the Chartist Convention and expelled. In later years he was a Baptist
preacher. Chartism's history and epitaph were written by another active member, Gammage, originally a cartwright from Northampton, then a shoemaker,
in later days a doctor. His book is often gloomy in tone: 'It is by no means a
pleasant task to wade through the mass of treachery, falsehood, and folly, that
engrafted itself on one of the noblest movements that ever engaged the energies
of a people.'[13]

It went with the heterogeneity of the working classes, and their uneven
development, that a number of the most prominent figures were drawn from
far outside their ranks. They too had their share of dissensions and disappoint-
ments. Robert Owen was a Welshman from Scotland. Like most others who
have come forward to save the people, he wanted also to save them from
themselves, to transform them. He offered them his assistance on condition of
their agreeing to 'renounce all violence and hatred against the possessing and
ruling classes'. Gandhi was to offer the same pledge on the same terms a
hundred years later. On his deathbed in 1858 Owen was still convinced that he
had been right, not the public: 'I gave important truths to the world, and it was
only for want of understanding that they were disregarded.' J.F. Bray, author of
'the last and most powerful manifesto of Owenism', was born in America and
returned there in 1842, convinced that the working class was on the wrong
road with its trade unionism and politics. Bronterre O'Brien, known as 'the
schoolmaster' or chief theorist of Chartism, was an Irishman, son of a once-
prosperous merchant, and a brilliant student drawn away from the bar into
left-wing journalism. In 1833 his emphasis on the necessity of political action
exposed him to a charge of hostility to trade unionism. Later on he fell foul of
'O'Connorism', a blend according to his loyal disciple Gammage of 'ignorance
and fanaticism'.[14]

Feargus O'Connor was another Irishman, with a career at Trinity College,
Dublin, and the Irish bar, and as MP for County Cork, before he threw in his
lot with the English labour movement. He soon stood out as its foremost man
of action in the eyes of the northern millworkers, whose massed numbers gave
them preponderance, and made a contribution to the movement which,

whatever his failings, commands admiration. His critics accused him of domineering, and a man of his flamboyant temper, descending from a higher social level, might well be bent on asserting himself, and claim the first place as his due. They found fault too with his habit of indulging in insurrectionary talk. This may have had its uses in rousing hearers who wanted a simpler, plainer message than O'Brien or Lovett could offer them; but it served to keep O'Connor in the forefront as well. Prison may have undermined him, as it did others, more than he realised, and the final Chartist flare-up in 1848 found him unequal to it. Suddenly placed between excited multitude and embattled government, he looked 'pale and frightened', Lord John Russell the prime minister reported to his sovereign on 10 April, ate humble pie, rebuked the crowd for its 'folly'. From that moment his reputation was wilting, and between failure and mortification his mind gave way. His private resources had been swallowed up in his abortive land settlement scheme. When he died in 1855 the people remembered their former hero well enough to turn out in thousands for his funeral.

Ernest Jones, the son of an army officer with very distinguished connections, was an even more surprising recruit to Chartism. He joined late, not long before its collapse, and was soon one of O'Connor's lieutenants. His writings make an impression of sincerity as well as of brilliant talent, an impression confirmed by John Saville's well-known study of him. Gammage, with some rancour of class it may be, a self-educated man's envy of the silver spoon, judged him 'ambitious and mercenary', one who must 'command the movement, or he would reduce it to nothing', and full of disguised cunning.[15] On his side Jones was far from uncritical of his party. His military parentage may have done something to make him a realist about organization. Other movements, from Christianity to free trade, he was writing in 1848, had been spread by missionary effort, 'whereas Chartism has proselytised less than any other great principle or dogma in the world. We have not of late years taken much pains to make converts; lectures have been given – but mostly in obscure places and to the same audiences.'[16] Innumerable later movements have been open to the same reproach. Jones stood firm in that year, was imprisoned, and subsequently made desperate but unavailing efforts to revive the Charter.

A Chartist of fiction admired O'Connor as a 'glorious man . . . the descendant of the ancient kings, throwing away his rank, his name . . . for the cause of the suffering millions!'[17] 'An Aristocrat is always most acceptable to the working class, even to Democrats', Gammage commented sourly on the speedy elevation of Jones. There may really have been some legacy to the industrial age from an older world where poor folk rebelling did like to have men of position – priests, squires, even lords – in the van, and might even compel them to take the lead. John Frost, the Radical transported to Tasmania after the 'Newport rising' of 1839, is said to have declared in jail that he was forced by extremists to put himself at their head. But much in the Chartist record has a bearing on problems of the psychology of leadership, or of the relation, peculiar and complex as some of these men saw it to be, between leader and led.

There was the impulse of all mass movements to believe and expect too much of their chiefs, strongest again among the northern factory workers with their vigorous but crude political consciousness. They were to be seen streaming in long processions to their open-air meetings, says Gammage, 'making the heavens echo with the thunder of their cheers on recognizing the idols of their worship in the men who were to address them.'[18] But to these idols it might feel as though they were in the grip of an irresistible force:

> I was the people's instrument [Cooper wrote] rather than their director . . . And it is thus, in all ages and in every country, whether on a large or small scale, that a popular leader keeps the lead: his temperament, nature, and powers fit him . . . to become the people's mouthpiece, hand, and arm, either for good or evil.[19]

'I don't lead; I am driven by the people', O'Connor declared. He was blaming the workers' rough ways and readiness to resort to force on 'those who have kept the workmen in ignorance and who degraded them.' Awareness of these defects may have helped to unnerve him in 1848. Other leaders as well were more apt to recognize deficiencies in the masses than the latter in them. O'Brien came to believe that there could be no quick transition 'from our present iniquitous and corrupt state of society into Owen's social paradise': much must first be done 'to rescue the people from their present brutalised condition of ignorance and vassalage'.[20] Jones warned his hearers in a speech of 1846 that 'while we desire to reform others, we must not be blind to the fact that we want reforming ourselves. That it might elevate the mind, and strengthen the frame of men, if they went less to the gin-palace.'[21] In a narrative of the Peasants' Revolt of 1381, one of several historical sketches he wrote during 1847 and 1848, he depicted a band of mutineers getting hopelessly drunk; he must have feared that the same might happen over again. In the end his rebels tamely submit, paralysed by 'hereditary fear' of those above them, and surrender their leaders to the king.[22]

Close to the people by virtue of his yeoman birth, and blessed with a sanguine temperament, Cobbett could sometimes at any rate feel more confidence in his public than most of the popular leaders. Englishmen he declared only wanted 'to live like men, and not like hogs and dogs . . . There never was a working people in the whole world, so reasonable, so just, and so easily satisfied.'[23] On a Rural Ride in 1826 he 'found the working people at Frome very intelligent; very well informed as to the cause of their misery; not at all humbugged by the canters, whether about religion or loyalty'; while talking to ordinary folk at Ely in 1830 satisfied him afresh that 'there are very few, even amongst the labourers, who do not clearly understand the cause of their ruin'.[24] He was addressing farmers as well as labourers, and his tours and meetings convinced him that both were very ready to agree with him, and to act together against the old gang of landlords and stock-jobbers. But he too had his misgivings, and was not always so hopeful.

All this time urban, middle-class Radicalism was waging its campaign against the old gang, for parliamentary and economic reform, a struggle separate from that of the workers but impinging on it at many points. Labour support was often sought, but most often by demagogue politicians in search of catspaws. The scene in *Felix Holt* where the Radical agent cajoles a set of bemused coalminers into promising strong-arm assistance on election day is a good epitome of how the masses were encouraged to demonstrate, even riot, during 1831 and 1832 for a Reform Bill which would do them no good. As Borrow was to write of 'Pseudo-Radicals' in *The Romany Rye* (1857): 'They egged on poor ignorant mechanics and rustics, and got them hanged for pulling down and burning', while they looked on from a safe distance. Later on there were genuine proposals of alliance from a left wing of the middle classes, men like Joseph Sturge at Birmingham. At a joint conference there in 1842 O'Brien argued that denunciation of the middle classes might be abated because they had grown less hostile to labour since 1834: 'now vast numbers of them not only recognise us as an integral part of the body politic, but they have actually paid court to us.' Opponents condemned all this as 'an act of treachery directed against the working class, and as an attempt to weaken or obliterate the class war'.[25] Disillusion had sunk deep since 1832; and manufacturers were not prepared to pay for labour's political backing with concessions in terms of wages and hours. Cobden inveighed against trade unions as 'founded upon principles of brutal tyranny and monopoly. I would rather live under a Dey of Algiers than a Trades' Committee.' Much to his disgust the bulk of labour held aloof from his campaign against the Corn Laws; he believed that intriguers were deluding the workers, and accused the latter of 'allowing a parcel of lads, with hired knaves for leaders, to interrupt their meetings.'[26] He was failing to understand what Mill saw very clearly – the total alienation of the working class: 'the *sourde* animosity which is universal in this country towards the whole class of employers in the whole class of the employed.'[27]

Reluctance on the part of the industrialists or their spokesmen to make any better offer to the workers left the way open for thoughts, or fancies, of inter-vention on their behalf by aristocracy, as deus ex machina. A Scots peasant, Carlyle, was the odd standard-bearer of this paternalism. His feeling about the workers comes out in his praise of Plato – 'With what disdain he speaks of the great unwashed and their blatant democracies!'[28] One of the seer's pipe dreams, in the first of his *Latter-day Pamphlets* of 1850, was of an heroic premier presenting the unemployed with a scheme for enrolling them into labour battalions: 'Disobey the rules, – I will admonish and endeavour to incite you; if in vain, I will flog you; if still in vain, I will at last shoot you.' A notion that the workers were famishing for leadership from above – not simply to welcome an individual who left his own sphere to join them – had a long lease of life in other minds too. Disraeli concocted a model factory, ventilated on a new plan, employing two thousand workers, with model housing attached; all the work of a Mr Trafford, younger son of an old landed family, who was guided by 'the baronial principle, reviving in a new form . . . a correct conception of the relations which should subsist between the employer and the employed.'[29]

Ruskin might have been recalling this fable when he satirized the upper-class dream of an ideal existence in a lovely mansion and park supported by a mill whose workers 'never drink, never strike, always go to church on Sunday, and always express themselves in respectful language.' Yet Ruskin himself could succumb to the same kind of fantasy, as when he assured a genteel audience: 'The people are crying to you for command . . . You think they don't want to be commanded; try them . . . "Govern us", they cry with one heart, though many minds. They *can* be governed still, these English . . . They love their old ways yet, and their old masters, and their old land.'[30] This rigmarole was addressed not to the Horse Marines but to the Royal Artillery Institute at Woolwich. A generation later Gissing would be furbishing the old legend afresh: 'Profoundly aristocratic in his sympathies, the Englishman has always seen in the patrician class not merely a social, but a moral, superiority . . . Very significant is the cordial alliance from old time between nobles and people.'[31]

On a more practical level paternalism manifested itself chiefly through the Christian Socialists. These men were prepared to collaborate with labour on humanitarian grounds, in opposition to the Poor Law of 1834, or for factory legislation and restriction of working hours. Kingsley and others even gave active support to a strike of Manchester ironworkers over piecework and overtime. On this plane too those who took the lead had their tribulations, if seldom as severe as Oastler's when philanthropy landed him in jail for debt. They were depressingly few, for one thing, though it is true that upstairs as well as downstairs in society an energetic group may have disproportionate influence. When Ashley (later Lord Shaftesbury) took up advocacy of the ten-hour day he hoped that many of his class would join him, but scarcely any did.

In parliament he 'regarded himself as the choice of the workers', but in his eyes socialism and Chartism were 'the two great demons in morals and politics',[32] and a good half of the purpose of all leadership like his was to guide labour away from its own path. Between such a man and the rank and file, relations could only be precarious. They broke down in 1850 when he decided to accept a modification of the Ten Hour Act. He had what he considered valid reasons, but he wrote in his diary: 'Expect from manufacturing districts a storm of violence and hatred. I might have taken a more popular and belauded course, but I should have ruined the question; one more easy to myself, but far from *true* to the people.' Indignation did run high, all the more because he had made the decision without consulting the workers, and a Lancashire committee passed a resolution deploring 'the infatuation which led to the cause of the factory workers being intrusted to Lord Ashley.'[33] By this time, also, Chartism was on the wane, and with it the atmosphere of crisis which had gained Christian Socialism a hearing among the well-off. 'When this boisterous pressure was withdrawn, nobody troubled about *Parson Lot* [Kingsley], or the scruples of Maurice and his friends.'[34]

'We say to the great minds of the day, come among the people, write for the people, and your fame will live for ever.'[35] Ernest Jones was anticipating Mao's call to the writers. Chartism had many of its own, but not of a calibre to be heard outside the movement. Of the others, a few novelists did try to write about the working classes, though scarcely *for* them, and as sympathetic critics rather than allies. What stands out in their thinking is a contradiction none of them could resolve between the harshness of daily life for labour and the futility or worse, to their minds, of its more impatient efforts to emancipate itself. Instead public opinion, that slumbering giant, was somehow to be aroused, and somehow to find a way of solving the insoluble. Strife between capital and labour was regularly deplored: each ought to recognize its obligations to the other. To Elizabeth Gaskell, writing *Mary Barton*, 'The most deplorable and enduring evil' from the depression and strife of 1839 to 1841 was the 'feeling of alienation between the different classes of society'. In Harriet Martineau's story *A Manchester Strike* the men's leader Allen and the employer Mr Wentworth are both meritorious human beings, and she ends with the words: 'When will masters and men work cheerfully together for their common good?'

Allen has been pushed by his fellows into taking the lead, reluctantly because he has a family and fears to be victimized, and after its failure cannot get his job back and has to spend the rest of his life as a street-cleaner. A far more lurid picture of a strike occurs in Mrs Gaskell's *North and South*, with a riot against an employer who is importing Irish blacklegs: 'As soon as they saw Mr Thornton they set up a yell – to call it not human is nothing – it was as the demoniac desire of some terrible wild beast for the food that is withheld from his ravening'. Trade unions still had a secret-society flavour which lost nothing in middle-class imagination. Mary Barton's father and friends took 'one of those fierce terrible oaths which bind members of Trade Unions to any given purpose', and drew lots for the duty of committing a murder. Disraeli conjured up in *Sybil* a ritual of robes and masks for the initiation of a new devotee vowed to carry out all union behests, including 'the chastisement of Nobs, the assassin-ation of oppressive and tyrannical masters.'

In 1848 Kingsley issued a manifesto to the 'Workmen of England', asking them: 'Will the Charter make you free? Will it free you from the slavery to ten-pound bribes? Slavery to beer and gin? Slavery to every spouter who flatters your self-conceit?'[36] The contrast between bitter wrongs and the folly of trying to set them right by force came out most strongly of all in his *Alton Locke*, in 1850. A farm-labourers' riot – 'the old crust of sullen, dogged patience' exploding into 'reckless fury and brutal revenge' – is easily routed by a few armed men. The half-reluctant hero, an artisan whose education has the familiar double effect of deepening his sympathy for his class while putting a distance between him and it, finds himself to his dismay in a London garret 'full of pikes and daggers, brandished by some dozen miserable, ragged, half-starved artisans ... the untaught, the despairing, the insane; "the dangerous classes", which society creates, and then shrinks in horror, like Frankenstein'.

In *Barnaby Rudge*, in 1841, Dickens drew a melodramatic picture of the Gordon Riots; in *Hard Times*, in 1854, he wrote with more discretion. By now the danger of a violent upheaval was receding, and he had made a sally from his London to see things in the industrial north for himself. In his description of a workers' meeting, the men are misled in their purpose of sending a workmate to Coventry for refusing to come into their plans; but there is a chairman to see fair play, the culprit is given his chance to speak, and the men are 'gravely, deeply, faithfully in earnest ... these men, through their very delusions, showed great qualities, susceptible of being turned to the happiest and best account'. There is a Carlylean inflexion in Dickens's language here, as if he were at a loss for words to express something novel to him. But in his essay on 'The Working Man', in *The Uncommercial Traveller*, he was to declaim against one of Carlyle's sins – 'that great impertinence, Patronage', and to praise the workman for 'the instinctive revolt of his spirit' against the floods of patronising talk bestowed on him.

The honest toilers of *Hard Times* contrast forcibly with the agitator, Slackbridge, who is egging them on in pseudo-heroic accents – 'Oh my friends and fellow-countrymen, the slaves of an iron-handed and a grinding despotism!' Slackbridge is cunning, vindictive, inferior in every way to his untutored hearers. He belongs to a gallery of such portraits: the figure of the agitator was a bogy to the better-off classes, because it jarred with their creed that the poor ought to wait for public opinion to do its work instead of trying to work out their own redemption. There ought to be no representatives coming between workers and masters, wrote P. Gaskell; such men were picked in hours of excitement, likely to throw up 'the brawler, the factious man, the specious scoundrel'.[37] Mrs Gaskell could feel with Mary Barton's embittered father, and the 'hoards of vengeance in his heart against the employers', but she could not help adding a censure on ringleaders who inflame such passions. Her London delegate coming to organize the Manchester workers 'might have been a disgraced medical student of the Bob Sawyer class, or an unsuccessful actor, or a flashy shopman', and began with bombast 'in which he blended the deeds of the elder and the younger Brutus' – though he was businesslike enough when he came to the matter in hand. In later, less perilous times the sinister agitator would turn into a mere soapbox spouter like Anstey's bellowing republican: 'Hour turn'll come some day! We sha'n't *halways* be 'eld down, and muzzled, and silenced, and prevented uttering the hindignation we've a right to feel!'[38]

George Eliot, an impressionable young observer during the 1840s, could welcome the February revolution of 1848 in Paris, but had no desire to see it emulated on her side of the Channel. 'Our working classes are eminently inferior to the mass of the French people', with little 'perception or desire of justice', only selfish greed: 'a revolutionary movement would be simply destructive.'[39] *Felix Holt* came out in 1866, when political emotions could be recollected in relative tranquillity. Its moral is that labour ought to have leaders of its own, who will remain faithful to their class while rising above its weaknesses, as Felix (a skilled craftsman, not a mill hand) is resolved to do:

> Why should I want to get into the middle class because I have some learning . . . That's how the working men are left to foolish devices and keep worsening themselves: the best heads among them forsake their born comrades, and go in for a house with a high door-step and a brass knocker.

He is clear-sighted about the drunken habits of the neighbouring colliers, and he tells a workers' meeting that they are not yet fit for voting rights; he wants them to have power, but only for good and constructive purposes (as usual, left undefined) – 'and I can see plainly enough that our all having votes will do little towards it at present.' His gospel, like his creator's, is public opinion. It is a symbolic part of this idealist's fate to be injured in a senseless mob riot he tried to restrain, and to be accused of provoking it. In 1867 George Eliot distilled his and her philosophy into an 'Address to Working Men, by Felix Holt', inculcating the lesson of every class's 'responsibility to the nation at large'.

Mark Rutherford's *Revolution in Tanner's Lane*, equally remarkable in its way, came another twenty years later. It might be called an elegy for obscure and unavailing martyrs:

> Who remembers the poor creatures who met in the early mornings on the Lancashire moors or were shot by the yeomanry? They sleep in graves over which stands no tombstone, or probably their bodies have been carted away to make room for a railway which has been driven through their resting-place.

At this date the uproar of past days could appear meaningless incoherence; what stood out was

> the undisciplined wildness and feebleness of the attempts made by the people to better themselves . . . the spectacle of a huge mass of humanity goaded, writhing, starving, and yet so ignorant that it cannot choose capable leaders, cannot obey them if perchance it gets them.

The two characters we admire are both out of tune with the movement they have joined, one set apart from it by self-education and Calvinist fervour, the other by birth. Zachariah is disgusted by the imbecile applause of the streets for a Bourbon prince about to return to France on the fall of Napoleon – 'the mob crying out, "God bless your Majesty!" as if they owed him all they had' – and ruminates: 'As for the people so-called ... I doubt whether they are worth saving'. When heated demands for action arise among the friends of the people, Major Maitland warns them 'that not only were the middle classes all against them, but their own class was hostile. This was perfectly true, though it was a truth so unpleasant that he had to endure some very strong language, and even hints of treason'. Zachariah gets into prison, Maitland loses his life when an ill-planned Blanketeers' march is attacked by the yeomanry. Rioters break into an inn cellar, and are then quickly mastered; a stock episode in the political novel. 'I ain't a Radical. I ain't', says a thirsty plebeian in another Rutherford novel: 'Wy, I've seed in my time an election last a week, and beer a-runnin' down the gutters. It was the only chance a poor man 'ad. Wot sort of chance 'as he got now?'[40]

Whatever their weaknesses, it appears that the first generations of the proletariat were capable of some vision of a world cleansed and renovated, and of the mighty put down from their seats. As their descendants became habituated to the mill, the slum, the industrial existence, shades of the prison house seem to have closed on them. There used to be a Russian adage that the peasant must be boiled in the factory pot before he becomes a revolutionary; but it may be equally true that if he is kept in it too long the revolutionary juices are boiled out of him. After mid-century the labour movement was stiffening into 'labourism', content with what improvements could be got by trade unions, and relinquishing any design of transforming society. Part of the cause must be looked for in the abandonment of its own 'mission' by the industrial bourgeoisie, which it signalized by throwing its hat in the air for the Crimean War and ditching Cobden and Bright in the election of 1857. Henceforth each class was satisfied to find a place in the existing order, and to tail politically behind the one in front of it.

Many old Chartists were now, as one of them at Halifax wrote in 1859, 'so thoroughly disgusted at the indifference and utter inattention of the multitude to their best interests that they too are resolved to make no more sacrifices in a public cause.' A legion of such former stalwarts shook their country's dust off their feet and emigrated. Jones remonstrated, and called on 'the tyrant-scourged pallid workers' to stay in England and make further sacrifices for their class. Yet he often showed remarkable insight into the springs of mass action, the urge of material benefit required to fire the train, to attach a multitude of men and women to progressive causes. Between this and the call to heroic abnegation there was a deep-seated incongruity which has haunted socialism from the cradle. Emigration had an evident affinity with retreat into merely economic struggle, and Jones was indignant at this too, all the more because it meant that the better-placed workers – 'that worst of all aristocracies, the aristocracy of labour' – were practising a self-help which ignored the interests of the less fortunate. '*All Trades-unions are lamentable fallacies*', he declared.[41] On 12 May 1865 Engels reported to Marx: 'It seems to me that he has no longer any real faith in the proletarian movement as a whole.' O'Brien had lately died in poverty and neglect. In 1869 and 1870 Thomas Cooper found the northern millworkers better off, but 'noticed with pain that their moral and intellectual condition had deteriorated'.[42] No doubt there was some nostalgic mirage in his memories of ragged toilers enthralled by debates on justice and socialism; but times really had changed.

In this climate Positivism had a part to play with the working class like Christian Socialism in the Chartist epoch. Its highly elitist thinking could infuriate an old working-class Chartist and secularist like Holyoake, converted though he might be in his later years to collaboration with Liberalism. He derided the heaven offered to the workers by Comtists as a model pigsty, 'where the straw should be clean, the trough copious, the wash abundant, and where the Comtist priests would oft come and graciously pat their sleek backs, provided they did not squeal to get out.'[43] This was too sweeping a criticism, at least of men like Frederic Harrison, whom George Eliot, an admirer of Comte, consulted about the political side of *Felix Holt*, and Professor Beesly. Their object was 'the creation of an organised and all-powerful public opinion' guided by men of wisdom, but they looked to the workers as the class 'best prepared to receive large principles', because least corrupted by property. In this spirit, these two could be during the 1860s 'quite the closest and most influential advisers of the trade-union movement.'[44] They furnished also some of the scanty knowledge of the working classes gained by a new and somewhat anaemic generation of progressive intellectuals.[45] Beesly would have liked the unions to widen their horizons and be readier to take political action; in later years his influence on the labour movement faded.

When Samuel Plimsoll went into Parliament in 1868 to press for protection for seamen against the owners of 'coffin ships', and failed to carry his bill or to get a Royal Commission, he turned to the trade union movement for support. 'For years I was in very close contact with him', George Howell records.[46] No such contact had been sought by Captain Marryat when he wanted to get life in the navy made less evil for seamen, and appealed to middle-class opinion in 1836 with his *Mr Midshipman Easy*. One of his aims, doubtless, was to ensure naval loyalty at a time when order was under threat, and the novel was also a satire on the democratic notions swallowed by Jack Easy's foolish parent. Old Mr Easy is a figure of fun, though his patent machine for altering the shape of men's skulls, and with it their characters, might serve as a warning against all mechanical or bureaucratic reformism.

When labour grievances broke out menacingly again, union leaders found an unexpected patron in Cardinal Manning. As head of a minority church, he wanted to enlarge its numbers; as scion of a wealthy family he wanted to shepherd labour away from socialism. In his biography of Cobden in 1881

Morley could credit the advent of a more civilized, less brutish trade unionism 'in no small degree to an active fraternization, to use Cobden's own word, with the leaders of the workmen by members of the middle class, who represented the best moral and social elements in the public opinion of their time.'[47] Well before this date Bright had been arguing that it was time for the working class to be given the vote, and maintaining, as he did in a speech at Birmingham on 29 January 1864, that there was now a more peaceful atmosphere, a wider acceptance of law and order: 'are not magistrates and all men in authority held in better regard than they were thirty or forty years ago?' There was enough agreement with this for him to carry the Reform Bill of 1867, against the rearguard headed by Robert Lowe with his alarmist talk of the ignorant and inebriated masses and his doctrine of elite rule – very close to Dr Johnson's definition of good government in 1773 as one where 'the wise see for the simple, and the regular act for the capricious.' Over this issue labour came back into politics, but with far more limited aspirations than in Chartist days. A vote now meant the right to ask for more porridge, not a new world.

One sequel was the Education Act of 1870. Bright pointed out in his speech at Edinburgh on 5 November 1868 that, though Britain led in so many fields, 'in the education of the people, of the working classes, we are much behind very many of the civilized and Christian nations of the world.' Teaching and learning had always been a debatable land between the classes, and on both sides there were contradictory attitudes. In *Mary Barton* we hear of hand-weavers round Oldham working away while 'Newton's *Principia* lies open on the loom, to be snatched at in work hours, but revelled over in meal times, or at night.' Factory life was only too likely to wipe out such thirst for knowledge: the new existence might lead towards better material rewards, but the old dying crafts could do more at times to stimulate mental alertness. Manchester workmen might be splendid at their duties, Brougham told the Mechanics' Institute, but they were deficient in 'love of scientific knowledge and useful learning'. This was in 1835, when Radical spokesmen were brimming with confidence, and he could proclaim that 'whatever improves men's minds tends to give them sober and virtuous habits.'[48] Conservatives had their doubts, like the Reverend Dr Folliott in Peacock's novel *Crotchet Castle* in 1831, indignant about the way his haystacks had been set on fire and his house broken into 'on the most scientific principles. All this comes of education.' E.P. Thompson quotes an old grumble that 'charity schools are nurses of Rebellion.' As time went on employers were in a quandary. Technical advances required literate workers: 'On the other hand, as the far-seeing ones clearly saw, an educated working class sooner or later made for radical changes ... Education meant bigger immediate profits, but it was gambling with "revolution".'[49]

On the other hand again, education from above could be the means of instilling into working-class children ideas proper to their station. Cobbett felt misgivings about this when he visited New Lanark: his comment would apply still more obviously to any state-run primary education – 'it fashions the rising generation to habits of *implicit submission*, which is only another term for civil and political slavery.'[50] Teaching ragged boys and girls from mining villages to sing 'Happy English children!' was evidently meant to convince them that the working class had nothing to complain of.[51] Education as it emerged was of very poor quality, likely to perpetuate mental inertia and hinder any rising above the level of 'labourism'. Reciprocally, labourism damped any desire for more knowledge. As one self-taught and highly literate workman came to realize, late in the century: 'There was very little enthusiasm for education among the working classes themselves, though popular shibboleths and party catchwords were shouted loudly from their platforms.'[52] He was conscious that his own attainments made him a stranger in the eyes of his fellows. '"I can't stick him: you never see him without a book", was a remark made about myself at a Congress.'[53] Such experiments as the founding of Toynbee Hall in 1884, which he helped to bring about, had little or no leavening effect on the lump. Working-class withdrawal from the political arena and from the national culture went together. One more feature of the retreat was a fading of the militant anti-religious or anti-clerical spirit of earlier days. Workmen might not be religious, but it was easy to prejudice them against anything that could be called atheistic.[54]

Cobden had endeavoured to convince businessmen that votes for workers would not bring socialism, but would turn them into 'conservatives', willing to 'elect their chiefs from a higher class than their own.'[55] His prediction was to be verified, as Gladstone, a late convert to extension of the franchise, saw. In his philosophy, expounded in an article of 1878 in the *Nineteenth Century*, however many might vote the few must rule: 'It is written in legible characters, and with a pen of iron, on the rock of human destiny, that within the domain of practical politics the people must in the main be passive.' Realistic enough about capitalist democracy, the People's William observed how acquiescence on the part of the working masses might turn into 'subserviency': 'We cannot be surprised if the mere desire to please the employer or landlord, as such, steps into the vacant or lethargic mind.'

'Deference voting' did indeed come naturally to many sections of the working class as well as of the lower middle class; labourism could lend a morbid degree of truth to the legend of the masses pining for upper-class 'leadership'. Lancashire mill hands, as the Webbs described them in *Industrial Democracy* (1897) were well organized, but politically naive compared with, for instance, the miners; engrossed with their chapels and cooperatives, they were ready to take their opinions on other things from mill owners and land-owners.[56] There was of course India with its markets to provide a bond of interest between cottonworkers and their employers.

It was a paradox of these decades that while labour was drifting away from any socialist ideal, a number of intellectuals, especially among men of letters, were moving towards it. They were disillusioned with their society, deprived of forward momentum by the inertia of the bourgeoisie, and turned with more or less hopefulness towards the working class, if only as an unknown quantity. Mill, if very tentatively, pointed the way, under the tuition of Harriet Taylor, whom he married in 1851. She softened his animus against socialism, and persuaded him to write that 'The poor have come out of leading-strings, and cannot any longer be governed or treated like children.'[57]

But a bridge to span the wide chasm was not soon built. Ruskin was typical of a good many intellectuals in being capable of much searching criticism of things as they were, but far less of seeing how they could be bettered, and what part the workers could play in the process. How, he asked in a lecture in the late 1860s at a Mechanics' Institute, was the manual worker to be 'comforted, redeemed, and rewarded? . . . Well, my good, laborious friends, these questions will take a little time to answer yet.'[58] It was for thinkers like himself to find the answers, he implied. He was one of several whom the Paris Commune, like the revolutions of 1848, pushed further left, making him more definitely a socialist if still a paternalistic one, while it horrified the bulk of respectable opinion. Another was George Meredith, who wrote that 'The people are the Power to come', and by the people meant the working class.[59]

In a more distinctly political and organized form the intellectuals of the Social Democratic Federation were trying to bring labour's mind back from bread and butter to higher things. Tom Mann, the pioneer working-class socialist, says that when he objected to the SDF's sweeping dismissal of trade unionism, its leader Hyndman exclaimed 'What were these precious unions? By whom were they led? By the most stodgy-brained, dull-witted, and slow-going time-servers in the country.'[60] There was a regrettable measure of truth in this dictum, but it is not one that a trade unionist could accept. Hyndman moreover was an 'aristocrat', and not of a sort to be congenial to labour. To a Scottish worker-socialist who encountered him at an Edinburgh meeting he seemed to belong to 'a world far removed from my humble environment and not at all like the disciple of Marx . . . He gave us a few words of advice how to behave and work for the social revolution and the party and we left quite unmoved.'[61] A brother Scot summed him up more bluntly as 'a vain, egotistical old peacock'.[62]

William Morris and his friends broke away from the SDF in 1884 to form the Socialist League. He too rejected trade unionism as irrelevant to socialism, and also rejected parliamentarism; which left the great task, 'the making of Socialists', too much abstracted from workaday life. In *Signs of Change* (1888) he paid tribute to Chartism as 'thoroughly a working-class movement', set going by 'the simplest and most powerful of causes – hunger', but in its goals too one-sidedly political.[63] In the utopian *News from Nowhere* in 1890, looking back on the revolution as something already got through, he ascribed it to idealism instead of hunger: 'the great motive-power of the change was a longing for freedom and equality', which touched the masses too, even though 'the slave-class could not conceive the happiness of a free life.' All this was remote enough from how labour in his Britain was really feeling, and in fact, after years of hopeful endeavour during the 1880s, Morris was deeply pessimistic at the end of the decade.

Young intellectuals in the 1880s fancied, as Shaw said, that 'Socialism had only to be put clearly before the working classes to concentrate the power of their immense numbers in one irresistible organisation.'[64] This was proving an illusion on a par with that of the Narodnik students who tried to throw their arms round the Russian peasantry. Socialists, the Webbs objected in *Industrial Democracy*, lacked any intimate knowledge of trade union wants, while they brandished revolutionary programmes incomprehensible to the plain man.[65] Talented trade unionists, as in other countries, prized their sphere of work because it was their own, not shared like the management of political movements with men from outside whose superior training gave them the advantage. Snowden recalls in his autobiography that older trade union officials were undisguisedly hostile to the ILP in its early days, and the only insults Keir Hardie met with when he entered the House of Commons came from labour camp-followers of Liberalism.[66]

Mann convinced himself that 'the real educational work on labour questions is now going on mainly in the thousands of trade union branches and trades councils that exist in all centres of industry.'[67] Hence he called for decentral-izing of government. In fact England already had more of this than most countries, and it did make for labour participation in local business. But this might push bigger issues out of sight. Living among Lancashire workers in 1883 the future Beatrice Webb, not yet a socialist, found them diligent in matters of their own district, which they understood, but indifferent to anything further away: 'Parliament is such a far-off thing, that the more practical and indus-trious lot say that it is "gormless meddling with it" (useless), and they leave it to the "gabblers".' This she welcomed as 'one of the best preventives against the socialist tendency of the coming democracy.'[68] They were prophetic words.

Fabian Socialism, starting in 1884, was as much a response to labour's political atrophy as a design to bring it about. Fabians had none of Marx's or Morris's 'faith in the people', but it is not clear that in the long run the presence or absence of such faith has made much difference either to the people or to the advance of socialism. And while labourism helped to mould a sober municipal-socialist mentality at one end of the scale, at the other it helped to produce by force of repulsion a bevy of highly individualistic socialists, among whom Shaw was only the most eccentric and perhaps the most talented. He was converted by *Das Kapital*, and set out with a desire to preach to the workers; his first open-air speech, to a couple of loafers on the grass of Hyde Park, may be said to have struck the keynote of his experience of them. Subsequently he came to the conclusion that 'proletarian agitation' only appealed to 'sects of idealists and cranks': solid trade unionists were interested in mundane things alone.[69]

Shaw's extraordinary medley of sense and nonsense may be put down to lack of the ballast that a strong popular movement (or belief in it, whether well founded or illusory) could have given him. For want of this he often sank to being no more than an entertainer of the middle classes. His brigand band in Act III of *Man and Superman* (1903), with its comic anarchist and three wrangling social democrats, might almost be intended to reassure timorous capitalists that they had nothing to fear. His faith in socialism persisted, but it was a highly bureaucratic one. Nationalizing industry would not affect the workers in any way, he held. 'To them the change will be only a change of masters.' Near the end of his biggest political work he wrote what may be taken as both his first and last word on his fellow men. 'Capitalist mankind in the lump is detestable . . . Both rich and poor are really hateful in themselves. For my part I hate the poor.'[70]

H.G. Wells was never a devotee of Marx, and had no liking or respect for the working class to live down. His origin from a social level just above it left him with an ingrained repugnance, recognisable in his *Time Machine* nightmare of helots turned by ages of servitude into cannibal beasts. It was dawning on the upper classes, he wrote in his Fabian essay, 'This Misery of Boots' in 1907, that they would be 'happier and more comfortable' under socialism:

> Much more likely to obstruct the way to Socialism is the ignorance, the want of courage, the stupid want of imagination of the very poor . . . But, even with them, education is doing its work; and I do not fear but that in the next generation we shall find Socialists even in the slums.

Bizarre as this may sound, and deceptive as was Wells's notion of socialist enlightenment floating down like manna, not many working–class socialists have been produced by any other recipe. Easy optimism ended for him, as for so many others, with the Great War. Myriads of those caught up in it, he reflected, were doing no more thinking about it than a pet monkey in a house on fire. He like Shaw came to a conclusion gloomy but hard to dispute: 'The human mind is an instrument very easily fatigued. Only a few exceptions go on thinking restlessly – to the extreme exasperation of their neighbours.'[71]

Other socialists outside the labour ranks formed a variegated bevy. Some were only following a fashion, like G.K. Chesterton who joined, as he tells us in his autobiography, only because 'not being a Socialist was a perfectly ghastly thing.' Edward Carpenter was a Tolstoyan figure, 'a middle class man who wandered the streets in sandals and broad hats copied from the American poet Walt Whitman, who tried to live intimately with people of a lower social station and combine intellectual and manual work.'[72] Cunninghame Graham, injured and arrested on Bloody Sunday in 1887, the year when he helped Keir Hardie to found the Scottish Labour Party, was a laughing cavalier with a

strong dose of cynical humour, better fitted than graver men to survive in the
left-wing wilderness: his wanderings carried him into many other strange
lands. Belfort Bax wandered into many corners of history, and cherished a
socialist 'religion' based, as he wrote in *The Ethics of Socialism*, on an

> objective social morality, of which we see the germs even in the working classes of
> today when at their best – and when they are not, as they are to a large extent in this
> country, completely brutalised by the conditions of their life.[73]

One early middle-class Communist who got into parliament adapted himself
to these conditions by going about

> unkempt and unshaven, wearing a dirty collar and clothes, trying to look 'prolet-
> arian'! He was an example of . . . the type that believes one has to use the most
> vulgar swear words when speaking; to be regardless of dress and a stranger to soap;
> and wear hobnailed boots and corduroys.[74]

Bax was hopeful enough to think that socialist ideas were penetrating the trade
unions, breaching 'the solid front of true British stupidity, of which, unfortunately, hitherto they have been the embodiment'. In fact, what a critic had said
long before of Lovett and his friends, that they had no more influence over the
workers of London than of Constantinople,[75] might have been said now of
these socialists. Two works of fiction, by a socialist workman and an anti-
socialist with working-class relatives, provide commentaries each as bleak as
the other. Robert Tressell the house-painter carries us into a frowsy world
where a few devoted socialists strive with faint success to lighten the gloom of
ignorance and nonsense, and toil-worn women skimping their families on
bread and margarine grow angry at the thought of 'the wicked Socialists . . .
trying to bring Ruin upon them.' He, like so many other novelists, describes an
election when ragged workers throw themselves with senseless excitement into
cheering for one or other of their rival exploiters [76] – an excitement sublimated
since then, it often appears, into enthusiasm for football teams. In Gissing's
*Demos, a Story of English Socialism* (1886), the working class is dangerous as well as
ridiculous. An ardent young socialist workman, Mutimer, comes into money
and drifts apart from his class, while striving to fulfil his ideals; he is denounced
as a renegade. In the end Demos, tired of palaver, is ready for 'a good wild-beast
roar, for a taste of bloodshed': Mutimer's house is besieged by a mob, and he is
hit by a stone and killed while – a neatly ironical touch – a party of police is
hurrying to the rescue.

Some could still believe in an unfolding alliance between elite and mass. J.A.
Hobson saw the 1910 election as displaying an advance of rationality,
Liberalism fortified by 'associated labour power'. In their confidence in mind's
unfolding ascendancy over brute forces such men 'exalted their own role'.[77] It

has been a chronic inclination of intellectuals to see a movement of the many in their own image. More frequent were misgivings, deepened by the exploration now spasmodically in progress into the lower social depths. Glimpses of lurking horrors caught the eye, like 'the crowded couch of incest in the warrens of the poor' in Tennyson's 'Locksley Hall Sixty Years After'. Against this background many doubts arose as to whether England's adulterated democracy could really bring the classes together, except at their worst points.

Trollope described a London election campaign in a novel of 1864 – *Can You Forgive Her?* – in a vein close to Carlyle's verdict on politics as 'beer and balderdash'. A few years later he tried one for himself, as Liberal candidate at Beverley, and his autobiography records it as just as disgusting. This was early in the new dispensation, but though bribery gave way as time went on to other modes of inducement these were often little more refined, and a long purse was as potent as ever. Watching voters at a London County Council polling station in a poor district, confused and tired, one of them drunk, Graham Wallas experienced 'an intense conviction that this could not be accepted as even a decently satisfactory method' of choosing a city government.'[78] 'Thirty years ago', G.W. Russell wrote of democracy in 1909, 'it was an ideal which ardent and generous souls honestly worshipped . . . Beyond all question the result has been disappointment and disillusionment.'[79]

What was flourishing instead was Tory demagogy, an easier and cheaper substitute for Christian Socialism whose nostrum was turning social resentment into anti-foreign feeling. J.M. Barrie was to make fun in *The Admirable Crichton* of an amiable earl who held monthly tea parties where his family had to wait on the servants, a ceremony equally irksome to both sides. But in the form of Primrose League jollities this kind of hobnobbing had a large share in Tory strategy. 'The most dangerous demagogues', a Liberal commented wryly, 'are the clever Conservatives who despise the people.'[80] In the years before 1914 progressives from the working class or from outside it often suffered from the same despondency. 'At this moment the Roman decadent phase of *panem et circenses* is being inaugurated under our eyes', Shaw wrote in the preface to *Man and Superman*. Frederick Rogers was conventionally patriotic, but a meeting with leading Cooperators during the Boer War left him disgusted: 'I was hardly prepared for the solid unbending Toryism of the older men, and the meek acquiescence or flippant contempt of the younger ones, in relation to social affairs.'[81] By this time a high Anglican, Rogers turned to Conservatism towards the end of his life. In Galsworthy's novel of 1911, *The Patrician*, an old Chartist stands in a crowd waiting to hear an election result announced, and there are 'tears rolling down his cheeks into his beard' as the Radical candidate is beaten: 'You wouldn't remember forty-eight, I suppose. There was a feeling in the people then – we would ha' died for things in those days.'

Marx and Engels cast the horoscope of the working class at a time when to most it seemed no more than a useful or troublesome drudge. How precisely, under what impulses or compulsions, it was to perform its task of transforming society and abolishing class, is an intricate question which they never fully answered. But as time went on they grew impatient to see it setting about its task in good earnest. Engels could sound as disillusioned as he reproached Jones with becoming. Of the 1868 election he wrote to Marx on 18 November: 'Once again the proletariat has discredited itself terribly ... Everywhere the proletariat are the tag, rag and bobtail of the official parties.'[82] On a more humdrum level he was conscious of awkwardness in the way of cooperation with it. 'Woe be to the man', he warned his friend Florence Wischnewetzsky in a letter of 9 February 1887, 'who, being of bourgeois origin or superior education, goes into the movement and is rash enough to enter into money relations with the working-class element. There is sure to be a dispute', and suspicion that he is out to make a profit.

Marx's last years may have been overshadowed by a failing conviction of the proletariat being equal to its mission. He had called spirits from the vasty deep; perhaps there were moments when Hotspur's ironical rejoinder to Glendower struck on his ear – 'But will they come, when you do call for them?' Writing on 9 April 1870 to Meyer and Vogt he gave it as his mature opinion that the decisive blow at the British ruling class would have to be launched in Ireland, not at home. 'Every industrial and commercial centre in England now possesses a working-class population divided into two *hostile* camps, English proletarians and Irish proletarians ... This antagonism is artificially kept alive and intensified ... by all the means at the disposal of the ruling classes.'[83] There had been political as well as economic gain to capitalism from bringing over Irish blacklegs. His disciple Kautsky, after several years in England, wrote scathingly of the working class there and its lack of any desire to revolutionize society, which alone, he argued, could give any working class an ethic and ideals of its own (or, he might have added, class consciousness in the fullest sense):

> The emancipation of their class appears to them as a foolish dream. Consequently, it is foot-ball, boxing, horse racing and opportunities for gambling which move them the deepest and to which their entire leisure time, their individual powers, and their material means are devoted.[84]

Years went by, and another voice was to be heard lamenting that the modern British workman, preoccupied with demarcation disputes, was as 'hopelessly Conservative' as the handicraftsman of old: 'The great fault of the mass of wage-labour is the failure to think scientifically at all. The most elementary questions are often beyond their understanding.' Above all, they were destitute of any knowledge of history, of great changes having taken place in the past and therefore being possible again in the future.[85] Without memory of yesterday there can indeed be no vision of tomorrow, and in this light history is indispensable to progress. Not surprisingly against this background, elitist attitudes were tenacious among more or less progressive social thinkers. J.M. Keynes dismissed Communism on the ground that it 'exalts the boorish proletariat above the bourgeois and intelligentsia who, with whatever faults, are the quality of life and surely carry the seeds of all advancement.' Beatrice Webb found Beveridge alarmed by the shocks of 1940 into recognition of the need for social planning: 'But as of old, Beveridge is obstinately convinced that he and his class have to do the job, and the Trade Unionists have to be ignored and the wage-earner *ordered* to work.'[86]

A century before this the old Radical Bamford was looking back gloomily on what he could only see as a record of failure and folly: 'Groping in a mental and political twilight, we stumbled from error to error, the dim-eyed calling on the blind to follow.'[87] Socialist parties in our own day, if equally candid, would have not many fewer shortcomings to confess. But whatever the defects of leadership or programme, it would seem that socialist consciousness has always been restricted to a very few, and that the bulk of the working class (as of every other, it may be) is inert except when activated by some direct material stimulus. This in turn would imply that most collective conduct is 'behaviouristic', and most of history mechanically determined, with little room for dialectical subtlety of combination and change except at corners and fringes, whence forces may on rare occasions emerge and intervene decisively. It must be added that in spite of long investigation the true nature of classes remains not much less mysterious than the cloudy figures of Blake's prophetic poems, masked actors of the drama of history.

# Notes

1. Sir G.O. Trevelyan, *Life and Letters of Lord Macaulay*, 1876, ch. 10.
2. A.R. Waller and A. Glover, eds, *Collected Works*, vol. III, 1902, pp. 37–8.
3. A. Trollope, *The Last Chronicle of Barset*, 1867, ch. 12.
4. G. Gissing, *The Private Papers of Henry Ryecroft*, 1903, part 4, no. 14.
5. St Loe Strachey, 'Infringing a Political Patent', 1895, in M. Goodwin, ed., *Nineteenth Century Opinion*, Harmondsworth 1951, p. 69.
6. D. Cecil, *Melbourne*, London 1954 edn, p. 72.
7. Lord Brougham, *Letter to the Marquess of Lansdowne . . . on the Late Revolution in France*, 3rd edn, 1848, p. 89.
8. M. St J. Packe, *The Life of John Stuart Mill*, London 1954, pp. 101, 298.
9. Rev. G. Ewing, *The Duty of Christians to Civil Government*, Edinburgh 1799, pp. 12–13.
10. P. Gaskell, *The Manufacturing Population of England*, 1833, pp. 282, 106, 19, 93, 105, 275.
11. M. Beer, *A History of British Socialism*, London 1929, vol. I, p. 235.
12. J.S. Mill, 'The Claims of Labour', in *Edinburgh Review*, vol. 81, 1845, p. 503.
13. R.G. Gammage, *History of the Chartist Movement 1837-1854*, 1854, new edn, Newcastle 1894, pp. 266–7.
14. Beer, vol. I, p. 173; vol. II, p. 174, vol. I, pp. 236, 204.
15. Gammage, p. 400.
16. John Saville, *Ernest Jones: Chartist*, London 1952, p. 106.
17. Charles Kingsley, *Alton Locke, Tailor and Poet*, 1850, ch. 33.
18. Gammage, pp. 282, 94.

19. Ibid., p. 408.
20. Beer, vol. II, pp. 129, 20.
21. Saville, p. 90.
22. Y.V. Kovaleva, *An Anthology of Chartist Literature*, Moscow 1956, pp. 350, 353.
23. W. Cobbett, *Tour in Scotland and in the Four Northern Counties of England*, 1833, p. 55.
24. W. Cobbett, *Rural Rides*, Everyman edn, 1912, vol. II, pp. 73, 231.
25. Beer, vol. II, p. 125.
26. J. Morley, *The Life of Richard Cobden*, 1881, vol. I, pp. 249, 299.
27. Extract in M. Palmer, ed., *Writing and Action*, 1938, p. 289.
28. D.A. Wilson, *Carlyle to Threescore-and-Ten*, 1929, p. 248.
29. B. Disraeli, *Sybil, or the Two Nations*, 1845, book 3, ch. 8.
30. J. Ruskin, *The Crown of Wild Olive* (lectures of the 1860s), 1906, pp. 105–6, 181–2.
31. G. Gissing, *Henry Ryecroft*, part 2, no. 22.
32. J.L. and B. Hammond, *Lord Shaftesbury* 1923; Harmondsworth 1939 edn, pp. 29, 55.
33. Ibid., pp. 135–6.
34. Ibid., p. 248.
35. Kovaleva, p. 312.
36. S.E. Baldwin, *Charles Kingsley*, Ithaca, NY 1934, pp. 43–4.
37. Gaskell, p. 304.
38. 'F. Anstey', *Voces Populi*, 2nd series, 1892; 1912 edn, p. 145.
39. J.W. Cross, *George Eliot's Life*, New York 1885, vol. I, p. 131.
40. 'Mark Rutherford', *Catharine Furze*, 1893, ch. 16.
41. Saville, pp. 74, 196, 194–5.
42. Beer, vol. II, p. 221.
43. G.J. Holyoake, 'Impatience in Politics', 1877, in Goodwin, p. 222.
44. R. Harrison, 'Professor Beesly and the Working-class Movement', in A. Briggs and J. Saville, eds, *Essays in Labour History*, London, 1960, pp. 209, 213.
45. See C. Harvie, *The Lights of Liberalism: University Liberals and the Challenge of Democracy 1860–86*, London 1976, pp. 147 ff.
46. G. Howell, *Labour Legislation, Labour Movements and Labour Leaders*, 1902; 2nd edn, London 1905, p. 265.
47. Morley, vol. II, p. 229.
48. *Speeches of Henry Lord Brougham*, Edinburgh 1838, vol. III, pp. 161, 171.
49. T. Johnston, *The History of the Working Classes in Scotland*, Glasgow 1929, p. 288.
50. Cobbett, *Tour in Scotland*, pp. 208 ff.
51. See R. Colls, '"Oh Happy English Children!": Coal, Class and Education in the North-East', in *Past & Present* no. 73, 1976.
52. Frederick Rogers, *Labour, Life and Literature. Some Memories of Sixty Years*, 1913; ed. D. Rubinstein, Brighton 1973, p. 52.
53. Cobbett, *Tour in Scotland*, p. 239.
54. See O. Chadwick, *The Secularization of the European Mind in the Nineteenth Century*, Cambridge 1975, ch. 4: 'The attitudes of the worker'.
55. Letter to *The Scotsman*, 25 January 1858, in Johnston, p. 258.
56. B. and S. Webb, *Industrial Democracy*, 1897, p. 259.
57. *Life of J.S. Mill*, pp. 307, 312.
58. Ruskin, pp. 50–1.
59. See Jack Lindsay, 'The Commune of Paris and English Literature', in *Marxist Quarterly*, July 1954.
60. Dona Torr, *Tom Mann and his Times*, London 1956, p. 207.
61. J. Clunie, *Labour is my Faith. The Autobiography of a House Painter*, Dunfermline 1954, vol. I, p. 92.
62. T. Bell, *Pioneering Days*, London 1941, p. 38.
63. William Morris, *Signs of Change*, 1888, pp. 102–4.
64. Torr, p. 180.
65. B. and S. Webb, p. 539.
66. Snowden, *Autobiography*, vol. I, p. 75.
67. T. Mann, 'The Development of the Labour Movement', 1890, in Goodwin, p. 210.

68. Beatrice Webb, *My Apprenticeship*, 1926; London 1929 edn, p. 139.
69. G.B. Shaw, *The Intelligent Woman's Guide to Socialism, Capitalism, Sovietism and Fascism*, 1928; London 1929 edn, p. 478.
70. Ibid., pp. 383, 489.
71. H.G. Wells, *War and the Future*, London 1917, pp. 182-3, 187.
72. Sheila Rowbotham, 'In Search of Carpenter', in *History Workshop* no. 3, 1977, p. 126.
73. E.B. Bax, *The Ethics of Socialism*, 2nd edn, n.d., p. 18.
74. Bell, p. 263.
75. T. Rothstein, *From Chartism to Labourism*, 1929, part 1, ch. 5.
76. Robert Tressell, *The Ragged Trousered Philanthropists*, 1914; London 1955 edn, ch. 48.
77. P.F. Clarke, 'The Progressive Movement in England', in *Trans. Royal Hist. Soc.*, 5th Series, vol. 24, 1974, pp. 168-9.
78. G. Wallas, *Human Nature in Politics*, 1908, pp. 229-30.
79. G.W.E. Russell, *Collections and Recollections*, series 2 1909, p. 78.
80. J.A. Spender, *The Comments of Bagshot*, 1907, p. 23.
81. Rogers, p. xxii.
82. Dona Torr, *The Correspondence of Marx and Engels*, London 1934, pp. 251-2.
83. Ibid., pp. 288-90.
84. K. Kautsky, *The Social Revolution*, 1902; English edn, Chicago 1916, p. 102.
85. Clunie, vol. II, p. 111.
86. P. Addison, *The Road to 1945*, London 1975, pp. 37, 118.
87. H. Dunckley, ed., *Bamford's Passages in the Life of a Radical*, 1893, vol. II, p. 184.

# 8

# Herbert Norman's Cambridge

The most stimulating environment may be the one with the greatest mixture of elements, and the Cambridge of the inter-war years was full of contrast and incongruities. Today, by comparison, it is more uniform, academically on average more respectable, less intriguing or exciting. In those days it had room for curious personalities, even eccentrics. Seriousness and frivolity, brilliance and stupidity, cobwebs and novelties, were to be found side by side. It was still a haunt of the jeunesse dorée, who were there to amuse themselves in a playground of snobbery and upper-class lotus-eating. Edwardian self-indulgence was having its last fling. For college seniors, a luxurious mode of living was sustained by the genteel practice of underpaying overworked college servants. Newcomers from more modest social backgrounds reacted sometimes admiringly, sometimes critically. There was a growing influx of them, among students and more gradually among teachers. Meritocracy was coming in, and individuals from the humblest families might soar by way of Cambridge or Oxford to high posts, fortunes, knighthoods, even gaiters. Others were less easily assimilated (a fact that their tutors found exceedingly hard to comprehend); the establishment was apt to strike them as smugly self-complacent, pretentiously genteel, over-anxious to keep up the pose of 'effortless superiority.'

It often seemed as if the Great War had never happened. Yet in reality the old world of before 1914 was now hollow and brittle, the country was groping its way painfully towards a different existence. Cambridge was a microcosm of this process. The university was highly paternalistic, standing in loco parentis to undergraduates in a fashion no university nowadays dreams of. Gowns had to be worn at lectures, as well as in the evening in the streets, which were patrolled by proctors. Bedroom windows on the ground floor were heavily barred, and young men and women were kept as far apart as possible. No woman ever had a meal in the hall of Trinity College until the present queen was given lunch there after her coronation. Yet there were two women's colleges, and heated debate and controversy after 1918 led to partial incorporation of their students into the university. They were not regular members of it, and not entitled to wear gowns – it took another world war to shake the walls of Jericho as far as that – but they could attend university lectures, sit for examinations, and take degrees. There were dire warnings, eagerly denied by feminists, that once allowed university membership women would want to get into men's colleges as well – as they have lately been doing. Their unequal treatment must have helped to push a good many girl students towards the political left, and one campaign early taken up by socialists was for the admission of women to that celebrated Cambridge institution, a club and a debating society, the Union.

Religion was another area where Cambridge was in a state of flux. Howarth[1] quotes from the diaries of A.C. Benson, master of Magdalene College, an account of a Church of England service where he noticed dignitaries nodding or snoring all around him – 'A disgraceful scene of infinite futility and grotesqueness.' In the Cambridge Inter-Collegiate Christian Union (CICCU – pronounced 'kick-you') was preserved a simple evangelical creed, muscular Christianity of the Victorian empire-building sort. A newer, more unwhole-some version of its non-intellectualism was 'moral rearmament', whose founder thanked God for Adolf Hitler. More reasonable, more sensitive to social problems, more open to what is now called 'dialogue', was the Student Christian Movement.

In spite of much frivolity and mediocrity, there were departments of knowledge where what Cambridge was thinking was of importance to the whole world. There was a galaxy of talent, even genius – more than at any time in its history – and some awareness of this may have helped to sharpen the faculties of the rising generation. In certain sciences especially, startling advances were being made. In the Cavendish Laboratory the way into the atom was being explored, Pandora's box about to be opened. Mathematics was another very strong field; so was astronomy, as books for the general reader by Jeans and Eddington, and on relativity by that banished Cambridge philosopher Bertrand Russell, made the public conscious.

Equally significant in a different way was a new conception of the social responsibility of the scientist. It was emerging chiefly in association with fresh ideas in biology, the science of life instead of, as physics has come to be, the science of death. J.B.S. Haldane, who had been at Cambridge in the 1920s, was already well known, a fellow of the Royal Society and professor in London, when his book *Materialism* was published in 1932. At Cambridge, Needham and Bernal were the scientists most heard of among progressives. A recent writer has emphasized the influence such men were having on the young men round them. Laboratory life and its team work facilitated such influence, and a number of young research workers of those days were to become distinguished scientists in their turn, and carry forward the social ideals they were imbibing. These found a kind of manifesto in Bernal's big book *The Social Function of Science*. It included sections on 'Science and Fascism' and 'Science and Socialism', with warm praise for developments in the Soviet Union. It came out in 1939, just before the outbreak of a war that was to give the writer a social function of a sort he little expected, as scientific adviser on the preparations for the Normandy landing.

In arts subjects and social sciences, currents of change were making themselves felt from a diversity of angles. English literature was presided over by 'Q' – Sir Arthur Quiller-Couch – who had written novels once popular but by the 1930s forgotten. In Leavis it had a literary critic of a radically new species, but Leavis was something of an Ishmaelite; ill at ease in orthodox Cambridge, he went about defiantly, without a tie. In economics, the theories worked out by J.M. Keynes as an alternative to socialism were only very slowly making their way. He brought from Italy the Marxist economist Sraffa, who had fallen foul of Mussolini; and there was actually a Communist lecturer, Maurice Dobb, who was not, however, given a fellowship at his college (Trinity) until many years later. Economic history had lately been recognized as an independent subject. Its first professor was Clapham, about whose book on modern Britain a reviewer made the joke that if Clapham ever found himself in hell it would not be long before he produced a report showing that it was not really so bad a place as it was made out; some localities were distinctly cooler than others. A more exotic figure was Postan, who came to Cambridge from far away, and knew more about Marxism than the home-grown conservatives.

At Cambridge and Oxford, life revolved around the colleges, though the more important lecturing was increasingly organized, like the laboratory work, by the university. Tuition was left to the colleges and followed an archaic pattern; a history student had to compose a weekly essay and read it aloud to his tutor, who might or might not know something about the subject. Trinity was by far the biggest and richest college, with the longest list of great men of the past, as various as Newton and Byron, and a quite long list of remarkable men among its fellows now, though some of these were old or aging. Sir James Frazer, the anthropologist, must have been the oldest of all; the master was Sir J.J. Thompson, who had been one of the atomic pioneers. A.E. Housman, the professor of Latin, was a remote, self-isolating figure, devoted to arid textual criticism, though the poetry he had written in youth was more widely read than any other English poetry of modern times. G.M. Trevelyan, the Regius professor of history, belonged to a worthy Liberal tradition of other days.

Among the other Trinity historians, none of whom did much writing, R.V. Laurence upheld a tradition of conviviality going back to the toping and ease of the eighteenth century. When one went to his room with an essay he would be found in an armchair, gouty limbs swathed in bandages, half the floor covered with empty bottles. A fellow Epicurean, Lapsley, lectured on medieval constitutional history – unaided by any notes – with ardour and gusto, but wrote nothing. His snobbery, unchecked or perhaps fostered by an American origin, was well known; it was understood that he did not much care to be visited by anyone below the rank of viscount. In addition, there was a Catholic priest, an Anglican clergyman – F.A. Simpson, so much in demand as a fashionable preacher that he acquired a private plane to fly him up and down the country – and an Anglican lay-preacher, G. Kitson Clark, at one time secretary of the county Conservative Association; he had a nervous horror of Marxism, or socialism in any guise.

To the censorious eyes of young people coming under the spell of socialism, this old Cambridge was part of an ancien régime about to be swept away – as it largely has been in fact since those days. At best its teaching seemed trivial, irrelevant, with no answers for the enormous problems and perils weighing on the world, and with little show of even recognizing their existence. It was quite in tune with the government of the time, the self-styled National Government or right-wing coalition, mostly Tory, which began with a landslide election in 1931, following a financial crisis which, in the light of later research, seems to have been somewhat artificial, but which paralysed a timid Labour cabinet and pushed Ramsay MacDonald and other leaders into abandoning their party and joining hands with the Tories. In 1935 the National Government was re-elected, with a smaller majority; MacDonald had been replaced by the Conservative leader Baldwin, who was succeeded by the disastrous Neville Chamberlain.

Its policies, at home and abroad, were of a sort to inflame left-wing feeling. It had no cure for the massive unemployment brought by the slump, the economic depression that suddenly descended on the capitalist world in 1929. Such a state of affairs was unfamiliar then, not taken for granted as it is coming to be nowadays, and unemployment was far more painful than now, when it is cushioned by the welfare state. Allowances were meagre, and the so-called means test made things worse, at a time when the rich were still living with their old prodigality. One of the experiences that did most to swell the Socialist Society at Cambridge was the sight of the hunger-marchers, a contingent of whom passed through the town in February 1934 on their way from the north of England to London. Students joined them at Huntingdon, a dozen miles north, and walked back to Cambridge with them. At Girton College, on the outskirts of the town, some of the women students provided refreshments; they were lodged for the night in the Corn Exchange, and bus loads of socialists went to London to join in their demonstration meeting in Hyde Park.

Between hungry unemployed and gluttonous college banquets the contrast was vivid. Something could be learned about living conditions in the town from college employees, porters and bedmakers. With about eighty thousand people, it had always supported itself a good deal by working for the university, but was now developing some light industry. Trade unions were gaining ground, there were strikes, of busmen for instance, and in elections the Labour party was making a better showing in what had been a Tory stronghold. Left-wing students canvassed for it at election-times, at least those who were not too far left: to Communists, in those embittered days, the Labour party was as much anathema as the Conservative. Within its national ranks there was a left-wing minority movement; one of its prominent figures was Sir Stafford Cripps, after the war a right-wing chancellor, but leader of a Socialist League within the Labour party (from which he was expelled for a while) at the time when he came to Cambridge to address a big public meeting. A bodyguard was provided to protect him from attack, thought to be meditated by Tory students; the meeting stirred up much excitement, applause from one side and heckling from the other. It was the same at another meeting where the speaker was Ellen Wilkinson, who had been a member of the Labour cabinet, Britain's second woman cabinet minister.

On this occasion some of the arguing was about foreign policy. Foreign horizons were overshadowed by the rise of fascism. The coming to power of the Nazis in January 1933 was quickly followed by the Reichstag fire, the Dimitrov trial, the 1934 purge, persecution of Jews, and before long rearmament and conscription. In February 1934 there was fighting in Vienna, with the clerical-fascist dictator Dollfuss using the army against the Social Democrats. Nazism, like Italian and Austrian fascism, found many admirers in Britain – Tories, often in high places, who liked it because it put an end to socialism and trade unions, even if they had some decent minor objections to some of its other doings. Rather too sweepingly, all Tories were suspected by the left wing of sympathy with fascism and of thinking that it would be a wholesome medicine for Britain too. There had been a first attempt at a fascist movement in imitation of Mussolini, under aristocratic leadership, in the early 1920s; now a far more determined effort was being made by Sir Oswald Mosley.[2] Refugees from fascism abroad were numerous, a good many of them in Cambridge and the other universities, and some of them, chiefly those belonging to left-wing movements, politically active. Socialist students on holiday on the continent made contact with like-minded people in countries like France and Spain, where they breathed a headier atmosphere.

War was the darkest shadow falling across Europe and Britain. A deep anti-war spirit survived into the thirties from the Great War, and there was a conviction that with the new and terrible weapons that were rumoured, any fresh war could only be blindly destructive. For the left it would be the result of capitalist greed and plotting, as 1914 – there was an increasing realization – had been. A landmark in Cambridge politics was a protest one night early in November 1933, at the Tivoli cinema, against the showing of a film called 'Our Fighting Navy', which was regarded as war propaganda; it led to a riotous counter-demonstration outside. This was followed by an event that made more stir, an anti-war procession through the town on Armistice Day to the war memorial. All left-wing and some religious groups took part. It was attacked by a swarm of conservative students, with eggs and tomatoes, and other missiles, but in spite of a running battle succeeded in reaching its goal and holding an open-air meeting. In subsequent years a November 11 march became an annual event, never interfered with again. The Cambridge Anti-War Exhibition was an impressive endeavour to warn the public of the horrors another conflict would entail, very much like the warnings of anti-nuclear campaigners today against the atom bomb. 'Scholarships, not battleships!' was a favourite slogan of demonstrators.

All these feelings about the bad state of our world, and the possible nearness of doomsday, were brought into focus by events in Spain – the three years' civil war set off in the summer of 1936 by the rising of Franco and his fellow-generals against the liberal Republican government. The spectacle of an international fascist crusade, with German and Italian forces in Spain along with the Foreign Legion and a horde of Moors brought from Spanish Morocco; the farce of 'non-intervention', sponsored by the British government; the improvised International Brigade fighting on the Republican side, in which a number of Cambridge and other British students served and several were killed – all this stirred up feeling that was all the more intense because of a conviction of Britain's and Europe's fate also being at stake. Tory prejudices in favour of the Spanish fascists and their aristocratic spokesmen were unconcealed, and added to left-wing detestation of the government. There was nearly as much indignation with the more backward Labour leaders, whose attitude over Spain was hesitant and shuffling. A good part of the time and energy of all progressives, not socialists only, went into organizing meetings and collecting funds for aid to Spain. Not far from Cambridge new refugees were living, a colony of Basque children.

All these pressures were multiplying socialists, and pushing many of them towards Communism. This was already taking root in the university by 1930, and all through the thirties was gaining ground remarkably. Those who led the way at first were from well-to-do families, typically – as in John Cornford's case – of the academic elite. On the one hand, they felt ashamed of their comfortable place in society when so many in the country and in the world were so badly off; on the other, they felt secure enough to be able to take some risks with their future. In some families of the elite the whole younger generation caught the flame; at Trinity for instance, the daughters of the dean of Chapel. As the movement spread, it drew in a cross-section of Cambridge students, undergraduates and researchers from every social background; it seemed to have answers to an equally mixed array of problems, at home and abroad, in face of which bourgeois thinking was bankrupt. ('Bourgeois' was a term habitually used to denote everything capitalistic, reactionary, or simply stupid.) In the gathering atmosphere of crisis, individual motives or psychology were felt to be of no account; only the practical collective result mattered. Freshmen began to arrive with political consciousness already acquired at their public or grammar schools. By the time the war came there were more than two hundred Communists, when the party nationally still had not very many thousand members.

In any such situation there are always some who are in a movement because it is in fashion, and they want to be in the swim. But in general, these Communists were very much in earnest, dedicated to what they regarded as their mission. It was not a 'student movement' in today's sense, when the university population of the country is vastly greater and has its own trade union organizations. Cambridge undergraduates were mostly not suffering from economic hardships, and though the left wing might be critical of the way the university was run, its concern was far more with the way the country and the world were going. They organized themselves with an efficiency which, looked back on after many years and much other experience of people working together, was really remarkable. In those years when Europe was increasingly divided between rival camps, Communist and fascist, each highly monolithic, discipline and uniformity seemed indispensable virtues. That capitalism was in its final stage appeared self-evident; the question was whether it would drag civilization down with it in its collapse, and the only way to avert this end was to build up rapidly a force and an ideology, based on the masses, which would be capable of replacing it. The party was a twentieth-century ark, designed not to rescue a handful in a perishing world, but all humanity.

It would be absurd of course to depict these Communists as perpetually wrapped in such thoughts, never giving way to more cheerful moods or lighter occupations such as falling in love. All the same, the moral pressure of the collective on the individual was firm. All paid a yearly levy or 'income tax', in the form of a regular percentage of their means, part of which went to subsidize the hard-up party in the East Anglia region; in addition there were always extra contributions wanted for causes like Spain. Each college had its own 'cell' (it was only after the war that the CP gave its local bodies the less foreign-sounding name of 'branches'); cells met weekly, as study groups, and to hear reports from representatives of the secretariat, and in a businesslike way checked up on the fulfilment of individual assignments. Among these 'contact work' always held a high place, the duty of keeping in touch with prospective recruits – who were often taken aback, when they became members in turn, to discover how systematically their shepherding towards the party had been conducted. 'Aggregates' were periodical meetings of the whole body; there were special ones for 'activists', though a good deal of activity was expected from all.[3]

Proceedings were rather more conspiratorial than they need have been, in emulation of Bolsheviks of Lenin's day working underground; but if they were not being spied on as persistently as some supposed, a number of college tutors were uneasy and inquisitive. In the practice of infiltration into other bodies, setting up 'fractions' inside them, manipulating unsuspecting liberals – in a style sometimes counter-productive – there was a certain pride in behaving in an un-British fashion, discarding conventions and good manners as bourgeois nonsense. In a more above-board way, speakers or speakers' notes were supplied for any meeting of any society where invitations could be got, as a means of 'putting the party line': the party had an opinion, actual or still to be worked out, on everything under the sun. Members went out into the town to deliver copies of the *Daily Worker* to subscribers, or distribute leaflets at factory gates. They took part in poster parades to advertise the *Worker* and in demonstrations in Cambridge or London, lobbied MPs, and turned out in force as hecklers at meetings of the Blackshirts, who had not much concrete support in the university or in the district, but were hopeful of winning it.

In all this the USSR was the grand inspiration. Communists looked up to it nearly as undiscriminatingly as their conservative teachers denigrated it. Most diatribes against it were so patently prejudiced and ignorant that they reacted with an opposite refusal to believe that anything could be amiss under Stalin. From 1928, the five-year plans were launching the first planned economy in world history, and they had enormous success on the industrial front, quadrupling production in a period when in the capitalist world it was falling by anything up to half. Of the leading countries, Russia alone was firmly anti-fascist. It alone was giving arms and diplomatic backing to the Spanish Republic; the national secretary of the CP, Harry Pollitt, had a powerful case to make when he came to speak on Spain, after a visit to Madrid, in a debate at the Union.

A bad side of all the seriousness, and the sensation of crisis, was the sectarianism which made it quite usual for Communists to denounce Labour party supporters as 'social fascists', and universal for them to view Trotsky as a fiend in human shape. It helped to provoke a breakaway of the more moderate wing of the Socialist Society, which was affiliated to a militant Federation of Student Societies set up in 1932; in 1934 a separate Labour Club came into being. This schism was overcome, and the two wings came together again in 1935 in a Socialist Club, though within it the Communists maintained their own very definite existence. In the same year, the 7th World Congress of the Third International gave a call for cooperation with other parties in popular fronts against fascism, and on the international plane for collective security. But the legacy of sectarian division was not easy to overcome.

Communists were not seldom accused of being as fanatical about their creed as if it were a new religion, and there was no doubt something like a religious flavour in their make-up. To most of them, a combination of Christianity and socialism like Joseph Needham's seemed bizarre. Yet many of them came from a religious background; and in their sense of duty to be always diligently at work they could be said to have some resemblance to Milton, toiling in his great taskmaster's eye, even if the eye was watching them from the Kremlin

instead of from heaven. But established religion and churches – very different
in those days from what they have since come to be – seemed to them mostly
reactionary humbug, which Russia had done well to cast off. Most German
Protestants welcomed or submitted tamely to Hitler; Italian Catholics
applauded Mussolini's conquest of Abyssinia; the attitude of the Spanish
Church during the civil war (for which many years later its national assembly
was to express contrition), and of Catholic churches everywhere, was violently
pro-fascist. All the same, in places like Cambridge there was a dawning recognition by each side of better features of the other side, and some friendlier
exchanges were taking place.

Most of a left-wing student's political reading was sternly practical. A
journal like *Inprecorr* ('International Press Correspondence') strengthened his
consciousness of belonging to a world-wide movement, of having unknown
comrades who were waging guerilla war in Brazilian forests, as well as others
who were building socialism in the USSR. The Left Book Club, launched by
the publisher Gollancz, was in full swing. Progressive bookshops were
sprouting up and down the country; one was started in Cambridge in the mid
thirties, surpassing sales of literature by the Socialist club.[4] Of Marxist theory,
however, there was far less available than today, when left-wing students are
often surprisingly well versed in it. There was a 'Little Lenin Library' – cheap
reprints of tracts by Lenin, of whom more was known than of Marx. Until
about 1934 or 1935 a term like 'dialectical materialism' had a mysterious sound,
like a conjuror's spell.

In the next few years things were changing. One reason was that Communist party students formed something of an intellectual as well as political
cream. Their code included the principle that time had to be found for
academic work too, and that one way to win collective respect was to be at the
top of the examination lists. A good proportion did take first-class degrees, and
in later life some of these reached the top of their academic trees. Especially
among those reading subjects like history or economics, political interest and
intellectual curiosity converged and set them trying to discover or work out
for themselves approaches to their problems in Marxist terms. This was true of
none more than the two leading spirits, those very remarkable individuals
James Klugmann and John Cornford.[5] Already before the latter's departure to
Spain, history students under his lead felt strong enough to try to create a
forum for discussion of history on lines opposed to the prevailing orthodoxy,
and to challenge a hostile set of lectures on the USSR by a very conservative
scholar, Reddaway, who was obliged to agree to a debate with his critics. It was
the first time such a thing had happened in Cambridge, perhaps in any British
university.

In the country, Marxist ideas were beginning to be thrown up by a few
writers like Ralph Fox or Christopher Caudwell, whose pioneer *Illusion and
Reality* was only published in 1938, after his death in Spain. John Strachey –

after the world war a Labour minister – was then very close to the CP, and was writing books on the economics of capitalism and socialism which many read. They helped to inspire a few ambitious learners at Cambridge, humorously known as 'the Bible class,' to try to struggle through *Capital*. Dobb was an inspiration closer at hand. By this time there was a small CP group of dons, one of them a writer on German literature and history. Klugmann might have been the equal of any Marxist scholar Britain has produced. After graduating in modern languages, of course with distinction, he embarked on research into the social basis of French Romantic literature; but this was interrupted when he was drawn away into full-time work in Paris as secretary of the World Student Movement (*Rassemblement Mondial des Étudiants*), then by the war, after which he devoted the rest of his life to the party's service, chiefly in its educational department. He died in 1977.

A good many on the left were fond of music, in which Cambridge abounded, but they liked to think of themselves as practical, down-to-earth people, for whom the annual figures of coal and steel production in the USSR were more important than any number of symphonies in the decadent West. Anything progressive in the arts, however, was sure of a welcome. Paul Robeson drew many to London one year to see him acting in *Stevedore*. A small cinema, the 'Cosmopolitan', showed foreign and experimental films; among its patrons was Herbert Norman, whom I remember saying that everyone needed some 'mechanism' as a safeguard against depression; for him, films seemed to have this function. Among Soviet films seen in those years were *The White Sea Canal* and Eisenstein's *Ivan the Terrible* and *Thunder over Mexico*. Novels of revolution or social protest found readers – works like Malraux's *La condition humaine* (Man's Fate), about the Chinese counter-revolution of 1927; or *The Cannery Boat*, by the Japanese writer Kobayashi, murdered by the police; or, a little later (1939), Steinbeck's *The Grapes of Wrath*.

Those with serious literary interest read *International Literature*, which was mostly Soviet and not always easy going. Several small left-wing journals were trying to blaze a trail towards a new, socialist kind of poetry and fiction; in memory they seem to have been carrying on an endless dissection of every fresh attempt and concluding that there was something amiss with it. One visiting speaker at a left-wing meeting was Stephen Spender, then in the very socialistic phase of his *Forward from Liberalism* (1937); a phase which, as with other writers admired at the time as progressives, like Auden and Isherwood, turned out to be only a flash in the pan. Like the poets of the Romantic era, they proved politically unstable by comparison with many other left-wing intellectuals. Cornford, more than most of the left, wanted to fuse politics with imagination, as well as with thinking. He wrote verse himself, even in Spain; and in one of his first essays, written between 1933 and 1934 for *Cambridge Left*, he found fault with Spender as too much abstracted from life. Art and action should be inseparable, the artist must throw in his lot with the people. He and others were saying what Mao said a few years later at his writers' conference at Yenan. Cornford predicted a 'revolutionary literature,' which has not in fact got far, either in the West or in China; the difficulty of turning art into propaganda, or propaganda into art, is more intractable than it looked in the 1930s. But he was closely followed at Cambridge by two others who have since contributed to Marxist theory, Raymond Williams and Arnold Kettle.

In the inter-war years, scarcely anyone guessed that the British colonial empire was destined to disappear so soon. It looked majestically rock-firm. Its virtues were an article of faith with Tories (and with many Labour leaders), and official Cambridge believed in it unquestioningly. Yet unrest was spreading in many parts of the empire, and it was deepened, and nationalist movements like those in India or Egypt were invigorated, by the economic depression, which hit the Third World harder than the industrial countries. Of facts like these very few in Britain were aware. Partly from insularity, partly because colonial issues seemed remote compared with those close at hand in Europe, only a few on the left, even among its intellectuals and students, felt any close concern about the colonies. Occasional happenings drew attention, like the sentences imposed in 1933 at the end of the Meerut conspiracy trial in India, a prosecution of Communists and trade unionists on charges of sedition. Three of the accused were Englishmen, one of them a former Cambridge student. The Socialist Society collected signatures for a protest about the convictions. But the imperial event that made the greatest impression on Cambridge students, socialist or other, was one unconnected with the British empire – the Italian invasion of Abyssinia in 1935. One morning, an Abyssinian flag was seen flying from a pinnacle of King's College chapel, hung there by some unknown climber, a difficult and dangerous feat. Honorary membership of the Union was conferred on the exiled Emperor Haile Selassie, who received a prolonged standing ovation from a packed house when he came to receive it.

Cambridge offered plenty of chances to meet an exotic array of students from Afro-Asia. There was a time in the 1920s when two Indians were passed over for the tennis captaincy because of their colour, but in general race relations were good. One of Cambridge's better qualities was a sort of republican equality and fraternity. One or two efforts were made to start discussion groups with Africans about what socialism could mean to African countries. There was a Chinese society with forty-odd members, some of them from Malaya or Singapore, and the best known of them tennis players; but the Japanese invasion of China was something that stirred them all, and there was some knowledge of the part being played in the resistance to it by Mao and the Communists. For socialists, one of the great books of the 1930s was Edgar Snow's *Red Star over China*, about the Chinese soviets and the Long March. There was an Anglo-Japanese Society too, at one of whose meetings the head of a college gave a talk, approving (as most British conservatives did) the occupation of Manchuria as part of a Japanese civilizing mission.

The Indian society, the 'Majlis' or Assembly, with a membership of something like a hundred, was one of the university's long-established bodies; Jawaharlal Nehru had been a member when at Trinity early in the century. Some of the Indians were well off, with a sprinkling of princes; most were from professional or official families, and there were a number of probationers for the high-ranking Indian civil service. But all were affected more or less emotionally by nationalism, and a good many were willing to take an interest in socialism or even Communism. Gandhi's second civil disobedience movement in 1930 had led to the Round Table Conference in London; in 1935, after a protracted filibuster by the die-hard Winston Churchill, a new Government of India Act marked a further instalment of constitutional concessions, which the National Congress thought very meagre. Against this background, young Indians could see the force of what Nehru had long been saying, as leader of the progressive wing of Congress, that there must be a programme for the benefit of the miserably poor workers and peasants to mobilize wider mass support. In other words, socialism was a necessary part of the struggle for independence.

Herbert Norman was already acclimatized to Cambridge when I got to know him, but his Canadian and Japanese antecedents put him in an exceptional position, from which he could view the world more broadly than most of us, immersed in our European cauldron, were able to.[6] He was of course following events in the Far East.[7] But his practical work consisted of trying to attract some of the Indians towards the Communist party. It was not easy; psychological barriers and mistrusts were strong. One of his converts told me later on that he had been suspicious of all white faces, but Herbert won his confidence with the clinching argument that he was not an Englishman, but a Canadian.[8] Indian students were under official watch, and the business of putting together a small group had to be gone about very discreetly. Another recruit had some experience of the need for secrecy, having been arrested in Calcutta as secretary of a student body suspected of terrorist leanings; his family was allowed to send him to England as an alternative to prison. His father had been a famous nationalist who gave away most of a large fortune to patriotic causes; a nephew of his, with a Scottish wife, is active in left-wing causes in India today.

I first learned of the group when Norman, its founder, before leaving Cambridge, invited me to take over from him the responsibility of liaison with it.[9] I was engaged in post-graduate work on Anglo-Chinese relations, which gave me more interest than most party students had in Asian and imperial affairs. Similar groups were coming into existence in other universities, chiefly Oxford and London. The party functionary in charge was Ben Bradley, one of the Meerut prisoners, who had been sent out to India to take part in trade-union organizing. Through him, and a young Englishman in the Indian civil service who had turned Communist and come home to undertake party work, there were exciting glimpses of the small outlawed Communist party of India struggling underground.

Herbert's strategy, in line with party policy of the time, had been for the group to 'capture the Majlis', by getting members elected to the committee. This was achieved without much difficulty, and the result was a more lively, stimulating programme of discussions and lectures, in place of mere social gatherings, with stress on political issues. One of our friends was president of the Majlis when Nehru, in the autumn of 1935, was released from prison because of his wife's illness, and came to Europe. Hearing of Nehru's arrival in London, he took the initiative of telegraphing an invitation to him to visit his old university, and collected subscriptions to cover expenses. Over tea Nehru met the group, in my room, and discussed the Indian situation with them; in the evening, after dinner at the Union, there was a public meeting at which he addressed a mostly sympathetic audience. It could scarcely be guessed that day that in a dozen years he would be prime minister of India. His daughter Indira, also to be prime minister, was with him, and stayed in England as a student at Oxford. She did not do much there in politics, but several women joined the Cambridge and other groups; for Indian women, socialism could appear a double emancipation.[10]

Groups like ours in Cambridge not only acquired a degree of influence over Indian students, but could do something to give British students and others comprehension of Indian national aspirations. One who became the first Indian president of the Union carried a motion in a debate that 'the continued existence of the British empire is a menace to world peace.' He was the son of a wealthy feudal landowner, and had been at school at Eton; he was one of two from the group who were imprisoned for a time on their return to India, and one of three who devoted all their time for a good many years to work in the Communist party there, under very spartan conditions. His sister, from Oxford, did the same, and is now a Communist member of parliament. One of his brothers, following a different track, rose to be commander-in-chief of the Indian army. Indians in London undertook work for the India League, run by Krishna Menon, later a cabinet minister under Nehru. He opened a conference in London, largely organized by the Cambridge group with much counsel from James Klugmann, which set up a federation of Indian student bodies in Britain. Marxists in London, Sajjad Zaheer and others, had the chief hand in planning the Indian Progressive Writers' Association (IPWA), which made a considerable stir in literary circles in India before the war. Zaheer, who died a year or two ago in the USSR, became in 1947 at the Partition secretary of a new Communist party of Pakistan and, not surprisingly, was very soon in prison. It was an Indian Muslim at Cambridge, a few years before our time, who invented the idea and the name of Pakistan, taken up after 1935 by Jinnah and regarded by us as highly retrograde. As socialists, Muslims and Hindus worked side by side.

In retrospect, it is clear to survivors of the thirties that their hope, or rather certainty, of a speedy advent of socialism in Britain was illusory; it might be compared with the faith of a minute Scottish sect a hundred and fifty years ago that its adherents would be translated to heaven while still living. It went with a very uncritical, almost mystic belief, instilled by the party, in the working class and its mission to transform society. Things were seen too simply, too much in black and white. Some illusions may be necessary to any positive, active movement. Nevertheless, many of the fundamental issues confronting that generation of the left – fascism, imperialism, Spain – really were in essence simple, and it was right about them. And it was, after all, the USSR that defeated the Nazi army and liberated Europe. Convictions formed at Cambridge in the thirties were often formed for life, whereas the student excitements of more recent years seem to leave little permanent trace on most participants. Not many Communists of those days grew into conservatives; a notable proportion have continued to be associated with progressive causes, from within the party or outside it. To them, the Cold War and American hegemony seemed evidence of a new menace, not unlike that of fascism, to be resisted. Vietnam came to be for them what the Spanish Republic had been.

As Marxist theorists, many of them, along with newer comers, were soon making much more headway than before the war, above all in history. Historical Marxism has made perhaps more progress in Britain than in any other country, East or West. Dobb's most original work, which came out in 1947, was an economic history of England. He took part in a Marxist historians' group formed soon after the war, divided into sections among which the one concerned with sixteenth- and seventeenth-century Europe went furthest. Eric Hobsbawm was one of the Cambridge undergraduates of the thirties who figured in it, Christopher Hill one of those from Oxford. The group gave everyone the feeling that he was learning history over again. They began, in the pre-war spirit, by wanting their work to have a very practical value to the party, for instance through studies of local history and working-class struggles. These expectations were not fulfilled; the unity of theory and practice, that bedrock principle of the thirties, seldom finds a straightforward application. More generally, the ideas that were being developed, largely through collective discussion and sometimes heated argument, have had an appreciable influence both on other scholars and on readers of history. In this process, still going on, Herbert Norman might have found the place most congenial to him.

## Notes

1. T.E.B. Howarth, *Cambridge Between Two Wars*, London 1978. A Cambridge historian; no sympathy with the left, but well informed and well written.
2. Mosley launched his British Union Movement in 1931. Aldous Huxley had depicted something very like it in advance, in his novel *Point Counter Point*, 1928. H.G. Wells's fantasy of a

dictatorship plunging Britain into war, first with the USSR and then with the USA, *The Autocracy of Mr. Parham*, came out in 1930. An American parallel was *It Can't Happen Here*, by Sinclair Lewis, 1936.

3. I myself joined in November 1934, and remained a member of the party until 1959; since then I have thought of myself as an independent Marxist. At Cambridge there was no special ceremony of admission; among London students (I learn from Professor John Saville) a new entrant had to present himself, in a somewhat cloak-and-dagger fashion, at a strange house.

4. I had been in charge of these sales for some time. The bookshop was run by a jolly Australian, Maclaurin, who had lost a teaching post at York through being caught by the headmaster in some tipsy frolic. He was killed in Spain. Norman, who knew him well, deeply lamented his death.

5. I am grateful for my good fortune in having had these two as my chief political mentors; they must have been well known also to Herbert Norman. Both were at Trinity, and Klugmann and I – and, incongruously, A.E. Housman – lived close together for a long time in a dingy college annex, Whewell's Court. See N. Wood, *Communism and British Intellectuals*, New York 1959, p. 85: 'A large number of the intellectuals were centred, during the thirties, at Trinity College, Cambridge'; and Samuels in P. Rieff, ed., *On Intellectuals*, Garden City, NY 1969, p. 215: 'The centre of communist activity was Trinity College, and its leaders were James Klugmann and John Cornford.'

6. I do not remember being conscious that he was four years older than I was, but these years must have made him a degree more mature than most of those he was with.

7. He was in touch with a variety of Japanese, and I was impressed by the fluency with which he conversed with them in their own language, sometimes in a small Chinese restaurant at Tottenham Court in London where he taught me how to eat with chopsticks.

8. There is a hint in this incident of the skill he deployed later in diplomacy. With his quietly engaging manner, and fondness for company and conversation, he was ideally suited to the task allotted to him.

9. Norman had to be careful not to advertise his own political doings. An unlucky accident was his being visited in his lodgings, when unwell, by Kitson Clark, a conscientious tutor, who was plainly shocked by the left-wing books he noticed there. When Norman was leaving Cambridge, and had to ask for a testimonial, Kitson Clark gave him a very unfavourable one, which he showed to me; it included a slighting reference to his having acquired 'a certain amount' of knowledge of the classics at Toronto – Toronto clearly was not Cambridge. He decided to remonstrate, and Kitson Clark eventually substituted a rather more useful certificate.

10. Through such channels Herbert Norman's political work, even if confined to a brief span of his life, and of course mingling with many other influences, can be said to have had some lasting positive results, like both his academic and diplomatic work.

# 9

# On Treason

Some drooping memories of Cambridge before the war have been revived of late by various writings. One is an autobiography, *Reading from Left to Right,* by a Canadian, Professor H.S. Ferns.[1] Few socialists of the Marxist persuasion – practically the only sort of people I got to know at college – seem to write memoirs; most of them probably feel that there are always more useful things to be done. Henry Ferns deviated from socialism long ago, but became a distinguished historian. His book, both entertaining and informative, looks back over a lifetime of abrupt, unforeseeable changes of outlook. Then there have been three books concerned with another Canadian of our time, Herbert Norman, a Cambridge Communist who turned into a respected member of his country's diplomatic service, was hunted by the Cold War pack, and ended, a suicide, at Cairo. He has become something of a symbol of Canadian independence from America, but scholars from both countries took part in a conference held a few years ago to assess his life and work. I was invited to speak about his time at Cambridge.

The conference papers, edited by Roger Bowen, have been published, and Dr Bowen has also written an appreciative biography. Japanese studies being his subject, he is well qualified to weigh up the writings on modern Japan of Herbert Norman, a missionary's son who grew up there. Very different is a viciously McCarthyite attack on him by an American, J. Barros (who has had the bad taste to thank me for some small assistance I gave him before I discovered what he was up to).[2] This has stirred up some controversy, and Barros was very effectively dealt with in a long review in the *Canadian Forum* (November 1986) by Reg Whitaker of York University. Henry Ferns, too, had a word to say about him in the same issue of the paper.

And there has lately been another outburst of barking and braying about 'Cambridge traitors'. It has come to be a perennial resort of reaction, when it is left without any fresher topic for claptrap, to indulge in these spasms of virtuous indignation about the wickedness of a small number of idealists of years ago. William Empson was stirred to an opposite kind of ire by one of many hack works, *The Traitors* by Alan Moorehead, who 'specifically denounced them for having had the impudence to obey their own consciences', instead of understanding that a citizen's duty is 'to concur with any herd in which he happens to find himself. The old Protestant in me stirred.'[3]

I went to Cambridge, to read history, in 1931, and stayed seven years. My undergraduate time was passed in premises – staircase I, no 2 – on the ground floor of the Whewell's Court annexe of Trinity College. Close by were two incongruous neighbours: A.E. Housman, anchored by misanthropy to this out-of-the-way spot, and James Klugmann, the chief Communist student organizer, and later a lifelong party worker. I.2 was not an ideal residence. When a gust of wind blew, the small fire, over which toast could be made with the help of a long fork and much patience, threw out billowing clouds of smoke, enough sometimes to drive me out into the court gasping for breath. During vacations mice nibbled at the backs of my books. Most of the thoughts of years in that cramped room have vanished, as they no doubt deserved to. Traces of sundry things have survived a half-century, the best of them books. Early in my second year I was reading for the first time Boswell's *Hebrides*, a cherished companion ever since; it was a tea-time luxury, accompanied by one daily cigarette, a limit I was not wise enough to keep for long, and I can still see the electric blue of the October sky as dusk gathered. Later on I moved to a nobler abode, in Great Court, on the top floor of a staircase beside the main gate. Here I was surrounded by the 'mighty dead', and could listen on summer nights to the fountain's murmur, and on spring days walk out, when work stuck fast, and look at the daffodils by the riverside.

In those days the deportment of senior Cambridge was oppressively genteel and ritualistic. Sciences flourished, as some had always done; history was in a stagnant condition, and at Trinity in particular was heavily overlaid by conservatism and clericalism. There was in general a stifling atmosphere of closed windows, drawn blinds, expiring candles, sleepwalking; outside, a mounting tumult of history in the making, instead of history laid to rest in neat graveyard rows of dusty tomes. With amenities such as the Backs, Wordsworth's *Prelude*, and a second-hand bicycle on which to explore the placid countryside, I was reasonably content, attended lectures as by law obliged, and took their stale fare for granted, like the weather. I became a socialist, then a Communist, before graduating to Marxism, the historical materialism that has been my Ariadne's thread ever since. Slow conversion may last longer than sudden enlightenment; and convictions, as Nietzsche said, are the backbone of life.

We had no time then to assimilate Marxist theory more than very roughly; it was only beginning to take root in England, though it had one remarkable expounder at Cambridge in Maurice Dobb, to whom a section is devoted in Professor H.J. Kaye's recent study of British Marxist historians.[4] We felt, all the same, that it could lift us to a plane far above the Cambridge academic level. We were quite right, as the rapid advance of Marxist ideas and influence since then has demonstrated. Our main concerns, however, were practical ones, popularising socialism and the USSR, fraternizing with hunger marchers, denouncing fascism and the National Government warning of the approach of war. We belonged to the era of the Third International, genuinely international at least in spirit, when the cause stood high above any national or parochial claims. Some of us have lived to see multinational capitalism, instead of international socialism, in control of most of the world: but at the time we had not the shadow of a doubt that capitalism was nearing its end. It was both too abominable, and too inept and suicidally divided, to last much longer. Socialism would take its place, and mankind be transformed not much less quickly.

At such a time, punctilios of 'loyalty' to things of the dying past seemed as archaic as the minutiae of drawing-room manners. And it was about the defenders of the old order that a strong smell of treason hung. We saw pillars of British society trooping to Nuremberg to hobnob with Nazi gangsters; we saw the 'National' government sabotaging the Spanish Republic's struggle, from class prejudice, and to benefit investors like Rio Tinto, blind to the obvious prospect of the Mediterranean being turned into a fascist lake and the lifelines of empire cut. From Spain the vibrations of civil war spread over Europe. The frenzied enthusiasm of the French right for Franco was the overture to its eager surrender to Hitler in 1940. Amid that tumult the sense of an absolute divide between 'whatsoever things are good' and everything Tory was easy to acquire, and with some of us has remained unshakeable. Our watchword was Voltaire's: *Ecrasez l'infâme.*

Feelings like these were to carry a small number of our generation, from Cambridge and elsewhere, into acts of 'treason', in the lawyer's meaning, not the only or best one. Those acts, amounting in sum to very little, have been sedulously embroidered and exaggerated, and the public has been continually reminded of them. For good measure, politics and sex have been mixed up, as if radicalism went hand in hand with homosexuality. In fact, an innocent could live in left-wing Cambridge without ever suspecting that such a thing existed, outside of Classical literature. The aim of all this pseudo-patriotic hubbub is to distract attention from the distempers of our ancien régime, keep people from thinking about the nuclear war they may well be drifting towards, and make them fancy that without zealous leaders to fend off a legion of spies and subversives, all would be lost. It also helps to nourish the illusion of Britain as a great power, with priceless secrets to be stolen. Writing books about secret-stealers is an easier way than most of earning a living; it benefits from the vogue of spy films and novelettes, symptom of an uneasy society in need of the reassurance of happy endings. 'Truth is sometimes stranger than fiction', as Mrs Thatcher said when telling the House one of her whoppers. It can certainly be made to look stranger and more fearsome.

I have no doubt that the extent of Herbert Norman's departure from rectitude was to start a small Indian Marxist group at Cambridge, which I inherited from him when he left. Some of its members were closely watched while at Cambridge, and arrested as soon as they went home. Norman had grown up in the Japanese countryside, still half-feudal, and must have been better able than the rest of us to imagine what life was like for Indian peasants under the British rulers who were obstinately denying independence to the country – Churchill most obstinately of all.

Guy Burgess was one of those – James Klugmann and John Cornford were the chief – who helped to induct me into the party. We belonged to the same college, and hence to the same 'cell'. I remember Burgess as a rather plump, fresh-faced youth, of guileless, almost cherubic expression. I heard him spoken of as the most popular man in the college, but he must have suffered from tensions; he smoked cigarettes all day, and had somehow imbibed a notion that the body expels nicotine very easily. He told me once a story that had evidently made a deep impression on him – of a Hungarian refugee who had been given shelter at his home, a formerly ardent political worker reduced to a wreck by beatings on the soles of the feet. I came on Burgess one day in his room sitting at a small table, a glass of spirits in front of him, glumly trying to put together a talk for a cell meeting that evening; he confessed that when he had to give any sort of formal talk he felt foolish. I never saw him after our exit from Cambridge. He did what he felt it right for him to do; I honour his memory.

Individuals who saw something of the machinations of government from the inside must have seen much to disgust them. If details of whatever secrets they gave away are still being hushed up, it must be because they were secrets discreditable to their superiors. We are always hearing nowadays of 'sensitive papers'. Paper is not sensitive, but those who write on it often have good cause to be, and prefer to blush unread. Anthony Blunt was quoted in his *Times* obituary (28 March 1983) as saying that he acted during the war 'from a conviction that we were not doing enough to help a hard pressed ally.' It is a political if not mathematical certainty that the same men who were adamant against collective security before 1939 were hard at work after 1941 to ensure that the conflict would end with Russia bled nearly to death, as exhausted as Germany. They were treacherously imperilling the whole allied war effort and the chances of victory. When another Cambridge man, Leo Long, made his public recantation in November 1981, it appeared that what he had taken part in doing was to give Moscow more British information about German troop movements than the British government chose to give it. Why did he feel obliged to sound so shamefaced? As he said, the information could do no harm to Britain.

If it is the case, as alleged early in 1982, that Maclean was trying at the end to influence Britain away from support of the American intervention in Korea, he was doing something very praiseworthy. It seems that Norman, by that time head of the Canadian mission at Tokyo, fell foul of General MacArthur, whom he had hitherto got on quite well with, by trying to dissuade *him* from intervention. At home, Sir John Pratt, dismissed from the Foreign Office for opposing the Korean War, stumped the country, in spite of his age, and denounced it in fiery terms. I was his chairman at a big meeting in Edinburgh when he referred to his campaign as one of invective against the government: 'invective', he said very truly, belonged to an old, honourable tradition that ought to be revived. It is indeed a mark of political decadence that there has been so little of it against Mrs Thatcher's regime: none since the war has more deserved it.

Treason has never been easy to define precisely, a fact illustrated by the long series of Tudor laws about it. It is an accusation easy to bandy about, but one that can be levelled in different directions. Antony in Shakespeare's play succeeds by his demagogy in turning popular feeling against the conspirators, and sets the crowd shouting: 'They were traitors!' They had plotted against a usurping dictator; Caesar had plotted against the Republic. In recent years Rome has been cannonizing batches of Catholics whom Queen Elizabeth's judges sentenced as traitors. Two centuries ago British conservatives were abusing yankee rebels in the same strain. During the French Revolutionary wars Tory Britain had open arms for all French reactionaries who were plotting against their own country, and welcomed them as allies against it. All the modern empires regarded resistance as treasonable, and employed multitudes of native collaborators, who in the eyes of nationalists were betraying their own people, like black policemen in South Africa today. A Russian who abandons his native land and settles in a hostile country is always credited with the most laudable motives, like the archetypal author of *I Chose Freedom*.

An honest Soviet dissident like Sakharov is, unquestionably, to be admired. So are the few Englishmen in British India who gave aid to nationalists or Communists. One of them, Michael Carritt, has written a light-hearted account of his brief career in the Indian civil service.[5] At vastly greater risk, a few Frenchmen in Algeria gave aid secretly to the rebels. Admirable too, though unlikely to be admired by Tories or Reaganites, is the young Chinese dissident Wei Jingsheng, jailed for fifteen years on charges including the giving of information to foreign journalists about the attack on Vietnam.

Toryism's record shows an elastic conception of loyalty, inspired by fidelity to the interests of class or party much more than of nation. Winston Churchill's father Randolph, when the Tory party was blocking the way to home rule for Ireland, coined the slogan 'Ulster will fight, and Ulster will be right' – a call for insurrection. In 1914 it was repeated by Carson, when a Liberal government was again about to concede home rule, or what is nowadays called devolution, and numbers of officers refused, with whole-hearted Tory approval, to take part in any coercion of Ulster. What would they have thought if their men had refused to take part in suppression of a colonial revolt in Africa or Asia? The object of the army mutiny, as it was very properly called, was to preserve Tory ascendancy in Ireland; the effect was to ensure the loss of most of Ireland to the United Kingdom, and the partition with its legacy of endless trouble. At the time, the Ulster affair may have been one of the factors that induced Germany to gamble on war, and induced the Liberal government to join in the gamble, as an escape from its embarrassments.

With this precedent in mind, it is easy to understand why it went without saying that British officers would decline to act against white rebels in Rhodesia. Ian Smith and his followers were levying war against the Crown; they received unstinted sympathy from the overwhelming majority of Tories. A speaker at a Tory Conference who ventured to criticize them was howled down. Wilson as prime minister once ventured to remind parliament that there were penalties for treason, or connivance at it; no Tory took any notice, and no action was taken. Since they own England, Tories naturally feel entitled to do as they like. Their encouragement of Smith was accompanied by wholesale evasion of the embargo imposed on Rhodesian trade: this, too, went unpunished. Tories have continued to cherish fraternal feelings towards the white savages of South Africa, their partners in upholding the natural right of capitalism to exploit its victims: quite indifferent to the moral damage to Britain, but also to the material losses to be expected from an alienation of black Africa and most of the Commonwealth.

It was the end, as Gaitskell said, of a thousand years of history when Britain was hustled by the Tories into the Common Market, and the abandonment of part of its independence. No referendum was held, because everyone knew that the vote would go against it. When Reagan carried out his bombardment of Libya, to please his right-wing voters and warn all other objectors to the American hegemony, Mrs Thatcher deemed it 'unthinkable' that Britain should decline to join in. Would it have been equally unthinkable if Reagan had been bombarding the USSR? Men were tried and hanged at Nuremberg for the kind of crime that this precious pair were committing. It seems clear, moreover, that Britain has taken part in undercover aid to right-wing insurgents in Nicaragua, in breach of American as well as international law.

Most friendships, said Dr Johnson, are either partnerships in folly or confederacies in vice: the Anglo-American connection is both. Toryism has been selling British independence for a mess of pottage, or of nuclear explosives, and at a time when America's many better qualities are in eclipse, when noisy reaction, political inanity, aggressive jingoism, hold sway, and arms dealers and the Pentagon, Eisenhower's 'military-industrial complex', are selling mankind's future for thirty trillion pieces of silver. Mrs Thatcher has been happy to play to the American gallery with her long string of anti-Soviet tirades, like the one so loudly applauded at Washington four years ago. How anyone, incidentally, can listen with pleasure to that detestable voice is one of our modern mysteries. Politicians are often given away by their voices, and that proportion of her career which has not been carefully concealed from the public has been one long hiss or scream.

When Franco began his rebellion and brought Moorish mercenaries and foreign troops and bombers into Spain to make it safe for landlords, capitalists and priests, almost all Tories cheered him to the echo. From their attitude then it may be imagined what it would be in a parallel situation at home. Human affairs, *res humanae*, are uncertain and obscure, as we learned from our Latin primers: but it is as certain as anything human can be that informal exchanges of views are always under way across the Atlantic, on a variety of confidential levels, to ensure that if ever Britain's 'nationalists' decide that the time has come for action they will not find themselves alone. There will be an open door not only for American forces, but for Germans, Chileans and other champions of free enterprise. The sell-out to America has masqueraded as a quest for the holy grail of a 'special relationship': here is its reality.

By way of a small rehearsal, during the 1983 election American money was made use of for 'dirty tricks' purposes against opponents. So was information, true or false, from MI5. The secret-service organizations, or rather secret societies of the right, which the public is induced to pay for without asking what they are doing, form a special submarine cable between Toryism and its American congeners. Vastly more serious than the allegation that a handful of their members have been agents of Moscow is the fact that, collectively, they are agents of Washington. It has been belatedly coming to light that they were involved in a plot to 'destabilize' a Labour government – a plot impossible for them to have conceived without the approval of high Tory personages and in collusion with American colleagues. If this was not treason, what ever can be? Destabilizing foreign governments has been a tactic through the centuries: it has been left to the USA to make it a cornerstone of foreign policy. Labour's leaders were too timid to make any real protest, though the question was one of British independence as well as of their party's fortunes. The people concerned are now bent on preventing any enquiry, and have spent a good deal of the taxpayer's money to that end.

While deafening us with shouts of liberty, our rulers are swathing us in all manner of invigilation, two-footed or electronic. Tory governments in the past, too, were addicted to use of police spies and agents provocateurs against progressives. Police spying was ubiquitous in all Western colonies or semi-colonies, and habits formed there have persisted. Kell, the founder of MI5, was in China at the outset of his career, and then for some time in Tsarist Russia. Like Bulldog Drummond's Black Gang, it always saw its business as hunting subversives of all sorts, including trade unionists.

A clique of politicians and generals manoeuvred 'democratic' Britain into the alliances that landed it in the First World War, and a similar process is going on underground today. The BBC correspondent Alastair Cooke once remarked that in Washington ceremonial gatherings are always being held in honour of foreign visitors to whom nobody has anything to say, while decisions are taken by small groups, often through telephone calls. It is hard to see how anyone could be a 'traitor' to the Washington plotters and their European jackals, any more than to Nazism. If we want to discover who is really undermining British welfare and safety, we need look no further than Downing Street.

The Tories came into office determined to sell off a vast stock of national wealth, at cheap rates, to their party and its financial backers, and to any voters who could be bribed: in other words, to plunder the nation they profess so much devotion to. By now an immense sum has been deftly transferred from the public domain to the pockets of Tories and, in good measure, their friends abroad. There was a foretaste of what was to come when Amersham International, the radioactive isotopes business, was sold in February 1982 at a price £23 million below its market value. The government was accused of making a fool of itself, but it was the taxpayer it was making a fool of, and what was politely termed mere ignorance and stupidity, venial faults in any Tory administration, ought to have been branded as a swindle. This year two Tory MPs, caught cheating when other public property was on sale, had to agree not to stand for re-election: they were given a pat on the back by their party chairman for making 'honourable' amends for an 'error of judgment'.

This sort of national asset-stripping is not new, except in scale. Indeed the history of capitalist property accumulation everywhere has consisted largely of 'privatizing' public resources, giving away North American forests to railway corporations, for example. Plundering the state has been a besetting temptation to men in power. No sooner was the breath out of Henry VIII's carcass than the noblemen who surrounded his young son were laying hands on generous acreages out of the Crown lands, on which the government depended for a good part of its revenue. During the eighteenth and early nineteenth centuries parliament was busy voting the village common lands off the map, mostly to be added to the estates of the landowners who were doing the voting, and the rest of their species. In old Scotland, where royal minorities were always happening, a king had the right on coming of age to take back lands granted away from the Crown during his nonage. A similar right ought to be vested now in the British public, to be exercised when – if ever – it comes of age.

Human nature being nearly as frail as Tories always tell us, when dismissing socialism as a pipe dream, it ought to have been insisted on that ministers, MPs, and all others responsible for the privatizing – or privateering – operations, should submit to a self-denying ordinance, like parliament in the Civil War.

There ought to have been the fullest guarantees that none of them or their families or hangers-on would benefit personally. No such assurances have been forthcoming. There has always been room in the City for conjuring tricks of a more or less unsavoury kind, but hitherto a decent reticence has been observed. Now, dizzy with success over the vast hoard of pearls scattered before the swine it is grunting with indiscreet loudness. We are coming closer to the monstrous regiment of stockbrokers that Marx saw in Bonapartist France in 1853: 'the whole state machinery transformed into one immense swindling and stock-jobbing concern.'[6] And this goes with a further disastrous decline in industrial activity, and its relegation to the background by the sway of speculative finance, the most parasitic, semi-aristocratical, cosmopolitan type of capitalism. From stealing village commons our profiteers went on to rob villagers in Asia and Africa; now they have come back to plundering *us* again.

In 1982 when there were American outcries about information leakage for fifteen years from Cheltenham to the Russians, the *Guardian* made the comment that this flood appeared to have done no perceptible harm. Life seems to jog along just the same whether the official secrets mystification is being eavesdropped or not. Much the same can be said of the whole spy scare, kept going for reasons mostly remote from the ostensible one. Searching for spies and traitors to explain why things are as they are is always a search for excuses. 'We are betrayed by what is false within': not Mrs Thatcher's 'enemy within' – miners, for instance, who object to being thrown out of work and have to be ridden down by police stormtroopers with horse and hound – but the falsity engrained in the entire fabric of capitalist society. The real anti-patriots are those who deepen and worsen it, for their own benefit. They are far more of a danger to Britain than any givers-away or sellers of 'sensitive papers', chiefly concealing no more than official trumpery and balderdash.

Morally, the 'treason' of the thirties cannot for a moment be compared with the morass of crooked dealing, profit-gorging, deception, looting of national resources and indifference to national welfare, that make up the world of Thatcherism. The latest bright Tory idea is to let agriculture follow industry into decay, and turn loose a barbarous horde of 'developers' over what is left of the countryside. One way or another, the country is being drained of vitality, while constantly assured that all is well, because national security (or official secrecy – to Mrs Thatcher the two terms are synonymous) is being vigilantly preserved, and no soldiers with snow on their boots are marching along Whitehall. So far as our unemployed and old people, at any rate, are concerned, they must be feeling like the famished labourer in the anti-Corn Law cartoon: 'I be protected, and I be starving.'

'If treason prospers, none dare call it treason,' and so far Thatcherism has prospered and been allowed to practise its philosophy. Mrs Thatcher takes it upon herself to lecture the nation on its moral shortcomings, and blame its permissiveness for sapping the foundations of law and order. She lectures the

Russians on the subject of human rights. On the Anglo-American view, human rights are essential for socialist countries, but can be dispensed with in Latin America, South Korea and elsewhere because there the people enjoy the supreme felicity of free enterprise, alias capitalism, which makes up for every drawback. Mrs Thatcher has had only the kindest words for the Indonesian regime, built on the bones of the hundreds of thousands massacred in 1965, and conspicuous for its conquest of the former Portuguese colony of East Timor, where at least a third of the population is reported to have been killed or driven into exile, with the help of Western arms sales and diplomatic support. Future historians, if any survive to look back on all this, will find our 'civilisation' the hardest of all to comprehend from the language of its statesmen, more indecipherable than any Egyptian hieroglyphics.

If every nation gets the government it deserves, hard though it may be to think of any nation deserving a government like Britain's in recent years, these years speak ill for the British people, or a large section of it. For some years after the war, Tories could claim that they were not as bad as they used to be: with some truth, because they were not allowed to be. Since then, they have been allowed to behave worse than ever, and have flourished accordingly.

Garaudy, the French Marxist and former Communist, wrote of his and my generation, with our eyes on Hitler, Franco, McCarthy; 'We were fighting absolute evil: how, then, could we not feel that our cause was the cause of absolute good?' Painful experience showed that the second of these beliefs was in part illusion. But our ideals and aims were valid, and mean as much now as they did then. If we have not been invariably right, our opponents have been almost infallibly wrong, in anything where public morality or human progress is concerned. After a decade or two of uneasy recovery following the war, economy and society are sinking into another quagmire. None of our fundamental problems have been solved, and on present lines never will be. In Rome, in times of emergency, a 'final decree' of the senate gave plenary power to the consuls to save the state. In Britain now, a government once elected, even by a minority of the electorate, can feel free to claim plenary power to do whatever it likes, and without telling anyone what it is really doing. It is to Britain's credit that the majority of voters have always been against Thatcherism: but we have been learning that a minority government can do the country immense harm, moral and material, much of it beyond repair. The system of representation that allows this is indefensible, the case for a change has become unanswerable. The alternative is going to be a dictatorship of the rich.

## Notes

1. H.S. Ferns, *Reading from Left to Right*, Toronto 1983.
2. R.W. Bowen ed., *E.H. Norman: His Life and Scholarship*, Toronto 1984; Bowen, *Innocence is*

*Not Enough: The Life and Death of Herbert Norman*, Toronto 1986; J. Barros, *No Sense of Evil*, Denau 1986.

3. W. Empson, *Milton's God*, London 1961, pp. 230–31.
4. Harvey J. Kaye, *The British Marxist Historians*, Oxford 1984.
5. Michael Carritt, *Mole in the Crown*, privately published 1985.
6. Article in *Daily Tribune*, New York, 14 June 1853.

# 10

# Socialism, the Prophetic Memory

Buddhist metaphysics, the highest wisdom of Asia, solved the paradox of our isolated yet incomplete selves by dismissing the 'self' of consciousness as an illusion, and seeing all 'true' being as part of one unity. Marxism, the highest achievement of Western thought, agrees – at least in regarding human beings not as mutually exclusive atoms but as entities continually borrowing and giving, and in this sense each infinite as well as finite. It is the heir of a long European evolution where the relationship between individual and social has always been a practical as well as a philosophical issue. Here from very early times there has been a dual, antiphonal development, nowhere else nearly so pronounced: on the one hand the single human integer with its rights and claims, on the other the collective organisation. In place of the Asiatic State, external in nearly every way to its subjects' lives and impinging on them only by magical pretension or by compulsion, there arose in Europe the Mediterranean city-state, the alter ego of each citizen, a partnership extending, at any rate in the lofty conception of a Pericles, to every corner of life. It raised natural gregariousness to a higher plane, elevating man from a merely social being to what Aristotle called a political animal. Both individual and collective were thereby enlarged: a genuine political spirit can arise only through interaction between the two. Since then the two have been growing, through interplay or collision. Today finds us in another of those recurrent epochs when their rival demands are felt to have become incompatible. To escape from this by abolishing the collective, as anarchism desires, would enfeeble the individual; to suppress the individual, as fascism desires, would stultify the collective.

From the point of view of socialism, it is a question of depriving a limited number of men of a 'freedom' based on a bloated power over the community's economic life, in order to liberate the growth of countless others, both as individuals and as members of a meaningful community. Property has always been the vital third term. The ancient *polis*, and its successor the medieval city-republic, both of them ancestors of the nation-state of western Europe, were collective owners on a large scale of land, food reserves, public buildings sacred or profane; above all, perhaps, of the town walls and forts which guaranteed their security. Such common possessions did much to generate the concept of a *res publica*, a 'commonwealth', scarcely glimpsed outside Europe, and with it that of a *patria* for the citizen to identify himself with. But within this whole the unfolding of individuality was being furthered, on some sides of its complex structure, though on others hindered, by the proliferation of private property. The Greeks, who debated everything, debated this explosive force, generated within the late clan and the early city-state growing out of it, which threatened to disrupt them. In Sparta the dominant class practised a kind of State Communism; it could be admired by conservatives elsewhere like Plato, whose ideal Republic reflected an aristocratic disdain of vulgar competition for wealth. In a more democratic spirit a dislike of private property, as an unnatural novelty, was perpetuated by the Stoic philosophers, and outlived its attic cradle. 'A broad current of communistic sentiment runs through the mental life of the Roman Empire in the age of Christ.'[1]

At the opposite pole was an unbridled competition for wealth, as the empire obsessively expanded and the republic degenerated; along with this expansion, property was coming to be endowed by Roman law with a mystically absolute, unfettered right. Social conditions bred mass resentment and calls for the land to be taken back from its greedy monopolists and reallocated as the common good required. These calls for an 'agrarian law' were among the spectres haunting nineteenth-century Europe. Property triumphed, but the memory of a time before its advent, before class division, lingered, bathed in a sentimental glow, in legends of a golden age of the dim past. There was no way for men to find their way back to it, or resurrect it; they could only wait for the 'great cycle' of time, the endless return of things, to restore it, as Christians were to await their less remote millennium. Collective ownership of land may never really have existed, at least after land came under regular cultivation, and before that time what men had to share was mostly hunger. Educated Romans knew enough about Goths or Scythians to be realistic about primitive poverty; but they could imagine no other refuge from the corruptions of wealth and sophistication than the daydream of primitive simplicity. They drew a nostalgic picture of an existence full of hardship and of virtue, free and equal and fraternal.

The common man was less apt to hanker for austerities that he was only too well acquainted with. His daydream of the past was the one romanticized by Virgil, of a time when nature produced unbidden, and men enjoyed plenty without the curse of toil. It was compounded of the genuine fellowship of older days, and of modern wealth, the happiness of the rich man who neither toiled nor span and yet was arrayed like Solomon. A like illusion showed itself in the New Testament maxim that men should take no thought for the morrow, but trust to luck. Primitive man to this day has had no need to be taught such fecklessness; it is fostered by habits of group life and dependence, which only the stern discipline of individual work and self-sufficiency has been able to counteract. A Frenchman living among Eskimos, in the harshest of environments, was astonished at their inability to practise self-restraint by rationing their food supply on a long journey.[2] Chinese Communists found it hard to introduce tribesmen like those of the Cool Mountains to any orderly routine: they were accustomed to work by fits and starts, and as seldom as possible, and the notion of a team reckoning up its members' quota of labour and sharing the produce in proportion to work done struck them as mercenary, unfeeling.[3] Communism was having to bring them the work ethic of Calvinism or capitalism. Something of the same childlike irresponsibility was to be seen in the loafing Sicilian or Catholic Irishman of the last century, by contrast with the north Italian or the Ulsterman. Each type suffers from its own maladies, which socialism hopes to cure by merging the two in one.

Like nations, classes have perpetuated something of the old social bond of the undivided clan, though at the cost of mutual hostility. Each maintained or created forms of association within which their members could enjoy a sense of partial re-absorption into a community. Sparta's collective land-holding found a counterpart, on a far greater scale and in more complex forms, among the feudal ruling classes that emerged from Germanic tribal infiltration into western Roman provinces. Feudal land ownership, by contrast with Roman property right, was indeterminate: the same acres belonged to a multiplicity of persons, with conjoint though very unequal claims; even the cultivators had some share. Monasteries and military orders were brotherhoods of members of the elite, holding land and buildings in trust. The same medieval spirit, of the privileged group leading its own corporate life, was to be seen in the town guilds and fraternities, which were professional associations and mutual benefit societies combined; they too owned collective endowments, much as the village had its common lands.

Templars and teutonic knights provided a model for the later officer corps of modern Europe, the Prussian above all, with their common table and identical costume; monasteries were to live on in colleges like those of Oxford and Cambridge, resolutely anti-socialist in our times while practising a version of socialism of their own. Aristocracy in modern Britain has herded together in the public school – in the exclusive club safeguarded by the democratic weapon of the blackball – and in a semi-nomadic lounging from country house to country house. Its men, though not its women (whether or not this proves women to have less of socialist instinct in them), learned to wear identical clothes every evening, a costume marking them out as society's officers or superiors. While the rich exchanged entertainment, the poor exchanged aid. The same custom of everyone within a social group being entitled to a share of whatever was going, which struck William Penn among the Red Indians,[4] likewise struck Dr Chalmers and his Kirk deacons exploring the bottomless poverty of Glasgow.[5] But the poor too have practised forms of social extravagance; a funeral in Lancashire, or a wedding in an Indian village – a feast due from the family to all its neighbours, the *baradari* or brethren. In all these shapes an ingrained collectivism, truncated and often rendered noxious by class division, can be seen asserting itself.

It was left to religion to prolong, in a more ghostly fashion, the lost integrity of the social whole. All the 'founded' religions have begun with an emphasis on their followers, as children of God, being of one family. Early Islam had a *bait-ul-mulk* or treasury of the people, replenished by plunder taken from non-Muslims. Christianity grew up with an exceptional measure of this 'social' sentiment, thanks to its complex inheritance of ideas, and its setting in a cosmopolitan society torn by class strife as well as strife of peoples, full of slaves and other expatriates to whom it offered a compensation for lost roots. Some of them in the early days pooled their resources and had common funds. Christianity was faithful to what may already at that date be called the European spirit, in being at once strongly individualist and strongly associationist; it endowed each man and woman with a precious soul, but this soul was to find salvation by doing good to fellow creatures. This helped to qualify the new faith presently for official adoption, and for eminent service as reconciler or harmonizer of classes, the prime social task in historical times of all religions.

This European religion was to be the parent or foster-parent of socialism, if a reluctant and even unnatural one. Not only did it preserve and deepen men's recognition of their interdependence, but more remarkably even if only abstractly, it also kept alive through many ages the belief, a legacy of the philosophers of antiquity, that private ownership was a corrupting innovation, and communal ownership the natural usage of mankind. Ideas when sanctioned by religion can have an astonishing tenacity. This one must have helped to keep the Church's conscience uneasy, and the duty of charity in mind. But the Church studied and prayed in a dead language, and presided over a society where literate and illiterate were very far apart. So far as carrying the principle into practice was concerned, it was satisfied with a symbolic, merely negative parade, the joint renunciation of wealth that monks were supposed to make. Monkish austerity seldom lasted long; and when envy of the rich by the poor sharpened, it was time for a more striking exhibition of voluntary poverty, as vicarious atonement for the sins of an unjust world. This was provided not by the clergy, but by St Francis, who dedicated himself from the moment of his conversion to the quest for *Sancta Paupertas*, as for a blessed lady.[6]

Embracing and idealizing poverty, Francis tacitly rebuked envy or hatred of the rich. The Church would know how to exploit his cult, and turn it into one more device for bamboozling the poor and reconciling them to their lot. Meanwhile Aquinas, born in 1227, the year after Francis's death, came to the rescue of orthodoxy by explaining that Communism was, indeed, the ideal, but had only been practicable in the state of innocence: in man's fallen condition its place must be taken by legally sanctioned private property.[7] Property was thus smuggled in as a regrettable necessity. A line of descent can be seen here from the thinking of the upper classes of antiquity, uneasy under the burden of their wealth; the Christian doctrine of man's sinfulness and fall from grace had offered them a sort of comfort. By the propertied classes of his own time Aquinas might well be hailed as the 'Angelic Doctor'. He was in a way anticipating the Marxist historical scheme of primitive Communism followed by an era of private ownership, but he was ruling out its sequel, the return to Communism on a higher level, discovering the modern objection, so dear to conservatives that human nature is not good enough.

Francis came to terms with the Church, and was rewarded with a title and a gaudy tomb. Other zealots refused to do so, and were persecuted as heretics,[8] to wealthy prelates any preaching of poverty sounded like a reproach. In the later Middle Ages there was a proliferation of sects with a leaning towards sharing of goods, or more frequently, towards rejection of any goods. The name of one of them, the 'Family of Love', is revealing. They were trying to hold on to the brotherliness of a social order partly remembered, partly imagined, in an epoch when it was being eaten away by the search for money and luxury. Their emotional fervour was kindled by the sight of selfish riches which seemed to show that all property, even the least, must in some degree corrupt men and set them against one another. In moods of religious exaltation stimulated by economic and social tension, acceptance of shared penury as the best of blessings, because it preserved human brotherhood, could be very potent.

But many ideas or sensations must have jostled together in discontented minds, among them the thought of relieving the rich of their superfluity in order to relieve the hunger of the poor. To the healthy materialism of the ordinary man, with his utopian daydreams of ease and plenty,[9] pauperism, however spiritual, would have little appeal. Its attractions may have been strongest for those already penniless. Rebels like Wat Tyler's men in England in 1381 had something to defend against their rulers. After the revolt John Ball, the democratic priest who took his Christianity too literally, was hanged. In the Hussite national resistance in Bohemia in the first half of the fifteenth century a species of war-Communism was practised by the most extreme faction. Social unrest and mystical doctrines often intertwined as the Middle Ages neared their end, as in south-west Germany. Mysticism has been serviceable to all religions, but also perturbing, because by removing barriers between man and

God it may undermine those between man and man, and cast doubt on the solidest of them, private property.

In western Germany the disturbances which culminated in the Peasants' War of 1524 to 1525 were largely, like the risings in England in the same period, a defence of village commons – pasture and woodland – against encroachments by the lords. In other words they were a defence of a socialist element embedded in the traditional economy, threatened now in Germany and elsewhere by neofeudalism, in England by nascent agricultural capitalism. Newer experiments in common ownership were tried by groups of craftsmen and mineworkers, under pressure of nascent industrial capitalism such as had already provoked a blend of religious and social unrest in the Flemish manufacturing towns of the later Middle Ages. Anabaptism, that loose array of left-wing movements demanding a far more radical reformation of Church and society than either Luther or Calvin contemplated, was hunted down everywhere. It was denounced for wanting abolition of private ownership, as well as for pacifism and other mortal errors. For good measure, Anabaptists were charged, like the early Christians they sought to emulate, with wanting wives in common as well, and with enjoying them in common during the outbreak at Munster in 1533 led by John of Leyden. Classes, like nations, have been fond of accusing each other of degrading women (a modern British critic of socialism maintained that it would turn women into 'brood mares').[10] Perhaps some sectaries really did hanker after communal marriage, if only because their women might be almost the only belongings left them to share. Whether for women this would have been a step towards or away from emancipation may be debatable.

The same epoch of groping and confusion that gave birth to modern capitalism was also giving birth to its antithesis, modern socialism, though this was to be pushed for long into the background. And if new forms of Christianity, notably Calvinism, were mixed up with the beginnings of capitalism, others had as close links with those of socialism. Fresh interest in common ownership, as the means to overcome men's perennial discords, showed itself in speculation among thinkers as well as in action by the people. The two were far apart, but socialism as a conception might unfold the more readily for this. It was turning away from archaic reverence for poverty towards the thought of common ownership for the sake of the well-being of the majority. This thought showed itself in the 'utopias' that were being written in the sixteenth century, efforts – encouraged by the expansion of Europe's geographical horizons and contact with far-off civilizations – to transpose the never-forgotten golden age of legend into sketches of how society might be reconstituted.

More's *Utopia*, most famous of them all, was written in 1516. As a churchman employed by the State, More belonged to a type which might be said to float above private property in its ordinary manifestations: it was supported by public funds of diverse origin. Disgusted by the spectacle of rampant greed, and the expropriation of the English peasantry already under way, he repeated with renewed force the old conviction that private property was the root of all evil, that land (and everything else) should be collectivized. He was thus going far beyond the peasants, still struggling to defend their mixed economy. To Shakespeare, nearly a century later, utopian bliss could be no more than amiable fantasy, like the worthy Gonzalo's talk for the amusement of his companions on Prospero's island about how he would direct a common-wealth, where all should enjoy plenty without toil. In the forest of Arden Shakespeare conjured up a retreat where men could 'fleet the time carelessly, as they did in the golden world', but he did not disguise the ruggedness of this flight to the wilderness. Yet no invective of reformers against human greed for wealth and power has ever gone beyond Shakespeare's in the tragedies; in *King Lear* above all his vision of the social problem, unsoftened either by hope of possible change or by religious illusion, is abysmally pessimistic.

It was in Catholic Europe, where capitalism was developing much more slowly, that religious illusions could loiter longest. More gave his life for the papacy, not for the peasantry, but he was a precursor of the Counter-Reformation not only in its theology but in its social thinking, which revived here and there the old patristic mistrust of property. On this plane, ideas resembling those of Anabaptism could emerge at the opposite pole. Catholic writers reminded themselves that Christian tradition (like Islamic) regarded the land as belonging to God, and that it condemned private ownership as a man-made and malignant thing. In the Spain of the early seventeenth century, sinking into decay while landowners piled up huge estates and reduced the cultivators to pauperism, the churchman Pedro de Valencia called on the king to protect the poor against the rich, *los poderosos*, and to compel the proper cultivation of all land, even if it meant expropriating absentee owners and planting agricultural colonies.[11] Philip III had other things to do with his time. These finer flights of the Counter-Reformation were bound to be ineffectual, because they were merely appeals to the conscience of the great, divorced from any protest by the poor. More wrote his *Utopia* in Latin. Once more Catholic revival was utilized, instead, by the rich to quieten the poor.

With the fading of the old order its collectivist ingredients were dis-appearing or shrinking. Unleashed individualism could not be held in check by any prophetic images of socialism drawn on the clouds; it was something more crude and earthy that arose in the sixteenth and seventeenth centuries, to impose limits and keep social conflict within bounds. This was the emergent modern State, most often in the guise of absolute monarchy. Equipped with standing army, secret police and firearms, and with greater coercive strength than any before, it was further fortified by close alliance with churches every-where directed by it; with its aid these churches were themselves armed with a power of persecution – its acme the Spanish Inquisition – on a scale virtually unknown in history outside Europe. There could be no more complete negation of individualism than all this dragooning, no clearer illustration of how much else has to be sacrificed to untrammelled pursuit of happiness, when happiness means money. Yet the State and its ecclesiastical partner obscured the dominant economic interests which they largely served, and popular feeling could come to identify itself with them. Nationalism was far less natural or wholesome than the civic spirit of the old city-states, but it was growing far stronger than any sentiment resembling it outside western Europe. It could preserve, however distortedly, some part of a collectivist ethos which would one day help to make western Europe the cradle of practical socialism.

Human aspirations represented today by socialism have been in great measure constant through the ages, but the means men have looked to for their fulfil-ment have varied widely. For a long time after the opening of the modern era the belief that brotherhood among men requires community of wealth was overlaid by a new faith in private ownership and free enterprise. This could include a democratic leaven of peasant proprietorship, and fortunes, except in land, were still usually moderate. Mentally as well as economically the self-assertion of the individual was necessary for progress, but it was always haunted by a Faustian aura of guilt, of a primordial social compact violated. However heroically the new man has dramatized or romanticized himself, he has always suffered from misgivings about his wilful self-isolation; it has been the source of the travail, the angst of modern Europe. In the eighteenth century, whose laborious optimism hid a great deal of hypochondria, Pope tried to believe that there was no real contradiction, because providence had bidden 'self-love and social be the same'.[12] Poetry was showing the way to laissez-faire economics, and reversing the old Christian tenet that a man could only do good to himself by serving others: he was now to do good to society by serving himself. Such sanctifying of egotism bore a resemblance to Paley's argument from design, which proved the existence of a benevolent deity from the care he had taken to provide for his creatures' sustenance by arranging for them to eat one another.

In the bourgeois revolutions, in 1789 above all, the eagerness of an inchoate social order to appear as reconciler of personal and public welfare was carried to the most ambitious point. The messianic complexion of all grand revolutions, the desire of a class intoxicated by the sense of leadership to deem itself the vanguard of humanity, its own interest universal, is a familiar phenomenon. It is not all hypocrisy, for the bourgeois idealists who have inspired enthusiasm and made sacrifices were for the most part quite different men from the profiteers who carried off the spoils. The year 1789 may have opened the door to unrestricted capitalism, but its intentions were at least as much in harmony with socialism, and their frustration led at once to the first active attempt at socialism, the 'Conspiracy of the Equals' of 1796.

All the values that classical antiquity ascribed to its golden age, or to its noble savages, can be seen again in the three grand if vague watchwords of the Revolution. Liberty extended to various 'freedoms' that we have since then been compelled to distinguish more closely, among them 'freedom from want'. 'Tis against *that* that we are fighting', an ardent Frenchman exclaimed to Wordsworth as they watched a 'hunger-bitten girl' knitting with 'pallid hands' by the banks of the Loire, and Wordsworth joined him in looking forward to 'better days to all mankind'.[13] 'Equality' stood for another complex of associations, old and elemental or new and sophisticated. Burns with his 'A man's a man', Mozart's Sarastro with his call to every man 'to be a man', were paying tribute in almost the same words to the worth and the rights of the ordinary human being, which the Revolution undertook to vindicate; theirs was an individualism with higher, socialist overtones, like all the best in bourgeois ideology. In the subsequent passion of the middle-class Frenchman for equal civic and legal status it took on more cramped dimensions, behind which lay the glaring absence of any material equality. 'Fraternity', the third dimension of the Revolutionary trinity, was like that of the Christian hardest of all to define; yet it could be the most emotive and unbounded of all. The word 'brother' as used among Wesleyans or trade unionists perpetuates an older and commoner usage, still current in lands like India. In 1524 the German peasants argued that no man should be another's serf, because all men were children of God and therefore brothers. The kernel of George Eliot's humanist faith was a prayer for 'energy of human fellowship'.[14] It was an often-repeated story among socialists in the late nineteenth century that a Communard prisoner, derisively asked by his captors what he was going to die for, answered: 'Pour la solidarité humaine'.[15]

Ideals soon to be taken up by socialism can be recognized among the quickly blighted hopes of 1789, alike in the microcosm of the family and the macrocosm of world relations. One of these aspirations was for a freer, more equal bond between men and women, and parents and children, with more even sharing of family goods. It found its way into the civil code, but was sadly warped by Thermidorean reaction and Bonapartist dictatorship. In 1789 the National Assembly formally renounced war as an instrument of policy, and Europe applauded. Nations like individuals, it was assumed, had only to be relieved of the incubus of monarchy and aristocracy to get on happily with one another ever after. In 1792 a far from unwilling French government took up a European challenge to war, and France embarked on two decades of conquest. It has been left to socialism to fulfil all such disappointed hopes; it is the New Testament that supersedes all old ones – though like all scriptures, it is still a very incomplete one.

In the Paris of George Sand, she says, sooner or later in any conversation someone would say: 'Posons la question sociale'. It was the social problem engendered by industrial revolution, along with a new proletariat, and a new concreteness and immediacy of the socialist idea. This could not blossom in the countryside, even in England with its unique capitalist agriculture; though after it appeared it could be received eagerly by some rural workers, like the gangs of labourers on the latifundia of Andalusia. The rise of large-scale capitalist industry to a dominant place in the economy was polarizing society on fresh lines, and bringing in sight a possible future of machines owned and worked for the good of all. This could not only reduce labour and increase well-being, but could constitute a new bond of combination among men, and at the same time a release from the servitude of the factory run for private profit.

Socialism was indeed as obviously necessary, once steam machinery came in, as the replacement of private armies by a single armed force of the State had been three centuries before, when gunpowder came in. Without the driving force of private profit industrialism might have spread much more slowly, but in a far more orderly, rational style. Yet after another century and a half, in most of the world socialism is still only knocking at the door – in many countries, like Britain, not very insistently.

The idea made its way spasmodically, here quickly, there more sluggishly, and frequently taken up only to be forgotten. It had attractions for both the more progressive (morally progressive) of the educated classes, and the new working class, but they were still – like their ancestors, and too often their descendants – far apart, and each weakened by the lack of contact. Among the literate, some of the pioneers had no notion of converting society to their views, but like the Anabaptists before them were separating themselves from it, to make a life of their own. Disillusion following the too sanguine hopes of 1789 helped to inspire small groups to retreat as far as the American wilderness where the socialist cream of the Revolutionary milk could, so to speak, be strained off. Two years before Babeuf's Conspiracy of the Equals, the youthful Southey and Coleridge were planning a 'Pantisocratic' settlement beyond the Atlantic, whose name proclaimed the same principle. These utopias had a long lease; as late as 1881 we find a socialist refugee from Germany joining a colony in Tennessee, but soon quitting it.[16]

When it was time to think of remodelling society, instead of hiding from it in little oases, it was tempting to suppose that socialism could come about by peaceful penetration, here and there. That was, after all, how capitalism had been and still was developing. Cooperation, or 'association', seems to have been the original meaning of socialism when the word came into use in the 1820s. It could be started by small groups, but these would be living among their neighbours, and trusting to force of example to bring others eventually to emulate them, leaving capitalism to wither away. Only while industrial technology was still rudimentary could the programme be·at all realistic; after this stage socialism could only be established by the taking over of existing factories and mines. Another 'utopian' thought was of socialist measures, sweetened by a religious infusion, being adopted by governments, in the spirit of the enlightened autocrats of the eighteenth century, just as they could be induced to assist capitalism. Saint-Simon's disciples made some impression on Napoleon III, when in his days of exile he was looking round for a cure for the social problem, a nostrum to be his passport to the throne. They even thought it worthwhile to make approaches (so she told Kinglake) to that minor autocrat Lady Hester Stanhope, self-appointed ruler of a patch of the fabled East.[17] In China the same impulse showed itself when the reformer K'ang Yu-wei sketched out between 1884 and 1885 a utopian programme of universal peace, emancipation of women, and socialism.[18] A dozen years later he tried to carry it out, with the support of a youthful emperor; the latter was promptly dethroned, the reformer had to take flight.

Working-class responses were equally variegated. Capitalism took on differing complexions in different regions, under the influence of their past and of their social structure, and its proletariat, which Marxism was to think of too much as everywhere one and the same, was in reality at least as diverse. Neither self-conscious classes nor their political parties can come into being without a heavy admixture of features carried over from earlier times, or moulded by national temperament. The ironclad socialism of the Third International was to be very much the offspring of the First World War, and could only have grown from a soil as stony, as indurated to battle and martial discipline, as Europe's; outside Europe it has transplanted itself with most success in the Far East, in so many ways a second Europe by comparison with the rest of Asia. In the formative years of capitalism much, in the reactions of any workforce to industrial conditions and in its receptivity to socialist thinking, depended on how far it was made up of women and children; on its national or religious composition, which might be as little uniform as in Glasgow or Manchester or eastern France; on how many recruits were coming straight from the village, and what their status there had been, and what they had known of agrarian resistance; and on how many had been craftsmen. It would be affected also by the extent to which other artisans managed to hang on to their independence, as they did in London or Paris. All this heterogeneity of the labouring masses, in the crucial first generation or two, did as much as anything else to allow capitalism to consolidate its position.

Before the end of the 1820s there was 'an indigenous English Socialism', and writers like Gray and Hodgskin had 'laid down the main lines of Socialist thought'.[19] In England as elsewhere the movement was taking shape on two levels, which have never come very close together, that of the mainly middle-class thinkers – or dreamers – and that of the working people. Among the workers there was a medley of jostling sects, a millennarian ferment with all sorts of freakish religious notions once more mixed up in it,[20] heaven and earth churning together as in one of Turner's landscapes. Little by little amid this turmoil there dawned first a longing to destroy the machines before these monsters could gain sway over mankind – then an ambition to win control over the monsters, and make steam a boon to all instead of an enrichment to a few.

Heaven and earth jostled together in the mind of Robert Owen, an outstanding 'utopian' in every sense of the term, who did nevertheless drift towards a recognition that the blight of capitalism would have to be eliminated to make the world safe for something better. He drifted therefore into collaboration with a young trade union movement, a few of whose leaders envisaged the overthrow of capitalism by means of a general strike. But by this time British capitalism was so firmly in the saddle that to overthrow it must mean also overturning the State. William Morris was to dwell on Owen's failure to understand the impracticability of hopes like his 'as long as there is a privileged class in possession of the executive power.'[21] This country's relatively low concentration of State authority helped to conceal its decisive importance from socialists, most of whom have never yet fully opened their eyes to it; whereas over most of the continent the bureaucratic, military structure could no more be overlooked than the pyramid of Cheops in its desert. Local amateur magistrates, yeomanry, special constables, could provoke class resentment without this crystallizing into political hostility to the class State.

Chartists did recognise the vital need of political power for any new social dispensation. Many of them, however, when they thought of social change looked backward rather than forward. They wanted to resettle the people on the land, giving each family a farm of its own. This seems strangely atavistic, considering how long it was since most Englishmen had possessed any land. Peasant proprietorship was particularly dear to Feargus O'Connor, and one may wonder how much of its popular appeal entered England with the flood of immigrants from peasant Ireland, a country of land-hungry rack-rented tenants. The British Isles had to wrestle with the ailments of several eras of history at the same time. Later leaders of Chartism like Harney and Ernest Jones reached more modern and socialist conceptions, not without some help from Marx, but they came too late, when the mass movement was about to crumble. After 1850 industrial capitalism in Britain was strong enough to enforce acquiescence, flourishing enough to win it by doling out its proceeds a trifle more liberally, but above all perhaps established for long enough to achieve it by simple force of habit. The chaotic protest it aroused when its whips and scorpions were new died down as it became a thing of use and wont, and could seem the only imaginable mode of life. Socialism as an alternative had been a compound of many remnants of social life and experience now fading into the past. It was painfully slow to develop a new, autonomous consciousness; in this it has been more tardy than the march of capitalist technology, always lagging at least a stage behind.

Marx and Engels were fixing their hopes on the working class before the defeat of the revolutions of 1848 on the continent, and of Chartism in England. When they worked out their doctrine, in the following years, it was to counteract a mood of failure, by furnishing a guarantee of ultimate success for socialism, as well as to exorcise 'utopian' notions about socialism arriving by amiable agreement. Their 'scientific' teaching fused economics and politics. Its essence was the conviction that socialism must come, not from men acquiring any ideal preference for it, or resenting capitalist injustice, but because capitalism would be brought by the laws of its own nature to the point of collapse, and thus enable, or compel, the working class to put socialism in its place. It followed, or seemed to follow, that socialist teaching ought to be addressed to the working class alone. Others might sentimentalize, but only a class driven by economic compulsion could be the reliable vehicle of change. Part of this calculation was that the working class was destined to become a bigger and bigger part of the total, as the strata above it were proletarianized each in their turn, and that it would be burdened with increasingly unbearable conditions. As things have turned out, the manual working class has come to be a diminishing part of the population, in America less than half, and conditions have not forced it willy-nilly towards socialism. Its worst miseries, those brought by wars, have been shared with other classes, and capitalism's responsibility for them has been successfully disguised by its apologists.

Marxism always disclaimed any necessitarian belief in revolution coming of its own accord, but it was led by its 'scientific' logic into some undervaluing, not of the factor of human will, but of the ideas and ideals, the emotional wants left by religion and many other things of the past, which are needed to create the will to socialism. All these it was too much inclined to ignore as utopian fancies. In the process, intellect and emotion were too strictly set apart. Countless men and women have been able to identify themselves with the Marxist cause (though not always for very long) by an unconscious blending of their own emotions with its rigorous argumentation – as Marx himself must have done; the mass of mankind, and of the working class, may have required something more romantic, such as religion or patriotism offered. Tom and Dick are as much Don Quixote as Sancho Panza, and readier to follow rainbows and will-o'-the-wisps, crusades or football pools, than sober sense.

Earlier on Marx had made a forecast which turned out to be correct, but which later Marxism has never taken adequate account of: that in all coming social revolutions the petty bourgeoisie would play its part.[22] Unlike Calvin, who confined salvation to the chosen, Marx looked to socialism to enfranchise all mankind, by abolishing all classes. But in counting on the working class to perform the task virtually single-handed, he was making another dichotomy, akin to that between thought and feeling. There may have been a mis-calculation here on a par with Mazzini's belief that Italy could free itself unaided. Marxism has had a keener eye for the weaknesses than for the better qualities of the middle classes. In the shadow of 1848 and the years that followed, when everyone from mill owners to professors displayed a timid incapacity to complete their own bourgeois revolution, it must have seemed hard to suppose that any of them would ever be useful allies in the struggle for a socialist revolution. In any case most of them were supposed to be doomed to disintegration and absorption into the proletariat.

Marx and Bismarck both dismissed the middle-class 'ideologues' from history, with something like the same contempt, as mere blowers of soap bubbles. Certainly among such an assemblage as Owen's respectable well-wishers, cranks and religious oddities abounded,[23] and it has often been the case at other times when middle- and lower-class progressives have been in conjunction. Yet the utopian sects proved at least that there was an instinctive hunger for socialism among some of the middle, or literate, strata, as well as among the workers; that they too harboured aspirations which socialism alone could realize. They were dreaming, that is, of betterments in the human condition that their own historical trajectory could never bring about; all their idealists, from Hamlet on, suffered an acute sense of social disharmony, of the times being out of joint with no remedy in sight. And the paradox remains that Marx was devoting his best energies to a book which only very well-educated readers would ever understand, while he was impatient of efforts by self-taught workmen to devise a philosophy for themselves. Late in life Engels lamented a proneness of the workers to 'ineradicable suspicion against any schoolmaster, journalist, and any man generally who was not a manual worker as being an "erudite" who was out to exploit them.'[24] He considered that it was being left behind by then, but to this day it has never been fully overcome; and Marxism with its depreciation of everything 'bourgeois' must be said to have helped to foster the prejudice. In this alienation of classes lay another disunity that has helped capitalism – 'With all its crimes broad blown, as flush as May' – to divide and rule, to prolong its reign and multiply its ill-gotten gains.

Marxism shared with the later phase of Chartism the fate of appearing on the scene when in Britain a tide of mass militancy was about to ebb. Having been pioneer first of machine industry, then of the first struggles to get rid of it or to take it into custody, this country was to lead the way in reconciling itself to capitalism. Disputes over wages and hours could be energetic without threatening to upset the system. Similarly in the Middle Ages dogged defence of rights by a peasantry rooted in the soil was of a different character from the more desperate revolts of the disinherited. As time went on, indeed, trade union pressure could stimulate the economy into expansion, instead of paralysing it, by compelling it to widen its home market.

A brief fresh glow of socialist enthusiasm was marked by the founding in 1881 of Hyndman's Social Democratic Federation, which Morris joined in 1883 and left two years later to start his Socialist League. It was the time when cyclists made weekend forays into the countryside with leaflets to stick on cows' horns, for the edification presumably of farm labourers. Belfort Bax rejoiced in the thought that socialist ideas were finding their way even into the trade unions. 'The solid front of true British stupidity, of which, unfortunately, hitherto, they have been the embodiment, has at length, to say the least, been broken.'[25] But the antidote was to hand in the Fabian Society, formed in 1884, which speedily guided the movement back into safe conventional channels. One of its hallmarks was a thick-skinned indifference to foreign and imperial affairs; the same attitude has always been typical of British labour.

When Kautsky lived in England in the early 1890s he gained the worst possible impression of the working class, as more apathetic and inert even than in Russia; incapable of rousing itself to anything higher than football or horse racing, because it had renounced the goal of a transformation of society in favour of mere bread-and-butter 'practical politics', and by so doing had given up its soul.[26] Renewed combativeness in the years before 1914 was soon to show that British workers were anything but inert or submissive, but no economic struggles can rise, except in the moment of conflict itself, above a certain height. They could be no substitute for the sense of historical mission that Marxism had sought to kindle. Instead the working class was turning in on itself, forming an estate with a culture and social life of its own, coexisting with the capitalist realm. In short, it was relapsing into 'labourism'.

'Utopian' habits of mind of one sort lived on in the political attitudes of what it would be a misnomer to call a 'movement', in the Labour party's easy confidence in its ability to extract socialist tunes from the capitalist hurdy-gurdy, or turn the grizzly into a tame performing bear by a wave of the electoral wand. John Strachey remarked on the propensity of British and American socialism to forget all lessons of history, all hard-won ideas, and be obliged to start from scratch over and over again.[27] (He was soon to forget some of them himself.) This is only a special case of the inability of men in the mass to remember and profit by experience: we retain only the most generalized impressions, and have very little hold on the facts or events that gave birth to them. While capitalism has had a continuous development, and piled up an armoury of argument and expedient as well as a mountain of profit, socialism has come and gone, wearing all kinds of guises. This may have conferred on it each time renewed hopeful freshness, but has also rendered it liable to youthful illusions. Marxism has maintained continuity at some cost in over-fidelity to obsolescent ideas.

Rulers and ruling classes did not sponsor socialism, as optimists had expected them to do, but in face of the danger of socialism making its way without them they were edging towards the 'State socialism' patronized by Napoleon III and adopted by Bismarck, the 'collectivism' fashionable in late-nineteenth-century England. 'We are all socialists now', said Vernon Harcourt with humorous resignation. This was the starting-point of our Welfare State, the most effective substitute for socialism yet invented, often reminiscent of the philosopher's maxim in ancient China: 'Fill the people's bellies and empty their minds.'[28] It was a secularized rendering of the old religious acceptance of a duty of the rich to take some care of the poor, combined with the feudal paternalism not yet extinct in Europe's aristocracies. When Winston Churchill as a bright young Liberal politician toured Uganda on a bicycle, the duke's grandson indulged in a benign flight of fancy about this secluded bit of Africa as the right place for a trial of socialism, with all selfish money-grubbing businessmen kept out. 'The first, and perhaps the greatest, difficulty which confronts the European Socialist', he observed (and history must be said to bear out his words), 'is the choosing of Governors to whom the positively awful powers indispensable to a communistic society are to be entrusted.' In Uganda there could be no such obstacle, for it already possessed in its British officials a perfect set of governors – perfect because as aloof from their subjects as H.G. Wells's invaders from Mars.[29]

Europe, it may be remarked, was frequently disposed to look at itself like this in the mirror of a wider world. When the western hemisphere was discovered, reports of its tribal customs reinforced the conception of communal ownership as being part of the law of nature. When Marxism was mobilizing its arguments it soon delved into primitive society, as well as into history, for evidences of a prehistoric Communism of which modern socialism was to be the dialectical completion. Anti-socialist anthropology took up the challenge. Earlier on there had been a preoccupation with untutored man's notions about God, now there was more concern with his view of property. Conservatives in every country have liked to think of socialism as an alien importation (as all patriots have liked to think of sundry diseases) and they were anxious to confirm from the behaviour of man in the state of nature that socialism was unnatural. To the same observers nothing has appeared more 'natural' than the stock exchange, or the House of Lords. In mid-century China they could not fail to notice and dislike symptoms of a rough and ready Communism in the programme of the great Taiping rebellion;[30] and in our epoch Western determination to suppress any growth of Communism in the backlands by armed force marks a continuation of the academic debate about primitive society with new weapons.

Catholic Europe in the last century was less fully exposed to industrialism, and its reaction to it amounted to nothing more constructive than 'Christian Socialism', a species of feudal demagogy laughed at in the *Communist Manifesto*. (Today we are told of an 'Islamic' and even a 'Buddhist Socialism' of even cloudier complexion.) It resurrected the social teaching of the Counter-Reformation, but in a still more abstract, unmeaning fashion. Which way it was likely to turn under stress was made clear by the spread of 'clerical fascism' in the late 1920s and 1930s; and 'welfare' societies, of the more undemocratic or 'Martian' type at least, have been all too ready to lurch in the same direction. William Morris foretold something very like fascism in his picture of the

'Friends of Order' banding together to crush social revolt,[31] much as Jack London foretold it a few years later with his *Iron Heel*.[32] If socialism is the legitimate heir of the bourgeois revolution on its ideal side, the inheritor in our times of its sordid impulses, its violences, has been fascism. But this too has been a perverted species of socialism, as its title in Germany implied. It was a socialism for the middle classes, morbidly divided from and set against the working classes, but wanting, like them (though by very different means) to break out from the crisis of an anarchic egotism and find shelter within some organic society. There the workers themselves, after submitting to the loss of their selfish trade unions and parties, and being forcibly merged in the *Volksgemeinschaft*, would have their modest share of the rewards.

In the long run the masses were intended to get their share out of the loot of foreign lands. Nazi imperialism had a barbarian analogue in the tribe, when it took to preying on its neighbours. War has always owed much of its charm to its power of bringing men closer together: in an army at war both food and danger have to be shared, and all its members dress alike and strive for the same ends. It was in modern Germany that the doctrines both of socialist inter-nationalism and of the armed people, the nation in arms, grew most readily. They were rivals, but also mutual reinforcements. Fascism has been the climax of all the diseased striving of modern Europe towards an artificial restoration of social union.

In the sharp air of 1938, when his Marxism was at its keenest, John Strachey found fault with Fabians for putting the socialist case on grounds 'humani-tarian, moral and aesthetic, rather than scientific or economic'; and for address-ing it to all classes, instead of specifically to the working class.[33] Such an attitude has been recurrent at times when great events have been in the making. Talk about ethics and human duties has then seemed, as it did to Kirk zealots in Scotland, no better than 'a blether of cold morality'. In other, less urgent hours dogma has been felt to matter less, moral considerations more. But arguments like those Strachey deprecated have not always gone with a watered-down socialism. If Fabians used them, so did William Morris. And in a press interview in 1893 Engels jubilantly asserted that in Germany 'our ideas make headway everywhere, as much among teachers, lawyers, etc. as among the workers. Tomorrow, if we had to take over power, we should need engineers, chemists, agronomists. Well, I am convinced that we should already have a great many with us.'[34] In practical politics Engels was anything but a doctrinaire.

To call up new horizons something wider is needed than the self-concern of either a class or a nation. On the whole, socialism in Europe has been allowed to appear too closely linked to a single class and its bread and butter, or beer and tobacco; and paradoxically, a class not always showing much interest in it and scarcely entitled – or eager – to speak for all. Bax looked on the socialist workman as, by virtue of his socialist enlightenment, rising above his narrower class self to shoulder human aspirations at large,[35] but this workman has remained an exception, and 'labourism' has not been confined to Britain. On the other side, in the student or youth movements of recent years something of the inveterate confused excitement of middle-class efforts for progress has shown itself once again, fed by a curious medley of grievances over trifles and fundamental discontents. With all this, partnerships across class boundaries have continued to be fumbling and ineffective.

A way forward must take account of Europe's perennial groping towards a balance between individual and collective, a harmonious development of both. At various times our unstable continent has gone to both extremes in sacrificing one to the other, but in its healthier moods it has recoiled. It censures an aberration to which it is more liable itself than Asia, when it condemns 'Asiatic uniformity', the spirit of the ant heap. Its intellectuals have felt as strongly as its plutocrats a horror of being swallowed up in an anonymous mass. With well-educated Germany in mind, Kautsky could be hopeful of this reproach to socialism fading, in face of 'the rapid and unbroken rise of the proletariat in moral and intellectual relations.' Half a century before, he admitted, even socialist intellectuals might fear, as all the bourgeoisie did after the Paris Commune, that the coming to power of the proletariat would be a barbarian invasion, bringing a new Dark Age.[36] Some similar advance must be hoped for again, but a broader and deeper one.

So far as the ant heap – instead of chaos – is concerned, we may trust that individuality is by now sufficiently adult to dispense with the artificial brace of the ownership of fields or factories. Most men have always had to do without it; and for the majority to let their economic life be run by a few is as much an abnegation of responsibility as to let political life be run by monarchs or dictators, or moral life by bishops. We may also recall that just as the 'liberal' outlook has always contained a dash of social thinking, in the working-class outlook there has always been a dose of individualism, a hatred of factory regimentation and the reduction of craft skill to mechanical repetition. This disgust is being revived in our day by the spread of automation. An assembly belt is closer even than a barrack drill ground to the 'Asian ant heap'. Generations of embittered artisans looked to cooperation or socialism to deliver them from enslavement to the machine; and today socialism ought to be better able than capitalism to guide industrial life away from this nightmare.

Forms of workers' control will be needed as well as technological changes. Ownership of all means of production by the State, as proposed by Marxism, is no doubt essential, but it has had a forbidding look to workers as well as others: syndicalism, guild socialism, have expressed the desire to belong to a small tangible community, instead of to the 'broad masses' that Marxism has been too fond of talking about. Stalin was making a far too mechanical distinction, as he and many others often did, in his polemic against anarchism, which invites comparison with Calvin's against Anabaptism. 'The cornerstone of Anarchism', he wrote, 'is the *individual*, whose emancipation, according to its tenets, is the principal condition for the emancipation of the masses . . . The cornerstone of Marxism, however, is the *masses*, whose emancipation, according to its tenets, is the principal condition for the emancipation of the individual.'[37]

Morris was again seeing clearly into the future when he foresaw a capitalist world where all human values will be debased and 'the earth's surface will be hideous everywhere, save in the uninhabitable desert.'[38] With this other nightmare, on its physical side if no more, we have lately been coming face to face. There has been looming up too the prospect of exhaustion of raw materials, and, between this danger and that of global pollution, the prospect that capitalism is leading us into a blind alley, or across a broken bridge; that it *must* be working out its own nemesis, as Marx prophesied, though not for Marx's reasons. All this affects all classes (much of it affects all industrial civilizations, capitalist or other), and ought to convince anyone not shackled to vested interests of the necessity of thoroughgoing change. It may be that the evolution of the human race has not equipped it to disentangle itself from such a situation, and that even *in extremis* only an ineffective minority will try, amid the labyrinth of official deception and mystification, bribery and corruption, force and intimidation. If there is to be any hope, it must depend on a reawakening of ideas and ideals, the common inheritance to a great extent of the middle and working classes which Marx, himself steeped in them, took for granted or left in the shade of his 'scientific' schema. Engels wasted time when he tried to apply the laws of social dialectics to the inanimate world; and to scan human affairs by the measuring rod of physical science is equally futile. Marxism is counting on the working class, but this, too much turned in on itself, is evidently in need of fresh inspiration; though it remains true that no progressive impulses outside it will get very far if they are not in league with a strong and intelligent mass movement.

Middle-class man in the West has lost most of his religious ideology; ironically, Christianity and socialism have been drooping together, and the new-old faith of humanism has a message for both. Christianity has been catching fire again, here and there in the world, from contact with socialism, or with the problems that socialism brings forward; but socialism is in need of intercourse with the Christian ethic that ushered it into the world. 'Materialism' in the sense of mindless egotism is as much an enemy of socialism as materialism in a philosophic sense of religion. Many older socialists or Communists now living (how many, it would be worthwhile to enquire) came from religious backgrounds. Christian or Jewish; not a few of them have found themselves wondering whether a new generation, of whatever class, growing up cut off from it, will be likely to feel as they have done.

Rosa Luxemburg declared long ago that socialism could not be reached without a great moral renewal, which she feared Bolshevik rigidity might hinder.[39] Communist China with its small working class has been obliged to rely more heavily on human will and idealism. Its Cultural Revolution has been at bottom a design for a vast moral rebirth; it has sought to persuade hundreds of millions that they can live better and more happily by agreeing to live as one great family – to make real what religions have only dreamed of. Cabral in his little corner of Africa, with scarcely any working class to take part in the rising against the Portuguese, confronted a still more acute dilemma. There was only a petty bourgeoisie with 'the historical opportunity of leading the struggle', but this class could 'strengthen its revolutionary consciousness' only by aligning itself with a working class. His final conclusion was that 'if national liberation is essentially a political problem, the conditions for its development give it certain characteristics which belong to the sphere of morals.'[40] These cautious words can be repeated more boldly about every progressive cause everywhere.

When 'revolutionary' socialism is talked of, either of two meanings may be intended: the aim of a sudden catastrophic overthrow of the old order, or a reconstruction of society that may be slow and piecemeal but will in the end be all-embracing. As to the first, European socialism for the most part settled down early to acceptance of patient legal methods, in contrast with middle-class Liberalism which, often in alliance with national revolt, had a long and adventurous history of plots and uprisings; they find an echo today in the student movement, with its taste for direct action. In other regions socialism has displayed a similar fighting spirit, often again in partnership with national rebellions, because there it has been allowed no choice. To Marxists it has often appeared that radical change could only be brought about suddenly; slow sapping and mining may be unable to rouse the required fervour. Soviet experience may suggest, on the other hand, that forcible seizure of power, against not merely the will of the few, but a large dead weight of inertia or conservatism as well, must perpetuate evil features of the old order, beginning with a secret police. Idealistic socialism curdled into Stalinism, as naive Anabaptism was superseded by authoritarian Lutheranism and Calvinism.

It is another good reason for spreading socialism as widely as may be among the middle classes before it comes to power, that once in power it seems to find it harder to convince them. Altogether, the task of fitting men's minds and dispositions to a genuine new life has turned out to be a much harder one than socialism expected. China's self-imposed and heroic, if at times freakish ordeal, the Cultural Revolution, was recognition that genuine socialism can only be built from below, by a people roused to wish and work for a new society. At the opposite pole is what E.P. Thompson, speaking of Robert Owen's paternalism, has called in one of his many happy phrases 'planning society as a gigantic industrial panopticon'.[41] That Owen and Stalin thought so much alike suggests that the antithesis of 'utopian' and 'scientific' socialism – in many ways an unsatisfactory one – has less meaning than that of 'artificial' and 'organic'.

H.G. Wells in 1905 sounded extraordinarily like a forerunner of Mao when he insisted that socialism was no mere 'odd little jobbing about municipal gas and water', but meant 'revolution', 'a change in the everyday texture of life. It may be a very gradual change, but it will be a very complete one.'[42] There was a blind thirst in Europe for some sweeping change, some apocalypse; the middle classes, straggling along their road towards war and fascism, were fascinated by Nietzsche's gospel of a 'transvaluation of all values', his fantasy of a transfigured mankind with its economic system untouched. Fabians and kindred 'reformists', oblivious of all transcendental goals, suffocated socialism under the plodding humdrum business, the 'little jobbing', of today and tomorrow. A Dutch social democrat has eloquently dwelt on the loss of dedication and fire that overtook socialism when it exchanged the image of a new heaven and a new earth for the mess of pottage of small repairs to an old, worn-out dwelling. 'Socialism's worst enemy is its own cultural blindness and deafness.'[43] He reproached Marxist 'scientific' formulas with helping to cripple it by darkening its vision of utopia, the very thing to which it owed and still owes its own 'tremendous and revolutionary influence'.[44] More recently E.P. Thompson has written of how the New Left endeavoured 'to rehabilitate the utopian energies within the socialist tradition'.[45]

In 1898 Bernstein told the German Socialist Party that he no longer credited any sudden coming collapse of capitalism, but that he still held to the aim of the conquest of political power.[46] His doubts were repudiated, and he and his associates failed to discover an alternative route. In effect Western Communism since 1945 has been setting itself the same purpose as Bernstein's, of keeping alive the goal of a fundamental renovation of society and all human relationships, while discarding the prospect of a cataclysmic transition. How far it has been or will be able to keep clear of the creeping parochial numbness that goes with philosophies of gradualism is still to be decided. It may fortify confidence to recall that socialism in its human essence was a fact long before it was an idea; it is already very old, private ownership by comparison newfangled, capitalism a usurper of yesterday.

## Postscript (1987)

Private ownership of land, mankind's principal sustainer, has never been universal, and in many regions is comparatively novel, an Italian writer has reminded us.[47] In western Europe itself much land was still communal property down into the last century. It was disappearing into rapacious maws just when humanity was being confronted with the question of who should own the Aladdin's lamp of modern technology. Some countries that seemed capable of it failed to move on to capitalism; others, like Britain, have long had the ability and the need to move onward to socialism, yet stand spellbound, halted by failure of will or imagination even more than by tangible obstacles. Affluent societies have abundant fleshpots to stimulate private egotism, with the blessing of our new use of propaganda, and we scramble for better places in our old tumbledown world instead of trying to make a better one.

Our troubled century has seen many attempts at building socialism, two especially, with very considerable but far from complete success, in Russia and China. In both countries the builders had to fight their way to power, through civil war worsened by foreign intervention. Born amid the convulsions of the Great War, communism united harsher qualities with its virtues. Its hatred of social oppression was more apparent than its love of the victims; it inspired an impressive roll of martyrs, but it might have taken more to heart the words 'Though I give my body to be burned, and have not charity . . . .' All the same, emotions and ideals deriving from Christianity, and belonging to the more utopian side of socialism, never disappeared, hard as they might be to reconcile with Marxism's 'scientific' teachings, or its 'laws of history'. 'The Golgotha path of the German working class is not yet at an end', Karl Liebknecht said in his last message to his comrades, just before his murder.[48]

A critic of Leninism has dwelt on what was akin to religion, even to the mystical, in the Russian revolutionary spirit. No faith but Christianity has had such ability to transform itself into a secular movement of regeneration, without shedding its ardour. Lenin launched the Third International confident that the workers everywhere would be ready to make all the sacrifices demanded by the cause. Stalin, not a man much given to poetic metaphor, liked to picture the working class turning its back on the golden calf and plodding doggedly through the desert towards the promised land. Since then Christianity itself has given astonishing proofs of readiness to return to the wilderness. 'It is the few who take the Gospel literally that leave their mark upon the world', Hobhouse wrote of Christian Socialism, early in this century;[49] today the few are becoming many, and they have learned far more from 'real' socialism, which, in turn, now has lessons to learn from them.

Stalin applied himself to constructing, and after 1945 reconstructing, the material base of socialism in the USSR. The Mao of the Cultural Revolution concentrated on strengthening its moral foundations, by methods which likewise included much forcible dragooning. Stalinism found one typical expression in Katayev's novel about a team of workers and technicians straining every nerve to improve the performance of their concrete-mixer, and finally, the grand climax of the story, achieving a record-breaking twenty-four hour output.[50] Maoism set itself a harder target, complete social equality and fraternity. The sequel has shown that it failed to implant its ideals in the mass mind, though we may hope that it left many scattered seeds.

Mao has been well described as the last of the great utopian socialists. Somehow the two visions of socialism have to be brought closer together, the utopian or romantic and the scientific or realistic. Europe, and England not least, has been a home to both science and romanticism, which is at bottom refusal to accept the world of today as the only possible one, – desire to open gates, to climb walls, and discover what is beyond. Utopian dreams and romantic love or poetry are not very far apart.

There has been a third way to socialism, or apology for it, the nationalizing of ailing industries, as in Britain where they are now being fattened for the market and sold back to capitalists and their humble emulators. Retrograde as this is, a fresh start was overdue. These industries were run bureaucratically, by Labour and Tory governments alike; their workers showed no ambition to undertake any part of the arduous task or running them, little eagerness to make them prosper. Socialist consciousness cannot be counted on to grow out of simple trade-union activity, the Belgian socialist Hendrik de Man was saying half a century ago:[51] many Marxists have shared his misgivings, even if few have followed him on the downward path to fascism.

Increasing social mobility has brought classes into a state of flux, likely to continue until some urgent crisis clarifies and sharpens their outlines once more. New blood has been entering the always heterogeneous 'middle classes' from below (also from outside, by immigration), and some part of it can be expected to prove valuable and enriching. Now that the middle classes are growing so much more extensive and various, it is a pressing duty of socialists to take stock of them more attentively. They include the sections of society that are the repository of most of its general, as well as technical, knowledge. They include also the guardians of its accumulating treasures of art and thought: very particularly, of history, the painfully learned wisdom of that silent majority, the dead – always too quickly forgotten by the many, and in our mobile, mutable, fragmented existence more quickly than ever.

Our manifold 'good causes' are tended chiefly by dwellers in these inter-mediate social latitudes; movements concerned with the world's health, conservation, and so on, which may not look in any direct way towards social-ism, but all in their own ways help to expand awareness of the problems of our planet and our race. Their cumulative, converging effect must be to bring reali-zation of practical, as well as ideal, arguments for fundamental charge. Untu-tored, unrestricted greed may spell affluence for a minority of the world's population, but it is rapidly depleting the earth's resources, even those crucial to bare survival. Poverty is a menace as well as wealth: hungry peasants in Kash-mir or Madagascar are destroying forests, as well as profiteers in Brazil or acid rain in Scandinavia.

Concentration of capital and advanced technology are increasingly subord-inating politics to economics, civilization to the stock market, the individual to the system. A few financial overlords may appear to rule our destinies, as free as gods, but it is at the cost of losing their own human personality, of becoming mere creatures of greed and ambition; they and the common man alike are drawn closer and closer, willy-nilly, into the slimy coils. It has never been so true as today that only removal of control of the machines from owners nearly as robot-like as themselves can emancipate humanity, collectively and individually. In this light we can profitably recall the words of the *Communist Manifesto* about old relations of production becoming a fetter that has to be burst; only now it is not so much the forces of production that cry out for liberation, but the talents and energies of human beings, the teeming vitality of the human race.

# Notes

1. M. Beer, *A History of British Socialism*, London 1929, vol. I, p. 3.
2. G. de Poncins, *Kabloona*, London 1942, p. 101.
3. See A. Winnington, *The Slaves of the Cool Mountains*, London 1959. Cf. the passage of Virgil in *Georgics*, I, 121 ff. – in strong contrast with Eclogue IV – where Jove terminates the golden age in order to force men to toil, suffer, invent and develop.
4. William Penn, *Pennsylvania . . . A General Description* 1683, XIX.
5. Thomas Chalmers in H. Hunter, *Problems of Poverty*, London 1912, pp. 342 ff.
6. See the *Sacrum Commercium*, written by a disciple of Francis, para. 1, 2. When the saint went to the 'optimates et sapientes' he was roughly repulsed, and his ideas declared 'nova . . . doctrina' (para. 3).
7. Beer, vol. I, p. 14.
8. See Rev. M. Kaufmann, *Socialism and Communism* 1883, chs II, III, a work reflecting the revived interest of its period in socialism.
9. See A. Morton, *The English Utopia*, London 1952, especially chs 1, 2.
10. Quoted in H.G. Wells, *New Worlds for Old*, London 1908, p. 192.
11. See Pedro de Valencia, *Escritos Sociales*, ed. C. Vinas y Mey, Madrid 1945.
12. A. Pope, *Essay on Man*, epistle III, p. 318.
13. W. Wordsworth, *The Prelude*, Book IX.
14. J.W. Cross, *George Eliot's Life*, 1885, vol. III, p. 141.
15. E.B. Bax, *The Ethics of Socialism*, 2nd edn, n.d., p. 19.
16. R.A. Gettman, ed., *George Gissing and H.G. Wells Correspondence*, London 1961, p. 49 n.
17. A.W. Kinglake, *Eothen*, 1844, ch. 8. Lady Hester seemed to have some notion of becoming 'mystic mother' to the Saint-Simonian sect, but on this she bound him to 'eternal silence'.
18. See V. Purcell, *The Boxer Uprising*, London 1963, pp. 102 ff.
19. R.H. Tawney, Introduction to M. Beer, *A History of British Socialism*, p. xviii.
20. E.P. Thompson, *The Making of the English Working Class*, London 1965, pp. 799 ff.
21. William Morris, *Signs of Change*, 1888, pp. 102–3.
22. K. Marx, letter to P.V. Annenkov, 28 December 1846.
23. Thompson, pp. 797–8.
24. F. Engels, 'On the History of early Christianity', in *K. Marx and F. Engels on Religion*, London 1957, p. 319.
25. Bax, p. iv.
26. Karl Kautsky, *The Social Revolution*, English edn, 1916, pp. 100–2.
27. J. Strachey, *What Are We To Do?*, London 1938, p. 114.
28. Quoted in W.A.P. Martin, *Hanlin Papers*, 1st series, 1881, p. 99.
29. W.S. Churchill, *My African Journey*, 1908; reprinted London 1972, pp. 71–2.
30. W.S. Gregory, *Great Britain and the Taipings*, London 1969, p. 158, discounts the argument that it was the socialism of the Taipings that turned the West against them. But some Western strictures which he cites suggest that the argument has some force.
31. See William Morris, *News from Nowhere*, 1890.
32. See Jack London, *The Iron Heel*, 1907.
33. J. Strachey, p. 83, 90.
34. F. Engels, *Correspondence* (with Paul and Laura Lafargue) vol. III, n.d., p. 394.

35. Bax, pp. 102–3.

36. Kautsky, pp. 44–5.

37. J. Stalin, *Anarchism or Socialism?*, English edn, London 1950, pp. 9–10.

38. Morris, *Signs of Change*, pp. 138–9; ch. p. 29.

39. Rosa Luxemburg, *The Russian Revolution*, 1918; English edn, London 1961, p. 71.

40. A. Cabral, *Selected Texts by Amilcar Cabral: Revolution in Guinea*, London, 1969, pp. 88–90.

41. Thompson, p. 781.

42. H.G. Wells, 'This Misery of Boots', 1905; turned into a Fabian tract, 1907, section V.

43. F.L. Polak, *The Image of the Future*, London 1961, vol. II, pp. 309, 322. Cf. p. 326: 'the childlike and eternal longing for human fulfilment in another and better future is basic to man's mental structure'.

44. Ibid., p. 308.

45. E.P. Thompson, 'An Open Letter to Leszek Kolakowski', in R. Miliband and J. Saville, eds, *The Socialist Register 1973*, London 1973, p. 1.

46. E. Bernstein, *Evolutionary Socialism: A Criticism and Affirmation*, 1899; English edn, London 1961, pp. xxiv.

47. Paolo Grossi, '*Un Altro Modo di Possedere*', Milan 1977.

48. Karl Liebknecht, *Militarism and Anti-Militarism*, trans. and ed. G. Lock, Cambridge 1973, p. xvi.

49. L.T. Hobhouse, *Morals in Evolution*, 1906; 1915 edn, London, p. 522.

50. V. Katayev, *Forward, Oh Time*, 1932; trans. C. Malamuth, London 1933.

51. P. Dodge, ed., *A Documentary Study of Hendrik de Man, Socialist Critic of Marxism*, Princeton, NJ 1979, pp. 142, ff.

# Index

Abyssinia, invasion of 188
Act of Union (1707) 56, 59
action, and poetry 100, 119, 126 n68,
    127 n110
age, and social dissent 50
agitator, figure of the 163
Agnew, Sheriff 48
Anabaptism 209, 210
Anglicanism 66–7, 69–70, 74
Anglo-American alliance 198–9
Anglo-Japanese Society 188
Annandale, Earl of 47
anti-war activity, at Cambridge 182–3
Aquinas, St Thomas 208
Argyle 22
aristocracy 46–9, 146, 160, 206–7
Aristotle 204
armies, private 28
Arminianism 58–9
army, Covenanter regiments in 56, 57–8
Arnold, Matthew 135
arts, role of 96, 187–8
atheism 66
Attwood, Thomas 155
Auden, W.H. 187
Austen, Jane, *Persuasion* 71
automation 221
Aytoun, W.E. 60

Babeuf, François-Noël 213
Bagehot, *Literary Studies* 137
Baldwin, Stanley 181

Ball, John 4, 208
Bamford, Samuel 175
Baring, Rose 145
Barrie, J.M., *The Admirable Crichton* 173
Barros, J. 193
Barwick, Dr John 22
Bax, Belfort 217–18, 220
    *The Ethics of Socialism* 172
Baxter, Richard 70
Beesly, Edward 166
Beethoven, Ludwig von 135
Bell, John 49
Benjamin, Walter 2
Benson, A.C. 179
Bentham, Jeremy 75
Bernal, J.D. 179
    *The Social Function of Science* 180
Bernstein, Edward 224
Beveridge, W.H. 175
Bismarck, Otto von 217, 218
Black Act (1670) 47
Blake, William 123 n4, 135, 175
Bloody Sunday (1887) 33, 171
Blunt, Anthony 196
Boer War 34
Borrow, George 140
    *The Romany Rye* 160
bourgeoisie, Victorian 165
    *see also* middle classes
Bowen, Roger 193
Bower Captain R.L. 143
Boycott, Captain 53

boycott, invention of 33, 53
Bradley, Ben 189
Brahms, Johannes 135
Bray, J.F. 157
Bridges, Robert 137
Bright, John 131, 152, 165, 167
Britain
    foreign policy 196, 197
    self-image of 30–32
British and Foreign Bible Society 71–2, 73
British Union Movement 191
Broadhead, William 32
Brougham, Henry 31, 155, 167
Browning, Elizabeth Barrett 137
Browning, Robert 147, 155
Bruce, Robert 42
Buddhism 204
Bulwer-Lytton, Edward 129
    Rienzi 147
Bunyan, John 75
Burgess, Guy 196
Burke, Edmund 67, 70, 72
    Reflections on the Revolution in France 68–9
Burleigh, William 92
Burnet, Bishop 53
Burns, Robert 61, 212
Burton, Robert, Anatomy of Melancholy 79
Butler, Samuel 74
Byron, Lord George Gordon 31, 77 n51,
    110, 124 n36, 126 n79, 137, 153, 180
    Childe Harold 136
    Don Juan 136

Cabral, Amilcar 223
Cade, Jack 19
Calvin, John 74, 209, 216, 221
Calvinism 41–3, 51–3, 59, 70
Cambridge Inter-Collegiate Christian
    Union 179
Cambridge Left 187
'Cambridge traitors' 193–4, 195–7, 201
Cambridge University 178–97
Cameron, Richard 50, 55
Camoens, Luis de 137
Canadian Forum 193
capitalism
    resistance to 25, 31, 130
    and socialism 213–22
    and treason 201–2
'Captain Swing' 26, 29
Cargill, Donald 50, 55

Carlyle, Thomas 121, 130, 140, 173
    Oliver Cromwell's Letters and Speeches 31
    The History of the French Revolution 30
    Latter-day Pamphlets 160
    paternalism of 155, 163
Carpenter, Edward 171
Carritt, Michael 197
Carson, Sir Edward 197
Carter, Sir G.C. 143
Cassilis, Earl of 47, 48
Catechism (1647) 43
Catholic Northern Rebellion (1569) 21
Caudwell, Christopher, Illusion and Reality
    186
cells, Communist 184, 196
Cervantes, Miguel de 135
'Chain of Being' 84
Chalmers, Dr 207
Chamberlain, Neville 181
Chapman, George 80
    Caesar and Pompey 82, 93
    The Conspiracy of Byron 93
charity 73
Charles I, King of England 42
Charles II, King of England 55
Charles X, King of France 131
Chartism 5–6, 26–7
    and Christian Socialism 161–2
    and intellectuals 156–9, 165, 169
    outside of England 29, 30, 60
    and the State 215
Chesterton, G.K. 171
China, People's Republic of 222–3, 225
Chinese Society, Cambridge 188
chivalry, cult of 130, 140
Christian Socialism 161–2, 219, 225
Christianity 207–8, 222, 225
Churchill, Randolph 197
Churchill, Winston 34, 189, 196, 197, 219
civil disobedience 18, 36
Clapham, Sir John 180
Clapham Sect 73
Clark, G. Kitson 181, 192 n9
Clarke, Adam 72
class struggle
    and Coleridge 125 n39
    peasant, forms of 23
    and religion 67–70
    and Tennyson 131
    and Victorian novel 162–5
    and Wordsworth 108

*see also* working class
classes, and collectivism 206-7
Claverhouse, Graham of 49, 56
Cobbett, William 26, 69, 109, 159-60, 167-8
    *Political Register* 108
Cobden, Richard 131, 152, 160, 165, 166-7, 168
Cockburn, Lord 63
Coke, Lord Chief Justice 21
Cold War 191
Coleridge, S.T. 74, 213
    and Wordsworth 101, 106, 110, 119, 120, 126 n81, 135
collectivism 206-12, 219-20
Common Market 198
common people
    as historical agent 2
    ideas of 118
    middle-class attitudes to 153-4
    and Tennyson 140-41
    and Wordsworth 98-9, 104-5, 111-16, 120
    *see also* working class
commonwealth, idea of 205
Communism
    at Cambridge 183-97
    work ethic of 206
Communist Party Historians' Group 2, 3, 12, 17 n37, 191
Communist party of Great Britain
    founding of 35
    Kiernan's membership of 4, 15 n11, 192 n3, 196
Communist party of India 190
Communist party of Pakistan 190
competition, and human relations 78
Comte, Auguste 166
Conan Doyle, Arthur 143
conflict, resolution of 20
Connolly, James 33-4
Conservative party, and treason 197-202
conspiracy 25
Conspiracy of the Equals (1796) 211, 213
constancy, as virtue 89
conventicles 43, 45-6, 49
Cooke, Alastair 200
Cooper, Thomas 157, 166
Cornford, John 4, 183, 186, 187-8, 196
corporatism, medieval 206
corresponding societies 55
Counter-Reformation 73, 210

Crabbe, George 26, 28, 103
craftsmen, political role of 109, 157
Crimean War 32, 165
Cripps, Sir Stafford 182
Cromwell, Oliver 22, 44, 48, 75
cultivation, forms of 56-7
Cultural Revolution 118, 223, 225

*Daily Worker* 185
Dalhousie, Lord 142
Dalziell of the Binns 53
Darwin, Charles 72
Darwin, Erasmus 72
de Man, Hendrik 226
De Quincey, Thomas 74
deference voting 168
Defoe, Daniel 55
*Democracy and the Labour Movement* 3
Dickens, Charles 23, 130, 138
    *Barnaby Rudge* 163
    *Bleak House* 36
    *Hard Times* 163
    *The Uncommercial Traveller* 163
*A Dictionary of Marxist Thought* 11
direct action 2-3, 6, 18-37
disguise, use of, in protests 29
Disraeli, Benjamin 121, 161
    *Sybil* 25, 162
Dobb, Maurice 180, 187, 191, 195
Dollfuss, Engelbert 182
Dostoyevsky, Fyodor 99
Dryden, John 153
Dufferin, Lord 148

East Timor 202
economics 180
Eddington, Arthur Stanley 179
Edmonds, T.R. 156
education
    and Chartist leadership 156-7
    of working class 167-8
Education Act (1870) 167
Eisenstein, Sergei
    *Ivan the Terrible* 187
    *Thunder over Mexico* 187
elders, and social control 58
election by tumults 28
Eliot, George 212
    *Felix Holt* 28, 160, 164, 166
    *Middlemarch* 130
    *Romola* 147

Elizabethan drama 78–82
emigration 32, 165
Empson, William 194
enclosures 56, 200
Engels, Friedrich 124 n36, 166, 185, 220, 222
    see also Marx and Engels
England, image of 134, 147–8
epic poetry 135–6
equality, ideal of 212
Erasmus, Desiderius 80
Espartero, B.J.F. 31
ethics, and religion 67
Europe, compared with England 30–32
Evangelicalism 68, 70–75
Evangelical Magazine 71, 74
Eyre, Governor 139

Faber, G.S. 135
Fabian Socialism 170–71, 218, 220
familial relationships 85, 87–9, 107–8, 156,
    212
'Family of Love' 208
fascism 182, 219–20
Fawkes, Guy 21
Fenwick 113
Ferns, H.S., Reading from Left to Right 193
feudalism 19, 78–9, 206
Fifth Monarchy men 22
finance capital 201
FitzGerald, Edward 137
Football Association 33
Ford, John 94
Form of Presbyterial Church-Government 43
Fox, Charles James 107–8
Fox, Ralph 186
St Francis of Assisi 207–8
Franco, Francisco 183, 195, 199, 202
fraternity, ideal of 212
Frazer, Sir James 180
freedom 89, 97, 110
French Revolution 75
    English reactions to 66, 67, 154
    and socialism 211–12
    and Wordsworth 96, 97–8, 110, 119,
        123 n6, 131
friendship, in Shakespeare 91–2
Frost, John 158
Froude, R.H. 61

Gaitskell, Hugh 198
Galloway, Earl of 48

Galsworthy, John
    The Mob 34, 39 n60
    The Patrician 173
Galt, John 156
    Annals of the Parish 155
Gammage, R.C. 157, 158, 159
Gandhi, Indira 190
Gandhi, Mahatma 18, 36, 104, 122, 157,
    189
Garaudy, Roger 202
Garibaldi, Giuseppe 31
Gaskell, Elizabeth 163
    Mary Barton 24, 162, 167
    North and South 162
Gaskell, P. 155–6, 163
General Strike (1926) 35
German Socialist Party 224
Gilbert, W.S. 21
Gissing, George 154, 161
    Demos 172
Gladstone, William Ewart 144
    Nineteenth Century 168
Glorious Revolution (1688) 22
Gordon riots (1780) 23
Gorky, Maxim 99
Government of India Act 189
gradualism 224
Graham, Cunninghame 171
Gramsci, Antonio 9
Granville, Sir Richard 133
Gray, John 214
Grey, Sir George 143
Guardian 201

Hainau, Marshal 31
Haldane, J.B.S. 179
    Materialism 179
Halévy Thesis 7
Hamilton, Duchess of 49
Hamley, General 149
Harcourt, Vernon 218
Hardie, Keir 60, 170, 171
Harney, Julian 27, 215
Harper, G.M. 112
Harrison, Frederic 166
Haydon, B.R. 116
Hazlitt, William 69, 75, 76, 126 n79,
    128 n112, 153–4
Heinemann, Margot 12, 13
Hill, Christopher 2, 11, 191
Hilton, Rodney 2

*A Hind let loose* 51
history, knowledge of 1–2, 10, 104, 174
history from below 2–3, 7, 16 n18, 191
Hitler, Adolf 179, 186, 195, 202
Hobhouse, L.T. 225
Hobsbawm, Eric 2, 7, 191
    *The Age of Revolution* 11
Hobson, J.A. 172
Hodgskin, Thomas 214
Holyoake, G.J. 166
Hopkins, Gerald Manley 137
Horace 134, 148
Housman, A.E. 180, 192 n5, 194
Howarth, T.E.B. 179
Howell, George 166
Hughes Rev. J. 72
human relations
    in Shakespeare 82–95
    in Wordsworth 117
human rights 201–2
humanism 80
Hume, David 61
Hungary 31–2
hunger marches 36, 181
Hunt, Leigh 75
Huntingdon, Lady 70
Huxley, Aldous, *Point Counter Point* 191 n2
Hyndman, H.M. 169, 217

images, role of 30
imperialism
    and Cambridge Communism 188
    and Tennyson 130, 133–5, 136–7, 139,
        141–3, 148–50
Independent Labour Party 170
Indian Mutiny (1857) 32, 139, 141, 142,
    149
Indian National Congress 189
Indian Progressive Writers' Association 190
Indian students, at Cambridge 188–90, 196
individual and the collective 204–5, 211,
    221
Indonesia 202
Indulgences (1669 and 1672) 55
Industrial Revolution
    and socialism 212–17
    and Wordsworth 96, 108–9, 111, 122,
        126 n7
    and working class 154
Inglis, Fred 12
*Inprecorr* 186

intellectual life, and Calvinism 52–3
intellectuals
    and poetry 96
    relationship of, to working class 98,
        104–5, 118, 168–75
    role of 5, 9, 15
    *see also* the literate
International Brigade 183
*International Literature* 187
Ireland
    civil war in 35
    English policy on 155, 197–8
    resistance in 24, 30, 33–4
    and Tennyson 139
Isherwood, Christopher 187
Islam 207
isolation, human 80–82, 115, 211

Jacobinism 65, 66
James II, King of England 22, 48, 56
James VI, King of Scotland 41
Jeans, James Hopwood 179
Jeffrey, Francis 112, 140
John, King of England 19
John of Leyden 209
Johnson, Dr 81, 91, 167, 198
Jones, Ernest 9, 27, 34, 38 n35, 158, 159,
    162, 165, 174, 215
Jonson, Ben 80
    *Catiline* 82
    *Sejanus* 93
Jourdain, M. 18
Jowett, Benjamin 137, 139
*Jus Populi Vindicatum* 51

K'ang Yu-wei 214
Katayev, V. 225
Kautsky, Karl 174, 218, 221
Kaye, H.J. 195
Keats, John 126 n79
Kell 199
Kenmure, Viscount 48, 49
Kent, Edward, Duke of 73–4
Ket, Francis 20
Kettle, Arnold 188
Keynes, J.M. 175, 180
Kiernan, V.G. 1–15, 15 n11
    *The Duel in European History* 13
    *The Lords of Human Kind* 10
    *State and Society in Europe 1550–1650* 13
King, Mackenzie 148

Kinglake, A.W. 214
Kingsley, Charles 30, 161
    *Alton Locke* 27, 162–3
    *Hypatia* 147
kinship, in Shakespeare 81
Kirk, and Scottish nationalism 41, 42–3,
    44–6, 47, 58, 59
Klugmann, James 4, 186, 187, 190, 192 n5,
    194, 196
Knox, John 46
Kobayashi, *The Cannery Boat* 187
Korean War 197
Kossuth, Lajos 31

labour movement, Victorian 33
    *see also* Chartism; working class
Labour party 182, 185, 218
labourism 6, 9, 16 n13, 165, 168, 170, 218
Lamb, Charles 126 n79
land ownership, patterns of 46, 206
    *see also* property
Lapsley 180
Latimer, Bishop 20
Laurence, R.V. 180
law and legality, English emphasis on 21,
    32–3, 35–6
Lawrence, T.E. 130
leadership of labour movement 156–60,
    165–6, 168, 175
Leavis, F.R. 180
Left Book Club 186
Lenin, Vladimir 184, 186, 225
Leopold II, King of Belgium 143
LeRoy, G.C. 92
Levellers 52
Lewis, Sinclair, *It Can't Happen Here* 192 n2
liberty, ideal of 212
Liebknecht, Karl 225
Lilburne, Colonel Robert 44
literacy 124 n36
the literate 152–6, 172–5, 213
    *see also* intellectuals
literature and socialism 11–12
London, Jack, *Iron Heel* 220
*London Review of Books* 9
London University 193 n3
London Working Men's Association 157
Long, Leo 196
Louis XIV, King of France 55
love, in Shakespeare 86–7, 89–91
Lovett, William 157, 158, 172

Lowe, Robert 167
Loyola, Ignatius 73
Luddism 25, 32
Luther, Martin 74, 209
Luxemburg, Rosa 222
Lyon, John 53

*Mabinogion* 136, 147
MacArthur, Douglas 197
Macaulay, Thomas 26, 134, 153
McCarthy, Senator Joseph 202
MacDonald, Ramsay 181
Macerone, Colonel, *Instructions* 27
Machiavelli, Niccolo 80, 92
Maclean, Donald 197
Maclellan, John 47–8
magic 53
Magna Carta 19
Malory, Thomas 136, 142
Malraux, André, *La condition humaine* 187
Manchester 'Blanketeers' (1817) 36
Mann, Tom 169, 170
manners, calls for reformation of 71, 75
Manning, Cardinal 166
Mao Tse-tung 188, 223, 225
Marat, J-P. 27
Marlowe, Christopher 79, 86, 91, 93
    *The Jew of Malta* 80
marriage 88
Marryat, Captain, *Mr Midshipman Easy* 166
Martineau, Harriet
    *Cousin Marshall* 156
    *A Manchester Strike* 162
Marx, Karl 122, 166, 201, 222
    and Chartism 215
    *Das Kapital* 170, 187
    and poetry 96, 117
    *mentioned* 170, 171, 186
Marx, Karl, and Friedrich Engels 2, 4, 6, 10,
    13, 14, 104
    *Communist Manifesto* 219, 227
    on working class 173–4, 215–17
Marxism
    at Cambridge 180, 186–7
    development of, in England 194–5
    and poetry 117–18
    and religion 10–11, 225
    and socialism 204, 216–17, 218
Massinger, Philip 88, 90
    *The Bashful Lover* 91
    *The Old Law* 87

Matthews, Charles 97
Mayhew, Henry 29
Mazzini, Giuseppe 216
Meerut conspiracy trial (1933) 188
Melbourne, Lord 154
Menon, Krishna 190
Meredith, George 134, 137, 169
Methodism 7–8, 24, 65, 68, 70, 74, 77 n55, 155
Metternich, Prince C. 122
Meyer, Siegfried 174
middle classes
    and aristocracy 132
    relation of, to labour movement 160–65, 166–75, 214, 216–17, 221, 223–4, 226
    see also ruling class
Middleton, Thomas, Women Beware Women 79
Mill, James 155
Mill, John Stuart 155, 156, 160, 169
Milner, Dean 74
Milner, Lord 143
Milton, John 89, 135, 185
    Paradise Lost 112
    mentioned 96, 136
ministers
    intruded, treatment of 53
    Scottish, background of 49–50
A Mirror for Magistrates 19
missionary work, growth of 73
the mob, 22–3, 27–8, 34
Molière, 44, 80, 89
monks 207
Monmouth, James, Duke of 22
Montrose, James Graham, Earl of 43
Moore, Tom 30
Moorehead, Alan, The Traitors 194
Moorman, Mrs 119
moral force 36
morality
    democratization of 93
    and socialism 11, 220, 222–3
More, Thomas 4
    Utopia 209–10
Morley, J. 19, 166–7
Morris, William 4, 8, 33, 135, 147, 169–70, 215, 217, 219, 220, 222
    News from Nowhere 169
    Signs of Change 169
Morton, Leslie 4

Mosley, Oswald 36, 182, 191 n2
Mozart, W.A. 212
Mulgrave, Lord, Essay on Satire 153
municipal socialism 170
Muslim League 18
Mussolini, Benito 180, 182, 186
mysticism 208–9
myth, use of 147

Napier, General Charles 27, 139
Napoleon 26, 72, 74, 109, 112, 121, 154
Napoleon III 144, 214, 218
National Covenant (1638) 42, 45, 59–62
    and aristocracy 47, 48–9
    and peasantry 51–4, 56–7
National Government 181, 195
national revolts, British sympathy with 31–2
National Union of the Working Classes 27
nationalism 30, 36, 45, 211
    Scottish 42–7, 59, 60
nationalized industries 226
nature, concept of 119
Nazism 182, 220
Needham, Joseph 179, 185
Nehru, Jawahardal 189, 190
The New Reasoner 3
Newport rising (1839) 158
Newton, Sir Isaac 180
Nicaragua 198
Nietzsche, F.W. 130, 194, 224
Nonconformism 10–11
Norman, Herbert 4, 187, 189–90, 191, 192 notes, 193, 196, 197
North, Christopher 60
Notestein, W. 60
novelists, on working class 162–5

Oastler, Richard 161
O'Brien, Bronterre 157, 158, 159, 160, 166
O'Connell, Daniel 30
O'Connor, Feargus 157–8, 159, 215
order, as ideal, 31, 93–4
original sin, dogma of 70–71, 74
Orwell, George 120
outcast, image of 97, 120
Outram, General James 143
Owen, Robert 4, 157, 215, 217, 223
ownership, forms of, see land ownership; property
Oxford University 178, 180

Paine, Thomas 67
    *The Age of Reason* 72
Paley, William 67, 211
Pankhurst, Emmeline 35
Paris Commune 169
Parkes, Sir Harry 148
Parliament, aura of 25
past, and imaginative writing 147
*Past & Present* 7
Pater, Walter, *Marius the Epicurean* 147
Peacock, Thomas, *Crotchet Castle* 167
peasantry
    and class struggle 20, 23–4
    and Marxism 122
    Scottish 40–41, 43, 50–54, 56–9
    and Wordsworth 103–5, 106, 120
    and working class 155
Peasants' Revolt (1381) 19, 38 n35, 159, 208
Peasants' War (1524–5) 209
Peden, Alexander 46, 50, 53
Pedro de Valencia 210
Peel, John 29
Penn, William 207
Penruddock, John 22
Perceval, Spencer 73
Peterloo Massacre 26, 28–9
Philip III, King of Spain 210
physical force, use of 26–7, 33–4, 50, 54–6
Pilgrimage of Grace (1536) 20
Pitt, William 69, 73, 77 n51
Plato 205
Plimsoll, Samuel 166
poaching 23
poetic diction 103, 135
poetry 12–13
police, establishment of 29
police spying 199
politics 3, 156
    and personal relationships 83, 92–3
    and Wordsworth 97–8, 100–101
Pollitt, Harry 185
Poor Law (1834) 161
Pope, Alexander 211
Porteus, Bishop Beilby 66, 70, 72
Porteus riots (1736) 23, 59
'positive relationships', in Shakespeare
    85–93
Positivism 166
Postan 180
poverty
    and Christianity 207–8

    in Wordsworth 97, 99, 106, 113
Pratt, Sir John 197
Prawer, S.S., *Karl Marx and World Literature*
    12
Presbyterianism 47–8
privatization 200–201
progress, ideal of 31, 112
property, private and collective 205,
    206–11, 215, 221, 224–5
    *see also* land ownership; ownership
'the public', creation of 19
public opinion, role of 162, 164, 166

Quakers 72, 76 n37
Quiller-Couch, Sir Arthur 180

Rabelais, François 135
Radicalism 160
Rani of Jhansi 141
raw materials, exhaustion of 222
Reagan, Ronald 198
realism, artistic 107
Rebecca riots (1843–4) 29–30
'Red Clyde' 35
Reddaway, Peter 186
Reform Bill (1832), agitation for 25–6, 160
Reform Bill (1867) 139, 167
Reformation 42
religion
    at Cambridge 179, 185–6
    and class consciousness 40, 57, 61–2
    and collectivism 207–9, 210, 222
    and human relations 84
    Marxist interpretation of 10–11
    protest 21, 23, 24, 29–30
    revival of, and social change 65–75
    and the State 210–11
    Tennyson on 143–4
    working-class indifference to 155
Renwick, James 50
'Resistance Movement' (1971) 36
Restoration (1660) 44
revolutions
    of 1848, and England 30–32
    English 21–2
    and middle class 154–5
    and religious sectarianism 52
    *see also* French Revolution
Rhodesia 198
Riot Act (1716) 23
Robeson, Paul 187

Robespierre, Maximilien 27, 69, 98
Rogers, Frederick 173
Rothes, Duke of 49
Rousseau, Jean-Jacques 70
Royal Irish Constabulary 29
Royalists 22
Rudé, George 2
ruling class
    composition of 22, 146
    direct action by 26
    study of 7–8
Ruskin, John 130, 161, 169
Russell, Bertrand 179
Russell, G.W. 173
Russell, Lord John 29, 158
Rutherford, Mark, *Revolution in Tanner's Lane* 164–5
Rutherford, Samuel 50

Sabbatarianism 71
Sacheverell riots (1710) 23
Saint-Simon, Claude-Henri 214
Sakharov, Andrei 197
Sand, George 212
Saville, John 2, 3, 16 n13, 158, 192 n3
Schwarz, Bill 12
science, and social responsibility 179–80
Scotland, religion and nationalism in 40–61
Scott, Sir Walter 28, 56, 60, 82, 109, 131, 135, 140
    *Old Mortality* 49
    *Rob Roy* 56
Scottish Enlightenment 58
sectarianism, left-wing 185
sects, growth of Scottish 43, 52
Selassie, Emperor Haile 188
sex, and Tennyson 144
Shaftesbury, Lord 161–2
Shakespeare, William 12, 13, 79, 80–95, 123, 146, 210
    *All's Well That Ends Well* 86
    *Anthony and Cleopatra* 86
    *As You Like It* 86
    *Hamlet* 84, 86
    *Henry V* 84
    *Julius Caesar* 85, 86, 92, 197
    *King John* 91
    *King Lear* 86, 210
    *Measure for Measure* 86
    *A Midsummer Night's Dream* 86
    *The Tempest* 86

    *Timon of Athens* 86
    *Titus Andronicus* 86
    *Troilus and Cressida* 86
    *Twelfth Night* 81, 86
    *The Winter's Tale* 86
Sharp, Archbishop, murder of 50
Shaw, G.B. 170–71
    *Man and Superman* 171, 173
Shelley, P.B. 31, 117, 119, 124 n36, 128 n112, 135, 153
Sidmouth, Lord 74
Simeon of Cambridge 74, 77 n57
Simpson, F.A. 18
Sinn Fein 33–4
Sleeman 142
Smiles, Samuel 132
Smith, Adam 61
Smith, Ian 198
Smith, Sydney 75
Snow, Edgar, *Red Star over China* 188
Snowden, Philip 170
Social Democratic Federation 169, 217
social injustice, in Wordsworth 102, 107, 109, 127 n90
social mobility 226
socialism
    development of 2, 4, 14, 33, 204–27
    and peasantry 122
    and religion 11
Socialist League 169, 217
Socialist Society, Cambridge 181, 185, 188
Society for the Friends of the People 72
Society for the Prevention of Vice 71, 76 n31
Solemn League and Covenant (1643) 42–3
South Africa 198
Southey, Robert 77 n55, 120, 127 n102, 213
Soviet Union 185, 225
Spanish Civil War 183, 185, 186, 195
Sparta 205, 206
Spedding 135
Spender, Stephen, *Forward from Liberalism* 187
Spenser, Edmund 130
sport, Victorian cult of 33
Sraffa, Piero 180
Stalin, Josef 185, 221–2, 223, 225
Stanhope, Lady Hester 214, 227 n17
State
    modern, rise of 210–11

and religion 68–9, 70
and socialism 215
in Wordsworth 99
see also toleration
Steinbeck, John, The Grapes of Wrath 187
Stevenson, Robert Louis 54
Strachey, John 186–7, 218, 220
Student Christian Movement 179
student movement 36, 221
Sturge, Joseph 160
Suffield, Lord 28
Suffragettes 35
Swinburne, A.C. 135, 137

Taiping rebellion 219, 227 n30
Tawney, R.H. 4
Taylor, Harriet 169
Taylor, John 27
Teignmouth, Lord 72, 73
Ten Hour Act 161
Tennyson, Alfred Lord 8, 12, 129–50
    Idylls of the King 8, 132, 135–46, 149
Tennyson, Hallam 129, 148
tenurial conditions 40, 105
Test Act (1681) 48
Thackeray, W.M. 131
Thatcher, Margaret 9–10, 196, 197, 198,
    201, 202
Theocritus 143
Theodore, Emperor of Abyssinia 139
Third International 195
Thompson, Dorothy 2
Thompson, E.P. 2, 5
    on Blake and Wordsworth 17 n37
    on conspiracy 25
    on education 167
    The Making of the English Working Class
        12
    on Methodism 7, 11
    on utopianism 223, 224
Thompson, Sir J.J. 180
toleration, religious 45
toll bars, protests against 29–30
Tolstoy, Leo 99, 103, 104
Torr, Dona 3
Tory democracy 121
Tourneur, Cyril 94
Toussaint L'Ouverture 110
Toynbee Hall, founding of 168
trade unions 1, 162, 166–7, 169, 170, 172
tragedy 13–14, 94

treason 195–202
Tressell, Robert 172
    The Ragged-Trousered Philanthropists 28
Trevelyan, G.M. 180
Trinity College, Cambridge 180–81, 192 n5
Trollope, Anthony 131, 154
    Can You Forgive Her? 173
Trotsky, Lev 185
Twain, Mark 143
Tyler, Wat 208
Tyndale-Biscoe, Conan 143

Uganda 219
Ulster rebellion (1914) 34
unemployment 181
United States of America 199
    see also Anglo-American alliance
utopian socialism 4, 215, 217, 223–4, 225–6
utopianism 209–10, 213–14

Victoria, Queen of England 144, 145, 154
Vincent, Henry 29
Virgil 134, 205
Vogt, August 174
Voltaire 21, 195

Wales, direct action in 29–30
Wallace, Sir William 42, 54
Wallas, Graham 173
Walsingham, Sir Francis 92
war
    and collectivism 220
    and French Revolution 212
    nineteenth-century cult of 130, 133–4
    and popular consent 24, 32
    and Wordsworth 99, 100, 119
Webb, Beatrice 170, 175
Webb, Beatrice and Sidney, Industrial
    Democracy 168, 170
Webster, John 94
Wei Jingsheng 197
welfare state 218–19
Wellington, Duke of 28
Wells, H.G. 171, 219, 223–4
    The Autocracy of Mr Parham 191–2 n2
    The Time Machine 171
Welsh, John 50, 55
Wesley, John 8, 66, 68, 69, 70, 73
Western Rising (1549) 20–21
Westminster Confession 43
Whiggamore raid (1648) 45–6

Whitaker, Reg 193
White, Blanco 72
*The White Sea Canal* 187
Whitefield, George 70
Whitman, Walt 143
Wigtoun, Earl of 49
Wilberforce, William 8, 72, 73, 74
    *Practical View* 68–70
Wilkins, Bishop 72
Wilkinson, Ellen 182
William III, King of England 56
Williams, Raymond 188
    *Culture and Society* 15
Wilson, Harold 198
Wischnewetzsky, Florence 174
Wolseley, Viscount 149
women
    at Cambridge 178–9
    and the Covenant 49
    and socialism 209
    in Tennyson 144–5
Women's Social and Political Union 35
Wordsworth, Dr 74
Wordsworth, Dorothy 99, 100, 101, 106,
    120, 125 n55
Wordsworth, William 3–4, 12, 55, 96–123,
    212
    *The Borderers* 97, 100
    *The Convention of Cintra* 106

*Descriptive Sketches* 97, 101, 108, 115,
    117
*The Excursion* 101, 109–10, 112–16, 120,
    121, 137
*Lyrical Ballads* 101, 102–3, 103–6, 107–8,
    115, 119, 135
*The Prelude* 97, 98, 101, 105, 107, 110,
    118, 119, 120, 121, 153
*The Recluse* 106
*The Ruined Cottage* 100–101, 103, 110
*The White Doe of Rylstone* 97, 112
*mentioned* 129, 131, 132
working class
    and Chartism 26–7
    and education 167–8
    leadership of 156–60, 175
    and literacy 124 n36
    relation of, to middle classes 25–6,
        152–6, 160–75
    and socialism 5–6, 8–9, 214–23
    and Wordsworth 121
World Student Movement 187
World War One 35, 171, 200

Young, James 6
Young Ireland 30

Zaheer, Sajjad 190